*Liberalism, Black Power, and the Making of
American Politics, 1965–1980*

Liberalism, Black Power, and the Making of American Politics, 1965–1980

Devin Fergus

The University of Georgia Press   *Athens & London*

A Sarah Mills Hodge Fund Publication
This publication is made possible in part through a grant from the Hodge Foundation
in memory of its founder, Sarah Mills Hodge, who devoted her life to the relief and
education of African Americans in Savannah, Georgia.

Set in Adobe Garamond by BookComp, Inc.
Printed and bound by Thomson-Shore
The paper in this book meets the guidelines for
permanence and durability of the Committee on
Production Guidelines for Book Longevity of the
Council on Library Resources.

Printed in the United States of America
13 12 11 10 09 C 5 4 3 2 1
13 12 11 10 09 P 5 4 3 2 1

Library of Congress Cataloging-in-Publication Data
Fergus, Devin, 1969–
Liberalism, Black power, and the making of American politics, 1965–1980 / Devin Fergus.
p. cm. — (Politics and culture in the twentieth-century South)
Includes bibliographical references and index.
ISBN-13: 978-0-8203-3323-6 (hardcover : alk. paper)
ISBN-10: 0-8203-3323-9 (hardcover : alk. paper)
ISBN-13: 978-0-8203-3324-3 (pbk. : alk. paper)
ISBN-10: 0-8203-3324-7 (pbk. : alk. paper)
1. Black power—North Carolina—History—20th century. 2. Black nationalism—
North Carolina—History—20th century. 3. Liberalism—North Carolina—
History—20th century. 4. African Americans—North Carolina—Politics and
government—20th century. 5. North Carolina—Race relations—Political aspects—
History—20th century. 6. North Carolina—Politics and government—1951– I. Title.
E185.93.N6F47 2009
323.1196'0730756—dc22   2008049355

British Library Cataloging-in-Publication Data available

CONTENTS

INTRODUCTION

"Son, what do you want for Christmas?" a doting Black Power parent asked his adolescent son in a reprint of what the 1970 FBI report claimed was a Black Panther Christmas card. The son replied, smiling broadly, "A machine-gun shotgun, a box of hand grenades, a box of dynamite, and a box of matches." Black revolution, now instilled in a next generation of "extremist black nationalists" thriving on "hate and violence against authority," seemed America's fate for the foreseeable future.[1]

"To my mind," as *Newsweek* quoted FBI director J. Edgar Hoover at the time, "the big question for every American is whether he wants to support and defend our free society or let it be overrun and destroyed by visionary agitators." For Hoover there was no guessing where liberals stood on the problem. As the nation's domestic intelligence leader saw it, liberals "enabled terroristic violence at home" by aiding and making possible America's number one internal threat, Black Power. Indeed, since the late 1960s, it has been generally held that the efforts of liberal elites to accommodate the polarizing demands of black nationalists encapsulated, if not instigated, the unraveling of political and social consensus in the modern United States. As one historian answered Hoover's big question, yes, Black Power ran amok over liberalism.[2]

Black Power's most visionary agitator, Malcolm X, also shared concerns about liberalism's entente with Black Power. Yet he understood its effects somewhat differently than Hoover then and historians today. "It's like coffee," Malcolm X warned contemporary black nationalists of the permuting powers of liberalism, "strong and hot . . . until you add the cream." In time liberal engagement would "cool" a Black Power movement in both rhetoric and program until, he and other nationalists' feared, Black Power became "nonviolent, peaceful, [and] negotiating."[3]

Rethinking the big question of the unraveling of consensus in America, this book examines the relations between liberalism and black nationalism, from 1965 until 1980. It reveals that liberals helped reform Black Power so that by 1980 black radicals and their successors were more likely to petition Congress than to blow it up. Those very policies that moderated Black Power would also energize the New Right, as the Right's critique of liberalism—as an effete ideology emboldening anti-Americanism abroad and enabling such fifth columns as black nationalists at home—would grow in popularity among Americans. In sum, this book offers a fresh reading of both the relationship between liberalism and black nationalism and the implications of this relationship for the nation as a whole.

The book accomplishes this reading by mapping the liberal–Black Power entente in North Carolina—a progressive southern state and a center of the Black Power movement in the United States from 1965 until 1980. North Carolina's progressive core (Durham, Winston-Salem, Greensboro, Raleigh, and Chapel Hill) created the operational space for the state's developing Black Power movement. Amid the liberal climate of the urban Piedmont, individual nationalist projects representing a full spectrum of ideologies emerged and modified their programs to conform to the prevailing pluralistic ethos and constitutional order: Malcolm X Liberation University (MXLU), founded in Durham in 1969, embraced cultural nationalism; also in 1969, the Winston-Salem Black Panthers openly championed political organizing and action; the 1974–75 "Free Joan Little" movement coalesced in Raleigh around sexual politics; and the founders of Soul City, North Carolina, once the largest public project ever underwritten for an African American, promulgated economic nationalism until the community's demise in 1980.

Each of these projects was heralded nationally as a premier initiative of its kind; each openly repudiated violence and functioned within the established constitutional framework and pluralistic ethos. A more accommodating nationalism did little to stem reaction from the New Right, however. Instead, the interplay of black nationalism and liberalism further energized traditionalists such as Jesse Helms, who toppled the Nixon-backed Soul City project. In the end conservative insurgents supplanted not simply liberals and nationalists but moderates as well.

North Carolina's urban Piedmont is only one venue in which the liberal-nationalist interplay at large might be examined. Indeed, as the conclusion shows, the story captured here recurs across the United States. In New York, Los Angeles, Chicago, Atlanta, and elsewhere, liberal funding and legal backing made possible the programmatic rise and reform of Black Power think tanks, publishing houses, schools, and media. Even Black Power start-ups, like the grant-making Twenty-first Century Foundation, whose institutional raison d'être centered on weaning fellow black nationalists off liberal support, often owed their own existence to liberal venture capitalists and philanthropists.

Chapter 1 begins by providing the historical and spatial context in which black nationalism emerged and crested in North Carolina's most progressive geographic region, the urban Piedmont, during the late 1960s. The story then shifts to the creation of Malcolm X Liberation University, a project that demonstrates that not even cultural nationalists—renowned for their racial essentialism—rejected white support, but MXLU's story also foreshadows a more general backlash by the Religious Right against liberal support of Black Power.

Chapter 2 continues the story of MXLU to accentuate Black Power's evolutionary trajectory in the absence of liberalism's campaign of indulgence. It chronicles the university's contentious relationship with the black professional and upper strata in North Carolina—a relationship responsible for the school's loss of funding by 1973, despite cultural nationalists' toned-down rhetoric and behavior. Liberal withdrawal, in turn, actually spurred cultural nationalists' embrace of the antistatist politics of Marxism-Leninism. Rather than continue backing MXLU, whose earlier concessions had been deemed insufficient, liberals lent their imprimatur to another group: the once-revolutionary nationalist Black Panther Party (BPP).

Chapter 3 gauges the success of liberals' positive orientation toward black nationalism by reviewing their intercourse with the best-known radicals of the day, the Black Panther Party, during the Watergate era, when the United States faced its most important constitutional crisis since the Civil War. Despite polls showing confidence in public institutions at all-time lows and others hinting at the demise of the two-party system, the Black Panthers adhered to the legal and political system in surprising ways. Their transition to mainstream politics, of which the North Carolina Panther affiliate is a prominent example, was facilitated largely through the legal sponsorship of the American Civil Liberties Union (ACLU), with its philosophy of constitutional liberalism.

Chapter 4 focuses on the 1974–75 cause célèbre trial and acquittal in North Carolina of Joan Little, a black inmate indicted for the capital murder of the white jailer whom she identified as her rapist.[4] The state, trapped in its own rhetoric of cosmopolitanism, which historically had shielded it from the scrutiny often facing lower southern states, compelled the trial's removal from eastern North Carolina to Raleigh.

Chapter 5 contextualizes the Little case within the broader possibilities and pitfalls of cosmopolitan black nationalism. Nationalists' frontline role in the Little movement masked their own record on intraracial gender relations. In concealing their inner lives and problematic gender relations from a wider white society, nationalists behaved no differently from many of their white brothers. Black men, however, were subject to a far more negative interpretation than their white counterparts, and as whites learned of the dissonance between nationalists' rhetoric and reality, whites construed them narrowly as intellectually dishonest political opportunists, self-promoters, and profiteers. Nonetheless, despite the nationalists' private behavior and subsequent caricaturing by whites, their enlightened rhetoric and reliance upon the legal mechanisms of the state underscored Black Power's essential investment in constitutional government.

The final chapter shows how a more accommodating nationalism, rather than stem the ascendance of the New Right, in its interplay with liberalism helped energize the Right. The book closes with a discussion of additional cases that extend the analysis beyond North Carolina. Such cases, in conjunction with the North Carolina projects that are the focus of this book, suggest how and why liberalism succeeded, both nationally and in other western democracies, not only in creating space for ethnic and regional nationalists but also in helping these subnational movements renegotiate the terms of their membership in the nation-state.

This book unfolds as a dialectic and thus should be read as such. Chapters 1 and 2 provide the thesis, which is that liberalism created an operational space for Black Power. Most important to this argument is the fact that even those most assumed to be essentialists—cultural nationalists—engaged liberalism. Chapters 3 through 5 deliver the antithesis;

amid this space created by liberalism we find Black Power (in the form of the Black Panther Party, the most notorious radicals on the Black Power block) moderating its politics and agenda to conform within the pluralistic and constitutional ethos. What I attempt to show in chapter 3, for example, is how the ACLU beat back police repression on behalf of the BPP. This freed the party from suffocating state repression so that it could pursue its community service projects and run for local political office. "We wanted to do it earlier," one former Panther expressed, "but hell, we were standing in court all the time."[5] The North Carolina Civil Liberties Union helped to get the Panthers out of court so that they could regain trust in the community. Chapters 4 and 5 complement this while also looking at how black nationalists moderated their racialist rhetoric to embrace more liberal universalist and cosmopolitan sensibilities. The synthesis comes in the final microstudy chapter. Chapter 6 shows what happened despite liberalism creating space and Black Power modifying its agenda (e.g., most notably acceding to the government's terms regarding Soul City's interracial residential makeup and placing industrial recruitment ahead of residential recruitment, which McKissick believed helped doom the new town project). The synthesis is that the liberal–Black Power dialectic energized the rise of the New Right. Helms and his supporters described Soul City as a liberal boondoggle. Resummarizing the book's contents to provide this kind of overview reveals how the dialectic works between the subarguments.

In sum, liberal interventionism worked. Liberals' policy of engagement helped to reform Black Power. Black nationalists assented—toeing the political and constitutional line, and adjusting their programs and agendas to fit within the pluralist order. Despite their success, liberals' accommodation of Black Power cost them enormously.

Evidence for this argument, as it pertains to North Carolina, is gleaned from personal diaries, state agency records, interviews with leading activists and officials, and church, corporate, and foundational records. Of particular note are recently discovered taped conversations, never before transcribed or published, featuring controversial black nationalist Howard Fuller and his meeting with a group of liberals. This behind-the-scenes dialogue is as close as most people may ever get to listening to how liberals negotiated to win the peace with nationalists. I also draw on previously untapped congressional correspondence, court records, FBI files, and other federal records made available by invoking the Freedom of Information Act.

Materials outside of North Carolina enrich the book. Evidence from Black Power collections archived in California, Georgia, Pennsylvania, Connecticut, New York, and elsewhere amplify the commonness of the North Carolina experience. In addition I draw on the records of foundations sponsoring Black Power initiatives, notably the Ford and Rockefeller foundation collections. Presidential papers, from Johnson to Reagan, give readers a bird's-eye view, though often insular, of the rapprochement liberalism established with nationalism. Most fascinating of all, the Watergate Special Prosecution Force tapes, unsealed on December 10, 2003, bring listeners into the inner sanctum of the Oval Office to hear conversations between President Richard Nixon, George H. W. Bush, and Floyd McKissick, a leading black nationalist who had once rejected nonviolence as a dying, useless philosophy.

At issue are the standard interpretations of Black Power and modern U.S. liberalism. Scholarship in recent years has tried to explain the social and material awakening known as Black Power from the standpoint of what is described best as an "isolationist" school. With rich prose and exacting detail, William Van Deburg, Robert Self, Komozi Woodard, and Timothy Tyson, among others, have historicized the era for a new generation—challenging common assumptions about the nihilistic, criminal intentions of black nationalists and the canard of Black Power as an exclusively northern and West Coast movement.[6]

However, in their efforts to give voice to the Black Power movement, historians, political scientists, and sociologists have effectively silenced the dialogue between liberalism and Black Power. For example, in what is possibly the best isolationist book to date, *American Babylon*, author Robert O. Self stresses the agency of Black Power, noting that the Black Panther Party advanced "resistance and action almost entirely outside of liberalism."[7] Yet three sentences later he writes that Panthers Huey Newton and Bobby Seale penned Black Power's most famous tract, the Party's Ten Point Platform, in the offices of the war on poverty in Oakland. Unaware of how this fact unhinges his interpretive claim, Self ignores the larger question: why liberals who provided office space for Black Panthers are not providing operational space for Black Power. Indeed, the most memorable lesson for historians of the period, offered to Bob Woodward and Carl Bernstein as they investigated the Watergate break-in, seems to have escaped Black Power specialists: *follow the money*.[8]

By ignoring the liberal–black nationalist relationship, Black Power scholars have ceded the issue to mainstream historians and other nonspecialists. Historians of the Johnson, Nixon, Ford, and Carter years show breezy familiarity with the primary literature and scholarship of Black Power and have defined the movement and interpreted its meaning to the public.

These mainstream historians have recognized that liberalism created an operational space for Black Power, but they have often misinterpreted the nature and consequences of this relationship. Indeed, they often argue that liberalism's inability to tame Black Power contributed to, if not instigated, a social and political unraveling in America. The prevailing view is what one historian has called the story of how "black power ran amok over liberalism." The works of Allen Matusow, Steven Gillon, and Gareth Davies, to mention a few, reflect this disposition.[9]

Authors reflecting an array of ideological and methodological approaches have, in varying degrees, coalesced and adopted the unraveling thesis. Such book and chapter titles as *Coming Apart*, "The Collapse of the Rooseveltian Nation" and "The Spread of Anti-Americanism," "The Liberal Dream and Its Nightmare" and "The War Within," *America Divided*, and *One Nation Divisible* underscore the centrality of this school in recent U.S. history.[10] Arguably the best known articulation of the unraveling thesis is Samuel Huntington's *Clash of Civilizations*, which claims that liberal elites' countenance of black radicals fueled what he once called the "real clash" of civilizations between defenders of the West and black nationalists. And, if the most respected society of Americanists outside the United States offers any indication, the unraveling idea is today being outsourced, given that the British Association for American Studies has selected Michael Heale's *The Sixties in America* to its acclaimed paperback series.[11] Heale claims Black Power "spearheaded the attack" and "dismantling" of the traditional power structure in the United States. Nor has winning major book awards immunized authors, a Bancroft winner and Pulitzer finalist among them, from the de rigueur view that Black Power vitiated liberalism.[12]

In complicating these interpretations this book by no means suggests that the Black Power–liberal interplay was the sole, or even most salient, factor in the making and efflorescence of the New Right. As Matthew

Dallek, Lisa McGirr, and others have shown, modern conservatism found an audience in the suburbs well before Black Power entered the nation's lexicon or consciousness.[13] Beyond this, a spate of scholars has posited persuasive cases that the New Right was comprised of more than the sum of its opposition to civil rights. Michael Flamm, Byron Shafer, and Richard Johnston, to name a few, inform us that factors beyond race and civil rights led to Americans' disillusionment with the liberal policies and laws.[14] For some, particularly among working-class whites, it was a growing sense of alienation from putatively "out-of-touch" Washington embracing elitist policies like school busing, which white and blue-collar Americans opposed in not merely racial terms. Rather, the "elite" label resonated with so many Americans largely because it confirmed an existing perception of lawmakers, professional government bureaucrats, and judges embracing laws like forced busing that, in the words of political theorist and conservative pundit George Will, they "had no intention of ever being exposed to themselves."[15] Conversely, to others it wasn't an indifferent government but one too involved; it was an overweaning Washington ready to assume the role of locus parentis, dictating cradle-to-grave choices—whether federal aid for abortion, prayer in school, or as Democratic candidate George McGovern proposed in 1972, hiking capital gains rates on the inheritance (or "death") tax. The so-called silent majority bristled that their government was turning on them, ostensibly coddling criminals and other nonconformists engaged in acts of resistance, hidden or in plain sight, to the social order. Instead, from the conservative view, the Black Power–liberal interplay was emblematic of what conservatives and ever-growing number of Americans found wanting in liberalism: usually at the alleged expense of the law-abiding taxpayers, liberal elites were captive to a host of narrow interests, none more damaging than civil rights activists or Black Power dissidents.

When I refer to liberalism I mean the twentieth-century American ideology—manifest in individuals, institutions, and policies—that the promotion of greater social and economic equality is in the public's general interest. Essential to serving this general interest is a positive role for the broker state, which has generally meant the government though also including a participatory role for nongovernmental organizations. Of course, both blacks and whites subscribed to the liberal worldview. In its original parlance in the mid-1960s, the term "Black Power" was used interchangeably with "black nationalism," and that is Black Power's appropriation in this book. Finally, particularly in the book's conclusion I have taken some creative license with the term "soft power." I use "soft power" interchangeably with "liberalism" and a bit differently from its originally meaning in the early 1990s, when former state department official and political scientist Joseph Nye coined it. For Nye soft power meant "the ability to get what you want through attraction rather than coercion and payment." Soft power practitioners persuaded others, according to Nye, through American culture, political ideals, and policies.

Here I seek not to misuse "soft power" but to deepen its application. First, unlike Nye who focuses exclusively on world politics, I apply soft power to the United States. As mentioned above, black America required no introduction to notions of American culture, political ideals, policies, and their concomitant shortcomings. If all soft power offered black nationalism was the putative "attraction" of American culture, ideals, and policies, then it would not have gotten very far with Black Power. At minimum, familiarity breeds contempt. This would appear especially so in applying soft power to black America—given that history makes clear no other segment of U.S. society knew better how hollow such platitudes could ring. Thus, for any soft power practice to succeed with Black Power in America, a verbal investment in a group appeared more persuasive when accompanied with a financial one.

Second, in this domestic context I consider soft power from the position of nonstates. In particular it appears useful to view soft power from the perspective of those targeted by its policies, rather than how it is envisioned and articulated from the distant perch of policy makers. For example, Malcolm X seemed to understand soft power decades before the term was coined. He called soft power "friendly." Its allure was its "benevolent, philanthropic, friendly approach," an approach originating in postcolonial Asia and Africa, according to Malcolm X, before migrating to the United States. It once went by several different names: "humanitarianism" or "dollarism." In contrast, hard power for Malcolm X was, in the United States, the denial of certain rights; abroad it meant waging military battle against colonized peoples.[16] Given this more balanced methodological view—that is, taking into consideration the nonstate group's perspective—one is compelled to revise one's understanding of what soft power did and how it functions.

By highlighting the interplay of nationalists and liberals, this book corrects the growing body of monographic work that isolates the Black Power movement, ignoring in particular its interaction with liberalism. In underscoring how nationalism adjusted to the predominant political and progressive order, moreover, I challenge the widespread view of generalists that liberal elites accommodated the polarizing demands of black nationalists. In broader terms, my thesis challenges the scholarly view—reflected in broad currents of popular thought—that modern liberalism has failed. It does so by showing how liberalism helped to bring a radical civic ideology back from the brink of political violence and social nihilism, and the price liberals paid in the process.

Some scholars of Black Power may well view this thesis of liberal accommodation as relatively well known. Such specialists familiar with the personal and organizational records of the movement are not inclined to equate Black Power with separatism or violence and dismiss these linkages. Yet, statistically speaking, for most adult Americans Black Power meant precisely that—particularly after the murder of Martin Luther King Jr. In April 1968 51 percent of adult Americans polled believed that Black Power was a call for the use of violence or a separate society.[17] Fifteen months later, a Gallup-Newsweek poll revealed that roughly 60 percent of whites in middle America expected the dangers of racial violence to rise before getting better (25 percent thought it would go down).[18]

Nationalists were not necessarily concerned with disabusing the statistical man or woman of the specter of racial violence. "We are for revolutionary violence," Stokely Carmichael told the students at San Jose State University: "We are for spitting to killing, whatever is necessary to liberate us." Historian Jeffrey Ogbar writes that no groups shaped the Black Power movement more than the two groups most closely linked in the public's imagination with violence and separatism: the Black Panther Party and Nation of Islam.[19] Thus, for those who see Black Power through the looking glass, darkly, they occlude the permeability and protean quality of black nationalism.

Immersion, or embedding, if you will, often offered a different vantage point, however. Or at least that is the insight offered by that George Plimpton of Black Power, Tom Wolfe. In among the most widely cited books of its generation, *Radial Chic*, an embedded Tom Wolfe toured with black militants and liberals from New York to California. For Wolfe the most memorable experience was a January 1970 fund-raising party for the Black Panther Party hosted by Felicia and Leonard Bernstein, musical conductor and purveyor of progressive causes. That night, as Wolfe told it, began pregnant with revolutionary Panther rhetoric but ended with chardonnay-and-brie liberals mau-mauing black militants, who were "slowly backed into a weird corner." The dawn of this new decade augured neither a new day in Babylon nor an eschatological unraveling of Western civilization. Rather, cornered Panther spokesperson Don Cox explained to the Vanden Heuvels, Barbara Walters, and others huddled in the Bernsteins' posh Upper East Side duplex that he preferred diplomacy to dystopia: "We want the same thing as you, We want peace. . . . We want to come home at night and be with the family . . . turn on the TV . . . and smoke a little weed."[20]

Many modern U.S. historians (and many equally fine Black Power specialists) have collectively missed what Wolfe witnessed: liberalism's capacity to reform revolution. For a dean of U.S. history like Arthur Schlesinger, militants replaced Gandhi with Frantz Fanon, "contending that violence alone could bring liberation."[21] A similar conclusion appears drawn by an equally august William Leuchtenberg, in paraphrasing Herman Talmadge's complaint to Lyndon Johnson that presidential policy "was encouraging" Black Panthers to be in the business of assassinating police.[22] Historian Mark Lytle, taking a more isolationist tack, concluded black nationalists alienated themselves from liberals in an effort to wage guerrilla war.[23] Of course, what alarmed Bernstein partygoers more was not the putative guerrillas in the nation's midst but, as one Park Avenue matron put it, that "some simple-minded schmucks [might] take all that business about burning down buildings *seriously*."[24] More versed in the archival materials, some Black Power scholars may conclude that this book's view of Black Power—as protean and permeable, thus making it vulnerable to reform—is far from a pathbreaking insight. But to leave the analysis there elides a bigger epistemological paradox: How is it that a line of argument—black nationalism's openness to dialogue might expose it to reform—appears to be terra incognito to one set of modern Americanists but is a well-worn conceptual terrain to another set of scholars expert in precisely the same decades and same geographic space? Or to borrow from journalistic jargon: Do stringers of Black Power history like myself inform byline history written by generalists? Or has the checks-and-balance system within this subspecies of the historical profession eroded to the degree that what is now revelatory to one set of recent Americanists merely appears tautological to another? The studies that follow begin this critical dialogue.

Rethinking the liberal-nationalist interplay also invites us to revisit narratives of American exceptionalism. The liberal–Black Power entente clearly conforms to a wider, contemporary world of syncretization between liberalism and nationalism. As we see in the conclusion, during the 1960s and 1970s liberal democracies on both sides of the Atlantic proved a breeding ground for ethnic and regional nationalism. To understand Black Power in twentieth-century America it is useful to consider relevant European scholarship on the shared histories of liberalism and nationalism as twin ideologies of change against the forces of conservatism. My aim in recognizing the contribution of a wider community of scholars working on liberalism and nationalism is not to suggest that these ideologies merge seamlessly into the recent variations of black nationalism. If nothing else, the historical impact of race on liberalism, conservatism, and nationalism in the United States precludes seeing a seamless flow from nationalisms in Western Europe to black nationalism. Instead, my aim is to show how this most recent incarnation of the liberal-nationalist intercourse took shape in the unique time and space of cold war America; ultimately, I relate and establish Black Power's contribution to the unfolding epic of liberalism and nationalism.

The book also charts a fresh course in another important way. It views Black Power not as a snapshot from somewhere between 1968 and 1972 but as a story of change over time stretching across the 1970s. Only by exploring how it unfolded in this decade, after the intensity of the 1960s revolution and racial romanticism cooled, can we see what became of Black Power in the more byzantine world of nation and institution building.

I Hidden Histories of Remittance
Liberalism and the Making of Black Nationalism in North Carolina, 1965–1970

While at Chapel Hill a twenty-four-year-old graduate student in political science wrote a dissertation that, as one close friend explained, "changed him forever." Paul Wellstone's thesis, subtitled "Why They Believe in Violence," explored black militancy and its relations to liberalism in Durham, North Carolina. Based on findings from 175 interviews and surveys of local blacks, he argued that Durham was on the precipice of race war. Wellstone revealed that even Durham black women accepted political violence "and possibly guerrilla warfare" as a legitimate means of political expression. Wellstone, a suburban D.C. native and future Minnesota senator, conceded that some southern politicians and northern mayors were indeed correct: controversial liberal initiatives like the Community Action Program had in fact played an incubating role for black militant activists.

Yet that was only half of the story. He argued that engagement—symbolic acts, dialoguing, or direct material subvention—both nurtured and mollified Durham's Black Power insurgency, removing the climate of acceptance toward violence by channeling urban militants to nonviolent change.[1]

In the years to come Wellstone would emerge as a paragon of liberalism. Following his death in a 2002 plane crash, Great Britain's *Economist* told its transatlantic readership that American liberals had lost "the last of the 1960s generation" in the U.S. Senate.[2] But few know the context from which his politics emerged: the urban Piedmont, a context that is a useful though not unique place to study the liberal–Black Power interplay. In most northern and western American cities during the 1960s, the interplay between Black Power and community action programs was an essential part of the war on poverty. Many of the great controversies of the community action programs stemmed from the unbridgeable gap between the Black Power movement and the political system. Yet the relationship between Black Power and antipoverty officials was not a northern phenomenon, as many have assumed.[3] Rather, the impact of the maximum feasible participation clause in the Office of Economic Opportunity (OEO) Act extended beyond the West Coast and the North.[4] Racial liberalism in North Carolina's urban Piedmont provided fertile operational territory for a new generation of nationalist leaders like antipoverty employee Howard Fuller.[5]

Born in 1941 and raised in the housing projects of Milwaukee, Fuller, an African American, earned a master's degree in social administration and worked for the National Urban League in Chicago steering the unemployed to jobs, until he was invited to North Carolina. He arrived in Durham in May 1965 as the integrationist director of the neighborhood youth corps for Operation Breakthrough (OBT). Operation Breakthrough began under an initiative by then-governor Terry Sanford, and in an effort to secure federal dollars, was reorganized as part of the war on poverty's Community Action Program. OBT's raison d'être reflected that of community action programs nationally: improving services for the poor and fostering experimental educational programs.[6] To this end workers at the agency with assistance from Durham officials began organizing neighborhood councils with local blacks as representatives. Durham officials backed Operation Breakthrough in 1964 partly out of the belief that it could channel black protests. Instead, city officials' decision to establish neighborhood councils "let the genie out of the bottle," as one Durham historian put it, as indigenous blacks became more involved in actively finding solutions to ending poverty in their own city.[7] OBT was one of eleven community action experiments in North Carolina incorporated under the North Carolina Fund (NCF) and jointly financed by the OEO.

Background and Origins of the Great Society's First Statewide Antipoverty Program

As America's first statewide antipoverty program, what made the North Carolina Fund a reality in North Carolina were local liberals and a global foundation. The fund was an independent, nonprofit corporation, headquartered in Durham and introduced to the public by Governor Sanford on July 18, 1963. The most notable of the other founders was John Ehle. Novelist turned cultural attaché, Ehle persuaded Sanford to pay a visit to the Ford Foundation, looking "not for money but ideas" for eradicating poverty.[8] Enlisting Ford was a risky move for Sanford, as southern conservative politicians had consistently attacked the liberalism and internationalism of Ford and other foundations.[9] Ford agreed to support the fund, making it the first poverty program supported by the Ford Foundation below the Mason-Dixon Line.

Transnationals like Ford shared two operational traits. First, they tended to pursue a single interest. Second, they were apt to transfer problem-solving solutions from other sectors.[10] Ford saw the North Carolina Fund not as separate from but integrative to the whole of its world politics agenda, which since 1949 had focused on promoting peace. "Poverty, hunger, disease," a 1966 Ford report put it, "produce unrest and social instability, and these . . . produce a climate conducive to conflict."[11] Assistance was directed to problems regardless of national boundaries, Ford officials claimed. Marketing the success of democracy abroad was interlaced with social and political conditions at home. This was especially so as the 1960s social turmoil helped to unmask the consensus myths of the 1950s. The most enduring book of that generation, Louis Hartz's 1955 *The Liberal Tradition in America*, argued that even America's social revolutionaries, who in the past had "frightened the nation" with threats against the exist-ing order, actually did so "inside, rather than outside, the liberal process of American politics."[12] Concerns that Hartz's "one America" was giving way to Michael Harrington's Other America compelled Ford to focus more of its organizational energies stateside. Joining the Sanford administration in welcoming Ford were the family foundations of Z. Smith Reynolds and Mary Babcock Reynolds, two endowed philanthropies headquartered in Winston-Salem that opened their coffers to the fund. In less than a year the federal Office of Economic Opportunity would join as well, providing matching funds for the North Carolina Fund.

A collective vision "to turn North Carolina into a state laboratory of innovative approaches to the problems of poverty" attracted donors and central staff members to the program. Using Oakland as a model, the fund piloted such national demonstration programs as the Volunteers in Service to America and Head Start. The NCF's main purpose was to spend its six-year charter starting eleven self-sustaining community action agencies—none of which raised the hackles of conservatives more than Operation Breakthrough.[13] Clearly, during the early days of OBT, "upgrad-ing individuals"—that is, arming people with vocational and work train-ing—took priority as a prerequisite for the critical support of Durham's established city leaders. As months passed, however, the limits of such an approach became apparent. Training people for low-wage jobs and pro-viding ephemeral social services did little to ameliorate the overarching problems manifested in substandard housing, chronic underemployment, and daily struggles with such basic services as garbage collection and po-lice protection. As OBT workers quickly discovered, a well-rounded attack on poverty meant politically organizing the poor "to deal with their own problems." Mirroring community agencies throughout the nation, Opera-tion Breakthrough employees reinterpreted their mission as one in which "the people themselves" would "be trained to speak for themselves."[14]

OBT board members, including the mayor, bank and insurance officials, and university administrators, clashed with antipoverty workers over issues like representation of the poor on the board, and even whether the poor had any contribution to make except in an advisory capacity. The desire among OBT employees to engage Durham's dispossessed reflected the new strategy of its private sponsor, the North Carolina Fund, which had even sparser support outside the urban Piedmont.[15]

Politics of Place: Cultural Geography Matters

Black Power sought the most progressive spaces it could find. In North Carolina, this meant the urban Piedmont. Twentieth-century North Carolina was a tale of three divergent regions. Unlike the urban Piedmont and western parts of the state, agricultural-based eastern North Carolina more closely approximated the racial and cultural landscape of the Deep South.[16] "In the rural east," Jack Bass and Walter De Vries wrote, "not only was the region bypassed by the civil rights movement, but it was also a hotbed of Ku Klux Klan activity in the 1960s, and the Klan in North Carolina was larger and more virulent than in any state outside of Alabama and Mississippi during that period."[17]

Nothing exposed the stark regional divide inside the state more than the Voting Rights Act of 1965. All but one of the forty counties covered under the preclearance provisions of the act fell behind North Carolina's eastern iron curtain—in the counties east of Raleigh, black voting was rare. Not since the previous century had black voters seen anything akin to an election free from racial discrimination. That said, the election curtain had not fallen across the entire state. In fact, despite killing democratic elections by suppressing black suffrage in the east, North Carolina had the highest percentage of registered black voters in the South, nearly 40 percent. Those registered resided in the metropolitan region of the central Piedmont, which was only about 18 percent black. During the late 1960s and 1970s, when black elected officials returned to the legislature after seven decades, they came from this more politically active urban Piedmont. And ultimately it was outside of the black belt that Black Power would make its institutional home.[18]

Race was not the sole barometer of the region's social politics. U.S. representatives from eastern North Carolina consistently scored among the most conservative in the state and nation, according to the group ratings of the New Republic Magazine Index and the Americans for Constitutional Action. Similarly, no North Carolina congressman aligned himself more closely with conservative coalitions and more consistently opposed national Democratic congressional actions than lawmaker L. H. Fountain, whose second congressional district, located northeast of the metropolitan Piedmont, had the largest black minority of any North Carolina district.[19] Both labor's Committee for Political Education and cold war liberals at the Americans for Democratic Action gave Fountain a zero, as they did Wilmington's congressman, Alton A. Lennon. The liberal Eighty-ninth Congress revealed just how reliably right easterners could be counted on to be. In 1965–66, when the back of the conservative coalition of northern Republicans and southern Democrats was supposedly broken for the first time since the 1930s, as Congress voted into law 69 percent of President Johnson's Great Society programs, Fountain and Lennon bucked both their party and president by voting against Great Society legislation between 90 and 98 percent of the time.[20] During the mid and late 1960s, the two consistently jockeyed to make the *Congressional Quarterly*'s (*CQ*'s) list of the most southern of southern Democrats, unlike Piedmont progressive congressmen L. Richardson Preyer and Nick Galifianakis, who often found themselves at the opposite end of the *CQ*'s continuum, rated among the "least southern southerners."[21]

Few in eastern North Carolina saw value in encouraging greater political participation from poorer residents, particularly economically disfranchised black ones. Although the South's desire for federal dollars influenced even southern congressmen's support for the Great Society early on, these congressmen and their constituents remained wary of the most visible programs in areas like education, hospital construction, and job training, fearing federal support meant greater external scrutiny on matters of black equality.[22] Eastern congressmen such as David Henderson were among the most vocal in opposing OEO authorization, supporting legislation only after assurances of exclusive dedication to vocational and job training so that poor people could "become capable of earning a livelihood."[23] Others, like Fountain, saw to it that potential civil rights advocates in the Johnson administration were removed from influential positions within the OEO. It soon became clear that the views of eastern community action administrators conflicted with the evolving conception of poverty emanating from the NCF's central office in Durham.[24] For eastern antipoverty officials the goal, according to Tim Brinn of Nash-Edgecombe Economic Development Inc., was to "keep the Nash-Edgecombe area free from outside black power elements" and not to tolerate activists like Howard Fuller.[25] "What was really needed" to eradicate poverty, James McDonald and Thomas Hartmann of the fund explained to eleven project directors during a December 1965 training conference, "was to have a political coalition formed between poor whites and Negroes to give political power to the disadvantaged."[26]

The program director of Nash and Edgecombe counties feared that such views represented not merely the private grumblings of two disillusioned antipoverty officials, but the growing reality that the politicization of the poor had the institutional blessing of top officers at the fund, including its executive director, George Esser.[27]

Esser was a forty-one-year-old University of North Carolina (UNC) government professor plucked from academic obscurity by Governor Sanford to aid in drafting the 1965 Economic Opportunity Act. He proved an intrepid liberal on behalf of antipoverty warriors and would come to personify how urban Piedmont progressives were central in insulating Black Power. He confirmed the fears of the NCF's most conservative critics. Esser not only endorsed expanding operations to include political coalitions, but—in naming Hartmann director of the newly created community support department in 1966—sanctioned the fund's institutional advance. He designated the upstart department a clearinghouse for future NCF projects. Further exasperating program officials was the apparent fact that the community support staff would be charged with coordinating politics for local, state, and national elections and with policy making.[28]

In an attempt to stymie future political mobilization, Craven County Operation Progress and Nash-Edgecombe Economic Development administrators brought the personal testimony of Barbara Jean Cooper to the governor's attention. Cooper, a NCF field technician in Robeson County, objected to working for an antipoverty field representative running for the state legislature. Cooper resigned because, as she stated in a May 1966 hearing, the fund's growing ties with organized labor and social activists and its eagerness to challenge local political power structures demonstrated that "the poverty program [had] lost its main goals."[29] Cooper's testimony was used unsuccessfully by Nash-Edgecombe Economic Development and Craven County Operation Progress officials in a campaign to persuade Governor Daniel K. Moore to censure the North Carolina Fund.[30]

Competing perspectives reflected the political geographies within the state. Whereas eastern fund officials narrowly viewed the OEO's mandate, training workers for the area's labor-intensive low-wage textile industry, for example, NCF workers working in the center of the state took a more expansive view. Whereas easterners saw themselves producing a responsible, taxpaying citizen for the state, central fund officials looked to make a democratic one. And whereas easterners may have construed Tocqueville's

America to mean limited national government, central fund officials were moved as much by Harrington's America, tending toward the belief that ending poverty was intertwined with democracy in America. For the fund, whether democracy in America would be practiced robustly hinged less on manpower programs than on organized associations, like community action programs, at the local level. But this came at the cost of bringing in and providing some institutional cover for the state's most controversial black activist. From the outset, however, the radicalization that individuals like Howard Fuller brought to the organization was the objective of some officials in Operation Breakthrough.

Creating Space: Hiring Howard Fuller and Defending Speech

Howard Fuller was hired in spring 1965 by then OBT director Robert Foust, at the recommendation of longtime Fuller friend Jim McDonald.[31] McDonald and Morris Cohen, NCF director of training and a former college classmate of Fuller's, were anxious to see a black militant heading the agency's new community organization component. Fuller himself was eager to leave his bureaucratically laden appointment with the National Urban League in Chicago. He immediately took to grassroots campaigning in North Carolina.[32] By the summer of 1966 Fuller emerged as one of North Carolina's most controversial speakers, among the first to embrace Black Power publicly.

Until mid-July 1966 there was little acknowledgment of Black Power's presence in the state. This would change on July 20. Nearly four weeks after Student Nonviolent Coordinating Committee (SNCC) leader Stokely Carmichael's invocation of Black Power incited a national discussion of the future of the civil rights movement, Durham African American youth chanted "Black power" as they protested dilapidated housing conditions and the city's refusal to pave streets.[33]

Previously, the state's leading race relations official merely "dealt with the top class leadership of the NAACP [National Association for the Advancement of Colored People]." Now protests like those in Durham compelled the chairman of the state's race relations council (called the Good

Neighbor Council) David S. Coltrane to admit that Black Power "was trickling down to our State."[34] Black power was not as alien to the state as Coltrane suggested. Indeed, historians today even see the modern Black Power movement as homegrown in North Carolina, inspired by its native son Robert F. Williams, who headed a local chapter of the NAACP in North Carolina.[35] Williams's advocacy of armed resistance during the late 1950s through early 1960s spawned running debates with Martin Luther King Jr. about the merits of nonviolent integration. The life of Williams also lays bare the ways in which urban Piedmont liberalism in the 1960s helped to create space for Black Power. Williams, operating outside the urban Piedmont, was forced to flee North Carolina in 1961, whereas by the mid-1960s the newcomer Fuller, actively recruited into the state, had in the NCF a stronger base of institutional protection.[36]

Fuller's July 30 speech in rustic Woodland at the People's Conference on Poverty, ten days after the Durham march, shattered any ambiguity about the existence of Black Power in the state.[37] Fuller's brief but fiery oration not only brazenly endorsed Black Power during a storm of accusations concerning black radical insurgency within the fund, but it did so in the heart of eastern North Carolina—the geopolitical vortex of Esser's most strident critics. "All I hear is . . . don't none of you Negroes mention anything about Black Power," Fuller began the speech.[38] "Well, I'm going to talk about it." Fuller then called on the state to underwrite it, as government had a compensatory obligation to do so: "I'll tell you what, don't talk to me about the fact that . . . if something was all Negroes, then the Federal Government is financing Black Power. . . . Because all these years, every dime that has gone into Mississippi, North Carolina, Alabama, Chicago, has been financing white power, so why can't they finance us for a little while?"[39]

Financing Black Power was but a pipe dream without blacks first self-organizing to pressure the state from below, Fuller believed. For Fuller, organizing meant getting beyond both color and class. He regarded class-driven politics as a distraction, if not a divide-and-conquer subterfuge, for the black community: "It's time that you realize that the white man . . . doesn't make a distinction between the rich niggers and the poor niggers, all y'all niggers, when he get down to it. . . . So we gotta get together and you know this is a fact." During his four-minute speech Fuller questioned Washington's sincerity toward ending black poverty, Durham's progressive image, conflations of poverty with immorality, housing board policies, and "Negro Tom" professionals, whom Fuller accused of placing job security ahead of black unity.[40]

But Fuller piqued the local media most with his imagery that, to the mainstream white press at least, conjured visions of black violence and retribution. Fuller called for blacks to get a "baseball bat to fight the baseball bat that [whites] got in their hands." Second, invoking his variation of King's "I Have A Dream," Fuller dreamed of a day when he might look down on "two white boys shoveling ditches," as blacks had done for years on North Carolina's highways, he said, and tell them, "Keep on working." Such imagery, not of racial harmony but of fundamentally altered racial power relations in North Carolina, sent tremors about putative black retribution throughout the state.[41]

Zeroing in on these latter two points, the Woodland speech drew bitter condemnation from the state's leading dailies, the *Durham Morning Herald* and the *Raleigh News and Observer*, which admonished NCF officials that Fuller's subversive remarks—that drew a standing ovation from the more than 800 African Americans present—must be reproved.[42] Neither Operation Breakthrough nor the OEO in Washington saw cause for disciplinary action, however. William Pursell, a highly respected Baptist minister and new OBT director, explained that Fuller was not functioning in "an official capacity when he expressed his support of black power."[43] OEO claimed Fuller "was on his own time. He paid his own way to the meeting and, therefore, was not speaking under OEO authorization."[44] The NCF deputy director Nathan Garrett backed his subordinates by denying the slightest hint of impropriety in Woodland.

In fact, far from acceding to mounting public scrutiny, Esser and Garrett launched a search for legal and institutional safeguards to deflect subsequent attacks on the fund and its fieldworkers. Fearful that Fuller's speech and increased political activity jeopardized federal funding under the Hatch Act, which prohibited federal employees from political campaigning or openly advocating pending legislation, they quietly sought legal counsel from Moses Burt.[45] A black law partner of Congress of Racial Equality national director Floyd McKissick, Burt assured organizational officials that fund political activities were not in violation of Hatch. In fact, Burt added, since the NCF was not a federal, state, or local government agency but a private entity, it was completely exempt from the act. Although cautioning that "certain types of political activity," such as transporting voters to polls, still made the fund vulnerable to losing its tax-exempt status, Garrett recommended that NCF employees be allowed to participate openly in political organizing.

No longer constrained by Hatch, employees were now actively encouraged to engage in mass political education and activity. Many utilized fund facilities and equipment—except automobiles—to announce general elections and explain issues, so long as a particular candidate or policy was not endorsed. Field representatives were permitted to endorse public issues and candidates since, according to NCF officials, it was "difficult in some instances to determine when an employee is not on active duty." For safe measure, field representatives were asked to affix the disclaimer that their political advocacy was not made in any official capacity representing the North Carolina Fund.[46] So long as grassroots organizers functioned within these broad guidelines, Fuller and other fund employees were given carte blanche to raise the political consciousness of Durham and the state's most disfranchised.

The NCF's increased politicization strained its already tenuous relationship with other cooperating agencies, particularly in Craven County, home of the nation's first antipoverty experiment. Less than a month after the fund introduced the new political action and education policy, Robert Monte, executive director of Craven Operation Progress, quit. Possibly the only affront more objectionable than having to "stomach the verbal directives from Washington, [and] the Office of Economic Opportunity," Monte complained in his September 1966 resignation letter to Congressman David N. Henderson, "[are] the rantings of the people of the North Carolina Fund."[47] Echoing other disaffected antipoverty officials, Monte stressed the NCF's departure from its original goal of promoting individual uplift through job and vocational training. To Monte the fund's endorsement of civic activism among the poor had reduced the once-promising organization to little more than "a shield for the so-called 'black power' struggle."[48]

Monte's resignation prompted action from Henderson, who forwarded Monte's missive to OEO Director Sargent Shriver, Labor Secretary Willard Wirtz, and George Esser. In letters to the three Henderson expressed his dismay that the "primary concern . . . to enhance . . . earning power" among people of all races was betrayed in order to promote increased social activism. The congressman then reminded the antipoverty triumvirate that he was one of the few southerners who voted for the 1965 appropriation authorizing the OEO.[49] In a pithy rejoinder Esser reiterated his satisfaction with current NCF activism, particularly the "involvement of the poor . . . in planning, in policy-making, in program implementation."[50] The fund's director made it known to Monte and, among others, Shriver, Wirtz, and Henderson, that the NCF was no political mercenary interfering in local affairs. Rather, Coltrane of the Good Neighbor Council had invited both him and Garrett to eastern communities like Craven. Esser closed his retort by reminding them of Coltrane's prior entreaty for "mutual understanding of the different ways in which the same events were viewed by different people."[51] Such written encounters did little to bridge political differences; instead, the sides grew more polarized. By the fall Esser himself would become the chief target of fund detractors.

By October 1966 Monte was making his case to the governor. The solution to eradicating the chronic problems at the fund and discord more generally, Monte explained to Governor Moore, lay in removing Esser. It was Esser who remained silent as NCF officials encouraged the state's poorer citizens to work against North Carolina's congressmen and senators. When staff participation in voter registration drives took place without the knowledge of the executive director, Esser defended it. Proclamations of Black Power as a third political force in Durham were greeted with the director's compliance. Esser applauded a study conducted by a local professor sanctioning Winston-Salem's community action project as an effective agent for black political empowerment. Most paradoxically, Monte told the governor, Esser impugned fellow antipoverty officials for condemning the Black Power rantings of "anarchists" and "subverters" because they did not pursue further dialogue with such radicals—while permitting Fuller's Woodland speech to go unpunished.[52] Far from aberrant, Monte insisted that Fuller's Black Power speech was the logical culmination of the NCF's countenance of radicalization.[53] Despite a negative review spurred by Monte's charges, Esser and the fund would eventually be cleared.[54]

The Politics of Friendly versus the Politics of Exploitation: The 1967 Durham Disturbance

The mounting criticism of Fuller climaxed in late July 1967, following a march in downtown Durham to protest the city council's reluctance to deal with dilapidated housing conditions in the Piedmont's most famous black community, Hayti, an urban enclave inside Durham city limits. In Hayti, named for the French Caribbean country, black America had created its own nation. From the late 1800s until the Second World War, rural black migrants searching for tobacco and textile work descended on Durham and made Hayti their home. At its peak in the early twentieth century, well over a hundred businesses, anchored by black America's largest company, North Carolina Mutual Life Insurance, lined Hayti streets, earning the district the sobriquet Black Wall Street. Visiting in 1912, W. E. B. Du Bois boasted that there black men slept in houses built out of lumber that black men had cut and planed, woke on mattresses made by black men, wore suits bought at a colored haberdashery, returned home with victuals purchased at a local colored grocery, and cooked the meal on a stove built by coloreds; ill, the black man was taken to the colored hospital and later eulogized at a colored church, whereupon his widow received payment from a Negro insurance company to keep her children educated in a colored school.[55]

This black nation, Du Bois said, was clearly planted in liberal soil. Linking black Durham's "ambition and enterprise" to its location in "a tolerant and helpful southern city," Du Bois added, "I consider the greatest factor in [black] Durham's development to have been the disposition of the mass of ordinary white citizens of Durham to say: 'Hands off—give them a chance—don't interfere.'" According to Du Bois, whites of means, like Washington Duke, took part in symbolic and active benevolence—from building monuments to former slaves at Trinity College (now Duke University) to granting the local hospital $20,000 in start-up funds.[56]

By the 1950s and 1960s much had changed. As elsewhere in urban America, black Hayti had for years faced unresponsive local administrations and a black middle class more vested in property than community values, as evidenced by its collective flight. Left behind was a festering housing crisis for Durham's black poor. In the poorest Hayti neighborhoods 80 percent of housing, according to historian Christina Greene, remained substandard.[57]

Yet residents had nowhere to go; Durham's existing public housing had a waiting list of over 1,800 families. Durham's nearly all-white and all-middle-class Redevelopment Commission proposed remedying the housing crunch primarily by relocating Durham's black poor—a combined federal-state effort known as urban renewal.[58]

Many black Haytians had once welcomed urban renewal as a good-faith postwar policy aimed at revitalizing Hayti's black commercial district and gentrifying its blighted residential neighborhoods. But urban renewal in Durham increasingly meant social dislocation, as what was built or torn down seemed shaped to the uses of local leaders rather than dictated by the well-being of those most affected. Frustrations reached a tipping point on July 17, 1967, when plans were made public for a new freeway that would evict two hundred black and low-income families. The next night the remnants of black Hayti responded. Between 250 and 300 blacks marched, demanding enforcement of housing codes and ordinances to be included in decisions that affected occupants' lives (e.g., urban renewal).[59] Republican Congressman James Gardner, facing redistricting to a heavily Democratic Durham, capitalized on this opportunity by denouncing the NCF and calling for Fuller's resignation for helping to organize the protest march. "In the past we've had a very hard time confronting Mr. Shriver and Mr. Esser and people involved in the Fund because they immediately, categorically deny everything," Gardner told reporters.[60] Gardner demanded that the fund's three supporting foundations and OEO suspend both Fuller and Esser.[61]

The southern liberals running the two Reynolds foundations had no intention of caving in to Gardner. Foundation officers invited him to review grant procedures for himself since "he clearly had not done [this] before staging 'his' news conference." A statement from the laissez-faire Z. Smith Reynolds Foundation maintained that "the North Carolina Fund should have been free, as it was, to make its own trouble, if trouble it made."[62] With equal aplomb, Dr. William Archie representing the Mary Babcock Reynolds Foundation expressed his "great confidence in George Esser and in the N.C. Fund."[63]

Moderate and liberal whites holding or considering elective office approached the controversy differently. Durham mayor Wense Grabarek, an early supporter of the NCF's Operation Breakthrough, turned frosty, particularly as the probes escalated, while the fund's first chairman and former governor Terry Sanford became despondent. Seeking a safe public distance from the conflict, Sanford, considering a run against Senator Sam J. Ervin, refused to address either Gardner or fund activities.[64]

In a race for his political life, Durham attorney and freshman Congressman Nick Galifianakis, seeking to extricate himself from the "soft-on-crime" image saddling the national Democratic Party and the liberal moniker fastened on him by Jesse Helms, requested that OEO suspend Fuller's salary and reprimand Operation Breakthrough director William Pursell.[65] In so doing Galifianakis hoped to gain a significant bloc of backlash white voters who were put off by the Black Power rhetoric of Fuller. Conversely, black voters, Galifianakis calculated, had little choice but to support him. Redistricting was certain to make Republican House member Jim Gardner—who unseated a racially moderate incumbent by sidling up to the district's most reactionary electoral elements, publicly stating, "I don't disagree with a thing [Governor George] Wallace ever said"— his opponent in the next congressional election.[66] After a telegram from Galifianakis and later a few telephone calls to Sargent Shriver, the head of OEO did what Esser had refused to do: he suspended Howard Fuller. When the Office of Economic Opportunity Act was passed on August 20, 1964, creating the national antipoverty initiative, Sargent Shriver had assumed the agency's helm only after much persuasion from his brother-in-law Robert F. Kennedy and from President Lyndon Johnson.[67] More attracted to uplift solutions like Job Corps than political activism among the poor, Shriver preferred other programs.[68] By 1967 community action had been publicly tagged a national failure.[69] Critical headlines from the nation's premier dailies fueled skepticism about OEO and community action in particular, which soured Shriver further.[70] Compounding negative coverage were the frequent clashes of local community action programs with city administrations, which belied the Democratic Party leaders' goal of acculturating the poor politically.[71]

Many community action program leaders sought alternative political methods of empowering poorer citizens. This often ran afoul of the local Democratic apparatus. "What disturbs most mayors," Vice President Hubert Humphrey wrote Johnson, is the "belief that OEO is building and funding in the Community Action Committees opposition elements to the city administration."[72] Johnson administration officials took these complaints seriously; Johnson aide Joseph Califano and other presidential advisors thought removing Shriver was the solution.

Califano was an indispensable member of Lyndon Johnson's brain trust, in which there existed a friendly but clear division between the so-called Califano group and "the workers" like Shriver.[73] Such divisions were aggravated by Califano's proposal to Johnson for the complete reinvention of the war on poverty by eliminating OEO entirely, including Shriver's job, and transferring him to the Department of Housing and Urban Development.[74] By 1967 survival of the entire war on poverty program hinged on revamping OEO's image and approach. Shriver pursued this through a three-pronged campaign that emphasized the Economic Employment Opportunity Act's traditional agenda, refuted the agency's popular image as kowtowing to black demands, and afforded locally elected officials greater influence in privately run community action programs. Shriver hoped to win and sustain house moderates and conservatives, thus saving Johnson's war on poverty and salvaging his desiccating political career.[75] In so doing, he became more accommodating to politicians "who wanted the doctrine of maximum feasible participation toned down."[76] Neither Gardner nor Galifianakis, then, foresaw much problem in sacking Fuller in order to maintain the North Carolina delegation's continued support of OEO. Dismissing Howard Fuller, an antagonistic but relatively unknown part-time OEO tutor, to ensure future congressional support among Tar Heel representatives was, most thought, a facile quid pro quo. But when Shriver pressured Esser to fire Fuller for participating in a July 1967 near-riot in Durham, Esser rebuffed the nation's antipoverty czar with a polite yet unequivocal refusal. Shriver then exercised what limited control he had: over the written protestation of Esser, Shriver suspended Fuller without pay. Esser inquired if Fuller could at least resume his position as an instructor if the NCF agreed to continue paying.[77] His appeal was ignored.[78]

For a fleeting moment Shriver's reprimand pacified North Carolina's most ardent OEO critics. But Esser and others appeared to care little about placating Fuller's adversaries.[79] An incredulous Gardner apprised reporters at a press conference shortly after the OEO's removal of Fuller, "Esser turned around and rehired Mr. Fuller and paid his own salary by the Fund."[80] Esser also played an instrumental role in securing Fuller's paid lectureship at the University of North Carolina for the upcoming fall term. Gardner again demanded both be suspended.[81] The university's acceptance of Fuller was exploited by many as evidence of the school's affability toward dissidents.[82] Since November 1963 trustees and administration on the state's public campuses had regulated the appearance of visiting Communist speakers and other "potential pleaders of the Fifth Amendment." Now UNC made its facilities available to a deposed black activist regarded as too extreme even by the liberal-left standards of the Johnson administration.[83]

No pundit displayed greater zeal in seizing on the UNC hire than Jesse Helms. Audiences tuned in to the conservative's nightly editorials on North Carolina's radio and television stations. Those out of earshot could read the syndicated commentary in well over a hundred newspapers nationwide. Helms used his media megaphone to condemn "the liberal school on the hill" for the "hiring of a race agitator to teach," which he saw as another show of defiance under the guise of academic freedom and the aegis of the state's liberal press.[84] Administrators and faculty had anticipated such fallout and shielded their appointment against political infringement. UNC President William Friday counseled trustees, Governor Dan Moore among them, that Fuller was appointed according to "standard procedures . . . established" by the UNC Faculty Advisory Committee, and, more generally, that academic hires were the exclusive domain of the university; a realm where political vicissitudes had no privilege.[85]

Although area newspapers had been almost uniformly skeptical of Fuller since 1965, Gardner's politically transparent motives were too egregious for major Piedmont dailies to ignore. At a press conference assembled by Gardner, white reporters explained to the visiting congressman the social legitimacy of local black protest. "Let's talk about Durham, North Carolina," pressed a white reporter. "The Negroes say, 'We have tried the public works committee, the bus company, and everybody else for two years to get the public housing laws enforced, to get bus service, to get our streets paved, to get sidewalks put in. . . . We've had no action yet, therefore we have no choice but to go to the streets.' This is simply petitioning their government for redress." Gardner, thoroughly uninformed about the complaints, responded as if the reporter's request never existed: "Well, let's talk about Detroit."[86] The headline in the *Raleigh News and Observer*, "Gardner, the Exploiter," also summed up the editorial positions of the *Charlotte Observer*, *Greensboro Daily News*, *Winston-Salem Journal*, and other Piedmont dailies.[87]

A similar sentiment was reflected in the appeals emanating from the more moderate pockets of Durham's black middle class and elite. Lacking the social capital among poorer blacks accrued by Fuller in his two years of community activism there, Durham's black elite believed the young radical's ability to calm a rancorous crowd made him an invaluable public asset to Durham. Even the Durham Business and Professional Chain, traditionally estranged from political activism and long regarded as a bulwark of support for moderate black leadership in the city, urged the OEO to reinstate Fuller. Through Fuller economically deprived Negroes "had gained much-needed manhood and self-respect. To me, this is what the antipoverty program is all about," wrote Chain President F. V. Allison.[88]

In Durham the racial tensions climaxed in July 1967, when "racial polarization," historian Christina Greene notes, "engulfed the Bull City."[89] Faced with these extremes, many local liberals—notably those neither in nor running for office—sided with the group that defended Howard Fuller. Fuller could not have had a more dedicated defender than Esser. In these ways liberals helped to create an operational space—defending and defending the defenders of Durham's most visible Black Power advocate.

While Fuller would stay with the fund as a training director, he resigned from his UNC lectureship in February 1968, saying he could no longer accept the personal inconsistency of pressing others to "bring their talents and skills to the black community" while he remained at a predominantly white university. His decision was also undoubtedly triggered by pressure from the chancellor and UNC president following Fuller's participation and arrest in a campus demonstration.[90] Months later Fuller was one of six organizers banned from the University of North Carolina for helping to organize 250 campus cafeteria workers in their strike against Saga Food Service.[91] His suspension foreshadowed a series of repressive state laws through 1968 and 1969 curtailing the presence of controversial campus speakers and protestors.

For Fuller's black radical contemporaries, the assassination of Martin Luther King Jr. and the urban rebellions in its wake signaled the bankruptcy of the liberal integrationist agenda of the early civil rights movement. To them the slaying of a patriarch of pacifism was the culmination of intractable racial enmity within U.S. society. When questioned by a reporter about interracial activism just weeks prior to King's death, Fuller would echo the rising crescendo among black radicals: "Right now I'm in favor of black people getting a coalition among themselves." Control of black institutions and the community was "much more important than integration," Fuller told the reporter.[92]

Nationally, OEO's continued capitulation to moderate southern Democrats merely reaffirmed black militants' view of the limitations of racial liberalism. An October 1967 strategy meeting among Shriver, House Speaker Carl Albert, and various southern congressmen "to see whether further concessions should and could be made to round-up Southern congressional support" for future authorization of the agency set the agenda for the coming year.[93] Political expediency eclipsed the participatory ethos that once was the focus of OEO's community action programs.

By the end of 1968 a wary Fuller seemed set to sever any link to notions of racial inclusion. Still, he agreed to address the interracial Durham Council on Human Relations in late November. White liberals on the council still urged integration, but Fuller spurned the notion: "Mine is a kind of separatist philosophy," he told them plainly.[94] Despite Fuller's separatist stance, white liberals on the council still urged integration. "I would like . . . people just like this group here . . . [to] keep up the conversation between the two groups," a white male member wistfully commented. "Is coalition possible between blacks and liberals?" another earnestly wanted to know. Still another young white woman persisted: "Would this group perhaps not benefit from your association with us?" "Nah, you don't need me," Fuller replied, "I might as well tell you about how I feel about you. . . . I think y'all might really believe in the dignity of man and all that. But you don't have no power. You're just like me. Except they think you're crazy."[95] Radicals and liberals were marginalized from the city's power structure. For blacks to effect change they had to confront southern progressives and moderates in power like Mayor Wense Grabarek who, unlike liberals, were disinclined to urge desegregation but were nonetheless willing to accede to it, unlike hard-line conservatives who tended to take a more obdurate stance opposing such issues as school desegregation and voting rights.

Fuller emphasized the inadequacy of liberalism in Durham. "All I'm trying to do is get you to be realistic about what you can do and where you are. Now, whether you're going to have power in 1970? I don't know. 1980? I don't know. But, I know right now you don't have any."[96] Fuller believed the flaw was not liberal ideology per se but its lack of influence and access to resources. As Fuller increasingly saw it, the practical limits of liberalism—due to its marginalization in Durham, which left it vulnerable to co-optation—precluded it from materially improving the daily lives of most blacks. Interracial coalitions had also, at times, been inimical to the black community's welfare. If blacks, Fuller hypothesized, voted in their interest—for example, not supporting some liberal initiatives like school integration—white liberal support would quickly evaporate. Vacillating white moderates and liberals at places such as UNC, Fuller noted in an interview, were not really ready for total confrontation.[97] Thus Fuller's goal was to organize poor black people, "not meeting with a bunch of white people and . . . philosophizing."[98]

Establishment liberals, while perhaps holding some power, lacked the political will to engage in the protests necessary to reorient power relations within Durham. Liberals, Fuller warned, were not radicals. "If it's a question of you being really radical, then you're going to get in there and use whatever you can use out of that system . . . . To me that's the difference between the person who really believes in humanity . . . and one who's shucking and jiving." Liberals seemed willing to employ the rhetoric of racial equality as long as their social and economic position remained unthreatened.[99]

To Fuller nowhere were the shortcomings of racial liberalism more evident than in institutions of higher learning. A meaningful education, Fuller declared, "has to be put to use. . . . It's really not that useful if you can't use it to change society."[100] Simply allowing blacks to attend the state's historically white institutions did little to improve living standards for African Americans. As Fuller saw it, colleges like the University of North Carolina all too frequently invoked racial liberalspeak while colluding with nonunionized companies against predominantly African American cafeteria workers, as in the Saga example. Many students harbored similar reservations. Participating in an internship program that summer of 1968, students from across the state encountered the ravages of poverty in Durham's poorer black communities. Along with other students involved in earlier labor organizing of the mostly black nonacademic workers on campus, they began to confront the limits of traditional education in grappling with racial inequality. To black students especially, racial liberals showed little interest in addressing black students' academic and campus needs, as well as the needs of the African American community at large. At places like Duke, black students were neither encouraged to assimilate nor offered a cultural support network by the university. These issues would peak amid the battle for black studies at Duke in late 1968 and 1969.[101]

Duke University and the Black Student Movement, 1968–1969

Known as the Harvard of the South, Duke University's academic standing and growing cosmopolitan outlook had long challenged the Mencken moniker of the South as an intellectual and cultural "Bozart." Yet Duke still yearned to transcend its regional stature. Once a campus exclusively for the sons and daughters of the state's most privileged families, by 1969 North Carolinians comprised only a quarter of Duke's student population. Of the remainder, half of all Duke students were nonsoutherners. The university advertised its newfound multiculturalism to prospective students, particularly in its 1969 promotional literature that hailed "diversity as one of its greatest assets."[102] For the undergraduate population, which included 101 black students, becoming national in the late 1960s also meant at least a token change in its racial composition.[103]

Yet black students' concerns for a more purposeful education remained neglected by the administration. For two and a half years the Afro-American Society (AAS), a campus organization of black students, conveyed their numerous grievances. These were largely ignored. Duke president Douglas Knight, who took the Duke post on the eve of John F. Kennedy's assassination in 1963, was frequently compared to the late president. Both were young, northern erudite liberals vowing to usher in a new generation of change. During Knight's early administration the removal of "colored" signs and the admission of blacks into the undergraduate college denoted visible progress. Yet this auspicious beginning and Knight's "liberal credentials" were increasingly compromised by financial reliance on alumni and a lack of "moral courage . . . essential" in challenging trustees opposed to social reform.[104] To AAS advisor Howard Fuller, Knight was "the prototype of a weak liberal white man . . . trying to please everybody by giving everybody a little bit."[105] Committees formulated to grapple with campus racial issues through negotiation appeared equally ineffectual. By the end of the 1968 fall term these grievances remained unresolved. "We'd go to the appropriate channels. . . . That was all unproductive. The blacks were doing most of the leg work and getting the screws put on them academically," said one exasperated student negotiator.[106] Many students believed the situation was worsening, as the attrition rate for black students mushroomed to double that of their white counterparts.[107]

In early October 1968 the Afro-American Society at Duke had submitted only twelve grievances to the administration, which were still unresolved by late January 1969. The AAS also noted that plans to implement black studies programs had recently taken place at northern universities like Harvard.[108] By February, after four months of negotiations and student protests, Knight finally responded with a series of concessions, including the appointment of an advisor to address minority issues and the creation of a summer remedial program for students. But he failed to talk specifically about instituting a black studies program—the AAS's number one priority. "That is not enough," Mike McBride, AAS member fired back.[109] Students concluded decisive action was necessary.[110]

One of the earlier, minor concessions agreed upon by Knight proved costly. Knight had agreed to endorse and sponsor the Beauty of Black Week, which had already been planned by the AAS for early February 1969 to celebrate black culture and heritage. Among the featured speakers was activist and former Mississippi Freedom Democratic Party veteran Fannie Lou Hamer, who shared her harrowing experiences in the civil rights struggle in the Deep South. Hamer's account inspired seventy-five black students to march to the president's house. "It was a call to action," one student remembered.[111] Students were invited in by Knight, where for more than two hours they discussed the implementation of a black studies program. The next day, with little accomplished except the students' temporary pacification, Knight departed for a two-week visit to New York. Less than forty-eight hours later forty-seven black students seized the central records office in the Allen Administrative Building on Duke's West Campus. They had earlier contacted four or five sympathetic white reporters from Duke's leading student newspaper, the *Chronicle*. Student reporters disseminated the AAS press release to the national media.[112]

President Knight announced from New York that the university would not accede to any student demands, and he ordered students to vacate the administration building or face suspension and trespassing charges. Back at Duke, barricaded students released a list of demands to the Student Liberation Front, which copied and distributed the list to the approximately 350 students, faculty members, and administrators gathered on the main quadrangle.[113] An emergency faculty meeting convened on East Campus focused on the president's ultimatum to student militants and the more immediate threat of violence. Here the faculty's marginality became evident. Alarmed by Knight's implied use of force, one professor moved that the faculty request the president to "suspend the force of the statement until after deliberations of this faculty meeting," and several faculty quickly seconded the motion. Knight implacably refused. After evading questions about whether the police had been called, Knight finally responded: "If your research or your office were in that building you would have been concerned too." His callous disregard for Duke's black students astonished the most dispassionate faculty members.[114] Many grumbled that the East Campus emergency meeting was merely a diversionary strategy to keep them away from imminent police action on West Campus. Twenty faculty members rushed to the doorways of Allen "to put their bodies on the line." The majority, however, stayed silent or supportive of the administration. Knight thanked the faithful professoriate and reminded them that Duke "succeeds only if it has the loyal support of its faculty."[115] As sit-in protestors fled Allen, a campus melee among police, protestors, and white students ensued, only escalating tensions and attracting even more students to the campus. "When the police finally left, the reasonable, privileged, obedient white students of Duke University were stunned," observed a reporter for the *North Carolina Anvil*, a local alternative weekly.[116]

The hard-line position taken by Knight spurred a backlash among students. Between 15 and 20 percent of all students boycotted class the following day in a show of solidarity with black students. Duke faculty and instructors organized free university courses to discuss the takeover. The Free Academic Senate, a group of fifty predominantly young Duke instructors, was formed in response to "what has happened and the unresponsiveness of present structures." Professor Thomas Rainey angrily concluded that many professors at the emergency meeting had eagerly "sold out to the corporate structure," granting Knight carte blanche "to bring the pigs down on us." In a display of cross-racial solidarity, two hundred Chapel

Hill students conducted a forty-five-minute sit-in, and 125 UNC students traveled to Duke, chanting "UNC supports Duke."[117]

But Knight stood firm, insisting that the Allen takeover be viewed within a broader context. Rebellions on the campuses of Columbia, Berkeley, and Wisconsin had limited "our freedom to respond to militant students. In turn, other campuses are concerned about what happens at Duke."[118] Campus protests brought on unintended pecuniary consequences as well: according to the university secretary, Duke had lost hundreds of thousands of dollars from actual donors, if not millions in potential pledges, following a silent student vigil in the wake of Martin Luther King Jr.'s assassination in 1968. A more restrained administrative response to the Allen Administrative Building takeover might have resulted in devastating financial consequences for the university. In addition, Knight feared that if Durham police had not been mobilized, Duke trustees surely would have fired him.[119] He further feared for his safety and that of his family, not because of black firebrands but because of conservative and hostile whites. Experiencing physical and ideological vulnerability for the first time ostensibly gave Knight a more empathetic take on black student struggle. Despite expressing such empathy toward black students in his memoir, published thirty years later, it was not enough to have him defy a governor.[120]

Advisors to Governor Robert Scott influenced Knight with their domino theory. They warned the Duke president that "if the University gives in, within twenty-four hours demands" by student protestors would crop up on other North Carolina campuses.[121] On the advice of a high-ranking state official who feared exacerbating existing campus tensions while stressing a tough-on-militants public image, Knight rescinded an earlier agreement to speak to the student body in the aftermath of the Allen takeover. This time students were joined by faculty, administrators, and community activists who quickly occupied the vacuum created in Knight's absence.[122]

In the president's front yard an interracial throng of nearly a thousand supporters of black studies appeared. Knight, Fuller, black student leaders, and the newly formed Faculty Committee on Student Concerns worked on a plan until reaching a substantive agreement three hours later. By morning a press conference was held announcing Duke as the first major southern university to initiate a black studies program. Crisis in Durham had been averted, aside from an ostensibly minor quibble, the *New York Times* added: the issue of control of the program and curriculum.[123]

The Duke Student Movement in National Context

Duke typified student protest movements nationally. During the 1968–69 academic year there were 292 major student protests at over 230 college campuses around the country. One survey, published in a special issue of *Black Scholar*, profiled these protests: most occurred at four-year liberal-arts universities with a campus population of four thousand or more students, with blacks comprising 6 percent or less. Region mattered less than admission standards: the higher an institution's academic standards, the more probable it was that campus protests would occur. These universities, moreover, were either located in or near a city with a sizable black population.[124] Whites played a not inconsequential role in facilitating black studies. What made white administrators yield were durable, ramped up, interracial demonstrations in favor of black studies. Nondisruptive protests, like vigils, marches, and rallies, proved far less effective in persuading university administrators to reform policies than student seizures, takeovers, and strikes. Administrators generally considered black calls for more courses, black faculty, and cultural centers more legitimate than similar demands by their white counterparts, and thus blacks' demands had a higher probability of being fulfilled, 47 percent to 27 percent. But the most winning alchemy was racially mixed groups calling for black recognition: 50 percent of the time they achieved one or more of their demands. Paradoxically, interracial protests also served as lightning rods for police violence. Though violence erupted in less than 10 percent of major protests, police were most inclined to club or mace mixed-race groups. And police action appeared to ratchet up the possibility of violence on campus.[125]

On balance, most university administrators responded with a blend of reform and repression. Within this group, historically black colleges tended more heavily toward repressing and disciplining campus protesters than their white counterparts. The hiring of Nathan Hare, fired from Howard University for what the *Negro Digest* termed "his militant pro-black activities," offers a qualitative testimony to this. San Francisco State University president Robert Smith hired Hare to coordinate the nation's first black studies program in 1968. He "had not spoken with any one in the sociology department about the appointment," the president told critics upset at his unilateral decision. What was important, Smith maintained, was that Hare had a doctorate from Chicago, wanted to come to

San Francisco, and his hire would keep "the lid on the place" by improving relations with campus activists angered over the suspension of four Black Student Union leaders.[126] Duke, then, conformed to rather than led a wider trend—from the university's town-and-gown profile down to the common criticism that, whether from elite arrogance or pure fecklessness, it submitted to interracial student pressure.

Common Ground Lost: Black Studies and the Failure of Liberal Interventionism

Following the announcement of the black studies program, the Afro-American Society submitted four plans to the faculty committee requesting equal participation on the Afro-American Studies supervisory committee, whose purpose was to hire faculty and outline courses for the program. Duke's faculty committee responded by offering students three positions on their eight-member board. Leaders in the AAS wanted more equitable representation: "You have five; give us four and let us agree on one further member." The administration said "No."[127]

At this apparent impasse, more than 50 percent of the black student body threatened to withdraw from Duke. The same evening, at a torchlight march to St. Joseph's AME Church, AAS advisor Howard Fuller talked about the students' desire to form a new university that would, as he later wrote, "provide a framework within which black education can become relevant to the needs of the black community."[128] The name settled on by students, Fuller said, was Malcolm X Liberation University.[129] By week's end AAS advisers Fuller and Nathan Garrett, the new director of the recently formed North Carolina Fund–offshoot Foundation for Community Development, called a press conference to announce the opening of MXLU in Durham. They hinted, however, that the school's opening might be delayed, with students returning to Duke if a compromise agreement with the faculty council was reached. Despite forty-two students' verbal resolve to withdraw, only a third of that number actually did so.[130]

Opening as scheduled on March 17, 1969, MXLU remained open throughout the spring of 1969, offering weekly supplementary classes for students at Duke, North Carolina Central, and high schools, as well as members of the community. There they studied African history, principles of community organizing, and works by and about Malcolm X, and learned Ki-Swahili.[131] Throughout the spring and summer there were resource development meetings, planning MXLU's future with black students at other colleges—even while making the most of Duke's resources.[132]

Keeping an agreement following the Allen occupation, the Duke administration sponsored a two-day retreat to explore the question of black studies at Duke. Still aspiring to the Harvard model, Duke invited Harvard historian Martin Kilson.[133] The Afro-American Society brought in consultants from Federal City College, who themselves were organizing the Center for Black Education, a Washington, D.C.–based black institution of higher learning that was to be free from external control.[134] The weekend retreat fortified student alliances with Federal City officials and other founders of the Center for Black Education, which ultimately emerged, in spirit, as the northernmost branch of MXLU. The methodological difference between a traditional Western education and a Pan-African one was obvious, school founders argued: universities like Duke prepared students to participate in postcolonial oppression; as counter institutions, the Center for Black Education and MXLU designed a pedagogy for black liberation.[135]

As the summer months waned so did the possibilities of creating a mutually acceptable black studies program. A satisfactory resolution, thereby precluding MXLU's opening, withered rapidly under the inertia of Duke's supervisory committee, which conducted only three meetings during the spring term and summer in the aftermath of Allen. Following the unveiling of the committee's black studies program just days before the start of the 1969–70 academic year, few were surprised that the AAS resoundingly rejected the new curriculum. In a prepared statement released by the society, Adrenee Glover listed the group's disappointments. There was not one black instructor. There was no director. There was no budget. Only one new course, on African American literature, was introduced. "Most of all," the spokesperson for the AAS added, "there is no black control." Since the black studies program was interdisciplinary, its curriculum content, selection of faculty, and course descriptions all remained under the direction of the established departments of English, sociology, and history.[136]

During the same period, MXLU was transformed from a curricular corollary of Duke to a freestanding institution. While the supervisory committee assembled only three times in nearly six months, Fuller and

students convened countless meetings with school organizers, theoreticians, and activists in the state and across the nation. And in contrast to
Duke's ad hoc committee, which was bogged down in perfunctory exer-
cises like renaming courses, alternative school organizers secured new classroom spaces, recruited students, and expanded the course of instruction
to include nontraditional studies like martial arts. For MXLU organizers
institutional sloth validated apprehensions about the sincerity of Duke's
commitment to black studies, and accentuated the importance of black
control over the discipline.

In short, a confluence of forces propelled Duke to move from a final
vestige of Jim Crow higher education to become the first major university
in the South to announce a black studies program. Yet racial liberals, particularly Duke administrators, fundamentally misinterpreted the resolve
of black students and the importance of a scholarly methodology and apparatus—one that did not treat black studies as a functionally isolating
academic pursuit. Rather than participate, as they saw it, in a program
"controlled by the perpetrators of our oppression," black students opted
for a pedagogy that cultivated the knowledge and skills relevant for black
liberation.[137]

The Making of Malcolm X Liberation University

In Durham's decaying downtown black business district, the once-aban-
doned two-story brick warehouse—freshly painted in red, black, and
green—now became a schoolhouse for black revolution. Classes began
October 27, 1969, with fifty-one students enrolled from seventeen states.[138]
A few transferred from prestigious colleges and universities like Radcliffe
(then still a women's college), American, and Cornell; many were community citizens who wanted to contribute; and one or two were young
teenagers who had been disciplinary problems.[139] Most of them were fresh
from high school, and most, at least later, were from northern cities. Those
who could afford more than the $300 yearly tuition minimum were asked
to pay more. Financial assistance was provided, as Fuller phrased it, for
"any Brother or Sister needing it."[140] Though whites could not enroll they
furthered the alternative college in other ways; Duke Professor Jim Graham even taught courses. But it was an all-black institution. At the day-

long opening celebration, white reporters and cameramen were granted permission to peer through the building's windows, but Fuller warned it would be the last time they were allowed to do so.[141]

MXLU's significance lay beyond the South. The university headed a national network of primary and secondary Pan-African feeder schools throughout the Northeast and Midwest, including high schools in Youngstown and Milwaukee, an elementary school in Newark, and an early-education school in Atlanta.[142] The federation joined together in developing curriculum, sharing teachers and other resources, and cooperating in fund-raising.[143] In this way, the making of MXLU was a window into the governing culture of Black Power.

Throughout MXLU's brief existence the curriculum underwent substantive alterations. By the time the Pan-African university moved to Greensboro in October 1970, it would offer only four main areas of study: biomedics, teacher training, engineering, and communications.[144] It would also slash the number of students from fifty-one to twenty-nine, and extend its length of study to a minimum of three years for some fields.[145] Despite these changes MXLU's mission endured: "a black university designed to provide training to meet the needs of the black community."[146]

Inscribed on the peach-colored walls just inside the door was a quotation from Malcolm X that summed up the vanguard spirit of enrollees: a "new generation of black people who have become disenchanted with the entire system and who are ready now and willing to do something about it."[147] The first step toward eradicating "the impact of neocolonial hegemony" over blacks was severing oneself from the values and culture of white society. Black studies and black study groups were responsible for "not just talking about Africans living in Africa" but, as MXLU Council of Elders Stokely Carmichael challenged students, for interrogating the black world throughout the diaspora.[148] The next stage was to train a cadre of young brothers and sisters with the technical skills and information needed to transform Pan-Africanism from an amorphous ideology into a functional political-cultural-economic system. "When students come out of Malcolm X Liberation University, they will be in a position to offer their skills and services to our people wherever they are most needed in America, Africa, the West Indies . . . or Nova Scotia." "Wherever you may work," one speaker guaranteed the inaugural class of MXLU, "you will be contributing . . . toward the building of a strong African nation."[149]

MXLU's Primary Investor: Episcopal Funding
and the Religious Right Backlash

The martyrdom of Malcolm X attracted students to the university, but marketing Malcolm X as a cultural symbol to white donors in the late 1960s was a far more difficult sell. To many Christians funding a university bearing the name of a black radical Muslim was not an expression of interfaith dialogue but the sanctioning of militant Islam. Believing that America was God's instrument against communism, some local parishioners were mortified that Fuller categorically refused to profess Christianity or any religion. Telling questioners at a November 1969 meeting at an Episcopal church in Raleigh "it's none of your business," Fuller fueled fears that the school fronted for communism. His commentary on communism that night illustrated cultural nationalism's long-running ambivalence toward leftist politics. As he explained, the métier of the school clashed with the social realities of both communism and socialism: "There's a lot of racism in [communism and socialism] and I don't want any part of them either."[150] Fuller bristled at repeated suggestions of the White Left's influence over the university: "People think [communists and socialists] can just move in and take over anything."[151] Unlike the fear of a Communist menace masking as black separatism, no one expressed comparable fears about liberalism's ability to engage and co-opt. Indeed, it appeared the working assumption was the exact opposite.

The school's heretical eponym distracted potential donors from taking comfort in the counter-countercultural policies intended to govern campus life. MXLU, promised Fuller, was to be a pro–hard work, self-reliant academic environment. Beyond this, Fuller declared that in an era of rampant college-aged marijuana use MXLU would be a drug- and gun-free zone. And when it came to campus promiscuity, the student handbook put the point best: "This is not a free love hippie hideaway. . . . This is not a commune, or a Charles Manson gang bang atmosphere. African institutions have always had rules to govern behavior."[152]

The university's name, however, overshadowed overlapping bourgeois and African values expressed by Fuller and seemingly shared with church members who attended the November meeting. Urging Fuller to inoculate MXLU by using a less menacing name, one member blurted aloud what others no doubt thought: "Why not some other black man like Nat King Cole?"[153] In focusing more on name branding and rhetoric than on the conforming tendencies that group and organizational behaviors would probably have on MXLU students, grant critics missed how religious and quasi-religious groups like the Black Muslims and MXLU bore a "striking resemblance to the[ir own] old white, middle-class puritan morality."[154]

MXLU's early development came about through various kinds of support.[155] Local blacks donated money, resources, and time. Novice carpenters painted signs, laid bricks, leveled the cement floors, and lowered ceilings. Two houses in the community were secured for MXLU students to live in. In the university's first year Fuller raised approximately $60,000 for Malcolm X through numerous speaking engagements and donations.[156] Nationally, the Federation of Pan-African Institutions, the World Council of Churches, the Program to Combat Black Racism, Cummins Engine Foundation, and the Inter-religious Foundation for Community Development were listed as sponsors. However, the $45,000 grant that MXLU applied for and received from the national Episcopal Church comprised the single largest and most controversial funding during the school's first year.[157] The backlash this grant engendered reflected a burgeoning revivalist movement among religious conservatives.

Since 1967 the General Convention Special Program (GCSP) of the national Episcopal Church had awarded funding to various black groups across the nation. Every diocese was encouraged to create community development programs to assist in urban areas. Bishop of North Carolina Thomas Fraser appointed an Urban Advisory Committee in February 1969 composed of twelve Episcopal laymen, eight African Americans, and four whites. Seven members of the committee were members of St. Titus Episcopal Church, a predominantly black church in Durham. Fraser selected the Rev. E. Nathaniel Porter, the African American vicar of St. Titus, as group director. As a national grant, GCSP required only consultation with local dioceses. Nevertheless, Fraser, in agreement with Porter and the Urban Advisory Committee's recommendation, endorsed the GCSP emergency grant to MXLU. After meeting on September 20, 1969, and interviewing Fuller the following day, the committee again unanimously recommended that the full grant be awarded.[158]

Fraser agreed that MXLU fell within the guidelines of the church's program and was "quite appropriate for funding."[159] Before the first payment was received on October 2, however, the national church and Fraser would find themselves amid a firestorm of criticism from disapproving white laity. The internal dissension surfacing as a result of the MXLU grant revealed the underpinnings of the national philosophical split among Episcopal conservatives, moderates, and liberals throughout 1969 and 1970.[160]

Bishop Fraser hoped that the grant afforded a chance for parishioners to reexamine their personal racial, class, and religious myopia.[161] Pressure from Fraser transformed latent resentment against liberals who were "running and ruining" the church into the mushrooming of open rancor.[162] WRAL-TV editorialized that Bishop Fraser, the Diocese of North Carolina (one of three Episcopal dioceses in the state), and the liberal national church hierarchy banked "on the probability that citizens more conservative than he . . . will 'go along' rather than rock the boat with dissent."[163] Nothing could have been further from the truth.

Fraser had support among blacks and a sympathetic core of intellectuals, clergymen, and youth. Most North Carolina parishioners, however, regarded contributions to black nation-building projects like MXLU as illustrative of the diocesan and national church's disconnection from the views of devout lifetime Episcopalians, who were dedicated to the church but loathed black radicals like Fuller.[164] North Carolina Episcopalians threatened to quit the national church over the MXLU grant. Granting the money to militants for this "so-called university" undermined Christian society, declared a vicar from Raleigh's affluent North Hills section.[165] The Rev. Thomas Thrasher of Chapel Hill rued the lapse in judgment leading to the allocation.[166] Despite escalating reproof, the bishop defended his decision to support the national church and the local committee's award. "In my opinion," Fraser unrepentantly expressed in a letter to concerned clergy, wardens, and members of the diocesan council, "we have observed the democratic process."[167] But eventually North Carolina Episcopalians forced Fraser to take a harder line against the national church.

This challenge was by far the most difficult of the outspoken fifty-five-year-old pastor's career. For more than a decade Fraser had been a staunch integrationist, refusing to acquiesce to congregational separatist will despite the threat of disgruntled churchgoers withholding financial support. "We will be led by the cross . . . we will not be coerced by the dollar," a defiant Fraser was fond of saying.[168] His previous racial liberalism, however, made the MXLU grant more difficult to sell to the conservative general laity. Fraser undoubtedly would have been more persuasive if he had believed in the project himself. But unconvinced of the school's socially redeeming merits, Fraser lamented the alternative school's mission and what he considered to be Fuller's commitment to black isolationism.[169] Fraser's allegiance to the national church and commitment to Porter and the advisory committee, however, overshadowed his personal ambivalence toward Fuller and MXLU.[170]

At times Fraser appeared almost stunned that the modest grant elicited such vitriol from the laity and public at large: "In all honesty . . . much of the noise about Malcolm X Liberation University is all out of proportion to the size of the grant, the school and its possible influence."[171] Other clergymen, like Chapel Hill's Thrasher, were equally mystified that a disproportionately nominal award—$45,000 out of the national church's total budget of $14 million, or about 32/10,000ths of one percent—could bring the state chapter to the brink of withdrawing from the national church.[172] "Is this one mistake to be allowed to endanger that whole enterprise" of correcting past racial wrongs, he asked. Reactions to the grant decision, Thrasher believed, were symptomatic of liberals and moderates who opted for compromise and conservatives who threatened to "withdraw when things don't go to suit them."[173]

To more orthodox parishioners the funding of the university signaled larger concerns with what was perceived as the centralization of power, the loss of authority of local churches, and declining social values. Although the grant amount was miniscule relative to the national budget, the award itself symbolized for some the apparent triumph of an "out-of-touch" liberalism, nourished by the secularism of the 1960s, over the popular will of parishioners. For other white communicants, the grant symbolized not simply the loss of control to central authority but how diocesan liberals, in cahoots with national decision makers, had embarked the church on vehemently disliked "social crusades." That fear was exacerbated by the name of the university.

Conservatives attempted to starve the diocese, pressing Fraser to quit the national church over the grant. Statewide, 50 of the 138 parishes failed to reach the annual contributions pledged by church members.[174] The Diocese of North Carolina sustained reductions in 1969 church proceeds of $70,000 after the MXLU grant. Fraser had never witnessed statewide financial retribution like this. At one point the diocese reduced its support to the national church by 38 percent. He informed national church officials that congregational financial backlash rendered it impossible to propose a budget for the upcoming year because so many pledges were either conditional, reduced, or withdrawn altogether.[175] At St. Philip's Episcopal Church, within two blocks and full view of Malcolm X, pledges dropped $13,000 following the grant award.[176] Sharp disinvestment by white laity had palpable and immediate consequences. "Withholding the dollar from the church is the beginning of the end of spiritual life," a financially desperate Fraser pleaded to convention conveners in Salisbury, North Carolina.[177] Fraser's caveat was to no avail; programmatic casualties were inevitable. The diocese's National and Diocesan Program Fund, as well as other social programs, were either eliminated or eviscerated beyond recognition.[178]

This southern liberal bishop understood the practical realities and succumbed to popular communicant conservatism. An accommodating Fraser acceded to demands for more local control for future screening requests and backed off on aid to a low-income federation of black neighborhood councils named the United Organizations for Community Improvement—a grant he had enthusiastically endorsed a year earlier.[179] Fear of financial backlash persuaded the once-brash bishop to decline to canvass votes for greater black and youth participation for the upcoming diocesan convention. It was his responsibility, Fraser would later say, to "keep . . . good faith and credibility" with local members. This meant understanding the pragmatic limits—and financial costs—of southern liberalism.

Other southern Episcopalians simply rejected similar projects. The bishop of South Carolina, for instance, publicly refused to approve a GCSP grant intended for the Hilton Head community. Clergy in Texas and Virginia had already registered a formal rebuke in a resolution denouncing the national church's capitulation to the "black-jacking of funds" for James Forman's reparation tract, *Black Manifesto*.[180] Following a September national executive council conference, southern bishops and officials of Alabama, Florida, and Georgia voiced a similar collective displeasure with the Diocese of North Carolina's action, particularly with Esser's personal approbation of the grant.[181]

North Carolina and the Nation

The situation in North Carolina demonstrates a larger paradoxical point about modern liberalism. Liberal politics of inclusion, in this instance its support of Black Power in North Carolina, proved a political boon for the right. Among those whose social image was rehabilitated by such cultural politics was George Wallace, who surfaced as the national voice for blue-collar white ethnics in the Northeast and Midwest. Wallace exploited the period's perceived social and cultural unrest by rebelling against the conformity of the party system, attacking black radicals for urban violence and blaming their white allies for encouraging them.[182] Appropriating the polarizing language that guided him in Alabama in the early 1960s, Wallace employed the wedge words of "law and order," code for suppression of Black Power militants, and linked liberal permissiveness to the moral decline of America.[183] At the height of his popularity in late September 1968, one in five registered voters supported the Alabama governor.[184]

In Detroit and surrounding suburbs a reinvigorated white conservative movement emerged after 1967. Detroit Wallacites began "embracing politics to the right of Roman Gribbs," Detroit's moderate-conservative mayor, whom many whites considered too reticent to combat the perceived Black Power threat. "It soon . . . dawned on these white liberals," historian Heather Thompson observed, "that [their] plans to listen to, and even to fund, black radicals had seriously gone awry." Black militants remained relatively marginal figures in Detroit, writes Thompson, because they were not menacing enough and, unlike more politically influential whites, did not represent a true long-term threat to the social and political order. Questions about a social and moral breakdown helped George Wallace cultivate ethnic and blue-collar voters, particularly in midwestern states like Michigan, who blamed liberals for the 1967 Detroit uprising.[185]

Out west Ronald Reagan's firm stance against what white Californians widely perceived as the enabling role of liberalism in countenancing black militants on college campuses and elsewhere did little damage to his popularity in California's 1970 governor's race. Instead, in a state where Democrats outnumbered registered Republicans by nearly two-to-one, conservative apparatchiks credited Reagan's reelection to tapping into white populist sentiment against such militancy.[186] In New York Black Power was viewed through the prism of social unrest. Eager conservatives and anxious whites reacted against the Black Power movement and Great Society liberals, who were "blamed for responding to the grievances and demands of a militant minority while ignoring the fears and desires of a 'silent majority.'"[187] Gallup, Harris, Roper, and University of Michigan polls quantified what the New Right already knew: that political capital could be made among discontented white Democrats in the North and South, most notably by linking Black Power's rise to the supposed failure of liberalism.[188] "We are in a revolution, and it is characteristic of revolutions to go too far," proclaimed one North Carolina priest, summing up the views of both moderates and conservatives about putative liberal permissiveness regarding Black Power.[189]

Signifying this social revolution in North Carolina was the MXLU affair.[190] If the national church saw fit to fund MXLU over the desires of many local white Episcopalians, conservatives seemed to reason, no diocesan was immune from the reach of central authority. Nationally, Episcopal Church conservatives interpreted such funding initiatives in recent years as the usurping of the national church by liberal activists. Critics saw the national church driven mostly by agitating and autocratic New York liberals, who, circumventing the will of the people, brooked and backed Black Power without consultation or regard of local parishes. Yet congregants' sense of alienation, and the conservative cultural awakening that ensued, went beyond simple antimodernism. As an example, perhaps the most vociferous opponents of the MXLU grant came from a parish whose members were among the most adaptive within the Diocese of North Carolina, Raleigh's North Hills. With its easy access to the high-tech park of Research Triangle, North Hills became a popular residential destination for college-educated northern transplants, including many racial moderates. Often the complaint from these self-described color-blind critics, almost all white, was that in supporting a racially exclusive school, funders might inadvertently resuscitate Jim Crow. As Lisa McGirr, Martin Marty, and others argue, traditionalists were not unfettered antimodernists.[191] Indeed, some opposing the grant often advanced particularistic arguments that to later scholars might appear downright postmodern.

Throughout southern dioceses, nothing appeared to infuriate white Episcopalians more than "the idea that outsiders could be involved in decisions on matters in the geographical areas in which they lived, ministered, and exercised ecclesiastical jurisdiction."[192] The grant critics' primary objective was neither safeguarding local diocesan sovereignty nor a form of religious libertarianism, intending to wall the church off from secular politics. The recent past, for instance, had shown religious conservatives politically mobilized, lobbying state and central officers, often working in concert with the national church, to enforce greater moral stricture on such matters as gambling, prostitution, alcohol, and communism. Now, with the national church's social positions no longer dovetailing with theirs, moderate and conservative dioceses began to employ the claim of cultural pluralism as they called on the national church in New York to respect the cultural difference of the local parishioners in the South. "Local people," as one North Carolina Episcopalian explained, "feel that persons not resident in the South—such as the GSCP evaluators—are not acquainted with cultural influences and a clear understanding of the feelings that are aroused when grants such as this are proposed."[193] For racially conservative southerners, their opposition to forms of cultural relativist positions emanating from the left did not preclude them from positing relativistic arguments of their own.

Arguments about the impenetrable cultural geography of the South may have, in the short run, provided convenient multicultural cover for southern locals. But predicating their opposition to funding MXLU on regional difference concealed both the intensity and implications of what was a national problem. As the Religious Right looked to roll back the gains secured by liberal Protestantism—regarding abortion, gay rights, prayer in schools, separation between church and state, religious pluralism, and cultural tolerance—the provincial limits of a cultural geographic argument became self-evident. At best, cultural geographic arguments might offer religious conservatives a limited sphere of social influence in the South. At worst, cultural geography was reflexively defeatist and defensive, more about protecting what was left of the moral terrain than retaking the terrain annexed by cultural liberals during the 1960s. Religious imperialism, not multiculturalism, appeared to be a more successful route of return to cultural and political power. As many religious conservatives discovered firsthand in the late 1960s with MXLU, arguments steeped in regional distinctiveness or cultural geography magnified difference, isolating southern conservatives from potential conservative allies. Fellow conservatives who lived outside the South also objected to the cultural imperialism of religious nabobs, and shared conservative southerners' concerns over collapsing moral values.

By the early 1970s the culture wars appeared destined to split the country in two. The *Black Manifesto*, James Forman's call for reparations and predicting sustained guerrilla racial warfare inside America, exposed how local communicants in towns and cities across America, not just the South, were at variance with liberal lay and clerical leaders. Although mainline Protestant leaders in the Episcopal Church and other denominations accepted at least in principle much of the *Manifesto*, many parishioners rejected it outright: 92 percent of all Protestant churchgoers, according to a late May 1969 Gallup poll, refused any concession to Forman, threatening to withhold support if lay and clerical leaders acceded to *Manifesto* wishes.[194]

The resurgent Religious Right mounted a rigorous cultural defense to the challenge represented by a distant bureaucracy of elite cultural regulators perceived to be set on redistributing America's moral capital to black militants and youth.[195] With fears of cultural imperialism abounding, local congregants contested the alien cultural influences, which called not only for tolerance of Marxists and Black Muslims but for actively funding their endeavors. Conservatives called for cultural autonomy to shield them from out-of-touch liberals, whose modus vivendi clashed with that of socially conservative southern Episcopalians. Such an argument was at variance with facts in the Episcopal Diocese of North Carolina, where the local advisory committee unanimously endorsed funding of MXLU. For cultural conservatives the MXLU affair appeared a case of synecdoche, where the seeming erosion of shared national customs, values, and beliefs was a local phenomenon. The issues of centralization of authority, cultural relativism, and the social cost of liberal permissiveness were bound up in the funding of MXLU. These social cracks spread over race and war in the 1960s. By the mid-1970s, with the Vietnam War over and civil rights submerged, these fractures not only remained but, for the cultural right, grew intractably into full-blown division over abortion, ERA, and gay rights.

* * *

If, as Oliver Wendell Holmes once said, a page of history is worth volumes of logic, then North Carolina has much to reveal about liberalism and Black Power. The institutional rise of Black Power found operational space not in the state's conservative black belt, but in the urban Piedmont. There liberals hired and supported Howard Fuller, the state's most controversial Black Power figure, insulating him against local and national criticism before securing his employ at the University of North Carolina at Chapel Hill, the state's flagship university and the South's most liberal institution of learning. Eight miles away at Duke University, liberals on the faculty and in the administration underwrote retreats and conferences and established the South's first black studies program after pressure from below by black students. It seemed to its conservative critics that the Duke grant gave birth to a cadre of student activists, community organizers, and scholars. Out of this emerged Malcolm X Liberation University in Durham. Here, too, liberalism created an operational space for black nationalism, for its start-up capital took the all-black university from an idea to an institution.

MXLU seems the last place to expect a record of liberals creating operational space for Black Power, given the university's adherence to cultural nationalism and the standing of cultural nationalism among scholars as the thickest of all identity solidarities. It had appeared more resistant to incursions by ideological and ethnic others than competing strains of nationalism.[196] The natural solidarity of cultural nationalism also resonates among scholars examining Black Power. For Black Power critic Tommie Shelby, and one might add K. Anthony Appiah, black cultural nationalism was a hermetically sealed ideology whose chief property was its thick racial solidarity; so thick, in fact, that cultural nationalists were all but impermeable to what Appiah calls contamination. Such suffocating racial loyalty, the logic goes, choked off pragmatic interactions and engagements, as it militated for "an independent and autonomous community, with significant collective control over its sociopolitical, economic, and cultural life." For Shelby funding was a signifier of interaction and engagement and, thus, by extension contamination. At a book signing in Connecticut, Shelby told the crowd that Black Power did not take any money from whites.[197]

But black cultural nationalism seemed far more vulnerable to contamination than critics to date have realized. Even among hard-core essentialists of a leading cultural nationalist university in America, liberals interfaced with school officials in substantive ways, from securing personal employment to institutional investment. Rhetorical and philosophical notions underpinning racial notions of blackness should not obfuscate the real-world record of "blackhearted" projects' willingness to rely on liberal remittance. This seems particularly relevant for those whose arguments hang on rejecting cultural nationalism because of solidarities' unwillingness to be pragmatic.

Pragmatism gave liberals their entrée into the operational world of black cultural nationalism. MXLU officials turned to liberals not out of "jealousy, self-hatred, arrogance, greed, vanity, and pettiness."[198] Instead, school officials were compelled to address the practical. In following the money, scholars might go beyond theorizing the Black Power world to the praxis of what actually did and did not happen.[199] One can rarely assume that financial dependence leads to ideological independence. Instead, liberalism was capable of contaminating Black Power because neither were hermetic ideologies. Consistent with contrarian philanthropic giving, then and now, some believed in the cause; some believed in controlling the cause; and others only believed that a conservative alternative had to be worse. The racial loyalty of cultural nationalists should not be confused with impermeability—particularly when the contaminant was liberalism, a political philosophy with a core confidence in its ability to outthink and overcome competing ideologies via the power of reason and practice.

Scholars of Black Power also miss the cultural nationalist-liberal interplay. Black Power specialists opt to elide liberalism's operational role almost completely. As one leading Black Power specialist says of MXLU, it was founded as "the direct result of community activism and black student activism," growing out of the belief that African Americans had to gain control of "cultural institutions."[200] Given isolationist scholars' near-uniform rejection of liberalism, the notion of liberalism creating space for Black Power is akin to claiming Likud funded Hamas. This irony of history—that the school bearing Malcolm X's name owed its operational existence to liberal investors—too often escapes scholars of Black Power.

Conservatives certainly did not believe the liberal–Black Power interplay was fictitious. Indeed, it was precisely concerns regarding liberals and MXLU that helped fuel social conservatives. From the perspective of social conservatives and many moderates as well, both secular and religious liberals licensed programs that were, as one concerned North Carolina parishioner saw it, bent on "destroying Christian society." Secular moderates also turned, insisting that the interchange demonstrated that the so-called rights revolution had gone too far. Fear over the power of this interplay struck a national chord, as the social backlash against the space created by liberalism, couched in the language of liberal permissiveness, resonated well with East and West Coast cultural conservatives and a renascent or recombinant Christian right in places like Michigan and North Carolina.

The story told in this chapter—the hidden history of liberal remittance to Black Power in North Carolina—is not uncommon. Whether the focus shifts to the earliest (San Francisco State and UCLA) or among the most famous (Institute of the Black World) institutional expressions of Black Power, liberal subvention remains an inescapable fact of black nationalism and black studies.[201] What many, particularly contemporary conservatives and students of modern America, have underestimated was the openness of black nationalism. That openness, as we see in subsequent chapters, ultimately made black nationalism's vitiation possible. Perhaps Howard Fuller in an interview in 2000 best summed up the seductive soft power of liberalism and the limits it paradoxically placed on Black Power: "Our argument back then was power to the people. . . . You tell me how you empower people in America, if you don't ever give them control over the money."[202] Of course, liberalism paid in other ways. Liberals' policy of engagement helped contain MXLU, even as critics assumed Black Power ran amok over it.

2 "We Had a Beautiful Thing"
Malcolm X Liberation University, the Black Middle Class, and the Black Liberation Movement, 1968–1973

By 1974 the Black Liberation Movement, a struggle that crested in the late sixties and turn of the decade with the Black Power conferences and Gary, Indiana, convention, stood at its nadir. Embroiled in internal ideological clashes regarding the trinity of class, culture, and patriarchy, as well as revolution vis-à-vis pragmatism, the Black Liberation Movement imploded under the bifurcation of fragile coalitions. Few rifts were more indicative of the internal struggle within the movement than the escalating tensions between Marxist-Leninist nationalists and culturalist-oriented Pan-Africanists.

One can, if they wish, attribute much of this division to Howard Fuller's work in Durham and later Greensboro, North Carolina, particularly the formation of Malcolm X Liberation University. Or as the South's most prolific Pan-Africanist writer, Kalamu Ya Salaam, insisted in 1974: "To understand the current state of affairs, a prior knowledge of the development of MXLU and CAP [Congress of African People] is helpful, as those two institutions represent the most successful political thrusts of the Black Liberation Movement over the past few years."[1]

Yet it was Fuller's disillusionment and movement to the left—along with Maulana Karenga's incorporation of certain Marxian concepts—that inevitably influenced leading Pan-African activist and CAP founder Imamu Amiri Baraka's ideological embrace of Marx.[2] In turn, most intellectual observers agree, it was black elected officials and nationalists' reaction to Baraka's newfound class consciousness that ultimately triggered the liberation movement's final dissolution. In short, chronicling Fuller's ideological sojourn to Marxist-Leninism and the forces contributing to it is a sine qua non for charting the movement's national demise.

Once celebrated among fellow cultural nationalists as a chief theoretician of Pan-African thought in the United States, Howard Fuller, the ideological architect of MXLU, would jettison the teachings of Pan-Africanism for the self-described moniker of Marxist revolutionary.[3] Fuller's disillusionment marked the beginning of the end of the university's narrow nationalist focus. Yet this shift toward Marxism was not merely the result of his singular experience in Africa, as Ya Salaam and other cultural nationalists mistakenly suggest. Nor did his reevaluation of class matters in the black community take root in the "mother" continent. Instead, his reconsideration of the centrality of class within the black liberation struggle was at least as much a response to his lived experience in North Carolina. It was his near decade-long political engagement in North Carolina—and more precisely with MXLU—that predisposed him to a broader structural critique and laid the foundation for his revised leftist posture.

The point here is not to disregard the impact that Fuller's exposure to anticolonialist struggle in Mozambique and Tanzania had in his ideological evolution, an impact Fuller himself recognized. Rather, it is to place Fuller's travel and study in the context of the daily accretion of his and the university's relations with the black upper and professional stratum, first in Durham and then in Greensboro. Local circumstances command some scholarly consideration for three reasons. First, while Fuller personally believed that traveling and studies influenced his conversion, he also, borrowing from the influential speeches of Amilcar Cabral, nonetheless stressed the interpretive pitfalls awaiting those ignoring local realities. "If we do not deal" with local realities, Fuller later told Pan-Africanists in a mid-1970s position statement, then "we will be left saying that a peasant in Ethiopia and an auto worker in Detroit have the same historical experiences, and consequently their method of struggle will be the same . . . simply because we are of African heritage."[4] One might see how the daily accretion of what Fuller witnessed in Durham mattered, even in ways that Fuller and other MXLU officials may yet not recognize. To reject the importance of indigenous intraracial interactions would deny the premise of Fuller's ideological evolution itself, steeped in the belief that specific historical experiences must inform one's own critical analysis.

Second, the factors that facilitated Fuller's evolutionary trajectory need to be understood within a general climate of upper- and middle-class unreceptiveness toward MXLU rather than some direct causal link, as was made clear when Fuller cited his need for a better atmosphere as his reason for moving MXLU from Durham to Greensboro. Third, given the spate of community studies published since the 1980s, what one might glean by keeping local communities and grassroots work as a focal point, Charles Payne reminds us, compels at least a consideration of indigenous movements before a quick judgment is made. Local and national movements often fed off one another. Thus the development of MXLU captures one organizing tradition and the long-term commitment of ordinary men and women to nation building.[5]

Between 1969 and 1973 MXLU experienced ideological transformation. From its inception, the university's contentious relationship with segments of North Carolina's professional and upper black strata formed the critical backdrop of the school's migration away from its original narrow cultural nationalism. In Durham the city's up-and-coming black elite, established political leadership, captains of industry, and local academics fostered an adverse operational climate for MXLU. In search of greater operational and philosophical space, the university departed Durham for Greensboro less than a year after its founding.

MXLU's new location made little difference. Despite an auspicious start, the obstacles presented by Greensboro's black political, religious, and community leaders in undermining the university's institutionalization further illustrated the divergent agenda that alienated MXLU from the black middle class. By the time MXLU finally closed its doors in the summer of 1973, both the university and Fuller had reoriented their political philosophy, reflecting their experiences in Durham and Greensboro.

Thus to understand this transformation—and by extension the rift in the national Black Liberation Movement that Fuller helped trigger—one must inevitably turn to MXLU and the middle-class-oriented politics of the black upper and professional classes in Durham, and later Greensboro.

The Anatomy of Black Nation Building in the Capital of the Black Middle Class

In late 1960s Durham, a city where African Americans constituted nearly a quarter of the official voting registry and 85 percent of eligible blacks were registered voters, most had little influence on boards and commissions.[6] Despite the storied economic and modest political success of individual blacks and institutions, there were few effective social or economic programs for most African Americans in Durham. The most dedicated antipoverty organizations like Operation Breakthrough served Hayti, where unlighted gravel streets intersected with some of the nation's most squalid homes, many of which lacked indoor plumbing. Belying "the cult of progress" of the upper and professional stratum, the stark fact remained that the vast sector of black Durham remained on the city's social and economic periphery.[7]

Poverty for disfranchised blacks in Durham's famed Hayti community was not exclusively a matter of economic deprivation. Rather, theirs was one of access to channels of change. Though the civil rights movement had profited many in black Durham, the growing sentiment among poorer residents was, as one antipoverty worker expressed, an abiding sense that a decade of advances had passed them by "to benefit . . . Negroes with decent incomes and educations."[8] As Howard Fuller explained, socially alienated Hayti residents were confined by "the poverty of not knowing, of being 'left out' in community affairs, of lack of self-respect."[9] "The city's Negro elite," wrote North Carolina Fund staffers in a confidential in-house document, "were among those most bothered" by Fuller.[10]

Yet one was hard-pressed to find any visible opposition from black leaders when, on April 24, 1969, holdover aides from the previous Johnson administration's Office of Economic Opportunity approved a $960,000 grant to the antipoverty Durham-based Foundation for Community Development (FCD), part of which went to MXLU.[11] From this total FCD agreed to award $20,000 to MXLU. Both the award and amount startled many whites who vividly remembered Fuller's remark, earlier in the year, at the dedication of the university to "teach here why we must bring down capitalism."[12] The looming suspicion among many, one newspaper observed, was that "the foundation may be just a façade for Fuller's activities to organize and radicalize North Carolina's black students."[13]

Republicans especially expressed concern that under a GOP president OEO funding would eventually wind up in the possession of Fuller, a training director for the foundation, whose newly created university was reportedly located one floor above FCD's office. Both FCD executive director Nathan Garrett and the OEO chief of economic development Geoffrey Faux guaranteed party officials that Fuller would have no policy responsibilities in administering the grant.[14] This, however, did little to allay Republicans and skeptical whites.

While Democratic Governor Robert Scott conceded the award, telling reporters he "had no veto power" to prevent the grant, the Durham County Republican Party contested its allocation. With a more responsive administration in the White House, "strong" objections were registered by party leaders both in the state and region. Speaking for North Carolina Republicans, state party chairman Jim Holshouser urged that funds be withheld until further investigation by the Nixon administration. Meanwhile, neighboring South Carolina Senator Strom Thurmond warned the new director of OEO, Donald Rumsfeld, that funding known militants like Fuller would destroy public confidence in government programs.[15] Rumsfeld and special aide Dick Cheney agreed. They froze further FCD money until enumerated proposals for its use were made.[16]

Local GOP officials did not object to Durham receiving the grant, but the press reported that "party members [felt] it could be channeled through a 'more effective' agency."[17] There are better means "available to achieve this purpose," county Republicans advised in a telegram, "we suggest you familiarize yourself with the local situation."[18] This meant understanding the volatile influence of Fuller, as well as the potential of ensuring local Republican control over the project by way of more accountable black support. Moderate and conservative Republicans did not seek to preclude black participation altogether; they simply sought less radical participants than Fuller.

Since the mid-1960s Fuller had been hailed by adversaries and acolytes alike as the state's leading black activist. The appellation was apparently well deserved. Amid physical threats to himself and family, Fuller mobilized fair-housing rallies, protest marches, and university demonstrations. More important, he had earned the confidence of fellow activists and local residents. "I walked the streets of the most dilapidated sections," one observer noted, "and talked with tired Negroes on their front porches. Most all of them knew of OBT [Operation Breakthrough] and the residents' council and spoke well of them."[19] The success of grassroots organizing and black political power in Durham, community and fieldworkers claimed, was largely attributable to one man, Howard Fuller.[20] Fuller gladly accepted the responsibility. His job, Fuller boasted to a *Durham Morning Herald* reporter, "is to stir the people out of apathy."[21]

Some whites thought that such radical black populism ruffled more "responsible" and "law-abiding elements" within black Durham. Following the grant announcement, a local daily suggested that many Negro leaders privately opposed Fuller's militancy. Nonetheless, the reporter added presumptuously, they were afraid to speak out for fear of rebuke from within the black community. Few had the public courage of David Stith to challenge Fuller and FCD funding. It was Stith who surfaced as the more "effective agent" that local and national Republicans wanted.[22] A rising star among the black elite, Stith, president of Southeastern Business College in Durham, had a turbulent past with Fuller. Rancor between Stith and Fuller had lingered since their initial clash in 1967, when Fuller and others excoriated Stith for befriending Abe Greenberg, a Durham landlord who refused to bring rental properties up to code. A personal friend of Greenberg, Stith tried to arbitrate the dispute between lessor and tenants. Instead, Stith was taken to be Greenberg's vested ally.[23]

Prior to the dispute Stith claimed little social cachet with Durham's black residents in working-class and low-income neighborhoods like Edgemont. Well-dressed, suave, often seen driving his "off-the-assembly [line] Cadillac," it was difficult for Stith to be considered one of them. Not once prior to the Greenberg dispute had Stith worked with or consulted community leaders in Edgemont.[24] The prevailing view among Edgemont African Americans was that Stith's primary interest was taking the heat off his personal friend Abe Greenberg. As writer Osha Gray Davidson put it, area people saw Stith "as trading on his skin color to prove a solidarity with the black residents of Edgemont, a solidarity that did not, in fact, exist." Stith's newfangled role as community broker sparked protest outside the junior college president's downtown office by blacks carrying placards reading: "STITH, ARE YOU BLACK OR WHITE?" "UNCLE TOM STITH," and "GREENBERG'S NIGGER."[25] Angered and publicly humiliated, Stith pegged Fuller as the onerous protestors' ringleader. Later, in seeming retaliation, Stith tipped off local officials about the apparent use of public vehicles for political causes—an abuse of federal funds—by Fuller and other OBT employees.[26] Though the charge was eventually deemed unwarranted, OBT and Fuller in particular came under intense scrutiny because of the allegation.

With animus between the two unresolved, Stith found tantalizing Republican county chairman Darrell Kennedy's invitation to coordinate twenty "responsible, concerned white and Negro leader[s]" as an alternative "to be available as a recipient should FCD be denied the grant."[27] Calling the group Opportunities Now, Stith solicited the attendance of like-minded professors, physicians, attorneys, and factory personnel to the group's introductory meeting. Though publicly Opportunities Now denied any direct competition with FCD for funding, it became evident that the group wished "to seek the OEO funds."[28] Obvious to Fuller was that Stith, chairing Opportunities Now, had become the agent that local, state, and federal Republicans sought.

Lashing out against funding the rival Opportunities Now and Stith, Fuller told those at an antipoverty mass meeting in July, "There's nothing more amoral . . . apolitical . . . than Uncle Tom niggers like David Stith that exploit black people." Fearful of being "exposed" by Fuller and labeled as one of "my black enemies"—as the popular leader tagged Stith during the mass meeting—many distanced themselves from the Republican-supported alternative.[29] Following the group's inaugural meeting, three invited members—Dr. Joseph Campbell, Marion Thorne, and Dallas Simmons—issued a press release asserting no prior knowledge of the furtive mission of Opportunities Now. Stith and Republican County Commissioner Darrell Kennedy contended that all three had been consulted previously. One of them, they told *Durham Morning Herald* reporters, even inquired about becoming the new group's director. Intimidation and "pressure from the militant movement locally," rather than some benign misunderstanding, were the reasons "good and responsible" residents refrained from publicly aligning with Opportunities Now. Their withdrawal, a local reporter was told, was an "action of fear."[30]

Vacillation among would-be Opportunities Now proponents, however, was dismissed as a minor setback. Neither Stith nor local Republicans were deterred by the rescission. "Other people will be added to the group later," a resolute Stith opined.[31] Stith was correct. With unwavering GOP favor, Opportunities Now remained a viable grant recipient as an alternative to the FCD. With Durham already targeted by Nixon as one of ten cities for the president's pilot black capitalist project, funding was a fait accompli. The only remaining question was which organization would receive financial support. From the Nixon White House to local Republican operatives, Stith's group was favorably compared with FCD. Stith appeared to have a legitimate political future with the party. Despite his precarious relationship with the Edgemont community, Stith's espousal of law and order and black capitalism made him a model political vassal for Nixon Republicanism as well as an intractable foil for threatening FCD funding.

The ultimatum facing Fuller was clear. Even if Stith was unsuccessful in obtaining a grant, Opportunities Now's presence threatened to dilute the policies, organizational behavior, and possibly the personnel of the foundation. At worst, staying with FCD might mean surrendering a grant of nearly a million dollars. With little choice, on Tuesday, July 22, 1969, Fuller announced an indefinite leave of absence from the foundation. Satisfied with Fuller's departure, Republicans agreed to the FCD grant.[32] Before the university opened, however, other influential blacks would reject Fuller and MXLU.

In the weeks prior to MXLU's inauguration the maelstrom of class tensions bristled among varying factions, represented by Fuller on one side and elements of Durham's black bourgeoisie on the other. Lack of progress in many communities was thought to be caused by neighborhoods with already well-established indigenous leadership that, having for years served as the voice for black Durham, grew highly suspicious of the United Organization for Community Improvement (UOCI) and its fieldworkers. In exclusively black Lyon Park, for instance, where Fuller had coordinated since 1965, efforts to organize poorer residents met with resistance from the neighborhood community club members composed of property owners, leaders of the "better" church in the area, and other well-to-do residents.[33] "What I'm beginning to see," Fuller remarked, is "a lot of niggers in this town who are basically white. . . . Other than their color they ain't like us."[34] As MXLU prepared to open, Fuller continued pressing for community-driven accountability from local black leaders, especially on broader issues like improving tenant housing.[35]

Fuller and others inside FCD and UOCI thought that, with the presence of two African Americans on the housing authority, the board's days as the unchallenged fiefdom of its white director Carvie Oldham were numbered. Oldham, a former cotton mill executive, had a notorious reputation of blatantly disregarding the civil liberties of black housing tenants. Regularly upbraiding housing residents as "insufficiently servile," Oldham was known to have forced physical examinations on unmarried women he suspected to be pregnant. Housing officials, not physicians, frequently conducted such exams, poking young "women's abdomen[s] to determine if she was pregnant." Tenant complaints against Oldham for demanding impromptu apartment searches for men living with single women—a violation of housing and welfare rules—were routine. Fuller and UOCI director Ben Ruffin chose to wait no longer.[36]

Rather than rely on action by blacks on the housing board, Fuller and Ruffin called a meeting to discuss housing complaints and other critical community issues. The gathering, as recounted in the state capital's leading black newspaper the *Carolinian*, was little more than an ultramilitant siege on Durham's political establishment. Reporting for the *Carolinian*, Alexander Barnes blamed the alleged coup d'état on "black powerites . . . facilitating disintegration within the movement" in a "gasping effort" to wrest away political power. The "one aim in mind, solidarity," in Barnes's idyllic view, crumbled as Fuller and Ruffin shouted down NAACP members, rejected the statements of the head of the city's human relation council, subverted the orderly rules of parliamentary decorum established by Durham's former housing authority member, and belittled the city's first black board of education chairman as a leader handpicked by a select few. Shrewd black leaders like veteran city councilman John S. Stewart, anticipating the meeting to be a carryover from earlier strife-filled encounters, wisely refused the Black Power radicals' invitation, Barnes added. No doubt Barnes deemed Fuller and Ruffin particularly upstaging, given that Barnes was also Durham's chapter president of the NAACP.[37]

Angered by Barnes's charge of fragmenting the black community, Fuller accosted Barnes outside his downtown office. Fuller told Barnes that he was no different from any white columnist whose articles purposely misled the public. Fuller's attack on Barnes engendered a vituperative retort from the *Carolinian*. Protecting its own, the *Carolinian* insisted Barnes had reported reliably. Calls of "Uncle Tomism" from Ruffin evoked a similar strong reprisal from the loyal *Carolinian*, which editorialized that Barnes had been a victim of vitriolic remarks by two Black Power zealots. This incident quashed the potential for positive coverage by the *Carolinian* during the critical days leading up to the opening of MXLU.[38]

In his article Barnes dismissed both the UOCI and FCD as fledgling organizations overcome by leftist radicals. Urging readers to forget more democratic organizing, the Durham NAACP president argued that neither the mass-based UOCI nor the militant FCD held promise for blacks. Instead, Barnes advised readers that the Durham Committee on Negro Affairs (DCNA)—a local black political machine founded by North Carolina Mutual Life Insurance Company president Charles Clinton Spaulding in 1935 at a tennis club membered by the town's black elite—should provide "the nucleus by which the Negro could build its future hopes."[39] Barnes appeal for "one-aim solidarity" in the form of the DCNA, appeared to mask the diverging interests within the black community.

Though the DCNA earned recognition as one of the nation's most dynamic groups of its kind, over the years the committee had consistently refused to support reforms that would aid poor blacks. For a fleeting historic moment in the 1950s, the DCNA looked to embrace a more aggressive political posture, but by the late 1960s it was clear the DCNA was living on past glories, as its influence and prestige waned as a result of the effective organization of low-income blacks, particularly women, and amid ideological clashes in the black community between militants and wealthy black businessmen.[40] Nevertheless, the DCNA was insulated from criticism as much of its political effectiveness lay in substantial financial donations from either wealthy committee members or candidates endorsed by the committee. Poorer blacks, however, had no such comparable leverage within black Durham's most powerful political group.[41]

The DCNA provides a glimpse into the black professional and middle classes of Durham. For, although DCNA was open to all black Durhamites, the black professional and middle classes dominated the Durham-based pressure group from its inception.[42] However, the middle-class composition of the DCNA did not alienate it from working-class and underemployed blacks. For example, an endorsement from the DCNA has been, in the words of one scholar in the mid-1960s, "tantamount to electoral success for the candidate in almost every instance."[43] The DCNA, and its organizing of voting and registration campaigns for primary and general elections, was largely responsible for the fact that nearly two in every three voting-age blacks were registered, resulting in more registered black voters in Durham than almost any other southern city.[44] Yet the DCNA was unsatisfied with virtual representation. Since 1942 it had also encouraged blacks to run for local office. Many of its members also belonged to one of the city's leading black churches, White Rock Baptist Church. As the middle class dominated the DCNA, so did Democrats dominate Durham elections. Like the rest of the one-party South, the DCNA tended to endorse Democrats.[45]

It was on economic matters that the black middle class, in the institutional form of the DCNA, parted ways from much of black Durham. There DCNA's interests often converged with the pocketbook priorities of the city's economic elite, most famously in siding against Hayti protesters and with the chamber of commerce and local realtors on a municipal bond issue that would destroy black homes and property values by running a freeway through it to connect white-collar commuters to the Research Triangle Park.[46]

Perhaps no public issue better illustrated the DCNA's disconnect from poorer blacks than the November 1969 sales tax referendum—a ballot initiative, according to preelection surveys, that nearly 100 percent of working-class and lower-stratum blacks opposed. True to form, on Election Day black communities like Edgemont, which rejected the tax 109 to 21, voted against the referendum. Yet the DCNA, black Durham's leading political presence, was conspicuously absent in the weeks leading to the regressive flat tax referendum. Despite private discussions concerning the tax, DCNA spurned any public stance.[47] It also did little to mobilize black voters against the tax. Although restrictive speech legislation in the form of new election laws prohibiting political solicitation within 500 feet of polling sites hindered traditional mobilizing efforts of advocacy groups like the DCNA, these new laws didn't silence the UOCI—which was supportive of MXLU but less influential than the DCNA—from publicly expressing its dissatisfaction with the proposed tax. Nor was the DCNA able to dissuade the Democratic Party executive committee from placing an ad in the *Durham Morning Herald* objecting to the regressive tax.[48] In sum, as MXLU prepared its inaugural campaign, neither the DCNA nor the NAACP was a source of measurable support.

Even Louis Austin—editor of the *Durham Carolina Times*, the state's leading black newspaper, and often a supportive ally of Fuller in private—publicly rebuked the radical Black Power faction as "no better than the Ku Klux Klan." Such a call for "black or Negro separatism from the mainstream of American life," Austin predicted, "is certain to come to no good end."[49] Of special concern to Austin was the creation of MXLU, which he suspected was just another boondoggle fashioned under the pretense of helping disadvantaged Durham blacks: "Are we witnessing the birth of another facet of Negro '[C]adillac set,' this time masquerading under the honorable term Black? What are we in for? Are Black people, the little people to be disappointed again? Is this grand dream of a new order to dissolve into the old familiar nightmare of hypocrisy?"[50]

Most blacks, however, never actively denounced Fuller or the university he led. One NCF employee described the pensiveness of a local black magnate: he "talked about the growing push of organized young Negroes. He was defensive, spelling out in careful detail what he and the old-time Durham Committee on Negro Affairs had done to back up the push. How behind the scenes they furnished sage advice and legal assistance. How they were active politically and put Fuller on their Political Sub-Committee." But as Louis Austin admitted bluntly: "Fuller and his movement embarrass other Negro leaders, especially us older men, who don't stand up the way he does. Most of today's adult Negro leadership is hopeless. The future is in these young people."[51]

It is also not surprising that the strained relationship between Fuller and the black elite often went undetected by the majority press. During public speeches Fuller was known for banishing white reporters before berating other blacks' duplicity. "The cat from the *Durham Morning Herald*, he's a very nice cat," he told people at one gathering before a verbal assault on Stith, "but he works for the *Durham Morning Herald* so therefore I'd like to have him leave. . . . I didn't come to speak to no white people through the newspapers."[52]

Although Fuller was vexed by Stith's opposition, he was perhaps more troubled that other detractors lacked the college president's overt machinations. "There are a whole lot more like him that exploit black people," he warned angry UOCI supporters in the July heat, "but don't say it out loud." If blacks disagree with you, he warned, "they don't come to you. . . . They cut you up behind your back. They cut you up at them teas, and them book club meetings, and them church socials. . . . They don't ever say don't hurt [us] . . . but don't ever say do."[53] Just as southern liberalism's presence contributed to the operational space for MXLU's emergence, so the black middle and professional class's capitulation and retrenchment shaped an adverse climate for the university. Or, as Fuller pithily surmised regarding prosperous Durham blacks: "The problem is not a lack of money in this town. The problem is the reaction of some of us who have the money and could give it."[54] No one fit this profile better than Asa T. Spaulding.

"The Richest Negro in the United States": The Story of Asa T. Spaulding and MXLU

Venerated by the *New York Times* "as the richest Negro in the United States," Spaulding, former president of North Carolina Mutual, had long been an important Durham businessman and appointee on local, state, and national boards.[55] Joining the insurance company in 1933, Spaulding, second cousin to C. C. Spaulding and great-nephew to cofounder Aaron Moore, moved up through the ranks to become Mutual's president in 1959.[56] By 1968 Spaulding, recently retired from Mutual, turned his attention to politics.

Asa Spaulding's heightened political participation was no doubt buoyed by the increased militancy of local antipoverty groups like the mostly women-led United Organization for Community Improvement and Operation Breakthrough, whose early chief functions included extensive voter registration drives. For whites nationally and in Durham, Spaulding— who once boasted that he never marched in a civil rights protest in his life—seemed more tempered and was thus a more palatable choice than Fuller, who was known for leading frequent UOCI and OBT demonstrations in front of the Durham Housing Authority and city hall. Spaulding's personal motto, "Let's get things done—with as little noise as possible," was effective in indirectly challenging Fuller, as a climate hostile to radical Black Power agenda was quietly fostered.[57]

To Spaulding's credit, he was unswayed by letters from whites wanting him to remove Fuller from Durham.[58] Indeed, during the 1967 summer controversy Spaulding himself took part in a letter-writing campaign urging OEO head Sargent Shriver to keep Fuller in Durham. He also seemed generally supportive of resident struggles in places like Edgemont and southeastern Durham. Yet sitting with Spaulding on the board of United Durham Inc., a for-profit corporation to be owned and operated by low-income people, were white moderates and liberals. Moreover, the lack of representation of the poor on these boards was "difficult to discuss" because of the committee's penchant for secrecy: meetings were normally closed and no minutes were kept.[59] However, if Fuller's frequent maligning of the refusal of UOCI's board to accept greater participation of poorer residents on other boards and neighborhood councils suggests anything, it is that UDI's board, comprised overwhelmingly of the city's black and white elite vis-à-vis that of UOCI, faced even greater criticism.[60]

For the politically aspiring Spaulding, repudiating Fuller was certain to result in backlash from many Fuller loyalists. As Spaulding wrote to Shriver following the 1967 riot controversy, Fuller was a political asset. Spaulding would look to enlist such resources in his first political campaign.[61]

Along with the grassroots campaigning of antipoverty crusaders Ann Atwater and Ben Ruffin, Fuller's canvassing among black residents in the seven predominantly black precincts in Durham was central to Spaulding's election as Durham's first black county commissioner in 1968. Despite the credibility ascribed to Spaulding from Fuller's participation, Spaulding's support was less than seamless. A disaggregated look at the election reveals the fragility of Spaulding's constituent support in black Durham. In the at-large election, a more moderate J. C. Scarborough, the other African American challenger, bettered Spaulding in predominantly black working-class neighborhoods like Hillside, where blacks were 85 percent of registered voters. Conversely, Spaulding—while nonetheless lagging behind white candidates—received more votes than Scarborough in most predominantly white and conservative communities.[62] "It's obvious Skee-fie," as Fuller referred to Scarborough, is "not gonna get any votes in those kinds of precincts."[63] However, Spaulding got them, faring much better than Scarborough in precincts such as Oak Grove, which endorsed Goldwater Republican Jim Gardner in the governor's race. The same held true in the Holt precinct, where Spaulding's margin of victory over Scarborough was nearly two to one.[64]

Name recognition proved important but not determinant. Scarborough edged the better-known Spaulding in largely white districts like Pearson and Jordan, which voted overwhelmingly against Gardner. Moreover, Scarborough also fared better than Spaulding in precincts won by Wade H. Penny—the only Durham Labor Union candidate elected to the North Carolina General Assembly.[65] Weeks after the election Fuller wondered whether he had done the right thing canvassing for Spaulding, or if his political allegiance had been counterproductive to Durham blacks' self-interest.[66]

Fuller believed that not only were the interests of blacks and larger community divergent, but they often conflicted. "I think that unity is going to be put to a rather severe test when we begin to move away from things like voting," a clairvoyant Fuller told *Radish*, a statewide dissident weekly. "People who have resources . . . in a black community are going to be forced to deal with the question of whether they are now willing to deal in a unified manner with questions like a complete change in the educational process for black people, and in effect a complete change in ideology as related to integration."[67] Spaulding—with more resources and money at his discretion than arguably any other African American in the country—would not even bother to take this test.

Spaulding's election as county commissioner also signaled a departure from and transcendence of traditional race-conscious accountability. Serving "the community well," Spaulding wrote in a thank-you letter to Fuller, "*cannot be done without* serving the interest of the black people" (emphasis added).[68] In other words, Spaulding felt that local black needs would inevitably dovetail with those of the larger community. Following his victory he explained to his largely black constituency, "The most gratifying thing about my support is that it was so broadly based."[69] In this way, Spaulding let it be known that neither Fuller nor the black community should anticipate particular constituent reciprocity.

At times it seemed that only short-term expediency persuaded Spaulding to address the political concerns of the larger African American community in Durham, such as when his campaign committee appealed to registered blacks by imploring them to vote for Spaulding "otherwise, we will have no Black representation on our Board of County Commissioners."[70] Often, however, Spaulding appeared more comfortable transcending racial politics and allying with moderate and conservative white county officials. Spaulding prefigured what scholars now describe as postblack or postsegregationist regime politics, which flowered with an increase of black elected officials during the 1970s and 1980s, when candidates of color aimed to allay whites by allying with white moderate and conservative politicians. But in the late 1960s and early 1970s, Spaulding's efforts to secure whites' support was far from unexpected, particularly given his ambitions.[71]

Along with supporting such measures as an urgent resolution calling for the construction of an expressway, which displaced families living in the black community of Hayti, Spaulding actively defended and sought the political support of the county's most conservative white incumbents, most notably Dewey Scarboro, Ed Clement, and Howard Easley. Collectively, their conservative voting record—which included attempting to block the controversial hire of an allegedly better-qualified African American woman instead of a less-qualified white male as head of a new mental health center, publicly opposing the much-needed Lincoln Hospital that serviced blacks in Hayti, and thinly veiled hostility toward Durham Organized Labor—concerned nearly every segment of the black community.[72]

Rather than encourage criticism of white council members and commissioners' retrenchment, Spaulding privately urged the DCNA chairman to support them in their respective races, assuring a highly skeptical John Wheeler, chair of the DCNA, that a good rapport had been established. Even the relentlessly moderate DCNA, however, feared these Democratic council members to be too conservative, as did progressive local black council aspirants like William Bell and Nathan Garrett, who openly debated whether any favorable legislation could occur with Scarboro, Clement, and Easley on the board. Scarboro, Clement, and Easley's affiliation with the Democratic Party did not dissuade Spaulding, a major contributor to the national Republican Party.[73]

At times Spaulding appeared more disturbed by black militant insurgency than by the reactionary tendencies of nationally influential whites.

Since the McCarthy era Spaulding had long labored against "subversive elements" in the black community. In the emerging national activist context of the late 1950s—in which leaders like Martin Luther King Jr. worked toward politicizing southern churches for civil rights—Spaulding encouraged civil liberties antagonist J. Edgar Hoover to address the black congregation of White Rock Baptist Church in Durham. Such choices as testifying as an invited witness of the House Committee on Un-American Activities, in its 1967 search for subversive elements in racial disturbances, continued to curry much favor for Spaulding among conservative ranks.[74]

A long-time supporter of Richard Nixon, Spaulding served on the president's Cost of Living Council Committee, surreptitiously cautioning council chairman George H. Boldt to "hold the line" by suspending the "selfish interests" of the economically downtrodden and workers. Increasing wages and improving living conditions to ameliorate the nation's worst inflationary period since World War II was ill-timed, he advised Boldt: "attention can be addressed to remedying the inequities later."[75]

As the financially languishing MXLU faced foreclosure in spring 1973, Spaulding continued the search for worthy funding ventures for the Urban Coalition, a Boston-based organization dedicated to encouraging entrepreneurship as well as improving educational disparities in ghetto areas. Although under Spaulding's oversight coalition brochures and letters announcing the availability of funds reached newspaper publishers and college presidents like Clark University's Vivian Henderson, the independent black college in Spaulding's own backyard never made his mailing list.[76]

Yet there was no overt animus between Spaulding and Fuller. Rather, Spaulding's experience was vastly different from that of most blacks. Fuller's highly inflammatory Woodland speech, in which he dreamed of the day when whites worked for blacks, already represented reality for Spaulding, who was raised watching white field hands pick cotton on his family's Columbus County plantation.[77] As Spaulding campaigned for more blacks on boards of directors, local activists and community organizers often quipped that "Fuller objected to any black on any board."[78] Whether he wished it or not, Spaulding would find himself as one of the nation's chief thwarters of institutional Black Power.

In April 1967 forty-seven of black America's wealthiest business and professional leaders met at Manhattan's posh Harvard Club, pledging to raise one million dollars to inject new financial vigor into the Legal Defense

Fund's integrationist agenda.[79] The meeting and campaign were spear-headed by Spaulding and cofounder Percy L. Julian, a Chicago research chemist and highly successful director of Julian Associates in Oak Park, Illinois. Conveners, calling themselves the National Negro Business and Professional Committee (NNBPC), expected the million-dollar goal to be an "easy achievement."[80] The NNBPC represented a return to an older battle-ground in the movement—away from streets and front-page headlines back to an emphasis on courtrooms, administrative agencies, and legisla-tive halls. It was also designed to be a tactical shift from "group concept" organizing to one emphasizing personal responsibility.[81] Durham dailies touted the NNBPC as a much-needed corrective to some of the more "de-structive aspects of today's rights struggles."[82] The *New York Times* heralded the committee as an effective solution to Black Power extremism.[83]

The press's Quiet Champion label for Spaulding reveals that his rejec-tion of institutional Black Power was more subcutaneous than overt.[84] He privately feared encroaching self-determination doctrines like community control and independent political organizing. Even the 1972 National Black Political Assembly in Gary, Indiana, attended by mainstream black elected officials and the likes of integrationist-minded leader Coretta Scott King, disturbed Spaulding for its "separatist appeal." Concerned that such gatherings could "boomerang against minorities," Spaulding worked to see that the program and activities of the Legal Defense Fund (LDF) would replace them.[85]

Though he remained the Quiet Champion, Spaulding grabbed national attention. "He is the very antithesis of the new breed of militant civil rights activists," wrote newspapers across the country.[86] Associates in the corpo-rate world like James A. Finley of Moody Investors Services congratulated Spaulding for the "superb" timing of his mission to "neutralize the 'activ-ist' approach"[87] National civil rights organizations were equally grateful for Spaulding's contribution to challenging insurgent Black Power. "If our kind of leadership prevails," NAACP president Roy Wilkins wrote, "it will be due in large part to . . . persons like yourself."[88]

Though the NNBPC was primarily integrationist, it collectively held the view that funds would be sufficient to support all causes relating to the Ne-gro minority. With this charge in mind the LDF officially proclaimed itself "*THE* legal arm of the Civil Rights movement" (original emphasis), trying cases of all major civil rights groups and any individual with bona fide civil rights claims.[89] But the narrow scope of legal cases pursued belied LDF's professed broad-based declarations. While numerous cases confronted important racial discriminatory policies, few dealt with a legal interrogation of structural inequity and poverty.[90] Though seeking to disengage from the "wealthy" tags besetting them, the LDF and NNBPC reinforced such impressions by focusing the public's attention via press releases, surveys, and legal complaints on the underutilization of star black athletes on television commercials and claims of discrimination by black surgeons.[91]

In North Carolina, for instance, school and teacher desegregation—as opposed to discriminatory hiring and employment practices, exclusionary exemptions of poor and African Americans from jury service, safe and affordable housing, and unwarranted criminal search and seizure—totaled more than two-thirds of cases comprising the LDF North Carolina Docket Report.[92] Others in the NAACP leadership, like LDF board member Spaulding in rare public voice, crusaded for greater representation of "competent and responsible" Negroes on the board of directors.[93] Such antidiscriminatory campaigns contributed to the growing perception that the NCF was failing to represent the concerns of most blacks.

But it was not the cases pursued as much as those not pursued that strained LDF/NNBPC's purported agenda. Nowhere is this more acute than in the 1971–72 case of Angela Davis, when even the Young Women's Christian Association abandoned neutrality to defend the prominent American Communist. By contrast, LDF did not even submit an amicus brief.[94]

The myopic vision of LDF's brass sparked a mutinous clash with LDF legal interns. Interns attacked LDF director-counsel Jack Greenberg and its board for the corrosive effect of their stance on Davis and for the increasing hostility toward the Legal Defense Fund in general. The refusal to take a stand reflected the organization's unstated aversion for "the representation of any militant being prosecuted for his reputation for militancy, for his notorious philosophy or for espousing black liberation." No longer listening to the voices of the many, interns charged, the LDF was "betraying the black community and opposing the entire concept of black power."[95] To black radical activists like Fuller, the position of LDF leadership smacked of complete disregard for the needs of the majority of blacks. For his part, Spaulding expressed no qualms about siding with LDF's officialdom.

As social scientists have shown, individuals are more inclined to follow those they identify with and who share their values.[96] Consider Spaulding, whose failure to court MXLU's popular founder obviated a marriage of political convenience, a union that might have kept MXLU in Durham. Had Fuller remained he might have made a difference by helping Spaulding realize his open-secret ambition to be the city's first black mayor. The suspending of ideological differences by Black Power activists long enough to stump for establishment candidates who were making historic electoral runs was occurring elsewhere, most famously in Cleveland and Newark. Spaulding did nothing to keep MXLU or Fuller in Durham, however, and without Fuller canvassing again for him Spaulding had to win over the working and poorer black citizens of Durham, who were deeply ambivalent about the retired insurance executive. Quite possibly, then, it may have been Spaulding's inability to recognize opportunities to act in his own political self-interest that explains his and others' radioactive reaction to the school's founder.

No cultural hero, Spaulding failed to mobilize African American voters in his 1971 mayoral bid. Only 41 percent of registered voters in Durham went to the polls. Blacks were nearly as unenthused about the candidates as other Durham voters despite Spaulding's historic bid to become the city's first black mayor. Spaulding's loss marked the first time in twenty years that a mayoral candidate backed by Durham's black-labor coalition lost in an initial effort when not opposed by an incumbent.[97]

During the last few days of the campaign Spaulding complained, perhaps with some justification, that local radio stations, local press, and national wire services misstated facts by referring to him as "a black millionaire" in an effort to drive a wedge between Spaulding and potential black and white blue-collar workers. This may have cost him the election, Spaulding said.[98] But his unwillingness to make any overture to funding Fuller's university could have also played a detrimental role. As black Durham's most popular man of the people, Fuller's populist imprimatur could have helped militate against the black millionaire image, since Fuller had played an instrumental role in Spaulding's previous political success. The fact was that even though Fuller had moved forty minutes away, he still could have supported Spaulding. Instead, he chose not to. This contrasts sharply with Spaulding's Machiavellian mentor, Richard Nixon, and key Nixon strategists like Harry Dent, for whom finding common cause with groups of comparable backgrounds and political stripe appeared to be secondary to winning elections. Whether lacking either Nixon's pure ambition or

Nixon strategists' political acumen, Spaulding apparently missed one of his party's fundamental campaign lessons of the era: attempt to win over key constituents by financing leaders' pet projects. By 1971 Fuller, claiming a lack of operational space and support, had already departed Durham. In destabilizing radical Black Power, Spaulding alienated himself from the majority of local black constituents. Given the record number of blacks being elected across the United States at the time, swept to municipal office mostly by increased minority voting power, Spaulding's mishandling of Fuller and Black Power generally is perhaps even more significant.

Local Black Academic Elites and MXLU

Local black academics were similarly ambivalent if not antagonistic toward MXLU. Professors such as historian James Brewer counseled resource people and intermittently spoke as guest lecturers at the university.[99] However, Brewer's relationship with MXLU was highly unusual among prominent black academics in Durham and surrounding areas. "The brother in the ghetto feels . . . students here at North Carolina College [and] . . . faculty" do not care about him, "and it's true," Fuller gasped, embarrassed that white faculty and students at Duke consistently outnumbered blacks in tutorial projects and demonstrations.[100] He continued to believe that the failure of students to get involved was directly attributable to pedantic teachers.[101] Indeed, more common than Brewer's activism were the attitudes of Professors Earl E. Thorpe and William Couch, two among many whose revolutionary rhetoric was curiously incongruent with their militant participation.

Widely respected as one of North Carolina's most distinguished academics, Thorpe felt little impulse to defend black colleagues and bourgeoisie whom Fuller tartly ridiculed for their "refusal . . . to work with us."[102] Rather, Thorpe, history department chairman at North Carolina College, appeared the archetypal antibourgeois gadfly. An ever-swelling "crowd of complacent" Negroes remain psychologically shackled by the "church and white middle class values," he told a packed North Carolina College auditorium following a typically incendiary Howard Fuller speech the night before. Black power was begging, the notable historian sermonized, for the prodigal daughters and sons of "the black bourgeoisie and the black intellectuals to come home."[103]

At the same gathering William Couch, English professor at NCC, chastised his own colleagues. Eager to appease white segregationists who employ them, black college administrators sacrifice "education in favor of keeping peace and accumulating power, however local and limited," claimed Couch. Black instructors "invariably learn that great truth": loyalty, not competence, serves as the touchstone for advancement in Negro colleges. With black students victimized by administrative and faculty ambivalence, it was no wonder that black militants like Malcolm X were critically engaged intellectual products of prisons rather than universities. The solution to black academic fatalism, Couch stated, was overhauling existing black colleges so that Negro life, African history, and black awareness were central parts of a transformed curriculum.[104]

Thorpe's and Couch's armchair revolutionary harangues did not translate into investing their forty-plus years of accrued intellectual and social capital toward building MXLU. Despite his eloquence, Couch never parted from the snug academic haven of the local black college to teach at MXLU, nor did Thorpe use his considerable professional influence among black college professors to participate in any measurable way in MXLU.[105] Other faculty, like Cecil L. Patterson, a dean at NCC, rejected the university on philosophical grounds, and hoped—despite reluctantly agreeing to the initial grant from the national Episcopal Church—that MXLU would fade away.[106] Still others, like area black college administrators who publicly appeared cooperative, were furtively hostile to the radical change that MXLU represented.

To Fuller, few in the black academic community demonstrated Shaw University President James Cheek's zeal toward social commitment. Believed to be far more open minded than Albert Whiting of North Carolina College at Durham, Cheek sponsored a national conference on civil rights and antipoverty organizations for black college students, along with pioneering summer and curriculum programs for Fuller and students.[107] "He, to me, represents where black presidents ought to go." And, "he's the kind of individual that ought to be running the schools," Fuller said of the Shaw president in an interview.[108] Privately Cheek was less interested in facilitating Black Power groups like MXLU than stymieing them.

Unbeknownst to Fuller and others, since the Fisk University uprising in 1966 President Cheek had worked closely with State Bureau of Investigation (SBI) of North Carolina to "end the developing of the Negro colleges and universities in the country on a black power basis." As a state informant Cheek—best known as later president of Howard University after campus unrest there—was the eyes and ears of the SBI as well as highway patrol and Raleigh police chief—keeping them abreast of local college movements and activities, particularly what they deemed as Stokely Carmichael's and other radicals' efforts to take over colleges. Saint Augustine president Prezell Robinson, heading another Raleigh-Durham historically black college, also cooperated with SBI officials regarding the presence and rise of campus Black Power elements.[109] Fuller was far from paranoid when he suspected someone "was cutting him up at those teas." The bitter irony, as we see later in this chapter, was that the saboteur was one of his staunchest public allies: Alvin Blount.

Within months of beginning full-time operation in the fall of 1969 it was apparent that MXLU had to move. By February 1970 the *Durham Sun* with rare front-page coverage detailed how the "unaccredited university" was "beset by controversy and pressed for funds."[110] Weeks later Fuller announced MXLU's departure. Its relocation signaled to some MXLU's "insignificance as a community organization."[111] When asked why the university was leaving Durham, Fuller responded, "The only thing for certain is that we are going to have to have more room."[112] Fuller's search for space seemed as metaphoric as literal. As one reporter aptly put it, Fuller's search for space was not simply for additional administrative offices and classrooms, but for "a more acceptable climate in the black community," room not primarily away from whites—be they conservative, moderate, or left—but from the suffocating accommodationism of Durham's black upper stratum. Fuller's sojourn to "find more fertile ground for his school" led him to Greensboro, "where blacks have historically been more militant," though ultimately Greensboro too failed to offer necessary support.[113]

That spring, as MXLU prepared to move, the university would be forced to make concessions of its own in order to secure funding. On April 22, 1970, MXLU received its second largest grant, $35,000, from the Cummins Engine Foundation. It seemed a not unusual sponsorship given the school's emphasis on engineering and other applied sciences. But the funding came with strings. Only after school officials signed off on six preconditions designed to contain MXLU by depoliticizing the institution, was funding released. Under the guise of this grant, MXLU behavior was policed in the following ways. First, the grant stipulated that no monies could be paid to or used to benefit any government official. Second, MXLU officials were enjoined from lobbying legislatures (local, state, or federal) or seeking to influence the public on any legislative matters. Third, Cummins Engine Foundation monies could not be used to educate the public or to influence any election. Fourth, no portion of the monies could be used to register voters. Fifth, MXLU officials were enjoined from using the monies for travel or study. Finally, any money not used for purposes explained in the grant proposal request had to be returned.[114]

At minimum, MXLU did conform to the demands of the Cummins award. For a major selling point in subsequent funding appeals, as we see later in the case of the Episcopal Church, is that in subsequent months Fuller would be dubbed a model resident, eschewing local political agitation and activism. Fuller's local political de-escalation would be the single most important argument MXLU could make to potential donor organizations. "Black folks can start something and have it meaningful to them for a while, maybe two or three years," MXLU's public relations director, Chuck Hopkins, summed up his experience and expectation, "and then the foundations will co-opt it."[115]

MXLU in Greensboro

Though differences existed, black middle-class leaders in Greensboro recognized the value of young radicals like student Nelson Johnson.[116] Older black reformers, as historian William Chafe noted, shared Johnson's "objectives, if not his style."[117] Though rarely initiating grassroots organizing themselves, civic leaders like Greensboro NAACP president George Simkins and local financier B. J. Battle of American Federal Savings and Loans inevitably supported Johnson—once he took the first move. This made it easier for Johnson to not alienate black middle-class leaders—working on voter registration with the NAACP, cooperating with ministers on social welfare projects, and intentionally moderating his tone when addressing black audiences. Johnson's organizational dexterity in merging campus and community issues and in galvanizing broad support for students and cafeteria and sanitation workers were also promising signs for Fuller. More than any other single factor, the coalition-building talent of Johnson was the reason MXLU moved to Greensboro.[118]

With Johnson elected student body vice president in spring 1969, and later president, MXLU leaders felt that the university could draw greater support from students at North Carolina Agricultural and Technical State University (A&T) at Greensboro than it had from North Carolina College at Durham.[119] In the recent past many faculty members like A&T drama professor and *Carolina Peacemaker* publisher John Marshall Stevenson successfully coalesced working relationships with younger and more radical black sects in Greensboro. With the announcement of the Student Organization for Black Unity's relocation to Greensboro from Milwaukee, the city was promised distinction as the operational headquarters for black nationalism in the South.[120] When MXLU held a press conference formally confirming the move in late August 1970, "virtually the entire roster of established black leaders turned out to welcome the new facility."[121] However, the climate markedly changed as the university's arrival in Greensboro coincided with the volatile debate over integrating the city's school system.

By 1971 no issue was more socially charged in Greensboro than school desegregation.[122] Of the 152 school districts in the state, Greensboro was the largest of five North Carolina school systems violating federal civil rights guidelines. Because Greensboro was in noncompliance, federal funds declined precipitously from $1.5 million to $423,000. Most affected were cultural awareness training programs for teachers, which were eliminated altogether. For more than a decade school board officials, sticking to the legal advice of board attorneys and reflecting the segregationist will of local whites, had refused to follow any desegregation plan other than freedom of choice, which had led to 95 percent segregated schooling while perpetuating "unequal educational facilities and opportunities for black students solely on the basis of their race."[123] *Swann v. Mecklenburg Supreme Court*, in spring 1971, ended the legal machinations of school board attorneys.[124] Schools were ordered thoroughly desegregated by the beginning of the following school year.[125]

The implementation of school desegregation through busing was accelerated by the deaths of three pivotal freedom-of-school-choice adherents—the school superintendent, school board attorney, and school board chairman—within the span of three years. They were replaced by two

African Americans and Carson Bain, the city's former mayor widely respected as a "result-oriented businessman." Former chamber of commerce president Al Lineberry was elected chairman. Known as a white leader who worked conscientiously if not well, the pietistic Lineberry exhorted fellow committee members: "We are going to comply." "From that point forward, complete cooperation . . . marked the school board's posture toward desegregation." Though a few obdurate groups resisted, many white organizations sought to comply with *Swann* as well. "The greatest opposition," however did not arise from white Greensboro citizens but, according to Chafe, "came from within the black community."[126]

In responding to the majority of black community leaders endorsing busing, young black radicals like Johnson contended that wholesale school integration undermined black culture and leadership. Others in the pro-Johnson faction suspected that white leadership would use integration to control black schools. Established blacks' uncompromising desire for black children to attend school with whites merely reinforced that "the 'Negro' is the creation of the European. . . . [and] has no cultural history except what the European makes or creates for him."[127] Still, some considered it a diversionary device from more substantive issues like jobs and housing. The goal was "a quality education. . . . Integration was only a tactic," Johnson methodically rejoined to a black PTA group supporting busing.[128] Whatever the particular opposition to school integration, it inspired the wrath of black school board members and community leaders like Simkins and Dr. Julius T. Douglas, who spent their professional lives challenging racial segregation. Stevenson agreed.[129] MXLU and SOBU "should continue," Stevenson wrote, yet he cautioned readers that such nationalist tendencies were benighted relics of the past, a sad wish to "run back into the dark forest of segregation, of second-class citizenship."[130]

Even while Johnson and local OEO community development director Thomas Bailey ultimately played down their opposition to busing, "divisions of class and ideology" were surfacing in the black community over the issue. Although Fuller played a relatively minor role in the entire debate (he was in New York during the latter part of summer), to Greensboro black elite MXLU increasingly came to represent the limits of an ideology rather than a center for black liberation.

MXLU's emergence symbolized a programmatic contradiction to the modern civil rights movement that black leaders in Greensboro had been instrumental in orchestrating. The Pan-Africanist school came to be seen as not complementary to the intergenerational struggle against educational apartheid; nor was the revolutionary educational facility considered even an operational alternative. In many ways MXLU's institutional existence was increasingly recognized as a paradigmatic repudiation of the integrationist agenda mobilized during the Greensboro sit-ins in 1960. To be sure, Greensboro blacks had made great strides since then. The election of Julius Douglas, one of the original student members of the sit-in movement, personified a ubiquitous reminder of the gains as well as struggles of many black residents. With local compliance to court-ordered integration and the transformation of the school board, considered one of the last public vestiges of racial segregation, blacks anticipated that they, or at least future generations, would be integrated into the economic mainstream of Greensboro and the nation. Yet despite such progress, their recent foothold in municipal venues of power was delicate at best. Many feared that black community leaders' support for MXLU would be naively or duplicitously construed among whites as abandoning the cause of school desegregation for which they had long fought.

MXLU's lack of personal and local ties in Greensboro heightened the importance of its political and ideological views. These views often differed from black city leaders. "I would say the whole time we were in Durham, the community stayed involved," an official at MXLU remembered, in large measure because of the long-standing interpersonal relationships between many individuals and the black community in Durham.[131] In Greensboro, however, the university was treated with abiding skepticism.

Exacerbating concerns, Fuller's rendezvous with African liberation leaders in the late summer and fall 1971 fed fears among the moderate black leadership of Greensboro that MXLU was an extremist program with specious designs. His association with socialist liberation fighters in Mozambique and Tanzania revived concerns about MXLU as a possible training ground for subversive radical activity. The majority media needed little time to exploit such assumptions.

Searching to expand and institutionalize operations in Greensboro, MXLU encountered severe problems particularly among black leaders, who attempted to block the institutionalization of MXLU by thwarting the college's purchase of the financially troubled Palmer Memorial Institute, among the nation's oldest black preparatory schools, until it was forced to officially close earlier in 1971. Founded in 1902 by Dr. Charlotte Hawkins Brown, the Palmer Institute had suffered from years of mounting financial crises. By fall 1971 trustees watched as the school's indebtedness rose to $250,000, with another $140,000 due the next year.[132] Efforts at saving the venerable preparatory school failed. A nationwide fund-raising drive that fell far short of its $1.5 million goal, and a fire that destroyed the lists of contributors, forced the school to close its doors.[133]

In August 1971 MXLU sought purchase of the two-hundred-acre campus located in Sedalia, a small community just outside of Greensboro.[134] To MXLU, Palmer looked like an ideal site to implement instruction in cooperative farming, teach black people various skills, and provide a new training and conference center for blacks in North Carolina and beyond.[135] The financial woes facing Palmer trustees were far from insurmountable. In fact, MXLU tendered an immediate $50,000 cash down payment. Trustees, however, were less than enthused by the potential inheritors of the Palmer property. They ignored MXLU's first proposition; finding no other offers, trustees agreed to sell to MXLU in the last days of August. However, because not enough members were present to form a quorum, the board attorney nullified the decision.[136]

The notion of MXLU purchasing the Palmer property was unacceptable to many trustees. Board chairman Dr. Julius T. Douglas—after unsuccessfully seeking bids from other potential lessors like the Catawba Synod of the Presbyterian Church—resigned in protest over the tentative decision.[137] Desperate for additional offers, trustees chased other alternatives, contacting Bennett College, A&T State University, and the proposed Central North Carolina School of the Deaf. Greensboro NAACP president George Simkins, though without any serious bid proffered, hastened a proposal to turn the defunct school into a rest home. However, not a single competitive counterbid was made.[138]

Many Greensboro and Sedalia blacks did not object to the new school; they simply hated to see Palmer close. Perhaps just as many, with limited knowledge of the alternative college, wished to know more about its program. Still others stressed how divergent MXLU was from the Palmer tradition. Adding to the controversy were rumors that the school would bring guns, marijuana, and orgies to the area, forcing down local property values.[139] The overwhelmingly white attendees at a September community meeting expressed their disapproval of the sale. Petitions opposing the sale, possibly originating with whites, circulated around Sedalia and neighboring communities. Palmer trustees did little to combat the misinformation, instead inviting more bids.

Fuller raised the ante. MXLU returned with a new offer to lease the property with an option to buy, in addition to assuming all responsibilities for indebtedness. The university doubled its cash down payment. As a final gesture Fuller assented that the lease could be terminated, given proper notice and reasonable financial arrangements, if Palmer was ever able to reopen. The bitter reality for the university, however, was that trustees preferred Palmer's foreclosure to its sale to Fuller. Trustees continued to solicit additional bidders, and offers soon arrived from once-disinterested Bennett College, along with the United Holiness Church, and Skilcraft Industries. Simkins finally persuaded the Prince Hall Grand Lodge Masons of North Carolina to offer to convert the former school to a rest home. Greensboro resident and Democratic gubernatorial candidate Hargrove Bowles urged Governor Scott's office to reconsider the property as a future location for the Central North Carolina School of the Deaf.[140]

Fed up, MXLU officials begrudgingly agreed on September 3 to withdraw its bid if trustees could either keep Palmer open or find some other way to use the facility for educating African Americans. Director of Operations James L. Lee summed up, "Rather than engage in destructive arguments and mutual exchanges of character slander which threatened to tear the community apart, we are willing to withdraw our proposal to the trustees. We expected the reaction from whites. We always expect that. But we never expected the divisive action from blacks."[141]

To believe, as apparently Lee did, that the black elite and entrepreneurs should want to support MXLU may seem unusual, yet not unprecedented. MXLU had relocated to Greensboro largely on the belief that it would have stronger cross-class community support, a belief that was initially borne out by the welcoming MXLU officials received from black upper- and middle-strata Greensboroans.

Black American figures such as Booker T. Washington, Marcus Garvey, Elijah Muhammad, and Louis Farrakhan have all successfully melded petit bourgeois capitalism with programs of cultural preservationism or revival. In North Carolina at the time, Floyd McKissick's Soul City project captured this reinforcing coexistence of cultural and economic nationalisms—as its eponym was chosen as a genealogical reminder of a collective black psyche and spiritual past coupled with the city's aim to showcase black capitalism. If capitalism has a natural animus it is not toward race pride and preservationists like MXLU but toward so-called revolutionary or leftist nationalists, like the Black Panther Party.[142]

Lee's assumptions are consistent with ethnic and regionalist nationalist movements outside the United States. Industrial and commercial elites often forge alliances with emerging ethnic and regional movements for autonomy and independence.[143] In some cases, as in Scotland and western Canada, the economic advantage of greater independence and even separatism will be emphasized. Each stood to profit from mutual reinforcement of these ready-made identity markets. Walled off by Jim Crow for decades, black producers and professionals relied heavily on buying black insurance, groceries, real property, along with a host of goods and services.[144] In some ways the end of Jim Crow signaled an end to the racially centripetal force of segregation, loosening racial loyalties, both in the commercial sector between black producers and consumers as well as transclass strata commitments to collective racial uplift.[145] One should not blindly dismiss Lee as naive for expecting middle-class support, given what is known regarding the overlapping and reinforcing roles that cultural nationalism and economic interests play.

Lee spoke in place of the absent Fuller, who was attending a conference in Tanzania. The bulk of Fuller's August and September was spent in Mozambique, however. War and politics in Mozambique shook Fuller's worldview. "It had been my first day with FRELIMO [Liberation Front of Mozambique], and already," Fuller wrote in his diary, "some things were provoking deep thoughts within me." Specifically, Fuller noted how Mozambique's war of independence from Portugal imperialism compelled FRELIMO to accept aid from non-African sources—notably military aid from China, Soviet Union, Bulgaria, and Yugoslavia, along with humanitarian assistance from people (not governments) in the Netherlands and Italy, thus reconsidering common bonds beyond race. "I had personally conceived of our struggle as being against white people who represented and controlled the forces of imperialism. However, there was also no doubt in my analysis that Black people who represented the forces of imperialism had to be fought against as well."[146] What likely made it possible for Fuller to even entertain rethinking struggle was a predisposed worldview.[147] Fuller, then, not only could square FRELIMO's reasoning but could increasingly frame it as almost commonsense: "As I thought back on it, I clearly saw that much of my thinking had been conditioned by my life in the world's most racist society. . . . Given this particular situation we face in America, that was the valid analysis. Thus . . . it became a matter of the particular circumstances in which one found himself; this was one of the fundamental molders of ideological analysis."[148] Still, Fuller did not immediately reject racial essentialism. Fuller felt that his differences with Mozambique rebels over foregrounding race and Pan-Africanism did not put him "at odds with FRELIMO in any way."[149] Though he spent thirty more days there, his first impression was indelible. Any internal conflict Fuller penned while in Africa remained unresolved. He returned to America and Greensboro as a committed Pan-Africanist.

MXLU and the Loss of Its Primary Investor

Despite established black leaders eschewing the institutionalization of MXLU, the school remained in Greensboro and, between August 1971 and spring 1972, fortified its relationship with the Federation of Pan-African Institutions, a consortium of nation-building elementary, secondary, and higher educational academies dedicated to black cultural nationalism. With schools in places like Dayton, Ohio, and Newark, New Jersey, the federation nurtured an embryonic but developing relationship with local rectories and the national Episcopal Church. MXLU joined the other constituent institutions when the federation applied for national Episcopal funding. MXLU's pursuit of funding would capture the internecine struggle between the alternative revolutionary college and members of the state's upper stratum of blacks.

When in June 1972 the Greensboro Episcopal Committee and the Diocese of North Carolina opposed a second grant in the amount of $75,000 to MXLU, no one was surprised.[150] The backlash of conservative white Episcopalians after the first grant had been vociferous and financially devastating to the diocese. Fuller had anticipated the rejection, since he suspected there was "no level of black control" with decision-making authority inside the Episcopal Church. Few, least of all Howard Fuller, surmised that the most devastating criticisms were leveled by black officials within the church.[151]

Most damaging to MXLU was not the absence of white moderate and liberal support or white-controlled institutions, which Fuller always contended were "the real problems of black people"; rather, it was the pivotal capitulation of once-supportive blacks whose objections legitimated white moderates' decision to deny the grant. Not a single black member of the Greensboro committee defended the second MXLU grant proposal. Even the Rev. Carlton O. Morales, a vocal proponent during the initial grant, would join in formal disagreement.[152] Fuller was well aware of the rising tension with the shrinking number of black supporters like Howard Clement, an Episcopalian and Republican increasingly aligned with the city's conservative faction. Clement understood that his relationship with the radical university potentially threatened his professional advancement.[153] However, Fuller was unsuspecting of the ingrained resistance toward MXLU of other leading black officials in the Diocese of North Carolina.[154]

A second Episcopal grant meant an interview with the diocesan screening review committee, although Fuller was reluctant to comply. Dr. Alvin Blount, Fuller's personal physician and former MXLU consultant, coaxed Fuller to consent to the interview. A warden at the predominantly black Church of the Redeemer, Blount organized the interview. Blount assured whites present that he understood the black militant, or at least better than did white senior officials sitting in judgment that day. Blount detailed the warm friendship and professional relationship that had developed between the two. Fuller not only was a good individual, Blount insisted, but more important, there had been an "absence of any political involvement of Howard and MXLU since they had been in Greensboro."[155]

He vouched that the show of citizenship exercised by Fuller had made a difference at the university, where Blount had earlier volunteered as biomedical advisor. MXLU had always been a model drug-free campus, Blount attested, free of disciplinary problems. Fuller had strategically located male and female dormitories in different sections of Greensboro to safeguard against youthful indiscretion and carnal temptations.[156]

But the question of funding inevitably hinged on the committee's perception of Fuller. Blount closed his cogent testimonial by offering the charismatic but frequently misunderstood Fuller an opportunity to further sway onlooking skeptics. "I want Howard to tell us about . . . MXLU," he told the other six members present.[157] At the interview it seemed that, with Blount by his side, Fuller had no better advocate.

Days after the interview the committee reconvened to deliberate their recommendation. Though the committee did not have an official vote, it held great sway in the final decision of the national screening committee. The deliberation would once again find Blount in a central role—though one opposite that in the June 9 interview. Fuller had long suspected there was some saboteur eager to scuttle the second Episcopal grant, correctly surmising it to be Howard Clement.

But Fuller didn't expect MXLU to come under attack from Blount, whose inspiring testimonial during the first interview would disintegrate into silence and complicity at the second. Blount said nothing as one after another white committee member blatantly mischaracterized the university. When the question was raised if anyone favored the grant, no one, including Blount, expressed support. Blount and others responded to the committee chairman's suggestion of a noncommittal "no comment" with equal disfavor.[158] Blount aggressively postured as the grant's leading censor. In a stunning about-face, Blount pressed for aid to be withheld and the grant rejected. Blount complained that MXLU irresponsibly aroused further division between blacks and whites. "It was obvious . . . that the Church could not contribute money to help with this division since the Church has always supported reconciliation rather than division," Blount stated.[159] Fuller's trustworthy ally privately relished derailing MXLU funding.

Rather than leave his injurious remarks there, Blount attacked the entire grant procedure and the local churches' relationship with the national office. He objected to future committees receiving the New York–based GCSP grant recommendations prior to local screenings and reviews. For southern white sympathizers the current process had afforded convenient cover to fund unpopular projects under the guise of assenting to GCSP's wishes. If the procedural changes recommended by Blount were followed, it would eviscerate any protection for whites who considered supporting controversial projects like MXLU.[160] In the future, "the investigation by the Local Committee should be done first," Blount insisted to the delight of antagonistic rectors and wardens. Why Blount undermined MXLU at the committee's closed-door session may never be known; minutes from the meeting shed little light except to show that the local committee did not press him for justification.

Back in Durham, Episcopalian and dean of North Carolina Central University Cecil L. Patterson left no room for the bishop to misinterpret his position: "I am opposed to any additional funding of MXLU in Greensboro under any pretext or in any situation." Though he begrudgingly endorsed the first grant, Patterson reminded Fraser that from the beginning he "did not believe that Malcolm X was a viable concept." An unabashed Patterson offered: "I will be happy to repeat it to anyone who wants—or needs to hear it." "Incidentally," Patterson concluded, "I have talked with Howard Clement about this grant, and find (to my great surprise) that he opposes the grant also. He is much closer to the situation at Malcolm X than I am. . . . He no doubt has reasons different from mine, but I would give his opposition even greater weight than my own because of his close association with the current conditions."[161]

Fraser used Clement, Morales, Patterson, and others to justify his strongly worded opposition to the grant: "Those who gave us comments and observations were people who advised me to approve the last Malcolm X grant, people who supported the grant, and people who have been associated with MXLU in one way or another. All were unanimous . . . in oppos[ition to] the funding of any further grants to Malcolm X Liberation University."[162] The objections of prominent black Episcopalians proved that MXLU "had no strong appeal to the black community," Fraser suggested. Soon after receiving the bishop's recommendations, the General Convention Special Program vetoed the grant. The diocese's opposition not only thwarted indispensable aid essential for the upcoming fiscal year, but—because the grant was part of a larger grant—jeopardized funding for the entire Federation of Pan-African Institutions. After initially opting to appeal the veto, MXLU withdrew its application for funding rather than prevent or prolong grant approval to the Federation of Pan-African Institutions.[163]

Reforming MXLU: The Struggle between Liberal Interventionism and Institutional Autonomy

The diocese's refusal to continue funding MXLU should not be misinterpreted. It wasn't that MXLU was paying no dividends in the form of institutional moderation. Indeed, from the inaugural grant—which school officials' secured after vowing that MXLU would be violence free and then assuring grantors that students would avoid any activities that might invite local scrutiny—the liberal imprint was evident.[164] From its founding, university officials impressed upon the fifty-plus students enrolled at MXLU in 1969 the significance of policing their own behavior so as "not to bring pressure from the white community" in Durham on the school, which would not only attract unwarranted law enforcement attention but also jeopardize university funding.[165] Similarly, grant stipulations like those made by Cummins served to reinforce this. Moving to Greensboro only made MXLU officials more conscious of policing its organizational behavior.

In fact, by 1972, MXLU's president appeared to prioritize nonviolence and negotiating—the very outcomes the school's namesake, Malcolm X, had feared most would result from letting liberalism into a hot, strong, Black Power movement. Nothing illustrates this better than when, needing additional funding, the MXLU head took a second job in spring 1972 to run the Washington, D.C.–based lobbying wing of the Interreligious Foundation for Community Organizations (IFCO), a black-controlled funding outfit financed by thirteen predominantly white church agencies. In exchange for having IFCO funds at his disposal, the cultural nationalist–cum–lobbyist foreswore the use of revolutionary violence. Instead, Fuller, tasked with persuading U.S. corporations and the federal government to end its chrome ore trade with racist regimes in southern Africa, promised to get government and corporate America to the negotiating table by means other than the "bullet." As Fuller told reporters, they would achieve their goals by combining the ballot, moral suasion, and if necessary shareholder activism.[166] The pursuit of dialogue and shunning of self-defense had evolved greatly by late 1972 when, in the aftermath of the killings of two black Southern University students by Louisiana law enforcement officers, Fuller was part of a delegation meeting with Governor Edwin Edwards that urged verbal over violent exchange.[167]

International liberal interventionism reinforced grantors' regulatory control over MXLU's organizational behavior. Consider the World Council of Churches (WCC), headquartered in Geneva, Switzerland: as a result of a 1969 gathering in Notting Hill, London, it would underwrite MXLU along with liberation movements in Canada, southern Africa, and other countries. Concluding a five-year review of the WCC funding program in 1974, the auditor was unequivocal about the WCC's ostensible lax oversight despite the no-violence pledge affixed to any aid.[168] "The grants were given with no strings," the grant auditor told the black newspaper *Chicago*

Defender about the invisible hand of the WCC. "Except that they were not to be used for military purposes," she added. Oblivious to the organization's own constrictions, she assured the reporter, "the WCC exercised no control."[169] Here the Episcopal Church, IFCO, and WCC operated in classic Gramscian hegemonic fashion, wielding themselves as instruments of civil society that exercise power over a dissident movement culture in ways often unknown and unconscious to liberal interveners and, in this case, to MXLU.

Still, grantors pressed for greater concessions. With limited funds to allocate, grantors looked for a greater reform return on their investment in black nationalism, as the Episcopal grant committee discussed days after the grant hearing. Nationally, this is why grantors continued underwriting the Federation of Pan-African Institutions. In North Carolina, had those sympathetic Episcopalians believed backing Black Power was futile, they likely would not have thrown their lot in with America's best known radicals of the Black Power period, the Black Panther Party.

As for Fuller, his stance grew more radical. In the absence of liberal containment and intervention, Fuller's efforts toward moderation vanished as his actions grew more extreme: overtly consorting with African and Communist revolutionaries, urging violent overthrow of the state, and calling for the immediate destruction of American capitalism. These antistatist entreaties supplanted cultural and psychological arguments in Fuller's advocation of black liberation. Baraka soon followed suit, mirroring Fuller's new radicalism and reshaping himself in this image.

*   *   *

"I see myself as a human being who is both a product of the environment that I live in, and hopefully a person who is contributing to changing the nature of that environment. And because of that dialectic, it is always possible to have said something in 1972 that is no longer adequate to describe how I see the world in 1974," Fuller told a May 1974 audience of Pan-African conferees in Washington, D.C.[170]

A product of his environment, Fuller's worldview was shaped by the daily accretion of institution building in Durham and Greensboro in ways he could scarcely foresee. The university's contentious relations with North Carolina's black middle and elite classes served as a necessary foreground for Fuller's transformation, predisposing the school's founder to endorsing a structural critique, a position he came to embrace after his exchange with African liberation fighters. Study and travel influenced Fuller insofar as what he read and saw fit the frame of his lived intraracial experiences in Durham, then Greensboro. But change was only possible to those open to it. Fuller's conversion reinforces the openness of putatively isolationist thick solidarities like black cultural nationalism. Far from the isolationism attributed to cultural nationalists, Fuller's travel abroad, study, and empirical experiences—three essential traits of openness necessary for what some scholars call contamination—catalyzed his Marxian conversion. This was most evident after liberal interventionism.

Liberal interventionism by way of institutional funding hewed Fuller to the city's culture of civility, to borrow language from William Chafe's classic study of race relations. Indeed, as the second grant interview makes plain, even Fuller's critics could not ignore that Fuller had been a model community citizen. In rejecting funding, liberals removed its containment, and an unconstrained Fuller journeyed beyond the liberal orbit. Whether Fuller would have traveled this path if funding from the Episcopal Church had continued is unclear. History tells us, however, what ensued in the absence of liberal succor: Fuller's move to the left had a ripple effect felt throughout the cultural nationalist world, as fellow Black Power Brahmans Amiri Baraka and Maulana Karenga did likewise.

Not that soft power stopped engaging Black Power completely.[171] Rather, amid dwindling financial resources and an ascendant conservatism, soft-power practitioners focused attention on those Black Power programs whose reforms seemed somewhat more impressive. In North Carolina, for instance, that meant that liberal Episcopalians bypassed MXLU while underwriting the Joseph P. Waddell ambulance service, a program established by another Black Power group whose ideological trajectory was deemed more to liberals' liking: the once-revolutionary nationalist Black Panther Party. How the Panthers returned from the Rubicon of revolution, as we next see, is a story moving beyond liberals creating space to how liberalism helped reform Black Power.

School founder Howard Fuller, facing the street with hands on waist, talking with student at the first permanent location of Malcolm X Liberation University (ca. 1969), a converted brick warehouse located at the corner of Pettigrew and Ramsey streets in Durham's historic black business section. MXLU relocated to Greensboro by 1971. Courtesy of photographer Bill Boyarsky.

Joan Little at women's prison in North Carolina, February 1975. By month's end, Little would be out on bond and campaigning for her freedom. Courtesy of the North Carolina State Archives.

Floyd McKissick with Governor Jim Holshouser on his right. Soul City had no better booster than the governor, whose administration actively recruited industry, offered technical assistance and training, and served as a conduit for Soul City officials, putting them in contact with interested industries, and, when necessary, nudging high-ranking federal officials for program approval. For the governor, Soul City, in his words, promised to create "black-controlled corporations but to be open to people of all races. . . . Many of Soul City's citizens are certain to feel a spiritual kinship with those slaves [who once lived here]." Courtesy of the North Carolina State Archives.

Child at the Soul City dedication, November 1973. For the architects of the project, Soul City was an investment in present and future generations, expanding their quality of life and life opportunities by giving blacks rare hands-on experience in city governance and municipal planning and industry. Courtesy of the North Carolina State Archives.

Soultech I, a 73,000-square-foot industrial incubator. By August 1976, when the architectural drawing was done, Soultech I housed the offices of the Soul City Company, the information center, and the Soul City Foundation, as well as manufacturing space for the American National Housing Company and Warren Manufacturing Company. Originally envisioned as a centerpiece of black entrepreneurialism and industry for the area and nation, today Soultech I is owned by the medium-security Warren County Correction Institution, which opened in 1997 as the area's largest employer. Photo from the National Archives and Records Administration.

Jesse Helms at a rally for Ronald Reagan, July 25, 1975. Future Reagan rallies often had more of a Hollywood star quality, as Reagan's campaign would recruit celebrities like James Stewart and Efrem Zimbalist Jr. to stump for the erstwhile actor during the North Carolina primary. Courtesy of the North Carolina State Archives.

Reverend Benjamin Chavis and sister, Francine, a medical student at Humboldt University in Germany, at the North Carolina Black Leadership Caucus picnic held at Soul City, August 26, 1979. The Chavises joined nearly one hundred other families at Soul City to affirm their support for McKissick's embattled new town project. Thomas A. Johnson / *The New York Times* / Redux.

You can be Black, and Navy too.

Recruiting poster, ca. 1972, part of the navy's efforts to improve its image among young African American males in the aftermath of the racial uprising on the *Kitty Hawk* and elsewhere. When such ideas served its purpose, the nation-state too could acknowledge that civic nationalism was not incompatible with black nationalism. Courtesy of the U.S. Naval Historical Foundation.

THE FIRST CITY IN THE WORLD THAT'S BUILT AROUND YOUR FAMILY.

HUD advertisement for Soul City, ca. 1970. Far from the nihilistic image that often saddled the broader Black Power movement, Soul City was promoted as a racially open and family friendly community.

From Rebellion to Reform
Constitutional Liberalism and the Black Panther Party, 1968–1974

3

When citizens of Winston-Salem's north ward elected Nelson Malloy, a former Black Panther, to the board of aldermen in 1994, it marked sixteen out of twenty years that a Panther had occupied that seat. For an entire post–Black Power generation black Winstonians had looked on this municipal perch of political power as "the permanent Black Panther seat."[1] Even a four-year absence between 1986 and 1990 did not represent a waning of political confidence by the party faithful. Rather, these were years during which erstwhile Panther and incumbent Alderman Larry Little voluntarily vacated his post and handpicked his successor.[2]

By the late 1970s and early 1980s the Panthers' place in the African American community and city at large was secure. The city's majority press touted Little as Winston-Salem's most influential African American and, at the age of thirty-one, the youngest among the city's political elite. The city's black newspaper, the *Winston-Salem Chronicle*, selected the Panther alderman as its first-ever "man of the year."[3] At the pinnacle of his political success, however, the former party spokesperson chose not to continue as alderman: after more than a decade as a successful Democratic politician, Little enrolled full-time at Wake Forest University Law School. Malloy and Little's professional accomplishments, although perhaps the most celebrated, were not aberrations among former Winston-Salem Panthers. Hazel Mack, Robert Greer, Julius Cornell, and other branch veterans led socially and professionally productive post-Panther lives. Indeed, much had changed in the decade or so since local members were vilified by a jaundiced majority press and the city's only black publication simply ignored the local chapter altogether.

During the Black Power era black nationalism was inextricably linked to the criminal imagery of that generation.[4] According to scholarly and popular lore, black nationalists and other radicals were a nihilistic band of activists bent on rioting and social upheaval, functioning under the convenient but specious cover of championing racial justice and equality.[5] As J. Edgar Hoover said when he appeared before the 1971 House Appropriations Committee on Internal Security, it was a group draped in "self-made propaganda, depicting its role as that of an armed revolutionary vanguard calling for the overthrow of a fascist United States."[6] Others, like House Republicans on the same committee, insisted that the party was "a subversive criminal group, using the façade of politics and Marxist-Leninist ideology as a cover for crimes of violence and extortion."[7]

Such was not the case for the last official Black Panther Party chapter on the East Coast. When the North Carolina chapter dissolved in 1978, Malloy, Mack, and others had virtually erased the image of criminality surrounding Pantherism in Winston-Salem by transforming itself within the legal constructs of local, state, and federal law. From the vantage point of many, Panthers in the Winston-Salem branch had made the successful transition from radical revolutionaries to reformists. This transformation would elude the national office, despite party chairman Huey Newton's statement that such a transformation indicated the direction in which the party as a whole wanted to go.[8] That statement turned out not only to be instructive for the BPP but also telling for black American politics writ large. The story of the Black Panthers in North Carolina is an apt illustration of how, by the mid-1970s, post–civil rights black politics were increasingly incorporated into the processes of mainstream American politics, and of how and why liberalism served as a catalyst for this decade-long shift.

The latter half of the 1970s, in stark contrast to the period from the mid-1960s up to then, witnessed a marked convergence of efforts on the part of those involved in black American politics. Whether advancing independent parties or building coalitions, black activists met around and participated in electoral politics. Those casting their lot with mainstream party politics showed a decisive shift away from sectarian ideology to winning elections and exercising political power. Crucial to this transition, though seldom acknowledged, were liberals whose legal patronage facilitated Black Power's shift away from the politics of protest and toward the politics of pragmatism.

By examining the Winston-Salem Panther group, this chapter explores how black radicals made the transition to electoral and mainstream-party politics. In doing so they relied heavily on the appeal of constitutional liberalism. Nowhere is this more evident than in the local Panthers' relationship with the American Civil Liberties Union chapter in North Carolina (NCCLU). The legal sponsorship of the Panthers by the state's civil liberties union advanced party credibility and provided protection against the extralegal actions of local, state, and federal law enforcement. By curbing the legal authority that had been repressing the Winston-Salem Panthers, the Panthers embraced the Democratic Party machine and eventually won city office, establishing their members as municipal power brokers in the city for an entire generation.

This chapter reviews the interactions between the national Black Panther Party (BPP) headquarters and party organizers in North Carolina, and examines details of the Winston-Salem chapter. It offers an assessment of the Black Panthers that diverges markedly from the criminal imagery prevailing in much of the general historiography regarding the party. At the same time it complicates recent Black Power historiography, revealing in the case of Winston-Salem the contribution of liberalism to the Panthers' political legitimacy.

The BPP-ACLU connection did not signal so much a radical ideological departure for the party as much as it helped catalyze the party's stated desire to shift toward mainstream politics. "We wanted to do it earlier," as Panther Nelson Malloy pithily said of the branch's community building and electoral efforts. "But hell we were standing in court all the time."[9] The NCCLU, the state arm of the national ACLU, forced law enforcement to abate so the party could pursue its reformist agenda. Of course this reformist agenda was precipitated by a number of internal and external factors, ranging from a concern over the party's increased alienation from the black community to state repression and the incarceration of members and sympathizers. Although this chapter closes by focusing on the party's relationship with the ACLU, liberal legal support offers but one example of how liberalism facilitated the party's moderation. Take the Panther so-called community survival programs, launched to foster greater black support. Among the most celebrated of such initiatives was Winston-Salem's Joseph P. Waddell People's Free Ambulance Service. According to Bobby Seale, "[in] the Black Panther Party we created a Free Ambulance program, but the only chapter that had that was the North Carolina chapter in Winston-Salem because they got a [Episcopal Church] grant and everything with a health center, and created a Free Ambulance program."[10] Similarly, local physicians trained Winston-Salem Panthers to administer testing for sickle-cell anemia and tuberculosis.[11]

The party was also not antilegal or anticonstitutionalist. That said, Panther members lacked the legal expertise and clout required to sway public opinion or to compel the state to act constitutionally. For that they ultimately had to rely on experts friendly to Panther claims of constitutional abridgements. And when Panthers party to a suit did not use such experts, the results were disastrous—as Larry Little, the local Panthers' founding member and branch leader, proved when he was jailed on a charge of contempt. Thereafter, though, Little never undersold the value of expertise in law, which is why Little himself returned to school for a law degree, and later became a constitutional law and political science professor at Winston-Salem State University. Such acts of engagement—from liberal legal support to an Episcopal Church grant to the assistance of health-care professionals—aided the BPP's migration to moderation.

Charlotte

With its emergence from the 1940s as a banking and business center, Charlotte became a modern commercial beacon for the New South. Not surprisingly the fastest-growing city in North Carolina's Piedmont crescent grappled with problems endemic to metropolitan areas, problems that included crime. In August 1968 the big-city problems of the sprawling Queen City were announced on the front page of the *Charlotte Observer* in an article citing the Federal Bureau of Investigation (FBI) Union Crime Reports.[12] The annual report listed Charlotte as fourth (behind Little Rock, Baltimore, and Miami) in aggravated assaults. Of the cities in the Carolinas, Charlotte had the highest percentage of serious criminal offenses—murder, rape, robbery, aggravated assault, burglary, larceny of fifty dollars and over, and auto theft. Most disturbing, Charlotte had the second-highest murder rate in the nation.[13]

Law-and-order stump speeches of presidential hopefuls coupled with objections to legally mandated school busing met with enthusiastic support from many Queen City residents. Speaking at Central Piedmont Community College on September 13, 1968, for instance, Richard Nixon touched on many of the same complaints as had George Wallace in his campaigning among Charlotteans earlier. Such speeches reflected Nixon's 1968 southern strategy, designed to rally constituents, particularly whites living in the populous Sunbelt region, who were alarmed by lawlessness and criminal behavior among youth.[14] Echoing national themes, in late summer Republican gubernatorial nominee Jim Gardner outlined a plan for strict law and order in the Tar Heel State.[15]

Reports of criminal behavior and illicit activity did not subside after the November 1968 general election, or in 1969.[16] Rather, under headlines declaring that "Militants Defeat Selves by Rousing Masses' Fear of Anarchy" and "Violent Crime Rate Shames North Carolina, Charlotte," editorials as well as the news pages of the *Charlotte Observer* assured the high visibility of crime as a political issue among Charlotteans.[17] To many the links between crime and the Black Panthers were clear. The conservative commentator William F. Buckley Jr., for example, suggested that the Black Panthers' leadership maintained a narcissistic fixation on material possessions and that, despite their public anticapitalist rhetoric, they were willing to do whatever it took to get them. Buckley's depiction of Panther posturing as a thinly veiled guise for thievery and hoodlum exploits was simply one in a series of critical journalistic attacks on party members. Similar to the contemporary case of the Charlotte Three, in which law enforcement's portrayal of three black activists as common criminals muted broader community support, disparaging news features and columns about local Panther organizing fed the city's climate of fear and sensitized it even further to the crime issue.[18] Unlike the Charlotte Three, however, much of the negative publicity about would-be Charlotte Panthers appears to have been self-generated. The actions of would-be Charlotte Panthers did little to militate against the perception of the Panthers as criminal.

Although more than one Charlotte group attempted to organize a branch of the party, the largest effort—the Afro-American Unity Organization (AAUO)—was led by Jerome Clifton "The Fox" Johnson and Benjamin Franklin Chavis Jr.[19] The AAUO began affiliation discussions with the national party on December 16, 1968.[20] From the Panthers' earliest days in Charlotte, the FBI wanted any investigation "necessary to determine Black Panther activities and to place informants therein," but such intrusion appears to have played a less significant role there than in other cities.[21] The FBI did not have to intrude; would-be Charlotte Panthers destabilized their own organizational attempts.

While by mid-May 1969 AAUO had raised the necessary fees for Panther membership, the national party during this period "was engaged in a . . . [intraorganizational] purge to rid" itself, "according to the FBI[,] of 'informants and undesirables.'" The national office in Oakland, California, "instituted a moratorium on the organization of future chapters," but it did little to deter local organizing.[22] Johnson and Chavis, according to FBI surveillance, encouraged AAUO members to wear Pantherlike garb. Despite its lack of an official charter, the Charlotte group maintained its activities: selling Panther newspapers, making public appearances posing as Panthers, holding organizational rallies at the University of North Carolina at Charlotte, and collecting and walking around with unconcealed guns.[23]

On May 27, 1969, after receiving a tip from the FBI, the ATF (Bureau of Alcohol, Tobacco, and Firearms), the IRS (Internal Revenue Service), and local police officers jointly raided AAUO headquarters.[24] James Covington, one of the two members arrested in the raid, was charged with violating the Gun Control Act of 1968, which prohibited the purchase and possession of firearms by a convicted felon. When another would-be Charlotte Panther was questioned by police, special agents, and detectives, he offered no credentials indicating membership in the party but told them he was in training. He later informed officials that additional background information could be obtained from exiled Panther contact Eldridge Cleaver. As "jackanapes" masked themselves as Panthers, the local press celebrated the combined city-county-federal raid that subdued "Charlotte's beginning Black Panther movement."[25]

AAUO spokesperson Cordell Kennedy defended besieged comrades and attempted to explain the organization's relationship with the Black Panther Party. He claimed that while the AAUO agreed in principle with the ideals of the Panthers, there was no official affiliation. The *Charlotte Observer* buried Kennedy's clarification at the bottom of page five, while page-one headlines screamed "U.S. Agents Raid Black Panthers."[26] Any notion that the AAUO was a distinct and separate entity from the party was entirely lost the following day in a feature story reporting that the police's priority would be to investigate Charlotte Panthers.[27] For the third consecutive day the AAUO suffered guilt by conflation in local newspapers, with one misleading headline in the *Observer* claiming that "Black Panthers Reclaim 3 Guns, Plan to Sue Officers."[28]

Although Kennedy deliberately stressed that the AAUO and their constituents lacked Panther affiliation, individual members made no distinction between themselves and the party. In utter defiance of the AAUO's self-definition, AAUO activist Cordell Washington not only explained Black Panther principles but implied that AAUO members were in fact Panthers, and as such could dictate what the party would or would not do. As Washington told *Charlotte Observer* staff writer Bradley Martin, "Communism would never be permitted 'to infiltrate *our* party'" (emphasis added).[29] The AAUO's status had not changed, however; it still had not received a membership charter from the Black Panther Party.

Whereas Washington's renegade comments apparently eluded the national party's leaders, more outrageous actions did not escape their attention. Shortly after Washington's careless remarks in May, would-be Charlotte Panthers were arrested for "going [around] armed to terrorize the people" following a shooting incident involving white teenagers who had apparently hurled racial epithets at some local blacks. "Panthers Charged in Shooting," read the *Observer*'s front page the next morning. Two weeks later, five AAUO members, said to be "dressed up like Panthers," were implicated in a violent attack on the black owners of a popular drive-in eatery. At least one suspect, James Michael Black, claimed to be a Panther.[30] Perhaps the Charlotte organizing effort suffered its most embarrassing setback when allegations emerged that "former Panthers" were wounded in a local shoot-out with "current Panthers." Meanwhile, four AAUO members arrested in early August faced additional legal troubles for failing to appear in court. Such charges only distanced putative Panthers from the robust civil rights history of Charlotte, in which several political styles dominated the 1950s and 1960s. They included the legal activist approach of the NAACP. Nathaniel Tross, editor of the city's black newspaper, the *Charlotte Post*, was among those who embraced accommodation, moral suasion, and other forms of tactical engagement to sway whites and mobilize blacks. Even the newer, more confrontational activism also employed what is best described as a hybrid strategy. Consider the North Carolina Committee for More Representative Political Participation (MRPP) created by Reginald Hawkins, a local dentist and activist who twice ran for governor. Whether through the MRPP or when acting as an individual, Hawkins managed to balance a confrontational style with a willingness to operate nationally behind the scenes with, for example, the Department of Health, Education, and Welfare (HEW), the federal Department of Justice, and state and national Democrat conventions during the Kennedy and Johnson administrations in order to bring change in Charlotte.[31]

But the would-be Panther chapter in Charlotte never enjoyed broad-based community support from contemporary civil rights groups. Charlotte NAACP chapter president Kelly Alexander regularly criticized Black Power as separatist and racist.[32] Hawkins envisioned MRPP as an inclusionist alternative to the putative dystopia of Black Power. "In an era when black political power advocates began to reject the entire notion of equitable American democracy," as one expert on Charlotte explained it, "Hawkins sought to show North Carolina's African Americans that mainstream politics could be a force for civil rights into the 1970s."[33]

By September 1969 the national BPP office had lost patience. In response to rogue Charlotte behavior it called a press conference to expose all those in Charlotte who alleged membership in the party. The conference was followed by an article ("Panthers, Pigs, and Fools"), in the *Black Panther*, condemning disruptive elements in Charlotte such as James Michael Black. The article marked the national office's severing of discussions with Charlotte.[34] Five days later Chicago Black Panther field secretary Robert "Bobby" E. Lee addressed a gathering at the University of North Carolina at Chapel Hill to clarify the Panther position: "There is no Panther charter in North Carolina or South Carolina. . . . They're not Panthers, period."[35] The AAUO repeatedly found itself in trouble with the law and with the Black Panther Party leadership in Oakland.[36] The problems in Charlotte appeared to have less to do with law enforcement machination than with the dubious actions of would-be Panthers.

Greensboro

Panther organizing attempts in Greensboro began on its college campuses. With a long legacy intertwining education and student activism, Greensboro was home to the largest college-aged population in the state.[37] It was also the city where, according to the 1970 U.S. Census, students were more likely to complete four years of college than in any other city in the state.[38] Not surprisingly, then, the Black Panthers' effort to form a Greensboro affiliate began with the early 1969 efforts of Eric Brown and Harold Avent to recruit on two historically black college campuses, Bennett College and North Carolina Agricultural and Technical State University.[39] Over the Christmas holiday in 1968, Brown, an A&T undergraduate and son of a New York City police officer, invited Avent, a Panther organizer, to lead the formation of an area branch of the party.[40]

According to FBI sources Avent was a respected party mobilizer from either New Jersey or New York who frequently predicted that the South, and especially North Carolina, would be fertile organizing territory for the Panthers. As Avent saw it Greensboro would become a power base for the Panthers because, according to an agency source quoting Avent, African Americans "were treated better [in Greensboro] than they are in the . . . northern part of the country."[41]

For six months Avent coordinated Greensboro's basic operations: instituting a six-week training session, conducting Monday evening political education classes, compiling black leftist reading lists, and outlining procedures for disciplining members.[42] Unlike Charlotte, Greensboro appeared to be well organized. The Avent-led group even impressed AAUO functionaries Benjamin Chavis and Jerome Johnson of Charlotte, who traveled to Greensboro with a view toward replicating the local group's coordination and infrastructure. By June 6 Greensboro's potential branch of the Black

Panther Party counted thirty members, attributable largely to Avent, without whom, a local FBI intelligence memo remarked, "there [would] not seem to be much organization."[43] Ironically, it appears that the individual receiving recognition for Greensboro's auspicious beginning was suspected to be, and likely was, an agent provocateur.

From December 1968 to June 1969 all radical activity in the area was thought to be either influenced by or linked to what local law enforcement falsely believed to be the emerging Black Panther Party in Greensboro.[44] Beginning with Stokely Carmichael's address at A&T in December 1968 and climaxing with the tragic shooting death of Willie Grimes during a confrontation with the North Carolina National Guard and local police in spring 1969, any local conflagration was attributed to Panther activity.[45] Even the Greensboro Association of Poor People (GAPP), a grassroots antipoverty organization affiliated with the North Carolina Fund, could not escape suspicion even though its founder and leader, Nelson Johnson, widely repudiated Panther rhetoric and regularly eschewed cooperative campaigns with the group. Nevertheless, local FBI operatives continued to labor under the misperception that GAPP was a front organization for Black Panthers.[46]

Suspicion grew among community radicals about the motives of those who instigated conflicts. One individual suspected by many was Avent. "This feeling was never officially confirmed," admitted a local black activist, but "Avent only seemed to be around during rioting, picketing, and marching. He always caused trouble or was in the midst of trouble."[47] The mysterious Mister X—later suspected by many local Panthers and supporters to be Avent—encouraged training sessions on how to detonate explosives and on finding and shooting police.[48] At one point he urged all "to get guns and use them" at a memorial ceremony for Malcolm X. He also encouraged bombings, arson, police ambushes, and drug use. Any one of these things, observed another scholar, easily "made the Panthers liable to arrest." Though said to be the most dangerous individual involved with the protests, Avent was never arrested.[49]

Others were not so fortunate. Eric Brown was given a two-to-six-year prison term for ransacking a local market and stealing three cartons of cigarettes in retaliation for the storeowners' refusal to support student actions and striking cafeteria workers. Likewise, the alleged role of Nelson

Johnson in the May 1969 student revolt at Dudley High School earned the GAPP leader a misdemeanor conviction.[50]

Under Avent's watch of the would-be Greensboro branch, the FBI also gained extensive knowledge of its financial status.[51] Moreover, the volatile rhetoric of Avent and others was reported "to the Greensboro police department helping to create the attitudes that prevailed among police during the spring of 1969 toward black insurgents."[52] Avent's speeches were used regularly by police and media to dramatize extremism and violence in the Greensboro campaign. The local group grew alienated from protestors who were more mainstream. At one demonstration, in fact, Avent's appearance provoked sit-in demonstrators to cease their protest immediately. In early May 1969 Walter Brame of the Greensboro Redevelopment Commission questioned publicly if Avent was a Panther at all. Brame's desire to discover the nature of Avent's affiliation with the BPP appeared driven in part by his aspiration to lead the Greensboro branch himself. Brame contacted party members in New York and confirmed their reservations about him. Avent claimed to have joined the party during the second purge period, roughly from fall 1968 until summer 1969, but this was impossible: the party was not accepting members then. Brame and others fingered Avent as a phony.[53] Accused of being an informant, Avent disappeared. Though it tried, Greensboro never regained the organizational momentum it enjoyed under Avent. By fall 1969 national leaders found themselves revisiting the troublesome Panther situation in North Carolina. "We got some niggers . . . in Greensboro who are running around here propagating madness, propagating racism, calling themselves Panthers," stated national party organizer Bobby Lee. "We say you are either part of the problem or you're part of the solution, and these niggers are part of the problem."[54] Soon after Lee's address in Chapel Hill, BPP efforts at organizing in Greensboro ceased. Regarding a similar operation in Charlotte, FBI records later provided this insight: their activity in Greensboro "shows the value of having informant coverage to report on black extremism at its inception."[55]

For Charlotte, the backdrop of rising city crime rates followed by media reports of jackanapes—persons who violated party rules or who only endorsed Panthers as convenient cover for criminal wrongdoing and engaged in burglaries and shoot-outs—undermined organizing efforts in the

Queen City, fueling perceptions that the party was a criminal enterprise and not a vanguard for black liberation. In Greensboro alarms over informant infiltration halted the early, promising efforts of a city that envisaged the potential locus of Black Power in the South.

In these ways Charlotte and Greensboro conform to a broader pattern of the national party's disassociation with some nascent chapters around the country. In Omaha, Des Moines, and Kansas City, and other U.S. cities the national office forced closings as it did in Charlotte because of misconduct or violation of Panther policies. In others, concerns about police or FBI informants, implicated in violent altercations as was the case in Detroit, prompted shutdowns.[56] By May 1970 the Oakland office had apparently dropped several chapters for either failure to observe Panther regulations or for permitting themselves to be heavily infiltrated by the police.[57] The misconduct and criminal activity contributed to the party's public image as nihilistic, despite the fact that some of this was clearly the result of government infiltration. Although the extent and degree to which print coverage and the FBI influenced or misrepresented the behavior of official party members is debatable, it appears obvious that, as the Panther newspaper makes clear, the Oakland office deplored such negative publicity and rejected the culture of criminality suspected in North Carolina and across the nation.[58] Amid dashed Panther hopes in Charlotte and Greensboro, Winston-Salem provided perhaps the last opportunity for organizing in the state.

Winston-Salem: The Early Days

Following failed attempts in the Piedmont cities of Charlotte and Greensboro, the state's only official Black Panther Party branch, located in Winston-Salem, began in the fall of 1969 as the National Committee to Combat Fascism (NCCF). It received its full charter as a Black Panther chapter in April 1971. When the Winston-Salem chapter decided to cease operations in 1978, not only would it be the last surviving branch on the East Coast, but also its successes would reflect, and in many respects exceed, those of the national office. Never accruing more than twenty official members, the Winston-Salem affiliate at the height of its power had fifty volunteers and, if local police records are believed, more than a hundred active community sympathizers.[59]

Although at first Winston-Salem organizers challenged obstacles to structural and political equality in the black community, their members also attempted to reorient existing cultural practices. Embracing much of the counterculture of the late 1960s and early 1970s, they rebelled against long-established institutions and taboos. Their diatribes against conventional social mores alienated the party from the city's established black leadership. Friction developed especially with the local branches of the NAACP and Urban League, and with area churches—much more so than with either black or white merchants.[60]

Achieving the official designation of National Committee to Combat Fascism in late October 1969, the chapter received explicit instructions from the national BPP to avoid illegalities when conducting party activities and business. However, the national office condoned and at times contributed to the Winston-Salem group's negative image. In Oakland in the fall of 1969 for six weeks of leadership training, for instance, Larry Little, nineteen years old and soon to be the head of the Winston-Salem BPP branch, lit his first marijuana cigarette at party headquarters.[61] It was there that Little shared "puffs" with David Hilliard, Fred Hampton, and other Panther luminaries.[62] Smoking hemp, interrupting church services with profanity, and, as a redistributive action, "liberating" items from local business establishments refusing to participate in community or Panther programs—all these activities were characteristic of the BPP's countercultural excesses feeding the criminal image of the Panthers during the group's early existence until mid-1971.[63]

From the beginning, when original members first gathered in the Winston-Salem area in late 1968, Robert Greer and others championed an antiexploitative public stance by targeting for boycott stores that charged exorbitant prices or were unwilling to fund the free breakfast program.[64] Such was the case in thwarting the March 4, 1970, eviction of Polly Graham, an elderly local resident, a case that combined the group's earliest objectives: procuring better housing for the black community and protecting the East Winston community from economic, political, and law enforcement harassment. Graham's personal crisis would thrust the soon-to-be Winston-Salem Panthers into local prominence.[65]

On March 4, 1970, the police tried forcibly to remove Polly Graham from her residence following a rental dispute. Graham, citing a proceeding that condemned the property she lived in and allegedly instructed her for that reason not to pay rent, refused to leave. Instead, the long-time East Winstonian and veteran of the Reynolds Factory strike of the 1940s sought immediate assistance from the NCCF office. Moments later two armed NCCF members appeared at Graham's residence and took guard around the property; other members promptly returned her belongings to the house. Before long, Lee Faye Mack, an NCCF advisor and cofounder of the local Mothers for Black Liberation, told gathering residents: "Go get your pieces." Mack's exhortation moved even "old ladies," according to Little, to get "their double-barrel shotguns."[66] The standoff ended peaceably enough, however, after a local antipoverty worker paid Graham's rent and promised her that better housing would be found.[67] This, along with the Panthers' armed defense of Minnie Bellamy and Pauline Greer, two other elderly women threatened with eviction that day, soon mobilized neighborhood people.[68]

The response of Mack and the Panthers was not public theater. Such exhibitory courage in protecting encroachments against poorer black citizens without due process gave them a psychological lift. As in numerous other cities the radical emergence in Winston-Salem of organized blacks for armed self-defense instantly struck a chord and elicited strong expressions of support.[69] By summer's end the Rev. J. T. MacMillan of the NAACP would praise the Panthers' fearlessness and pursue an alliance with them. MacMillan, a moderate and presumably someone city leaders found a more palatable presence than the Panthers, had previously been ignored when he sought to bring attention to police brutality. One of the state's most prominent physicians, a protégé of plasma specialist Charles Drew, shared a similar experience:[70]

When rumors surfaced that the Klan was . . . going to . . . shoot in the houses of the big Niggers . . . I went downtown to [the] sporting store. . . . And I spoke a voice . . . that could be heard by everyone in the store, and said, 'I want a rifle. I want a rifle because I understand the Ku Klux Klan is gonna be coming through my neighborhood this weekend, and I'm not going to get on the floor anymore.' Everyone in the store looked up and stared at me. Prior to that time, I put my family on the floor, but when

I saw [the Panthers] stand up against the landlords, the police, and the Klan with those guns. . . . I attribute that courage to Larry Little and the Panthers.[71]

Black militancy was not stale rhetoric, bound to innocuous acts of daily nonconfrontational resistance. Rather, in order to sustain its emancipatory potential to African Americans and whites alike as a valid mode of political struggle, resistance needed to be palpable and imminent. If necessary the Panthers would wage physical struggle, not underground but in public view.[72] Paying lip service to armed self-defense was not enough. Demonstrating a willingness "to pick up the gun" was, they felt, the first step toward legitimization within the black community. Not coincidentally, it was only after the Graham showdown with the police that interest in the locally based NCCF began to swell.[73]

Not everyone responded positively. Landlord and Republican mayoral candidate Jerry Newton warned that the emergence of a small, armed black group bespoke "a darker day in Winston-Salem."[74] Newton, whose real estate company initiated Minnie Bellamy's eviction, lectured about budgeting, upkeep, nutrition, and making "themselves better citizens."[75] But in predominantly black East Winston, the eviction, followed by a Bobby Seale rally in May, was used as a vehicle to garner greater community support.[76] The rally was a huge fund-raising success, which even the FBI begrudgingly noted. It also thrust into the spotlight Larry Little, who outshone titular Winston-Salem leader Robert Greer and national Panther spokesperson Dhoruba Bin Wahad (Richard Moore).[77] This was followed in June with a boycott against store management of the A&P supermarket in Winston-Salem. The store had refused to compensate a black customer who had been severely injured at the store. The Panthers saw A&P's refusal as symptomatic of a broader issue: the store's callous treatment of its black patrons, manifested in exorbitant pricing and perceived discriminatory policies and hiring practices. "Either you make the A&P relevant to the needs of the Black community," a NCCF member admonished franchise owners, "or get out." The customer was compensated.[78]

Despite playing critical roles in the lives of many East Winstonians, during its first summer of affiliation with the national BPP office the NCCF group appeared destined to follow in the faltering paths of the Charlotte and Greensboro groups. During the summer of 1970 James Cato of the

Winston-Salem branch was arrested for larceny. In late July another would-be Panther, Anthony Cain, was arrested for trespassing. On September 11 two locals posing as Panthers were placed in custody for armed robbery. An anonymous caller threatened terrorist action unless the suspects were released. Another alleged Panther was charged with public drunkenness and with threatening "to chop off" the head of a resident in nearby Lumberton in early October.[79] Such wrongdoings did not go unpunished by the Oakland office. Some NCCF members, including Anthony Cain, were publicly expelled after police raided Panthers' local headquarters.[80] Despite efforts by the national office to stabilize the party's image through purging criminally minded members, recurring evictions in Winston-Salem beginning in November 1970 forced the frequent relocation of headquarters, exacerbating the group's reputation as volatile. By early 1971, as a former member recalled, the Panthers were forced "to re-evaluate [their] position on a whole lot of things."[81] Indeed, the first two years of their attempt to establish an official branch in Winston-Salem were wrought with legal and public-relations problems, many of which were self-inflicted.[82]

Winston-Salem: Why the Branch Survived

Winston-Salem's branch of the BPP survived while Charlotte's and Greensboro's did not for three reasons. First, Winston-Salem had stronger local support, evidenced in its successful fund-raising efforts and newspaper sales—a valuable revenue stream for the national office in Oakland.[83] This contrasted starkly with Charlotte and Greensboro, where chief organizers like Benjamin Chavis, Eric Brown, and Harold Avent were out-of-towners with no organic connections to these communities. Second, Little and others were not only the children of black Winston-Salem but they also defended—and in the case of Lee Faye Mack were defended by—matriarchs of previous struggles like Polly Graham, which only strengthened these local ties. Third was the simple matter of fortuitous timing: by the time Winston-Salem began organizing, the national party's great purge period had largely ended. These factors helped Winston stay open.

It is difficult to determine whether or to what extent problems in Winston-Salem could be attributed to new leadership. The discrediting factors included law enforcement's increased scrutiny precipitated by the branch's imminent designation as a local affiliate, belligerence by provocateurs and reckless Panther hopefuls, or simply negative media coverage generated by the mainstream press. Still, any reasonable interpretation of the Panthers as criminal seems premature unless understood in the light of police action and, at the state and federal levels, judicial and penal action. The question, then, remains how to characterize the efforts of local, state, and federal law enforcement to cage the Panthers.

Winston-Salem: Caging Panthers through State Repression

By March 1971 the Winston-Salem branch of the Black Panther Party had moved their headquarters five times in six months.[84] In most instances landlords simply wanted possession of the premises. After yet another eviction began, a feature on the evening news named the apartment of Lillie Jones, a Panther sympathizer, as the party's next local command center. "I came home that night and turned on the TV, and there was a picture of my apartment, and the announcer said that it was the new headquarters," Jones told a local reporter.[85] That morning twenty-five deputies had "spread out around the house and [with] weapons ready" had emptied her apartment. "It was obvious," the twenty-five-year-old woman said later, "somebody downtown had been watching me, watching who comes and goes at my place."[86]

Law enforcement's search of Jones's apartment produced no weapons, Panther members, paraphernalia, or materials of interest. Despite the absence of evidence of wrongdoing, the lessor demanded conditional possession of the premises. Jones was permitted to remain provided she immediately advanced $468, the equivalent of a year's rent, even though she had been living in the apartment less than three weeks.[87] "There is a conspiracy to keep us out of houses in Winston-Salem," Little said shortly after the Jones eviction. The police, he continued, were urging property owners to kick them out. The goal was not to have them evicted, Police Chief Justus Tucker wryly explained to the local media: "We want them in a place we know. We stopped two or three evictions."[88] Tucker's claim seemed inconsistent with the practices of the FBI and local police who frequently alerted landlords that "the Panthers are now located in [your] building." Landlords typically responded with immediate termination of the rental contract.[89]

Perhaps not coincidentally, subsequent FBI documents show that eviction yielded an opportune moment to search the premises, as on July 8, 1970:

> A deserter from the Marine Corps was apprehended . . . by agents of the FBI at Winston-Salem, N.C., where he was observed in the company of two members of the Winston-Salem National Committee to Combat Fascism, a Black Panther Party affiliated group. . . . Moreover, insurance companies informed property owners that their insurance would automatically be cancelled if any of their tenants were alleged Panthers.[90]

Responding to other suggestive letters from law enforcement, many businesses systematically disrupted NCCF's communication with local backers, branches and chapters, and the national BPP office. Southern Bell Telephone and Telegraph Company, for instance, abruptly disconnected Jones's phone service prior to eviction, despite her having paid a deposit just a week earlier.[91] Southern Bell also refused service to NCCF member Hazel Mack. Ochie Belle Little, suspected supporter and mother of an NCCF spokesperson, was warned by the phone company not to call Charlotte and Greenville, the Bronx and Corona in New York, and Oakland and Berkeley in California. Southern Bell notified her "that if calls were made to these places they would immediately disconnect [her] phone."[92] The local Panther "situation [was] bad," an attorney for the NCCF told Norman Smith of the North Carolina affiliate of the ACLU. The Winston-Salem police department was "using community economic pressure from every angle."[93]

The repressive tactics from law enforcement had few boundaries. Common strategies included blackballing Panthers from jobs, sending phony letters to employers resulting in dismissals, and arresting party members for illegal car horn use and, despite the driver's willingness to produce proper documents, for operating an automobile without registration.[94] Lee Faye Mack and Larry Little were just two who were approached by law enforcement and solicited as potential paid informants. Others were frequently set up to look like informants. "The FBI picked me [up] . . . when I was coming out of work," recalled Greer. "This was to show people I was an informant."[95] According to another Panther member: "My wife would get all these letters. . . . supposed to have been written from a girl, as if we had a relationship. At that particular time, all I did was . . . [go] to work and work for the party."[96] In conjunction with the U.S. Department of Justice, the FBI created a Panther unit to assist local police departments in containing groups like those in Winston-Salem.[97] By late summer of 1970 the Panther unit there had amassed a list of 115 suspected area members and sympathizers—including home addresses and phone numbers, employers, makes and models of automobiles, and license plate numbers—for the discretionary use of the Winston-Salem Police Department.[98]

Also during this period FBI director Hoover stressed the need to disrupt sales of the *Black Panther*, the party organ. While San Francisco and other FBI offices balked, the Charlotte division obliged. Disruption severely threatened a primary revenue source for the Winston-Salem group, since affiliates received half the proceeds earned from the weekly publication.[99] The FBI's disruption effort included incarcerating members. Taking NCCF peddlers off the streets, where they sold newspapers and solicited donations, was law enforcement's way of financially crippling the nascent branch.[100]

With Hoover's official sanction in early October 1970, the divisional director of the FBI in Charlotte, Robert M. Murphy, initiated a widespread counterintelligence campaign. Murphy authorized letters to more than two hundred assumed Panther supporters and contributors in Winston-Salem in an effort to besmirch the local branch. Letters were circulated as originating from the Committee of Twenty-five, supposedly a group of religious-oriented and "responsible" black East Winstonians that formed itself anonymously in order to avoid retribution from the hoodlum element. The "committee" branded the local NCCF members as Communist-inspired thieves, homosexuals, and community parasites embezzling party funds.[101]

The bogus committee even slandered the popular free breakfast program, claiming that the initiative indoctrinated innocent children "to drop out of school and get . . . education on the streets." Additional letters were sent in subsequent months that insinuated the statutory rape of children participating in the breakfast program.[102] According to confidential FBI records, the letter-writing campaign of the Committee of Twenty-five lasted at least into late 1972.[103] The external smear campaign was complemented with a similar program to disrupt the internal operations of the party.[104]

By winter 1971 the FBI's Counterintelligence Program's (COINTELPRO) internal writing campaign, as one author observes, "came to shattering fruition." For months FBI agents had sent forged letters from various Panthers to members throughout the United States—Chicago, Los Angeles, New York—and abroad. The international phase included a phony letter undersigned by European chapters coordinator Connie Matthews, living in Denmark, who purportedly wrote to the Panther central committee in Oakland that exiled Eldridge Cleaver "ha[d] tripped out," and urged "some immediate action before this becomes more serious."[105] Huey Newton, meanwhile, received bogus letters telling of assassination plots on his life. David Hilliard, chief of staff of the Black Panther Party recalled, "They created mass distrust."[106] North Carolina soon became part of the transatlantic campaign that united supporters of Huey Newton's newfound emphasis on community programs against expatriate Eldridge Cleaver's clamor for urban guerrilla warfare.

Written communication on national headquarters' stationery and bearing the signature of Panther hierarch David Hilliard arrived in Winston-Salem in February 1971; Winston-Salem members were astonished to find the national office abruptly denying it an official charter because of Little's poor leadership and conduct. The party's chief of staff, however, denied authorship. A month later the national office received an analogous letter, this time from North Carolinian Panthers, that Newton's "cheap, meaningless talk" and "lavish spending on himself" must end and that the BPP chair should be ousted and replaced with Cleaver. The Winston-Salem affiliate wanted action, the communiqué demanded. "Come home, Comrade Cleaver," Winston-Salem's Panthers-in-training supposedly implored Cleaver, analogous to McGovern's "Come Home, America!" cry in 1972. Such animus seemed far removed from the previous day's newspaper reports that highlighted the glowing rapport between Oakland and the Winston-Salem branch, particularly Little: "They hold [Little] in high esteem. . . . He does what he's told."[107] These acts of sabotage created a context for even bolder acts of constant harassment.

Nationally, raids on Panther chapters in such cities as Los Angeles, San Diego, San Francisco, Salt Lake City, Indianapolis, Philadelphia, and many others were the most successful and widely used law enforcement tactic.[108] The bureau worked closely with police departments "to develop a prosecutive theory against the Panthers."[109] To that end the FBI regularly conspired as police accomplices, implanting and paying informants. In Illinois one police official rapturously characterized the relationship as "the wonderful . . . cooperation and rapport that exists between . . . [the] Chicago [FBI] Office . . . and the Chicago Police Department." Such coordinated vertical operations between federal and local officials in Chicago, for example, which conducted four raids, led to the killing of Illinois Panthers Mark Clark and Fred Hampton by law enforcement. The two Panthers were apparently murdered while they slept; ballistic reports later showed that of the forty bullet holes found at the scene, only one was the result of a round fired from inside the apartment. The case came to symbolize how local and federal law enforcement often operated under the extralegal assumption that it could operate as judge, jury, and executioner. Winston-Salem appeared to fit well the broader pattern of extralegal assault against members, with law enforcement's covert war against the North Carolina affiliate climaxing with three major episodes in November 1970, January 1971, and June 1972.[110]

On November 27, 1970, less than an hour after the Winston-Salem NCCF members departed their branch headquarters for the Revolutionary People's Constitutional Convention (RPCC) in Washington, D.C., a Panther-sponsored New Left gathering, the building caught on fire.[111] Many in the media, including *Winston-Salem Journal* columnist Roy Thompson, who covered the Panthers extensively, accused local Panthers of deliberately setting the blaze to lure police officers into an ambush.[112] In denying the allegations, Little accused undercover agents of setting the fire and disguising themselves as firemen to remove files and equipment from the burning building.[113] After Fire Chief Paul Crim confided in Little that an incendiary device was found in the headquarters and had speculated that agents were the likely arsonists, Little quickly assembled a press conference at the fire station. Crim, however, refused to confirm his findings to the media. Pressed into responding, Crim finally acknowledged that "unauthorized persons" had entered the burning building, but he stopped short of substantiating Panther charges.[114]

"[It's] a damn lie," Police Chief Tucker shot back when questioned. "We did assist the fire department in removing items from the building, but they were all turned over to the fire department." The fire chief, however, denied that any of his personnel removed files. Allegations arose, and court proceedings eventually confirmed that a policeman, clothed in fireman garb, had indeed taken items from Panther headquarters.[115] Before the files were returned, they remained in police possession for more than three hours. According to a confidential police source, the Panthers' recovery of their property came only after the department made extensive copies of records.[116] Six weeks later a second seizure of a different sort occurred at Panther headquarters.

In January 1971 Winston-Salem members were besieged by nearly fifty law enforcement officers bearing a search warrant to recover a stolen meat delivery truck and its products: a ten-pound box of Sycamore sausage, a box of twelve one-pound packages of wieners, and a stick of bologna. Though the search warrant's authority was limited to "three specifically named and described items of meat," police seized almost every movable item from NCCF headquarters.[117] Trucks hauled off seventy-five items, in addition to weapons and ammunition, to the police station.[118] The police also arrested three Panthers-in-training.

Later known as the Winston-Salem Three, Julius Cornell, Grady Fuller, and NCCF spokesperson Larry Little were charged in connection with the larceny. Also facing criminal charges, a fourth Panther, Willie Coe, a high-school student, was "persuaded" by the Forsyth County district solicitor to turn state's witness. Though never charged, the fifteen-year-old was held in "protective" custody by the state for more than eight months. Coe was placed in a county juvenile detention center and later sent to a foster care facility at an undisclosed location. All three defendants would eventually be convicted, but only Fuller served time: three months in a county jail.[119] The Winston-Salem Three conviction, however, was subsequently cast in serious doubt. A forced acknowledgment by police of exceeding authority—along with a 1975 congressional inquiry, which unveiled evidence that the theft, in the words of the inquiry, "may have been set up by agents trying to provoke a confrontation"—publicly, if not legally, exculpated branch members.[120]

Most troubling to some at the time were the implications surrounding the untimely and disturbing June 13, 1972, death of Raleigh prison inmate and Panther comrade Joseph P. Waddell. Just twenty-two years of age, Waddell died suddenly following complaints of a stomach ailment shortly after lunch.[121] Despite his sudden death, medical records showed Waddell to be in excellent health; so did a routine physical examination, administered just before June 13. "He was very muscular and the lack of fat indicated that he exercised regularly," acknowledged Page Hudson, the state medical examiner.[122] Fellow Panthers, black community activists, and sympathetic whites found these particulars incompatible with the autopsy report certifying the official death as a massive heart attack caused by coronary heart disease.[123]

Skeptics attributed Waddell's death to a deliberate poisoning because of his growing reputation as a Panther section leader working on prison organizing for the party. Incarcerated since January 1971 for armed robbery, Waddell had spent much of his sentence in lock-up, a holding facility that largely segregated alleged troublemakers from other inmates. While there Waddell became widely regarded as an agitator for prison reform. Waddell was not only instrumental in raising the prison population's consciousness, but he also gained attention beyond the prison walls. Waddell eventually enlisted the support of NCCLU cooperating attorney Buddy Tieger, who brought even greater public scrutiny to allegations of physical abuse and the curtailment of constitutional rights in denying inmates Black Panther literature. In the aftermath of Waddell's death, reports of physical mistreatment surfaced from other inmates thought to be Panthers or seeking Panther literature.[124] Sparking additional alarm about the causes of Waddell's death was PRISACTS (Prison Activists), a cooperative program between FBI and prison administrators designed to check incarcerated Panther subversives and other black radicals.[125] Such state machinations intimated the repressive extremes that local, state, and federal government would go to neutralize the Winston-Salem branch's reputation.

The repressive acts of the state took their collective toll on the Winston-Salem organization. Bogus letters made it much more difficult to raise money and establish community-wide acceptance. Merchants who had contributed eggs or meat for the Panthers' free breakfast program stopped contributing. Other businesses and churches, according to Little, "became reluctant to support the program."[126] The portrayal in the media and to the public of members as thieves, narcotic peddlers, hoodlums, and pedophiles wrought considerable public damage.[127] Likewise, the socially stigmatizing specter of homosexuality hurt in a southern black enclave.

"A sampling of merchants" prior to October 1970 "revealed . . . that not only [did] some merchants, black and white, willingly support the breakfast program, but they [said] that the Panthers ha[d] been polite and appreciative." But after the collaborative FBI-police cabal took hold, former local supporters told Panthers-in-training like Malloy, "I can't get involved in this."[128] Black community leaders "on the fence in their thinking about the Black Panthers" were particular targets. In a national context the extent of criminal and penal repression still surfacing in the aftermath of the Pentagon Papers, J. Edgar Hoover's death, Watergate, and the public revelations about the FBI Counterintelligence Program made it more difficult for the public to trust aspersions heaped upon the party.[129] Not only were the extralegal tactics of local, state, and national agents more repressive than any the Winston-Salem Panthers actually employed, but branch activities—particularly after late 1971—belied earlier nihilistic propaganda propagated by the state. By 1972 the Winston-Salem Chapter would—through a political metamorphosis and revamped social agenda—refute the negative perceptions thrust upon them. The Panthers, however, required help.

Winston-Salem: Facilitating Change through Constitutional Liberalism and the Reformist Politics of Social Democracy

"We didn't have a lot of white supporters there in Winston-Salem." This was certainly so when Martin Kenner, a white emissary of the party's central committee, visited the city in the immediate aftermath of the January 1971 police raid. The white support that local Panthers received, while perhaps not comparable in either strength or numbers to other chapters, was nonetheless significant. The Panthers' Winston-Salem chapter outlasted the New York Chapter and every other chapter on the East Coast. It would do so, from early 1972 onward, by successfully transforming itself from a revolutionary confrontational organization to one stressing mainstream politics.[130] The trade-off for deescalating its program was greater social cachet, accrued primarily by providing a socially democratic agenda that featured a dazzling array—considering the limited funding resources—of community programs. Yet this was still not enough. The Panthers would ultimately view constitutional and legal challenges as the path leading away from its criminal image and toward political legitimacy, particularly among black Winstonians, academicians, activists, and legal professionals.

In both of these processes Panthers sought a narrow but deliberate role for liberals. Liberals welcomed the local branch's move toward a reformist political agenda. In abetting the decriminalized imagery of the party, sympathetic liberals allayed their own collective fear. For liberals Panther community survival programs and the participation of Panthers inside mainstream political and legal institutions signaled that social democracy could be a bridge—not to socialism but to a liberalism that was more durable, if not racially inclusive. Nowhere was the liberal role more evident than with Congressman Lunsford Richardson Preyer of Greensboro, who offered the Panthers not further isolation, like his conservative colleagues, but an olive branch. Preyer, who chaired the 1971 House Committee on Internal Security (HCIS) inquiry into the origins, activities, and goals of the Black Panther Party, would face stiff reproof for his views, however. The North Carolina representative and the inquiry he oversaw were "too sympathetic to the Panthers," went the primary criticism, which came mostly from nonsouthern congressmen and advisers.[131]

"If the HCIS' report on the BPP was called a Black Panther Party Report instead, that is produced by the party, it would not be far off the mark," a senior reviewer elaborated privately to the ranking subcommittee Republican after reading the first two chapters of the Preyer Committee Report. "The overall tenor of these chapters," he added, "cannot be characterized as anything but pro-Panther." It "reads like an issue of the BPP's official newspaper." "The report is unbalanced," opined the opening sentence of yet another evaluation team. The draft was so potentially harmful, according to one reader, he feared "the Committee's relationship with numerous police departments may henceforth and *justifiably* be severely strained" (emphasis added).[132]

When the HCIS published its final report two months later on August 18, 1971, its Republican members felt compelled to issue a statement of clarification. Ohio Republican John Ashbrook penned HCIS's minority view, which distanced the Republicans from the official findings and Preyer's summation: "This report, in tone and emphasis, is unfair to police and to the American people—especially blacks—who have to cope with Panther crime and violence."[133] Also misleading was the "grossly" inadequate attention given to cooperative relations between Panthers and Communists. In all, minority members said in closing: "The language of the report . . . sounds . . . more like a sociological rationalization for Panther violence" than like the language of the "small group of criminal misfits" comprising "a tiny minority of young Negroes . . . rais[ing] considerable funds from gullible whites."[134]

The HCIS report, however, was no romanticized defense of the party. In a summation appended to the report, Preyer shared many of his fellow house Republicans' misgivings about the Panthers, objecting in particular to the violent language of the group. But what distinguished Preyer and other HCIS members, like Massachusetts Congressman Robert F. Drinan and venerated southern liberal Senator Claude Pepper of Florida, was the absence of "a stronger sense of outrage," that dissenting minority Republican colleagues demanded. Unlike Ashbrook and others, there was no unilateral rejection of party members as incorrigible. In fact, Preyer seemed to retain tacit faith in the Panther's potential for political redemption.[135]

The problem with the Panthers as Preyer understood it was that "they are revolutionary radicals[,] not reformers."[136] In Preyer's view the Panther's platform lacked "talk of better jobs, more equal educational opportunities, better houses." A one-time Terry Sanford protégé, Preyer conceded that "originally the Panthers had some innovative community service ideas." Among those was "a Panther patrol which would tape-record police officers who were arresting blacks to insure—or prove the lack of—due process and fair treatment." To be sure, the group's revolutionary paramilitary posturing or "ghetto talk," as Preyer dubbed it, frequently undermined its effectiveness, but the party had potential. It was this possibility Preyer raised when, in closing, he urged the Panthers to "put down your guns and find your voices." The Winston-Salem branch appeared to have chosen this route. By mid-1972 they had exchanged bandoliers, black berets, and jackets for attaché cases and pinstripe suits. Military titles were also dropped, as "lieutenants" now became "coordinators." Following the January 1971 police raid Hilliard sent Martin Kenner to Winston-Salem, where he worked with a committee of mothers of the Panthers to win over church elders. As Kenner believed, "Mothers of Panthers should be going to churches on Sunday, saying: 'Support our children. Don't kill our children.'"[137] Yet the party's new image was more than merely a negation of criminal specter; it symbolized the party's inclusionist strategy.

Authors have previously suggested that nationally the Panthers' deradicalization was typified by increased centralization, greater reliance on institutions within the existing political system, and, following the Newton-Cleaver split, an emphasis on stronger relations with the black community—particularly through expansion of its survival programs.[138] Indeed, Newton swayed local affiliates to work within traditional community-centered organizations and establish coalitions, particularly with main-stream black community leaders and ministers. They were encouraged to formalize relationships by joining churches and civic and political groups such as the NAACP and the Urban League.[139] By 1972 the Winston-Salem branch had already created a working alliance with the religious-oriented and less radical North Carolina–Virginia Council for Racial Justice and the Southern Christian Leadership Conference. The SCLC's Golden Frinks, for instance, frequently appeared at local Panther rallies.[140] Panther party chairwoman Elaine Brown defeated her own assertion "that the Demo-crats would become Black Panthers before Panthers became Democrats" when she ran for citywide office under the Democratic banner and worked closely with a cross section of Democratic, and even some Republican, operatives at the state and national levels.[141]

Likewise, Newton's June 1971 reexamination in *Black Panther* of the vir-tues of the black bourgeois in "Black Capitalism Re-Analyzed" signaled the party's philosophical break from its revolutionary confrontational origins. Newton cast both black capitalists and black workers as indistinguishable victims of sprawling global capitalism, promulgating the transformative capacity of black private ownership—something ideologically repugnant in 1967. Newton reenvisioned black capitalists as primary supporters of the Panther survival programs. In return for contributions the party's premier ideologue proposed to carry respective business advertisements and urge community patronage. "If he does not make a contribution to the survival of the community," Newton predicted, in appropriating language more suggestive of a self-adjusting market economist than New Left theoreti-cian, "the people will not support him and his enterprise will wither . . . because of his own negligence." "In this way we will achieve a greater unity of the community of victims," Newton added, from "the people who are victimized by the society in general, and the Black capitalists who are victimized by the corporate capitalist monopolies." The Panther's new kinship with black enterprise, Newton argued somewhat naively, would "increase the positive qualities of Black capitalism until they dominate the negative qualities."[142]

In ideology and organizational behavior, no chapter functioned better than Winston-Salem within the confines of the party's new social demo-cratic scheme. In the twelve months following June 1971 Winston-Salem not only improved relations with black civic leaders and businesses, it initiated a host of social programs. Newton hoped the remarkable meta-morphosis of Winston-Salem would be typical of the party at large.[143] The branch touched nearly every segment of black Winston-Salem. Coordi-nating with area churches in 1972, the organization sponsored clothing giveaways. In addition, local members started a bus service for families to visit infirm loved ones as well as incarcerated relatives and friends lo-cated far from Winston-Salem. Panther community patrols escorted el-derly East Winstonians to banks and check-cashing centers. A free pest control program for vermin-infested houses was implemented. During winter months Panther members sold blood to purchase coal for the community's poor. African American and white physicians at Wake For-est University trained Panthers in sickle-cell and blood pressure testing. With improved relations, black and some white merchants resuscitated contributions in support of the popular free breakfast program, a branch staple since 1969.[144]

At its peak the branch enlisted more than fifty men and women to vol-unteer their free time while working full-time jobs. Winston-Salem Pan-thers also counted hundreds of sympathizers who contributed anywhere from ten cents to five dollars per week. Panther Survival Day symposiums attracted thousands interested in classes and seminars on political educa-tion, budgeting money, and the importance of universal health care. Free legal aid was also arranged for indigent residents.[145] In these ways Winston-Salem operationalized the agenda of the BPP national office in Oakland.

Such projects reaped positive results. Some two thousand public hous-ing residents attended the voter registration and Joseph Waddell Free Food Program on July 30, 1972, when the branch donated a thousand grocery bags of food. At the event Little "spoke at length about the importance [of] work[ing] within [the] political system," and announced future plans to run for public office. The Charlotte FBI division informed the national director that the forum "was the most successful project undertaken by the project to date."[146] During this gathering alone, according to the FBI, more than five hundred residents registered to vote. Two subsequent drives that year, in August and December, were nearly as well attended.[147]

There appeared to be beneficial fiduciary results. The group's implemen-tation of social programs was paralleled by a dramatic improvement both in amount and frequency of donations.[148] Likewise, by 1972 the party was involved in fewer legal and court battles, lessening the legal fees incurred by the group. For those legal cases in which Panther members were involved, they often retained pro bono representation. By 1973 the local press had even taken notice of "the high-heeled shoes, [and] the knit suit" styling of the Winston-Salem Panthers. "The former militance," declared a local paper, though still skeptical, "ha[d] given way to a new emphasis on social programs."[149]

Not much different from East Winston's black community, but perhaps for slightly different reasons, liberals too appeared buoyed by the party's democratically centered survival programs. Liberal acceptance of the revamped local party was clearly evident in support given to the Joseph P. Waddell People's Free Ambulance Service. Following a unanimous endorsement by the local Episcopal grant review team, the national church gave a $45,000 grant to the party, largely because "at no place in the application, field appraisal, or amended application [was] there any reference to the limitation of service on the basis of race." To white supporters the Panthers' patient building of health and social services, representing silent consent to a civic order while silencing racial rhetoric, was a significant factor in the ambulance program's appeal.[150]

The Episcopal grant helped the Panthers reorient services for nonemergency medical transportation, considered the community's most urgent need.[151] Panthers themselves staffed the ambulance. They received medical training from the local Red Cross and Surry Community College, whose college president downplayed an FBI visit discouraging him from enrolling Panthers in the medical program.[152] Local Episcopal bishop Thomas Fraser saw the grant as an opportunity to bring "together the responsible leadership of the churches and the responsible leadership of the Black Panther Party."[153] The program's immense popularity catapulted Panther coordinator and spokesperson Larry Little into becoming a major political player in the city.[154] Despite early reservations, Forsyth County commissioners voted unanimously to enter a franchise agreement with the Panthers. "What we see now," said County Chairman John C. Kiger, "is a group of people . . . working hard to gain community support."[155]

The ambulance service also generated national media attention, and to that end Little made "frequent appearances on television and [in] newspaper articles," as noted in the Winston-Salem group's FBI file. In February 1974 *NBC Nightly News* focused on the ambulance franchise as part of its human-interest story on the branch's efforts to reverse the Panthers' noted violent past. The transformation of the Winston-Salem group was bathed in a sympathetic national spotlight as a result of the broadcast—prompting the FBI to order the surveillance of the NBC reporter, Kenleigh Jones.[156] The good media didn't hurt locally, either: in the twelve months from January 1974 to January 1975 Waddell ambulance workers responded to 2,203 calls, mustered 23 outside volunteers who logged 8,146 hours, and drove close to thirty thousand miles.[157] The Oakland office of the BPP praised the ambulance service in its newspaper.

The raison d'être and popularity of the Winston-Salem Panther social services stemmed from a void created by government and by its refusal to either establish or allocate adequate expenditures to these social enterprises.[158] Through these programs the Panthers wished to demonstrate the potential of operating basic quality services at low public cost if broader political will existed.[159] In other words it wanted good government, one responsive to the needs of the people. In this way Winston reflected a national BPP agenda.

To trace the local appeal of the Black Panthers in the early 1970s is often to look at its network of social services, which largely supplanted unresponsive local, state, and federal governments. Thus a poor black family in East Winston might send a child to a Panther-sponsored breakfast, use a low-cost Panther medical clinic, and rely on groceries paid for by Panthers. Similar programs popped up in Panther chapters across America. Assuming the bureaucratic role of the state, as the Panthers did in Winston-Salem and nationally, heightened the group's appeal in local neighborhoods. At the same time, the daily pressures of administering these outreach programs worked to wear down the firebrands. It was one thing to complain about the Winston-Salem ambulance service, for example, quite another when the Panthers had to make an ambulance service run. "The terrorists among us," as *Reader's Digest* had described the party just a few short years prior, were now in the business of saving lives.[160] Oakland sanctioned such efforts toward moderation, praising in *Black Panther* the Waddell ambulance program and other community-based service initiatives. Finally, if the ambulance service, sickle-cell anemia testing, and similar survival programs were revolutionary political acts, then the people lending assistance to the Panthers—the Episcopalians underwriting the ambulance service, Wake Forest physicians teaching Panthers to administer blood tests, and even the local white officials who granted the ambulance service its license—were themselves committing revolutionary political acts.[161]

Despite programmatic strides made by the Winston-Salem operation, the members' criminal reputation still distorted the party's local public image and limited the group's effectiveness. Anti-Panther forces, Little believed, often dismissed party programs to expand social benefits and cooperative interaction with business as less of a desire to function within the political economy of capitalism than as public theater to mask the party's more extreme and sinister features. "I have always had to be [described as] the former Black Panther leader," a frustrated Little recalled later. "I'm also a member of the Urban League and the NAACP. . . . In terms of what I was able to do for the community as a member of the party, I have no problems with being a former Panther. But the FBI managed to give it [the party] a bad name."[162] Regardless of how many David Hilliard Free Shoe programs, citizens' police review boards, and citizen participation events the Panthers sponsored, it could not erase whites' collective fear of the Panthers as a possible fifth column; and a socially democratic agenda was not enough to legitimate the party in the eyes of black Winstonians. Neither was the depoliticization of the FBI, taking place at the national level, enough to usurp the threat of local law enforcement action. Panther effectiveness—both in terms of social programs and as a voice for poorer black residents within the political infrastructure—was limited by the constant threat of legal repression. As one local Panther put it, "We wanted to do it earlier, but hell[,] we were standing in court all the time."[163] The Winston-Salem Panthers' bridge to social and political legitimacy, then, inevitably hinged on its willingness to confront legally the institutions chiefly responsible for marring it: law enforcement and the judicial system. Only after a series of constitutional challenges did the police department's interference and subterfuges abate.[164] Initiating such challenges underscored the party's aim to operate within the mechanisms of the constitutional system. The former party for self-defense needed constitutional protection from the legal and criminal justice machinery of the state. The local Panthers sought this civil rights protection from the ACLU and its affiliated attorneys. Such protection would not only provide a necessary space for Panthers to continue their programs, but it would also facilitate the Panthers' move into mainstream electoral politics.

First Amendment victories in 1969 and again in 1972 involving police arrests for selling the BPP newspaper laid important groundwork for future Panther activities without overt law enforcement harassment. The second case was especially pathbreaking, as it ended with "promises secured from municipal officials not to bring new prosecutions for similar conduct."[165] These cases also foreshadowed the common constitutional ground shared by the ACLU in North Carolina and the Panthers.

The American Civil Liberties Union and the NCCLU saw the state and the U.S. Constitution as agents of protectivist intervention. So too, it seemed, had the newfound reformist members of the Black Panther Party. No longer suggesting an alternative constitution or radical transformation of the existing one, Panthers appropriated the legal apparatus to procure political rights. The party's convergent political philosophy with egalitarian liberalism, as expressed by national party leaders like David Hilliard and demonstrated through the Winston-Salem branch, proved a powerful lure for the nation's largest private law organization.[166] Thus the NCCLU's goal to make public "the special qualities of police behavior in their confrontations with the Black Panther Party" was an essential step in facilitating Panther political legitimization inside East Winston, and, in a broader light, strengthening liberalism through social democracy.[167]

In a series of court cases from 1969 to 1975, the North Carolina chapter of the American Civil Liberties Union sought to protect the criminal and constitutional rights of the Black Panther Party.[168] Following First Amendment challenges in 1969 and early 1971, the civil liberties union represented the party in March of that same year. Unlike earlier challenges, the NCCLU challenge of a thirty-day contempt sentence against Little invited national scrutiny of the North Carolina legal and criminal justice systems.

On March 8, 1971, Little stood trial for carrying a concealed weapon and pleaded innocent.[169] When the state district court denied Little's attorney a second continuance, Little chose to act as his own lawyer rather than accept a court-appointed public defender, a decision that proved to be an abysmal miscue for Little. The "court was biased and had prejudged the case and . . . [I am] a political prisoner," Little bluntly told the presiding judge, prompting his removal, a thirty-day sentence for contempt, and a conviction on the weapons charge.[170] On March 16 Norman Smith, general counsel of the NCCLU, petitioned the state superior court to overturn the contempt charge. Smith argued that State District Court Judge

A. Lincoln Sherk abused his summary contempt powers in judging and criminally punishing Little for his accusation of bias, and thus abridged the due process clause of the Fourteenth Amendment.[171] The state superior and appellate courts disagreed, however.[172] After the state supreme court refused to hear the case in June 1971, the NCCLU's Smith successfully carried its appeal to the U.S. Supreme Court.[173]

The Supreme Court's reversal in January 1972 was a watershed victory for the NCCLU and the Panthers. Even prior to the notoriety the case received before the nation's highest court, the Little contempt finding captured the attention of activists and the legal fraternity inside North Carolina. Whereas earlier Panther cases always received some attention, the Little hearing had commanded coverage by the *Twin City Sentinel* and even by the *Winston-Salem Journal*. Local activists were fixtures at the legal proceedings, and fascinated college students had trekked from as far away as East Carolina University in Greenville, a five-hour journey. Perhaps those most interested were attorneys, who at times had comprised as much as two-thirds of the courtroom's gallery.[174] When it came, the Supreme Court verdict and separate concurrence of Justices Warren Burger and William Rehnquist was bound to earn the notice of law professors, state supreme court jurists, and even a legal author writing about political prisoners.[175] In the period between the contempt charge in March 1971 and Supreme Court's ruling in January 1972, the NCCLU had established that they would not only protect the party's legal standing but also, when necessary, aggressively contest police and judicial action.

Shortly following its legal sponsorship of the contempt case, Norman Smith, the general counsel of the NCCLU on behalf of Panthers Deloris Wright, Larry Little, and Hazel Mack, took the offensive against the local police department and the city of Winston-Salem. Arguing constitutional abridgments by police in their illegal seizure and removal of Panther property in the November 1970 fire and January 1971 raid, the NCCLU pressed the Panthers' claims of legitimacy by unveiling the covert and illegal behavior of law enforcement.[176]

The courts sided largely with the plaintiffs.[177] "More than mere infringement of property rights is involved," Federal District Judge Eugene Gordon admonished city attorneys in refusing to kill the suit, "the plaintiffs . . . have alleged violation of freedom of speech and freedom from illegal search and seizure."[178] The middle district judge recommended a consent order;

attorneys for the city of Winston-Salem, who fought throughout the summer to prevent the case from going to the federal courts, eagerly agreed. The order required an admission that officers exceeded their authority and violated the Panthers' First and Fourth Amendment rights by seizing and photocopying items during the fire and police raid. If nothing else the case was a public relations coup for the party, since the order suggested that law enforcement, unable to get the case dismissed or remanded to a friendlier state judiciary, hoped to escape a public trial and revelations of extralegal tactics that might harm its public credibility.[179]

Just as important as the constitutional success itself was how the Panthers reacted to a perceived loss. In the consent order, for example, it took three years for the settlement to be reached mainly because the NCCLU and the ACLU were unable to get the local BPP to acquiesce.[180] Although Mark Harkavay, the NCCLU cocounsel, tried to convince them to the contrary, the Panthers saw the consent order as a bittersweet verdict.[181] In addition to the admission of police wrongdoing, the party desired monetary compensation—a claim the judge summarily denied. Little explained to the Panthers' counsel that the Winston-Salem branch had suffered far too much for a Pyrrhic victory:[182] innocent members had served considerable time in jail, the headquarters were destroyed, and records were burned and lost. Despite tensions that arose between counsel and client, the NCCLU remained a public ally of the Panthers. Little and others reacted to this legal defeat not by returning to the gun but by continuing to engage America's civic religion as well as exhibiting faith in the high legal priests preaching civil libertarianism. Few accused Panther attorneys of soft-pedaling in their defense of the Winston-Salem Three.

This case, which had its most significant moment in the aftermath of the original consent request in July 1971, highlighted law enforcement's controversial tactics. More generally it unmasked the extralegal efforts by municipal and county government to circumvent the Constitution. Although the NCCLU's bylaws prohibited it from lending formal counsel in any criminal trial, the organization did the next best thing. The Winston-Salem Three—Panthers Julius Cornell, Grady Fuller, and Larry Little, charged in connection with the stolen meat truck—tapped James Ferguson and Jerry Paul. Longtime ACLU-affiliated attorneys, Ferguson and Paul were two of North Carolina's most renowned legal minds committed to racial liberalism. As pretrial motions for the three men resumed in mid-September 1971, Panther defense attorneys subpoenaed FBI special agent David P. Martin, the local supervisor responsible for investigating Panther activity in the city. Forced to take the stand, Martin initially asserted immunity privilege when asked questions regarding surveillance activity of the Panthers. The FBI and federal attorney general's office insisted that no evidence against the Winston-Salem Three "was the product or result of any electronic surveillance conducted by the (FBI)."[183] This testimony was soon shown to result from the Department of Justice artfully parsing its speech. Such FBI machinations did not escape the notice of the presiding judge, however, who "refused to let the matter drop," and "ordered . . . over the strenuous objections of the state, any wiretap evidence against . . . [to] be produced within 24 hours." FBI documentation revealed that the Department of Justice had clearly relied on FBI counterintelligence and electronic surveillance, such as tapes of Panther phone conversations to Oakland, to build a prosecutorial theory against local members.[184]

Neither did the complicity of the FBI elude a local columnist who questioned the motives for "the massive and violent raid . . . on the Black Panthers." Nor was Congress oblivious. Years later, relying largely on official court records, it implicated agents in the fire and stolen records.[185] Last, and perhaps most important, revelations about the bureau's activities did not escape Panther sympathizers and East Winston citizens.

Only a few short years prior, hardly any Winstonian fathomed a local Panther running and winning electoral office at any level of government. But by late 1972 and 1973 the Panthers' fading criminal image was succumbing to news stories of community-centered survival programs, revelations about covert law enforcement activity, press clippings of constitutional challenges stewarded by the ACLU, and rumors of Panthers running for elected office. The immediate beneficiary, most assumed, would be Larry Little. After all, voter registration drives and numerous community rallies were a boon in marshaling an electoral base for the Winston-Salem chapter's most visible figure. In addition the party's volunteers were familiar with parochial issues and soliciting donations. Such backing made Little a formidable opponent against Democratic incumbent alderman Richard N. Davis. It also made the local Black Panther Party an emerging but potentially iconoclastic political lobby in the city. By March 1974, swayed also by the dictates of national headquarters and party members running for office in other cities, Little announced his plans to seek the alderman's seat in North Winston.[186]

Little's run was designed to institutionalize the Panthers' socially democratic program by capitalizing on its growing political power. "Our goal to transform the system is still there," Little expressed in an interview with the leftist Durham weekly *North Carolina Anvil*, "but our methods have changed." Little talked about achieving social change through classic reformist politics. "[We need streetlights] for the neighborhood, a hospital accessible to blacks, a police review board and other citizen participation programs," he told the reporter.[187] Little's reform-minded platform also pressed city government to strengthen drug counseling, build and fund more rehabilitation facilities, and improve manpower programs for youths.[188] Rather than campaign as a third-party or independent candidate, Little, like many Panthers nationally, opted for the old-guard apparatus of the Democratic Party.

Little's alderman campaign, however, came to a sudden end on May 7, 1974, with the Democratic primary election. The incumbent Democrat, Richard Davis, also black, narrowly edged Little by the slimmest of margins—eight votes. Little's defeat heightened the controversy that had simmered in previous weeks over a purge, ordered by the county elections board, in March of three hundred voters, following a cursory investigation of procedural irregularities of three registrars.[189] Barring suffrage was necessary because registrars did not properly register voters, contended Thomas J. Keith, chair of the county board of elections. Keith's decision stemmed from interviews with twenty-seven registrants, many of whom "gave inconclusive and confusing testimony" at a later appeal hearing. The purge most likely cost Little the election, as many of those who were disfranchised had registered during a Panther voting drive.[190] Once again the local Panther leader sought legal recourse through the NCCLU.

Norman Smith, still working as the NCCLU general counsel, challenged the purge of North Ward voters by the Republican-controlled county board of elections. Although the NCCLU did not contest the point that alleged procedural infractions might have occurred during the voter registration, it did challenge the drastic action of striking registrants without full due process of law. The board never met or heard the challenges of the three hundred voters, Smith explained later to the state supreme court. The wholesale elimination of registered voters was done and upheld "without proper notice, without hearing, and despite [the county board of elections] own concession that these voters had acted properly and in good faith."[191] Moreover, nullification occurred despite registrants and embattled registrars' sworn testimony denying wrongdoing.

Perhaps more troubling was the arbitrary manner by which the democratic process was subverted. Rather than remove all voters who were registered by the three embattled registrars, Keith picked and eventually disfranchised "only those voters who had the misfortune of having their registration cards sitting in a particular stack on [the] Chairman['s] . . . desk on March 11, 1974." As a result, from the testimony of only 10 percent of the registrants, three hundred lost suffrage. Smith made plain the collective concern of Little, the NCCLU, and three hundred aggrieved citizens to the state board of elections and then an appellate court. Even the chair of the board of elections admitted that these voters had been prevented from going to the polls "because of an error not [of] their own making."[192]

The state board of elections was unwilling to remedy this fraudulent election, however, although it agreed with the NCCLU that "voters held valid registrations and that the methods used by the Forsyth County board of elections to void those valid registrations violated" due process. By the time it reached the court of appeals on April 2, 1975, five months after the November general citywide election, the court deemed the Panther's claim "academic" and moot: "That general election has been held, and it is not now possible to give the petitioner the relief which he sought."[193]

The accusations brought against the county board of elections remained troublesome to many, however.[194] Little's challenge received support from unusual and unexpected places, including the *Winston-Salem Journal*. The one-time nemesis now argued that new elections—which clearly would have overturned the disputed election—should be held. This small change in the newspaper's position represented another step in the broader public's acceptance of the Panther's odyssey toward political legitimacy. Similarly, the new Winston-Salem Police Chief Tom Surratt, whose run-ins with party members once made headlines, reconsidered his own views of the organization. The Panthers were a "good source of conflict management" and their programs were a "good public service," Surratt would later tell white community leaders.[195] The local party's decision to accept the rule of political civility as prescribed by the establishment won them grudging respect.

The *Winston-Salem Journal's* acceptance of the party was particularly instructive in light of the reticence of the *Winston-Salem Chronicle*, a predominantly black-operated newspaper established in 1974. The party's transformation and the broader African American support buoying it transpired with little, if any, recognition from the *Chronicle*. Despite the party's well-known reform-minded goals, the *Chronicle* eschewed the still-controversial organization in its biweekly pages. One source observed that its editor and chief staff writer Ernie Pitt preferred coverage of debutante balls, church socials, and other congenial scheduled events to hard news.[196] Unable to rely on the local black press for positive coverage of individuals or the party, the Panthers relied on the ACLU and the U.S. Constitution. By the next election in November 1977, the attitude of the black press toward the Panthers would cease to matter: Little and the BPP received widespread support from the black community and won more than 80 percent of the black vote. Working with the ACLU and NCCLU to build a bridge to liberalism, Little and the party had successfully made the transition to political legitimacy.

* * *

When in fall 1988 Larry Little made his long-awaited appearance before the North Carolina Board of Law examiners to certify his public character and integrity in preparation for being admitted to the bar, the Panthers' former chairman feared his work for the party would jeopardize his acceptance into the state legal fraternity.[197] Little's Panther past never came up. The legal community accepted—though it is doubtful they ever embraced—his activities. The groundwork for Little's acceptance by the legal community was laid in previous years during the critical period of the early and mid-1970s. It was then that the local chapter, finally challenging the popular perception of party members, embarked on its journey toward mainstream politics.

The image of criminality undid the prospective branches in both Charlotte and Greensboro. Winston-Salem nearly met a similar fate; still, the party there survived, and established itself as arguably the most successful BPP branch in the entire country. To do this required transformation, which in turn required space and assistance. Unlike New Orleans and other cities where the main thrust of white support came from "the white movement kids," Winston-Salem's chief source of white support flowed from a different and institutionally deeper tributary of liberalism: the North Carolina chapter of the American Civil Liberties Union.[198]

First, in attacking constitutional violations encroaching on freedom of speech and assembly and on freedom from search and seizure, the ACLU in North Carolina aggressively protected the BPP from legal repression. In attacking the excessive actions of law enforcement, which were chiefly responsible for limiting the group's operational space and good name, the civil liberties union forced the police to abate. This space helped the Winston-Salem Panthers to pursue, largely free from extralegal harassment, a social agenda for the betterment of the community. Moderates and liberals endorsed the Panthers' deracialized reformist program—while opposing other black groups.[199]

Second, the legal stewardship of the NCCLU challenged myths about the party's willingness to work within the existing boundaries of the U.S. Constitution and other codified norms. Through it all, an image slowly developed of the Panthers as kinder and gentler. In publicly upholding the Panthers' constitutional claims, the civil liberties union also enhanced their own social legitimacy in the eyes of the white political and legal communities. The ACLU's twofold impact was essential in facilitating the BPP's absorption into the system. In the process the Winston-Salem Panthers entrenched themselves in city politics for the next generation as keepers of the "permanent Black Panther seat."

The significance of the Winston-Salem chapter lies not so much in its having unique aims as in that branch's ability to operationalize the Black Panther Party's national agenda. The story of Winston-Salem's development and transformation, relative to other chapters nationally, seems less a matter of kind than degree. Like Winston-Salem, other chapters pursued a path that looked like moderation, such as in Milwaukee where chapter members by the mid-1970s were lobbying their U.S. senators; in Dallas Panthers provided residents free legal assistance in consumer protection, tenant and housing problems, welfare, and food stamps; in the heartland Panthers of Des Moines, Kansas City, and Omaha launched drug treatment and rehabilitation centers. Moderation spilled into mainstream politics, partly inspired by municipal electoral successes in Gary, Cleveland, and Newark, ostensibly signifying blacks' political absorption into the body politic. Panther chapters endorsed establishment politics, normally under the Democratic Party umbrella, by running or backing political candidates. Strides toward mainstream electoral politics or social service orientation were captured in celebratory articles in the Panther's weekly organ promoting "these victories," as they all came with the blessing of headquarters in Oakland.[200]

Equally emblematic was constitutional liberalism. Beyond creating space, constitutional protection by liberals like the ACLU facilitated the Panthers' moderation—not just in Winston-Salem but elsewhere.[201] Using the courts was not unique. Indeed, the ACLU and other constitutional liberals mirrored a wider contemporary happening that made the courthouse "a channel for citizenship," in the words of sociologist Michael Schudson.[202] The results of ACLU channeling remain etched in the public transcript, as the record increasingly unveiled a Panther party actively imagining itself as heirs to America's civic nationalist tradition.[203]

But cataloging Black Panther conformity remains anecdotal without context. Placing the Panthers' transition in context means locating the party within a historical period that historians now commonly call "the greatest constitutional crisis since the Civil War": the Pentagon Papers, COINTELPRO, the Church Committee, Watergate, and other scandals all raised questions about the legitimacy of all branches of government.[204] Within black America especially, public revelations about government's role in the Tuskegee syphilis experiment in 1974 made fealty in the state a life-and-death choice. "Americans' general attitude toward the federal government underwent a sea-change over a period of ten years," Max Holland wrote, as healthy skepticism was supplanted by "corrosive cynicism."[205] Yet in this constitutional context, when the credibility of state institutions spiraled to its nadir, one sees the most dissident of all Black Power groups— the Black Panther Party—not proclaiming the bankruptcy of American constitutionalism but looking to invest in the existing political and social order. If scholars take seriously the old saw that contingency and context still matter in history, they might well apply them to the choices made by the most notorious black nationalist group—particularly at a moment when the nation teetered on the constitutional brink and some of the Left's most influential, Sartre and Mao among them, were holding steadfast that revolutionary change was still to be found at the end of a gun—in Watergate's America. It was not simply federal institutions in which questions of legitimacy were raised, but in local and state governments as well. In the weeks and months after Watergate, as we see in the following chapter, nationalists found themselves challenging North Carolina's government in its prosecution of Joan Little.

4

In Defense of Sister Joan
The Joan Little Case and American Justice
in the Cosmopolitan South, 1974–1975

In the predawn hours of Tuesday, August 27, 1974, a twenty-year-old black inmate serving a seven-to-ten-year burglary sentence in a jail in Beaufort County, North Carolina, fled her cell after killing a night prison guard. *New York Times* reporter Wayne King wrote, "The slaying of Clarence Alligood . . . might have" been an unusual but "simple case of murder and escape by a woman inmate except for what one law enforcement officer termed 'the peculiarities in the way [the guard] was dressed.'" As Joan Little (pronounced *Jo-ANN* but spelled *Joan*; no relation to Larry Little) hurried from the loosely operated facility, she left in her cell the dead, sixty-two-year-old white jailer, naked from the waist down, alongside an ice pick normally kept in his desk drawer. Also left in her wake was what the autopsy report later called "clear evidence of recent sexual activity."[1]

Pursued in a statewide hunt aimed at capturing her with any force necessary, Little turned herself in seven days later (September 3)—on the condition that she not be returned to the Beaufort County Jail. A nearly all-white grand jury convened in Beaufort and immediately indicted Little on capital murder charges.[2] Among the jurors was a man with the same surname as the dead jailer. "It'd take them five minutes to convict her down here," one of Little's attorneys commented to a reporter. Her attorneys' alarm was well founded. The state reportedly had the highest incarceration rates in the country. Its number of inmates on death row was also higher than any in the Union. The only two women in the nation sentenced to death since the 1972 Furman Decision suspended capital punishment across America were both held in North Carolina, so few doubted that gender would keep Little from receiving the death penalty.[3] In fact reports surfaced just prior to Little's surrender that a "shoot-on-sight" order was imminent.[4] Yet not only did Little avoid a capital sentence, she was acquitted in a mere seventy-eight minutes.[5] Little's victory, said her legal handlers, was predicated on moving the trial from "Jesse Helms country," as Morris Dees put it, to "the progressive urban areas."[6] By focusing on the state's response to the Joan Little case and movement, this chapter complements the articles and books that ably cover the movement marshaled in her public defense.[7] Little's case gained national attention because of both race and gender. The contacts of the Little camp with the Black Panther Party in particular played an important role in mobilizing legal, financial, and publicity efforts. Nearly one full year elapsed from the apparent sexual assault (27 Aug. 1974) to Little's trial (14 July 1975) and then to her acquittal (15 Aug. 1975).

The story of Joan Little's acquittal is also bound up with the story of the search for a cosmopolitan post–civil rights South, a specific moment in the experience of America's most distinctive region. This moment was perhaps most pronounced after King's assassination in 1968, when a more outward-looking sensibility eroded a regional one as the South's preferred frame of reference. This meant demonstrating to nonsoutherners that southern governments would no longer lend its imprimatur to a dual system of racial justice, though this did not mean that racial discrimination no longer existed. This chapter chronicles the state's acquiescence to community, national, and even international pressure. Specifically, it investigates how the state's claim to cosmopolitanism compelled its intercession on behalf of Little, a convicted felon and indicted murderer of a law enforcement officer.[8]

The Revolt against Modernity:
Why Not Beaufort? / What's Wrong with Beaufort?

Like much of eastern North Carolina at the height of the civil rights movement during the late 1950s and the 1960s, Beaufort was known as a hotbed of Klan activity, mightier there than anywhere else in the country outside of Alabama and Mississippi.[9] Though official membership had dropped by the mid-1970s, the virulence underlying the Klan's popularity persisted. "Cracker and racist comments by local citizens," noted James Reston, a transplant from Washington, D.C., who was teaching creative writing at the University of North Carolina at Chapel Hill and covering the Little trial for television, "are easy enough to hear in Beaufort County."[10] The Beaufort polity was, rightly or wrongly, judged as an insular people who were religiously fundamentalist, nativist, and isolationist in foreign policy toward places not threatened by Communism.[11] Their insularity mirrored the entire eastern region of the state.

Karen Galloway and Jerry Paul, two of Little's attorneys, set out to demonstrate that their client could not receive a fair trial in Beaufort. They did so in part by exposing the double standards that tainted the legal process in the county. Whites outnumbered blacks in Beaufort two to one, they pointed out, yet blacks were outnumbered nearly nine to one in terms of jury eligibility, which was then drawn from property tax rolls. The 1965 Civil Rights Act named Beaufort as one of the counties where less than 50 percent of eligible black voters were registered. In the eyes of many local whites, however, Beaufort in recent years had succumbed to the inexorable social forces of modernization. Townsfolk hinted that it had become a model of "racial progress."[12]

For many in the midst of rapid social change, religious fundamentalism had often provided psychological comfort.[13] Beaufort was no different, not even when it confronted a legal case based on uncertain evidence and dubious judicial proceedings. "Execution" was good punishment, the Beaufort solicitor once wrote to the editor of a local paper, whether it deters anybody or not. "The Bible not only requires [it]. . . . It demands it."

He added that "those who have difficulty making up their minds about it are those who have superimposed sociology on top of basic Christian ideals and traditions."[14] The intertwining of entrenched religious and political views impeded a cosmopolitan outlook.[15] The reliance on personal religious views to justify positions on such issues as capital punishment was perceived by secular onlookers as a vestige of the precosmopolitan South, and it revealed the "cultural lag" between Beaufort County and North Carolina's progressive heartland.[16]

If North Carolinians outside Beaufort shared the views of their eastern Tar Heel sibling, they gave little public evidence of this. For instance, notable political leaders, both black and white, publicly repudiated religious arguments for the death penalty. A petition supporting a criminal task force promoting the commutation of death sentences was signed by former governor Terry Sanford, mayors Howard Lee (Chapel Hill) and Clarence Lightner (Raleigh), and Wilbur Hobby, president of the state AFL-CIO and former gubernatorial candidate. H. M. Michaux initiated state legislation to that effect.[17] Throughout his term and to the consternation of factions on all sides, the governor said nothing substantive on the issue.[18]

In contrast the town press and public officials seemed impervious to both modern social convention and assumptions, or playing to a political gallery outside the state. An editorial in the local *Washington Daily News* in Beaufort eulogized the slain prison guard as "a man who gave his life in the line of duty."[19] The editorial did not explain or even suggest why Alligood was in Little's cell.[20] It did, however, substantiate Galloway's observation that "there are still people in the eastern part of the state who think she planned the whole thing."[21] Making the matter more controversial, the local sheriff's department waited four hours after discovering Alligood's body before contacting the North Carolina State Bureau of Investigation (SBI), raising questions about the possible contamination of the crime scene as well as speculation about a cover-up. "She stabbed him and stripped him," declared one town official, who all but dismissed the shoddy procedural practices that tainted the forensics, much of which had been compromised by local authorities who apparently tampered with the crime scene before the SBI's arrival.[22] "Dear God," a nationally syndicated black columnist wrote, "help Beaufort County, North Carolina, to prove that it is a trifle more enlightened than it was in the tragic era when the lynch mob was the law."[23]

The grand jury proceedings did little more than reinforce the community's image as a benighted backwater.[24] Dissatisfied with the potential testimony of one of their own expert witnesses, Medical Examiner Harry M. Carpenter, whose autopsy report indicated that sexual activity took place prior to death, authorities simply refused him the opportunity to testify, thus withholding any evidence of sexual misconduct from the grand jury. The prosecution replaced Carpenter with a pathologist who claimed there was no evidence of sexual relations that night, a view contradicted clearly by the forensic findings.[25] Adding to the impression of the miscarriage of justice were erroneous news reports that the grand jury indicting Little included no blacks, young people, or women. Still, that fourteen of the eighteen members of the grand jury were white virtually sealed an indictment against Little. During a Little rally in Detroit, Willie Mae Reid, the Socialist Workers vice presidential candidate, called what was unfolding typical "southern justice."[26]

Most Beaufort whites viewed the case quite differently. Deputy Sheriff Willis Peachey, the prosecution's star witness, felt more than a little pressure from local residents. He feared "he would never be able to hold his head up in Washington [the county seat] again" if Little was not convicted.[27] Even the prosecution could not deny that a Washington jury might be prodded and provoked by "deliberate and excessive publicity."[28] The deputy had proudly posed with ice pick in hand next to Alligood's corpse in the cell for local television cameras, which had catapulted him into the public eye and granted him instant celebrity status.[29] Accepting the local version of events surrounding the crime and hearing, many county residents resented the unflattering national spotlight. Perhaps most detestable was that a favorite local son, Jerry Paul, now one of Little's attorneys, had returned from Chapel Hill to focus it on them.

During his eighteen years in Beaufort, Paul, the son of a well-to-do couple, had shown no interest in civil rights or political activism of any kind. He was better remembered as a football star at the local high school and then briefly at nearby East Carolina University. He studied law at the University of North Carolina at Chapel Hill, which became pivotal in his young life. In his first year there he became radicalized while taking a criminal law class.[30] By the time he completed law school Paul recalled, "I said to myself, 'Do you want to make a lot of money or . . . look back twenty years from now and figure out what kind of human being you were?'" He chose a legal life protecting civil liberties and political rights in North Carolina. It rankled many of his former neighbors, friends, and family that Paul, now converted to the civil rights cause, regularly represented Black Panthers and other controversial groups. Paul's parents allegedly disowned their son-turned-activist-attorney, claiming, "You've become a traitor to your own race."[31] The boorish attitudes that made Paul an outcast in his hometown would ultimately draw him to return, as he did with a cadre of attorneys, experts, growing national sympathy, and a compelling story by his client.

In October, after denying a defense motion for a venue change out of the east, Judge James Pou Bailey granted a special venire that allowed jurors to be drawn from neighboring Nash County.[32] To most observers Nash was no different than Beaufort. Its jury pool was more than 90 percent white and male, despite the 1970 census showing that the majority of Nash residents were black and female.[33] Little's attorneys determined to show that inveterate bias, manifest in the racially skewed composition of the jury, was not exclusive to Beaufort County—or to Nash, for that matter. In their view the bias was pervasive throughout the entire eastern region of the state. They contended that only a radical move "far away from this rural part of the state . . . where, we believed, whites were prejudiced and blacks less outspoken than in the progressive urban areas" would ensure a fair trial.[34]

A survey of jury selection in twenty-three counties was commissioned by the defense. The survey, done in March 1975, portrayed eastern North Carolina as an area teeming with racist attitudes toward blacks—attitudes that led to discrimination and deeply troubling consequences. Their findings supported existing sociological interpretations that held that eastern North Carolina's demography—rural, culturally and ethnically homogeneous, and with few large cities where northerners chose to settle—contributed to the higher levels of racial prejudice harbored by residents in the counties surveyed.[35] The survey was significant to the Little case because the jury was the most crucial component of the trial. All the same, quantitative evidence validated what outsiders suspected life was like in Beaufort County.[36] The press and defense drummed one statistic in particular, noting that approximately six thousand Beaufort County whites supported the right of women to defend themselves against sexual attack, but when phrased in racial terms—does a black woman have the right to defend herself when the attacker is white?—the overwhelming majority of respondents responded "no."[37]

The study was based on the hypothesis that levels of overt racism were correlated to where one lived in the state.[38] The survey was a damaging commentary on Beaufort and the entire region. With respect to the facts surrounding the Little case, the survey made it evident that residents of eastern counties tended toward an interpretation that contrasted sharply with that of residents in Orange, the county in central North Carolina that served as the control for the survey. On the question of whether Little tempted the jailer into the cell, residents of Pitt County in the eastern region were three times more likely than residents of Orange to believe that she did. The study showed that urban Piedmont residents had been exposed to roughly the same amount of press coverage concerning the details of the case, and although they lived farther away Orange residents were slightly more likely to have heard about the trial—93 percent in Orange and 90 percent in Pitt. The survey supported the opinion that a change to any location other than in the urban Piedmont would not result in a fair trial. The survey raised obvious questions about the fairness of eastern North Carolinians, forcing the state either to provide a semblance of justice by removing the trial from eastern North Carolina or to have the reputation of the entire state damaged by keeping the trial in the Beaufort County seat of "little Washington."

By the spring of 1975 economic interests drove some in the Beaufort business community to press for the trial's removal. The aspersions cast on Washington brought a collective wince from the town's business establishment. One official from the chamber of commerce privately contacted the local prosecutor, William Griffin, and "implored him to accept any conditions to get the case moved out of the county."[39] Epitomizing this fear was a *New York Times* article that quoted a local industrial executive who made remarks about Little's sexual past, resulting in a furor in the national media. The reporter, James Reston, wrote: "For many of the whites in Washington NC the most comfortable accommodation to the facts is that Joan Little is a bad girl who enticed Alligood, a weak man, into her cell, with a premeditated plan of murder and escape. . . . 'I'll tell you one thing,' said Hardy Henry, an executive for the National Spinning Company, who lives in Country Club Estates in Washington, 'she wasn't defending her honor in that cell. She'd lost that years ago.'"[40] Of particular concern was the trial's potential harm to the town's leading industry—tourism.[41] Although at the time local tourism was doing reasonably well, grossing more than $7 million the previous year, the recession that hit much of the nation in 1975 magnified the significance of any loss that the local economy might suffer as a result of the unfavorable publicity.[42]

Some local black leaders as well as the white business community wanted the trial removed (and with it the media spotlight) out of the county as quickly as possible. Among those who pressured for a venue change was Louis Randolph, a key financial supporter in the Little case and Washington's sole black councilman. Randolph maintained that Little could have received a fair trial in his hometown but that practical and political consequences necessitated moving it out of Washington.[43] Randolph suggested that people would be "visiting" the "little sleepy town," as the *Wall Street Journal* referred to it, out of some freakish curiosity. He feared that a carnival-like atmosphere would swallow whole the tiny rural community of eight thousand, sacrificing the town's economy.[44] By comparison, a trial in Raleigh, said Randolph and others, promised to be a less dramatic show.[45]

Little's defense strategy hinged on the assumption that the state also had a stake in avoiding the bad press that a trial in Washington would create. "The institutions involved have seen that it's in their self-interests to see Joann convicted," Paul said in a February 1975 interview. "Her conviction is necessary to maintain the illusion that police officers are infallible. Her conviction is necessary to maintain the racist attitudes about black women and to maintain the arrogance of some whites."[46] Paul understood that the state held a competing interest—to protect its moderate image on race. The key was to challenge the state's self-proclaimed progressivism on race issues. "In 1975, it may be bad to admit that you're racists because we have this image; the nation comes down on you, and it's bad. And you won't get any industry at any time."[47] Paul carefully sought to fasten this racist image, whether legitimate or not, onto the state in order to prod state officials to offer Joan Little a fair and impartial hearing. Furthermore, Paul suggested Little's conviction would also be vindication for increased scrutiny of the state's criminal justice policies.

From 1970 through 1974, North Carolina murder rates had drifted slightly downward while nationwide figures were steadily climbing. While during that period sexual assault in the state had inched upward, both the rate of increase (2.8 percent in North Carolina compared with 7.5 percent nationally) and the aggregate percent (15.5 versus 26.1) compared favorably to the national average.[48] Placing North Carolina's crime rates in the context of neighboring southeastern states provides an even more instructive picture. During this five-year span not only did North Carolina see lower murder and rape rates than peer states, but it had lower rates in every major statistical category recorded by the FBI crime report and the U.S. Bureau of the Census: robbery, aggravated assault, burglary-breaking/entering, larceny-theft, and auto theft.[49]

The popularity of the law-and-order position in North Carolina was incommensurate with the statistical reality of crime's presence between its borders. Although North Carolina had not experienced any significant increase in violent crimes, its incarceration rate per capita was the highest in the United States. Florida, which ranked second among peer states, had an incarceration rate only half that of North Carolina's.[50] This suggests in part that a disproportionate number of prisoners were incarcerated for nonviolent crimes. Nationally, North Carolina ranked second in percentage of the total state budget allocated for the criminal justice system.[51] The racial aspect was conspicuous. Few Americans were shocked that blacks in North Carolina were overwhelmingly singled out for capital punishment, which for the past five decades had been administered in that state by lethal gas. A 1975 report on the impact of criminal justice policy on blacks in the state trial courts found that an unusually harsh "treatment of blacks relative to . . . whites occurred in the category of major traffic offenses."[52] Racial disparity occurred at each rung of the state's criminal justice system, from traffic violations right up to capital offenses.

By the end of 1974 a quarter of all death row inmates in America endured the wait in the Tar Heel State.[53] The vast majority were either black or Native American. It was one of only two states, moreover, in which death was the sole legal punishment for sexual assault.[54] In the wake of the U.S. Supreme Court's *Furman v. Georgia* ruling (1972), which found capital punishment cruel and unusual and in effect annulled it, North Carolina was one of at least sixteen states that revised and reimplemented their capital statutes.[55] The operational space for these rollbacks was created by the state's supreme court and general assembly, which in 1974, according to Hugh Bedau, "enacted a statute that was essentially unchanged from the old one except that it made the death penalty mandatory."[56] The U.S. Supreme Court disagreed.[57] In overturning a 1974 conviction the Supreme Court rejected the state's murder statute and in the plurality opinion presented by Justice Potter Stewart claimed the state had deviated from "the evolving standards of decency respecting the imposition of punishment in our society."[58]

No significant change could be expected in North Carolina, where no elected official wanted to be viewed as soft on crime. The state's political and judicial system exhibited not the vestiges of a premodern society but its hallmarks. Countering this historic reality was the mounting national pressure that led the state to realize its interest in a Little trial that had to be perceived as fair: justice had to appear swift but evenhanded, orderly but race blind. Order as well as justice took on greater value in post-Watergate America. In this light the state had a vested interest not only in the verdict but also in the perception that the process of obtaining the verdict was fair. "The state and its system of justice," *Raleigh News and Observer* editor Claude Sitton wrote, "will face the bar of public opinion while the defendant faces the bar of justice."[59] Insofar as the state was on trial in the court of public opinion, the power to acquit the state as well as the defendant rested with the jury. The national spotlight on the Little case motivated North Carolina officials to ensure a fairer trial, according to social scientist Laurence French.[60] A state once heralded by politicians, newspaper editors, businessmen, and intellectuals as a model of the New South's racial moderation and civility now appeared to activists and a growing number of Americans to be returning, in media parlance, to provincial justice. Few within or outside of government, and in or out of the state, believed that keeping the trial in Beaufort would satisfy even the appearance of justice.

On April 23 Judge Henry McKinnon quashed the defense motion to dismiss the murder trial on the grounds of racial, gender, and age prejudice in the grand jury selection.[61] This was hardly a surprise, given McKinnon's political and judicial conservatism.[62] In response fifty blacks staged yet another protest outside the courtroom. The ongoing protests—placard-carrying demonstrators were marching under the banner "Government Stop Killing Off Black People"—remained a serious concern for leading state officials. With no trial date set, SBI Director Charles Dunn told

Governor Holshouser there was no end in sight to these embarrassing demonstrations.[63] The only question was how the state would defend its image.[64] The answer came one week later.

"In the Best Interests of Justice": The Change of Venue

After arriving in the courtroom on May 1, Little met with the judge in chambers. Several minutes later Superior Court Judge Henry McKinnon and Little emerged and the announcement was made: the trial would be moved to Raleigh, in Wake County. Prior to the venue change McKinnon had denied all fourteen of the defense's previous pretrial motions.[65] In the judge's estimation, noted reporter Jim Grant of the *Southern Patriot*, "it would be difficult to find an unbiased jury in Pitt or Craven Counties, both adjacent to Beaufort County."[66] Cathy Roche of the *Washington Post* suspected that McKinnon was swayed by the statistical proof produced in the defense team's jury selection survey, which demonstrated "that publicity about the case was more slanted against the defendant in the [more racist] eastern part of the state than in the Raleigh area."[67]

Though persuasive and revealing, the objective and quantitative evidence was not what ultimately swayed McKinnon. Rather, what the survey did, or at least what McKinnon feared it had done, was confirm outsiders' impressions of and prejudice against the small southern town of Washington.[68] "It would [not] look good to the public. . . . That was the compelling reason," the judge later admitted.[69] Yet the conservative jurist deliberately chose not only to remove the case from Beaufort but out of the region completely. He denied that any political consideration affected his decision. Some, like social psychologist Courtney Mullin, who engineered the study, considered McKinnon's motion ruling courageous: "He's from eastern North Carolina, a political man. He has a lot of reasons not to say eastern North Carolinians are so prejudiced to a point that they can't be fair and impartial."[70] Despite McKinnon's disavowals, most members of the defense and prosecution teams believed political motivations to move the trial far outweighed pressures to keep the trial in Beaufort or any other part of eastern North Carolina.[71]

The prosecution, which had consented to a new site as long as the change was within the same judicial district or a neighboring county, was outraged. Seeking to have the motion overturned, lead prosecuting attorney William Griffin immediately filed an unsuccessful appeal to the North Carolina Supreme Court. Griffin claimed that a trial more than one hundred miles away placed undue expenses on county residents. He also predicated his appeal on the implications of unfairness that the trial's relocation might impute to eastern North Carolinians. This argument found an ally in *Washington Daily News* editor Ashley Futrell, who editorialized that McKinnon's decision had smeared and insulted the people of Beaufort.[72] In the end the state supreme court refused to overturn the lower court's ruling.[73]

After its own review, the U.S. Supreme Court upheld McKinnon's venue change decision and expressed only modest endorsement of his position, withholding enthusiasm for it, probably because the district judge had stopped short of striking the state statute that restricted venue changes to adjoining counties.[74] Although moving the trial so far from the original venue was unheard of in North Carolina legal history, the U.S. Supreme Court also considered the venue change important for what McKinnon's ruling did not say. McKinnon later surmised that the Supreme Court was disappointed that "I did not make a positive finding of prejudice" against eastern North Carolina.[75] Still, he nimbly averted the embarrassing courtroom exhibition of a trial in Beaufort without labeling fellow easterners as bigots or upsetting the existing state judicial and jury-selection process. In not assuming an extreme position, McKinnon balanced the competing interests of the defense, easterners, the broader public, and the federal courts. The continuation of proceedings in any eastern county would have invited federal intervention, troubling media images, and possibly civil disobedience—Little protestors had already vowed to disrupt the trial if it were held in Beaufort, likely triggering a mistrial and thereby prolonging the case.[76] Behind McKinnon's appeal to "the best interests of justice" lay interest politics, described by Daniel J. Singal as anchored "solidly in reality and . . . typically 'pragmatic' and 'nonideological' in character."[77] A visibly relieved McKinnon quickly excused himself from further trial proceedings for what he characterized as personal reasons.[78]

For the defense the new trial scene meant that Little would "understandingly and knowingly" forfeit her existing challenges against the racial composition of the jury pool and accept the jury pool as it currently stood in Wake County. Little, her defense, and her supporters were willing to take the risk. Her attorneys considered the venue change the most crucial of the fifteen motions argued by the defense.[79] Never losing sight of the desire to keep the Little case in the international spotlight, Paul, referring to the venue change, told reporters that "there were three victories for the people this week." The other two, he said half-jokingly, were in Cambodia and Vietnam.[80] McKinnon's move signified that the trial was no longer a provincial issue but a matter of concern for the entire state.

Growing support for Little, as one publication sympathetic to the defendant noted, "no doubt put strong pressure on the state to show the semblance of a fair trial."[81] Organized political efforts included nationwide rallies; a letter campaign drive led by the Southern Poverty Law Center; and the presence of hastily erected shanties forming Resurrection City III in "little Washington," targeting the failures of government and dramatizing economic and legal injustice. Congresswoman Yvonne Burke (D-California) introduced a resolution calling for an investigation by the Department of Justice. Along with Burke, Shirley Chisholm (D–New York) and John Conyers (D-Michigan) threatened to dramatize racial and criminal justice concerns for McKinnon, a judge already preoccupied with the bar of public opinion. They called for the Department of Justice to intervene and, in Chisholm's words, uphold "a woman's right to defend herself during sexual attack."[82] In response, the Civil Rights Division of the Department of Justice made known its intention to "monitor Little's case."[83] Finally, the damning evidence offered in the jury survey quantified and validated public skepticism about North Carolina's readiness to ensure justice in a racially charged case.[84] Little summed up the expectations of the defense: "I think the people in Wake County . . . are not as racist as the people in Beaufort County. I hope they will fulfill the confidence I have in them to make sure I get a fair trial."[85]

Though the defense had preferred Orange County, home of Chapel Hill and UNC, they deemed Raleigh an acceptable substitute.[86] Most assumed that Little would receive a more sympathetic hearing in the more cosmopolitan state capital "because women, blacks, and students appear in large numbers on the voter registration lists from which jury pools are drawn."[87] Unlike Beaufort County, however, Raleigh had a black population of only modest size, particularly for a southern city.[88] What made Raleigh a promising choice for the defense was not a sizable black electorate, since blacks accounted for only 25 percent of the residents of voting age and less than

16 percent of actual voters, but the mayoral election of November 1973 and the decisive role of the white electorate in it.[89]

In 1975 no place better symbolized the racially enlightened urban Piedmont than Raleigh, where Clarence Lightner became the first black elected mayor in a southern capital city that was predominantly white. The councilman successfully put together an unprecedented coalition of blacks, moderates, and white liberal voters to pull out a surprise victory over G. Wesley Williams, director of the Raleigh Merchants Bureau, who counted on the backing of downtown commercial interests. Unlike the election of Maynard Jackson that same year in Atlanta, where blacks composed 51.3 percent of that city's population, the election in Raleigh was characterized by support from whites, who were a decisive majority. Winning the votes of blacks and white liberals, Lightner's politics augured well for the birth of postblack politics, enshrined a decade later in victories by Douglas Wilder, Harold Washington, William Gray, and others. Lightner culled widespread support largely from white voters in suburban neighborhoods where race was a less pressing issue than urban sprawl and land-use policies.[90]

Black mayoral successes in Detroit, Newark, Cleveland, and other American cities may have spawned further white flight, as some authors have suggested, but not in Raleigh.[91] Since 1965 Raleigh's population had mushroomed by 36 percent. A slower growth rate was nowhere in sight, with predictions of the city's population more than doubling over the next fifteen years. A notable contribution to Raleigh's sustained growth was white in-migrants.[92] It was this segment that proved to be most significant in the trailblazing election of Lightner, who, as southern political analysts Jack Bass and Walter De Vries explain, fared "best among recently arrived Research Triangle Park employees."[93] More broadly, Lightner's victory signaled the impact that the mass influx of migrants had in moving Raleigh beyond the shadows of southern provincialism into southern enlightenment.

Because Raleigh was the state capital and had a high proportion of state employees, it was partially insulated from the rising unemployment rates that gripped the nation and much of the state.[94] Its unemployment rate was less than 5 percent, compared with 8.9 percent for the state, and was credited for the city's relatively smooth racial relations and its ability to attract and absorb northern migrants. Research Triangle Park (RTP) was central to the area's tight labor market. As the 1980s approached and throughout most of that decade, unemployment levels in the RTP area were consistently among the lowest in the United States.[95]

Still, Raleigh was far from a racial oasis. Only a few years before the Little case, William Knight, a black Raleigh councilman, was leading protests over city hiring policies.[96] The local community relations commission registered many complaints of racial discrimination in housing and employment. Most of the city's substandard housing was found in Raleigh's black southeast quadrant. Despite its relatively stable jobless rate, the city, a Raleigh official acknowledged, was "just submerged in employment discrimination complaints." The city also faced a suit from the NAACP Legal Defense and Educational Fund. Citing unfair racial grouping practices in the city's public school system, the suit charged that Raleigh had done little since officially desegregating schools in 1968.[97] The hiring practices of the fire department were the subject of investigation and subsequent lawsuits by the Equal Employment Opportunity Commission.[98]

In spite of Raleigh's mixed state of racial progress, Little and her attorneys preferred a city that looked both forward and backward over a putatively dyed-in-the-wool reactionary one. Raleigh was not Washington, D.C., Paul remarked, but it was a better venue "than . . . any we could have gotten in Washington, NC."[99] Others echoed the sentiment. "This is the best place for it because she wouldn't have gotten a fair trial in the eastern part of the state," one black Raleigh housewife said.[100] The national press remained skeptical of Little's access to a fair trial even after the move to Raleigh. "The trial could tell much about life in this conservative Southern city," predicted *Washington Post* reporter Douglas Watson, "and how much it has changed since the civil rights crusades and desegregation demonstrations experienced by the nation in the 1950s and 1960s." Its outcome, he suggested, had even broader significance as a gauge not only of legal equity in Raleigh but of "the quality of justice that can prevail in . . . North Carolina."[101] North Carolina had changed, state leaders insisted. The unprecedented venue change as well as the new location itself was proof of that. In distancing the trial from Beaufort, the state had also distanced itself symbolically from its reactionary past. Many of Little's supporters saw the venue change as the inexorable result and action of the "power of the people," pure and simple.

"All Power to the People": Critical-Mass Support in the Defense of Little

During its early stages, from August to December 1974, the Joan Little Defense Committee, whose main responsibility was publicity and fund-raising, had mustered scant support.[102] For nearly two months the campaign sputtered, failing to galvanize the mass publicity necessary to command the sympathies even of local leaders. Only in October would the campaign begin to experience an upturn. Desperate for media attention and with coffers emptying fast, Paul acted in classic southern liberal tradition, turning northward for assistance.[103] With the trial set for November 18, Paul renewed his contact with Nancy Mills, with whom he had collaborated four years earlier on a study of black out-migration in eastern North Carolina. Living in Washington, D.C., and working for the Institute for Corporate Responsibility, Mills agreed to help Galloway and Paul to get financial commitments and pitch Little's cause to women's groups in the nation's capital. Meanwhile, the judge granted a continuance requested by the defense, moving the date of trial from November 18 to the following April.[104]

About the same time, Mark Pinsky, a freelance writer in Durham, was contacted by the *Los Angeles Times* to produce a piece about sexual assault and its victims for the style section of the newspaper.[105] Catching wind of this, Wayne King, a southern correspondent for the *New York Times*, followed up with a full feature story on Little.[106] The December 1 *Times* report helped stir demands for a federal inquiry into the practices of small-town jails.[107] The story spread rapidly, meshing with Mills's fund-raising efforts. Before the new year began, an excited Mills told the Little defense team: "You've got the biggest case in town."[108] The $600 that had barely kept the team afloat quickly ballooned to $20,000.

The sympathetic piece in the *New York Times* finally gave the Little campaign the national exposure it sought. Alabama attorney Morris Dees joined the legal team after reading the *Times* article. A principal contributor to George McGovern's 1972 presidential campaign, Dees brought with him an assortment of political operatives.[109] From December 1974 through April 1975 the campaign's credibility and stature soared. Joining Dees and the *New York Times* in the ranks of Little sympathizers were the American Association of University Women, the National Association of Black Social

Workers, and the Southern Christian Leadership Conference.[110] Two million letters were mailed on behalf of Little by the Southern Poverty Law Center, a Montgomery, Alabama, charitable legal foundation conceived by Morris Dees in 1970 and headed by Georgia state legislator Julian Bond. The *CBS Evening News* devoted several segments to the case. National television exposure fed the media barrage in which every major newspaper from Atlanta to Chicago to California participated.[111]

The "power of the people" had other palpable and positive consequences for Little. Referring to the bond money raised on her behalf, she commented, "When I got the $115,000 bond, I did something that has never been done before in the state of North Carolina. . . . You don't get a bond on first degree murder." Little, then, rightly credited her supporters for her temporary freedom: "If it hadn't been for the power of the people, I wouldn't have been able to have made that massive bond of $115,000."[112] The people's power, in this instance at least, meant professors at the University of North Carolina at Chapel Hill, who in February 1975 paid the bulk of the bond cost by pledging their homes as collateral.[113]

Despite its success, or perhaps because of it, the campaign experienced its share of internal conflict. Members hurled accusations of financial mismanagement and deceit. Most of them were targeted at the campaign's chief organizer, Golden Frinks, after he misled donors about the destination and purpose of funds being collected.[114] Spurred by charges originating with Little attorneys, the SBI pursued Frinks for embezzling campaign funds.[115] Accusations hinted at the rising tension fostered by two competing visions, that of Little and her attorneys and that of Frinks, who complained bitterly that taking the "case out of Eastern North Carolina . . . was the worst thing they could have done."[116] With a strategic outlook more closely aligned with that of Little and her counsel, the Black Panther Party of North Carolina—whom Paul had represented many times and with whom he therefore appeared to be more allied philosophically—was brought in to replace Frinks in March 1975.[117]

The campaign rebounded quickly from the Frinks controversy. "I'm going to help defend Joanne Little by sending some money," responded Carl T. Rowan, syndicated columnist and former assistant secretary of state. "I hope they find my check at the bottom of a whopping pile."[118] By the first week of April, the Southern Poverty Law Center sent out two million letters, raising more than $150,000 by April 6, 1975.[119] Those not offering financial support joined civic and governmental bodies, including the Essex County Board of Freeholders in New Jersey, in petitioning Congress "to insure that justice is done in the case of Joanne Little."[120] Three members of Congress urged federal intervention.[121] Prompted in large part by Joan Little, Congresswoman Yvonne Burke reintroduced a bill to establish a National Center for the Prevention and Control of Rape. The bill, HR 3590 and 3591, promoted greater federal supervision and involvement in local and state rape crisis and prevention.[122] Also sent to the judiciary committee as separate legislation was HR 2323, which authorized an investigation into the violation of prisoner rights in state and local correctional facilities.[123] Receiving pressure from the Congressional Black Caucus and others in Congress, Assistant Attorney General J. Stanley Pottinger agreed to monitor North Carolina's action in the Little case.[124]

The establishment of the Joan Little Information Center in Washington, D.C., in April 1975 helped institutionalize the movement.[125] The Little Center was a bricks-and-mortar reminder that the trial illustrated a growing crisis with respect to sexual assault in America. Back in North Carolina the center and its presence in the nation's capital undoubtedly looked like little more than political theatrics intended to embarrass the state in front of the nation. An agitated secretary of corrections David Jones bristled at these developments, blaming them on "outside activists, liberals, radicals, and my favorite words, fools, because I think they are all the same."[126] More rallies focusing on state racism were planned for the weeks leading up to and through the trial opening, scheduled for April 14.[127] Little addressed a mass audience in the nation's capital just days after Ralph Abernathy of the Southern Christian Leadership Conference (SCLC) led two thousand marchers to "little Washington."[128]

Because public pressure fostered a climate of opinion that made judicial reform both possible and likely, the state proceeded with measures rarely seen in criminal prosecution cases in North Carolina. Even before the jury was selected, not fewer "than five Superior Court judges and the state Supreme Court [had] dealt with one aspect or another," with McKinnon dedicating a better part of the spring to deciding on pretrial issues.[129] Under state statute, the law restricted new trial sites to neighboring counties. Like many venue changes, the one that set the Little trial in Raleigh was as political as it was clearly extralegal. "The move to Raleigh," read a *Raleigh News and Observer* editorial headline, was "justified—despite the cost."[130]

Resolutions of the state supreme court, moreover, "came with unusual speed and in a manner that court sources said was unprecedented."[131] The courts and politicians were genuflecting to a small but vocal minority, some on the prosecution team protested. The heightened attention the courts gave to Little's case was more characteristic of political pragmatists than of legal purists. Courts especially understood how unremitting resistance, as the "garrison mentality" of arch segregationists bore out in the 1950s and 1960s, often hastened rather than arrested federal action.[132] In helping to abate federal involvement, the court's flexibility was less about weakness than it was about tolerance and realism.

Some letdown was evident when the trial's move to Raleigh was announced. In the ten weeks following the decision, contributions dropped to about one-third of what they had been earlier in the year. The *Washington Post* would later report that the Little team was $5,000 to $10,000 in debt. Neither Galloway nor Paul received income, and the other defense lawyers were being paid less than their normal fees.[133] Declining fund-raising totals did not diminish sympathies, however. More likely it seemed a sign that moving the trial outside of Beaufort mitigated supporters' worst fears.[134] If the state had hoped that the historic venue change would quell national interest in the case, such hope soon evaporated, particularly as the summer trial date neared.

Public scrutiny mounted as support for Little spread from the South to the black-church community in the North.[135] Speaking in June 1975 at a Baptist church meeting on Chicago's South Side, Little recounted the cruel treatment—according to her, months in solitary confinement, inadequate clothing and medical treatment, sleeping on cement floors—that she and other inmates experienced during her six-month stay at the Raleigh Women's Correctional Center.[136] That same month, a thousand marchers encircled the U.S. Department of Justice building before marching to the treasury and then gathering in Lafayette Square, across Pennsylvania Avenue from the White House. Once again activists had embarrassingly dragged North Carolina's problems to the nation's capital. The damage to North Carolina's reputation was serious since, unlike prior high-profile and politically charged criminal cases, this one found the state without a federal ally in its prosecution of Little.[137] Indeed, pressure for a fairer trial was more likely because the federal government threatened intervention against the state, not for it. Following up earlier federal inquiries into small-town prison conditions, Congressman Ronald Dellums (D-California) was joined by others in Congress in his effort to pressure newly appointed U.S. Attorney General Edward Levi for an "investigation to determine whether Ms. Little's civil rights" had been violated.[138] The Civil Rights Division of the Department of Justice had already threatened involvement on behalf of the defendant, adding that for now it would "stay out of the . . . way."[139] Peter W. Rodino, chairman of the House Judiciary Committee, faced demands from his constituents to protect the constitutional rights of Little by "insur[ing] that racial recriminations be totally eliminated from the system of American justice."[140]

North Carolina governor Holshouser's party and personal loyalties to the Ford administration may have also been a factor in wanting to avoid a standoff with the Ford Justice Department. Holshouser was chairing the president's southern campaign and therefore found it politically difficult to respond aggressively to the attorney general's office, even if his office wanted to. With his widely held reputation among political observers for dodging controversial issues, the governor was confronting between seven hundred and nine hundred letters urging Little's acquittal.[141] In short, the state would have to go it alone, at least publicly. Authorities were wary of the impact and significance of the case if it were protracted, but they also faced a Pyrrhic courtroom victory, since a conviction that faced reversal on federal appeal would be meaningless and potentially damaging to the reputation of the state in general and of its judicial system in particular. The process, as well as the trial's eventual outcome, had to meet a threshold of legitimate jurisprudence at the federal level.[142] In Little's case—as it was with the Wilmington Ten and Charlotte Three—the fate of the black defendant depended not so much on justice being done as on a critical mass of favorable publicity.[143]

Seeking to derail the defense, the Alligood family hired private prosecutor John Wilkinson to assist the district attorney. Though legally permissible, their decision was a public relations blunder. As trial reporter and author Fred Harwell later wrote, "Wilkinson was a doctrinaire reactionary with a suspicious view of history and human nature. He was . . . anathema to the defense attorneys, an incarnation of everything they saw themselves pitted against."[144] His hiring "cast an immediate shadow of vengeance over the proceedings," another courtroom reporter observed.[145] Although the North Carolina Bar Association denied the defense grievance that Wilkinson, who had once represented Little for shoplifting in 1973, represented a violation of attorney-client privilege, his presence at the prosecution's table was considered politically foolhardy.[146] Shortly afterward the state made its own public relations misstep by appointing Lester Chalmers, best remembered for defending the Ku Klux Klan in his private practice, as state assistant attorney general.[147]

With the trial set to begin after Independence Day 1975, protests were planned for July throughout the country. Support and fund-raising groups sprouted up from Vermont to Western Washington University. Rallies numbering into the thousands were coordinated in more than thirteen U.S. cities. Hollywood and Motown participated with benefit performances from celebrities like Lily Tomlin and former Supremes singer Florence Ballard-Chatman.[148] The Joan Little story resonated with different groups for different reasons. "I saw Little as myself—as did most black women that was there," said one black woman organizer. The National Organization for Women (NOW) Task Force depicted Little as a cooperative, religious, and serious young woman.[149] For many Little supporters, particularly predominantly white women's groups, this was an opportunity to demonstrate that their activism was color and class blind.[150] But even here geopolitics mattered: Durham NOW "discussed Little at monthly meetings with pity." In eastern North Carolina, by contrast, NOW spurned the Little Movement almost entirely, focusing energies on ERA passage.[151]

Little's cross-political appeal seemed to work. Letters, petitions, calls, and telegrams flooded the office of the state's newly elected attorney general, Rufus Edmisten.[152] It surprised few, least of all the local underground press, that the thirty-three-year-old Edmisten, whose higher political aspirations would put him in the governor's race within a decade, discussed with McKinnon the advantages of moving the trial outside of eastern North Carolina weeks before the April preliminary hearing.[153] The attorney general's office, Jim Grant wrote for the *Southern Patriot*, "has been sensitive to the immense negative publicity given to the state for allowing the case to reach the trial stage when all indications show that it should have been dismissed earlier."[154] Years later Edmisten would agree: "Had it not attracted some national attention, it would have been a routine case of murder."[155]

In light of the Little case Congress had earlier passed a series of joint resolutions providing for the Commission on Civil Rights to investigate the effect of local, state, and federal justice systems on women.[156] Now, two days after the trial's start, Congresswoman Burke called upon Congress for stronger federal action "against the crime of rape and in support of the victim." The Congressional Black Caucus made this issue a centerpiece of its 1975 legislative agenda.[157] Even the media acknowledged that, while North Carolina exercised little control or influence in Washington, D.C., it still maintained a measure of control within its boundaries.[158] In the wake of so many national demonstrations supporting Little, Wake County Court officials on July 14 imposed severe restrictions on future public protests in the vicinity of the courthouse, prohibiting assemblies, placards, and leafleting.[159] The ban was ostensibly designed to limit publicity, but its implementation also protected the state's image by implicitly affirming SBI Director Dunn's earlier comment that Little supporters had a predilection to rogue behavior and were prone to instigate violence.[160]

Some North Carolina officials saw the relocated trial and related costs as a strain on municipal resources and a potential blight on the city of Raleigh. City manager L. P. Zachary, well known for his candor, bitterly complained to Governor Holshouser that his tolerance for protestors unduly burdened Raleigh taxpayers.[161] Holshouser essentially ignored the city manager's complaints. As was commonplace since the 1950s in other mid-sized American cities like Raleigh, the conflict was between "localist politicians" and "cosmopolitan industrialists," and Holshouser's sympathies lay with the latter.[162] Urbanization and industrialization had linked the South more "with the social, economic and even political characteristics of the United States as a whole than at any other time since the Civil War," according to William C. Havard.[163] Touted as a model of the new breed of southern governors, Holshouser and a "thoroughgoing liberal" named Jimmy Carter bore the marks of youth, civility, eloquence, and media savvy. Their "new" New South politics, displayed most notably by an public acceptance of racial equality and desegregation, contrasted sharply with the politics of Ross Barnett, Orval Faubus, Eugene Talmadge, and other earlier political figures of the New South. The cosmopolitanism of Holshouser and his contemporaries, Havard argued, made them "capable of symbolically representing a considerable cross-section of . . . respective constituencies."[164]

America's next president, Jimmy Carter, had perfected his projection of a New South cosmopolitanism. Carter "passed himself off," in the words of Havard, "as a 'peanut farmer'" from the unassuming Georgia village of

Plains, while campaigning on a national platform that included universal health care and racial, economic, and environmental moderation. With respect to its history on race, Plains could be said to resemble Washington, North Carolina. Lore has it that Carter in his youth was the only white man in Plains to not join the Plains White Citizens Council. Beneath the nostalgia that Carter's self-conscious public image evoked there endured an inwardly looking pre–civil rights South, which possessed entertainment value, to be sure, in the images it conjured up of a traditional culture and morally obtuse attitude toward race relations. It was this undertow that loomed as Holshouser's possible undoing.[165] For the governor, Beaufort's problem was now the problem of Raleigh and all of North Carolina, and consideration for the state's reputation was likely to trump any short-term inconvenience to the city manager or Raleigh citizens.

Though many Wake court officials were miffed at the prosecution's case, vocal opponents faced immediate criticism from court superiors for speaking out. For example, after the July 10 edition of the *Raleigh News and Observer* reported that Wake County District Judge Carlos Murray was embarrassed that a prosecution case so potentially lacking in merit would be decided under his jurisdiction, he was strongly rebuked by superior and state officials, who felt that his public dissent intensified media exposure.[166]

The trial's national appeal remained strong after its Monday, July 14 start until it ended a month later.[167] In most cities, support for Little came from a broad swath of the political spectrum. It included the New Leftists of the National Alliance Against Racist and Political Repression and the Young Socialist Alliance; the Black Arts Movement and the black labor policy advocates in the Coalition of Black Trade Unionists; and the Coalition of Labor Union Women, the Women's International League for Peace and Freedom, and the National Organization for Women. Among the more moderate voices supporting Little were Wellington Webb, Colorado state senator and future Denver mayor, and of chapters of the Urban League and the NAACP. Jesse Jackson's Operation PUSH (People United to Save Humanity) joined in.

The gathering at Riverside Church just west of Harlem represented a veritable Who's Who of social activists, entertainers, and political leaders of the 1960s and 1970s—activists H. Rap Brown and Ossie Davis, house members Bella Abzug and John Conyers, Georgia state representative

Julian Bond, New York municipal court judge Bruce "turn 'em loose" Wright, Gloria Steinem of *Ms.* magazine, leaders of the American Indian Movement, and emissaries of the Attica Brothers and the Federación Universitaria Socialista Puertorriqueña.[168] Willie Mae Reid bluntly summed up the intense publicity: this was a deliberate attempt to let officials know that "it's not Joanne Little who is on the trial, but the racist, sexist judicial system of North Carolina."[169]

The best hope for Little lay in getting publicity, or so thought Anne Braden, veteran civil rights activist and cochairperson of the Southern Organizing Committee for Social and Economic Justice (soc), based in Louisville. As long as the people who ran the state wanted at all costs to maintain their image on racial issues and the eyes of the world were fixed on the Raleigh courtroom, Braden wrote in her open letter, the state would be compelled to act properly.[170] The international press lent credibility to the defense's claim that the eyes of the world were watching Raleigh. "Rape is as American as apple pie," the *Economist* magazine of London said in reference to the Little trial.[171] Journalists from Reuters, the British Broadcasting Company, the London *Daily Mail*, the Dutch publication *New Review*, and the Swedish *Dagens Nyheter* (Daily News) descended on North Carolina. Following one feature piece by a British reporter, letters began pouring into the London newspaper office "asking where to send money to aid the defense."[172] The United Nations had declared 1975 as International Women's Year, and editorials in *Freedomways*, the *Crisis*, and other publications picked up on this theme, reminding readers to keep the struggle for women's rights in global perspective.[173]

Broader issues, then, provided the subtext for the Little case, setting Little's guilt or innocence within a larger forum. In addition to the women's movement there were the Watergate hearings, whose political and legal fallout raised questions about a two-tier system of justice: one for minorities and poor citizens, another for high-ranking public officials and white-collar criminals who had access to the nation's best attorneys and the halls of power.[174] Amid the revolt against authority spurred by Watergate, COINTELPRO, and the publication of the Pentagon Papers, it made political sense for Governor Holshouser to lace his speeches with the theme of "good government." As the state's first Republican governor of the century, he appeared especially sensitive to gaining the public's trust, admonishing his audiences "to keep your government clean and honest."[175] Yet no matter how many such speeches the governor made, to many onlookers the prosecution of Little undermined his message.

Little's attorneys and spokespersons did not hesitate to contrast the penalty facing Little who, they argued, acted in self-defense, with the relatively mild punishment meted out to Watergate convicts.[176] Spearheading much of the cause within and outside the state was the North Carolina chapter of the Black Panther Party and its coordinator, Larry Little. Under the leadership of Larry, who replaced Golden Frinks as head of the Joan Little Defense Committee, the organization mobilized news conferences, rallies, and press releases.[177] As chairman, Larry Little eagerly situated the Little case within the cold war politics of the era, thereby associating the Little cause with other causes championed by the New Left. "We're not willing to see this sister placed on Death Row," he said to sympathizers in Richmond, Virginia. "It's Richard Nixon who should be in jail, and possibly Death Row, for the murder of the Vietnamese people."[178] Similarly, since 1971 the Attica prison uprising in upstate New York and the state's repressive response to it had provoked public discussion about prison reform, brutal application of law enforcement, and the degree to which public officials endeavored to cover up wrongs committed by government.[179] By retaining William Kunstler and Marvin Miller—attorneys for prisoners at Attica and for Native Americans at Wounded Knee, respectively—the defense ensured that Joan Little's connection to other New Left causes was more than rhetorical. The sterling leftist credentials of these two attorneys guaranteed the Little movement a central place in the international debate on racism, sexism, crime and punishment, and the rights of the accused. It also assured that the state's handling of Little's trial engaged a U.S., rather than traditionally southern, standard.[180]

Some white southerners outside North Carolina feared the case would detract from the growing reputation, not only of North Carolina but of the entire region, for progressivism and cosmopolitanism. "Before it is over," editor Tom Baxter of the *Atlanta Journal* warned, the trial's outcome could "have the greatest impact of any in the South since the civil rights slayings of the early '60s." Such commentary made its way onto Governor Holshouser's desk.[181] Making matters worse for him, on the eve of the trial the National Organization for Women closed its statewide convention with a press conference on the Wake County Courthouse steps, where it denounced the state's prosecution and declared Little's case "symbolic of the struggle of all women."[182] The governor, exceptional for being a southern Republican who supported the Equal Rights Amendment and worked closely with the bipartisan Women's Political Caucus, saw his hopes for appealing to voters allied with the women's movement fade.

Thrust into the political arena, Joan Little assumed folk-hero status. The black-gospel and consciousness-raising group Sweet Honey in the Rock produced Grammy-winning songs celebrating Little's heroism. The Louisville-based Southern Conference Educational Fund, a civil rights organization, also recorded and promoted songs about her.[183] An astute Joan Little was appreciative of her fame and of the nearly cult following that was developing around her.[184] It was "all the support and publicity," one self-congratulatory publication in Southern California asserted as the trial neared, that had transformed Little "from another victim of capitalist justice" to heroine in the struggle for freedom.[185]

The looming death sentence provided, strangely, an unforeseen benefit to the Little defense. A reduction in Little's sentence in either late 1974 or early 1975 would have undermined the defense's public campaign efforts. The prosecution's decision against the lesser charge of manslaughter or second-degree murder exemplified a criminal justice system that was overreaching, if not outright vindictive. Without Little's life in the balance, Richard Kluger wrote in the *New York Times*, "the case would never have attracted the attention it did."[186] The state itself unwittingly threatened to make Little into a martyr. The benefits that the threatened death sentence brought spilled over into other reformist causes. Little had created a spark at a time when political activism was widely felt to be declining.[187] The media helped: as many as four hundred newspaper and television and radio correspondents, national and international, applied for media credentials, intent on cramming into the courtroom's thirty-two-seat press box.[188] To the chagrin of the state, which wanted to keep a lid on publicity, the proceedings had to be moved to a larger courtroom.[189]

Little's life-and-death struggle was appropriated for almost every battle of the period. To gain support for the Left's war against global capitalist hegemony, or for a particular candidate in a race for a local school board, the Little case was employed to capture the sympathies of the public or at least of a particular constituency.[190] In an editorial the *Raleigh News and Observer* observed that interest in the trial clearly "went beyond the borders of this state and indeed beyond the boundaries of the United States."[191] North

Carolina, so careful to cultivate its reputation for progressivism, now saw that reputation withering under the glare of the international media spotlight. The strain on Wake court officials was evident. The state appeared sensitive to negative portrayals not only in the mainstream media but also, as the trial judge's press aide revealed, in radical or left-wing publications. After a cartoon in the *Militant* featured the state's prosecuting attorneys in the Little trial as two Klansmen, the aide confronted the publication's trial journalist, Cindy Jaquith. "Do you really consider yourself to be an unbiased reporter?" he asked. "I am completely biased on the side of Joanne Little, if that's what you mean," Jaquith quipped. "I think every woman has a right to defend herself from a rape attack." The bemused press aide replied: "But you haven't heard all the evidence yet. You're just like my wife. She thinks Miss Little is innocent too."[192] Little's trial was often intensely personal, striking a chord with women across racial, class, and political boundaries.

If officials like the judge, who most likely had his press aide do his bidding in accosting Jaquith, were so visibly roused by a publication whose readership was no more than a few thousand, one can only imagine the impact of commentary from North Carolina's most influential daily, the *Raleigh News and Observer*—not to mention editorials in the *Washington Post* and the *New York Times*.[193] Wake County district attorney Burley Mitchell vowed not to pursue the case further, regardless of the verdict. Too much publicity surrounded it, he told the Associated Press.[194] As the trial itself finally took center stage, the *Raleigh News and Observer* editorial page weighed in: "Precisely because this exercise will be regarded as more than another murder trial, there is reason to wish the decorum and sense of fair play . . . could be more widely seen and appreciated."[195]

Such charges reinforced the demand for full and open disclosure of the court proceedings. Claude Sitton, editor of the *Raleigh News and Observer*, claimed that courtroom television was the only way to satisfy that demand. "The need for a fair trial is almost equaled by the need to publicly demonstrate that fairness," he insisted. A publicly broadcast trial, Sitton calculated, would promote the impression of the state as something more than traditionally southern, especially given that those most likely to watch the trial would be more cosmopolitan in outlook.[196] The broadcast would ensure that the state's judicial system—and the values, attitudes, and institutions girding that system—would receive some credit for being open and fair from a national audience.[197]

Sitton, articulating an opinion he frequently presented in the *Raleigh News and Observer*, editorialized that "a good deal more than Miss Little's future will be riding on the outcome," and that it was "the Court [that was] on trial in [the] Joan Little Case."[198] Sitton saw the state's progressive reputation hanging in the balance, but the judge and jury would be neither in Beaufort nor Raleigh—it would be scattered worldwide. Could the state prove it had a cosmopolitan spirit? The *North Carolina Anvil*, a Left-oriented publication, had already dismissed the state's touted progressive image as myth.[199] Not surprisingly, so did the hundreds of Little supporters who showed up the first day of the trial. They remained a daily fixture on the courthouse mall until the trial's end.[200]

Throughout the trial the "outsider issue" continued to be a factor. Trial Judge Hamilton Hobgood's overarching concern about outside agitation in the courtroom came to a head when he dismissed one of Little's attorneys, Morris Dees. While some accepted the charge for which Dees was dismissed—he was alleged to have tampered with a witness[201]—those who thought Dees' dismissal was an effort to undermine the defense's credibility included the attorney summoned to replace Dees, William Kunstler, the colorful New York counselor to some of America's most famous activists. Kunstler's first words to the judge were "I'm glad to see the quality of justice in North Carolina has not improved"—a comment that ultimately led to his spending two hours in the Wake County jail, two floors above the court on a contempt-of-court charge.[202] As the *Washington Post* reported, "[the state] can say they lost the Little case because her lawyers were unethical, out-of-state agitators, and Dees' conviction proves it."[203] Hobgood's decision appeared to be on solid constitutional footing. Former Attorney General Ramsey Clark declined to try to persuade Warren Burger, chief justice of the U.S. Supreme Court, to overturn it. What was most upsetting to state leaders was not the legal complications spawned by Dees, but its public-relations aspect.[204] Embodying this concern was Terry Sanford. A friend of Dees since George McGovern's 1972 presidential campaign, Sanford, a former governor of North Carolina, had already granted full use of his Raleigh law offices to the Alabama civil rights attorney for the Little trial. Now, with Dees' dismissal from the trial, Sanford marshaled the best of his current and former legal associates to help him restore Dees' reputation. Meanwhile, another attorney "paid a visit" to Claude Sitton, who responded to the social call with an editorial apologizing to the American public and international community. It read in part: "Judge Hamilton H. Hobgood's actions . . . are regrettable. . . . The nation and the world may be pardoned for believing that Dees is the hapless victim of hometown justice."[205] The following day the Wake County district attorney's office dropped the suit that would have dismissed Dees. Beforehand, Dees recalled, this exchange occurred:

> I saw Burley Mitchell in the courthouse the next day and asked . . . him to drop the case. . . . I said that North Carolina had suffered unnecessarily from the bad publicity of the Little case. "This is a progressive state, but if you try me and some of the country's top lawyers come to my defense, you're gonna have even more bad publicity." I told him the editorial in the Raleigh paper showed the establishment in town didn't support my prosecution and that soon the *New York Times* and networks would follow.[206]

Coverage of the case by mainstream media around the world motivated the state to try the case more fairly than it might have otherwise. According to Dees, moving the trial in Raleigh meant "we now had the urban area essential to give us a fighting chance."[207]

Revolt against the Village: Jury Selection and the Verdict

In commanding the move to Raleigh, Judge Henry McKinnon understood the dramatic impact it was likely to have. An eastern North Carolinian himself, McKinnon noted: "I . . . had just served a year in Wake County and I knew well the composition of that jury [pool] . . . in both the legal steps taken and black jurors they had."[208] The venue change meant that black jurors were now easily available. The jury that was finally selected knew that "the eyes of the nation," as the *Militant* put it, "were on Raleigh."[209] In their demographic composition and in their verdict they struck a blow for southern cosmopolitanism and helped displace the provincialism that in the public mind had been associated with the possibility of a trial in rural Beaufort County.

Having successfully moved the trial to Raleigh, the defense worked with the team of jury consultants to identify preferred jurors. To this end the Fair Jury Project for Joan Little, a team of twenty interviewers encouraged by the impact of the previous study, conducted a scientific telephone poll, reminiscent of the twenty-three-county pretrial survey, just weeks before the trial. The survey of 954 randomly selected Wake county residents showed that those likely to be supportive of Little shared common traits in religion, schooling, and racial attitudes. In constructing this social-psychological composite, the jury consultants hoped to find the ideal jury—an all-black jury if possible, though they knew that was highly unlikely.[210]

The ideal white juror, according to the profile, was young, liberal, urban, and a registered Democrat. Their religious affiliation, if any, would be Episcopalian, Jewish, or Unitarian. Being formally educated and well read were important requisites in selecting whites. Ideal white jurors subscribed to or were frequent readers of high-end magazines like *Psychology Today* or urbane publications like the *Nation* or the *New York Times Book Review*. Jerry Paul put it plainly enough: "They've got to prove they're not rednecks."[211]

The defense's criterion for jury selection went well beyond this standard, however, when jury selection actually commenced. Although the defense accepted any black person available in the jury venire, it still closely scrutinized white jurors. The defense wanted jurors who held views that would make them an anathema to rednecks and who were eager to defend the values of cosmopolitanism. "When you watched Watergate on the television, where did your sympathies lie?" "Do you believe in interracial marriage?" "What sort of verdict would you hand down against Adolph Hitler?"[212] These questions asked of prospective jurors revealed their emotions and attitudes as well as their political sympathies. The defense sought Raleigh citizens who repudiated ethnic chauvinism and racial doctrine and also opposed the death penalty. They wanted a jury whose cosmopolitan identity was matched only by a deep-seated inferiority complex about the popular image of the native, traditional South as parochial.[213]

In winnowing the pool the defense purposely avoided white jurors who voted Republican; who lived in rural or small towns; and who were Pentecostals, churchgoing Baptists, evangelicals, or members of conservative denominations. Consultants had also recommended against the selection of juror candidates who "read little and what little they read," added one of Little's attorneys, consisted of "simple-minded" magazines like *Reader's Digest*. Whites without a college education and who worked in "humdrum" jobs were systematically avoided. If white southerners were going to decide Little's fate, it would be a white cosmopolitan southerner who met the defense's criteria for status, occupation, outlook, and religious affiliation. Could the defense find enough of them?

Neither formulating a preferred social profile for jurors nor hiring psychologists, as did the defense, the prosecution took a sharply different approach to jury selection. They made their selections based solely on personal knowledge of jurors and their courtroom experience.[214] Intoned prosecutor Lester V. Chalmers, "Maybe I know something they don't know. I've been picking juries for twenty years," he added with his rich southern twang.[215] Chalmers mistook theory for mysticism, however. In preferring tradition and instinct over rationality and science, the prosecution's anti-intellectualism embodied a scorn for social science's contribution to twentieth-century American legal life.

During jury selection the prosecution used eight of its nine challenges, each time to dismiss a black person, whereas the defense wound up using only two of its fourteen peremptory challenges.[216] The first of seven white jurors selected was Cornelia Howell, twenty-one years old.[217] The ninth selected was Jules Hudson, twenty-three. Both were college-educated and nonchurchgoing white Episcopalians. Like subsequent jurors they were registered Democrats.[218] Equally suggestive, both had ties—Howell as a waitress and Hudson as part owner—to the Irregardless Café, a popular vegetarian eatery and countercultural meeting place in Raleigh.[219]

Neither of the two white males impaneled was older than twenty-six. One, Mark Nielsen, was an erstwhile New Yorker who majored in drama and English at Kenyon College in Ohio. The future jury foreman boasted of being a loyal Democrat and regular reader of both the *New York Review of Books* and *Saturday Review*.[220] The other white male juror, Paul Lassiter, was a Duke University law school classmate of Karen Galloway, a black woman lawyer and cocounsel for the defense.[221] All told, six of the first eight selected voiced their personal opposition to the death penalty.[222] Only one of the twelve, a white farmer's wife, approved of capital punishment without any reservation.[223]

Donnell Livingston, a twenty-two-year-old African American majoring in history at historically black Fayetteville State University, was selected as the first of four alternates. Next came Ernest Neiman, seventy-seven, Jewish and the owner of a jewelry store in Raleigh. A former resident of Chicago with a master's degree from the University of North Carolina, Neiman swayed a skeptical defense with a stirring account of his first encounter with racial segregation—seeing toilet facilities marked for "whites only" as he traveled in the South—and its lasting impact on his life.[224]

The opening jury approached a racial and gender balance favorable for the defense—eight women and four men, seven whites and five blacks.[225] Whites, whose average age was 24.6, were comparatively younger than the African Americans, whose ages ranged from forty-eight to sixty-seven years.[226] The white members of the jury were mostly young, female, college educated, urban, Democratic, and opposed to the death penalty. Perhaps as important, they were, according to one Little attorney, people "who have known events beyond their community."[227] The proportion of women, blacks, and twentysomethings in the jury was higher than in the population generally.[228]

Little's attorneys publicly described the jury makeup as "fair." Slightly less stoic in its public response, the *Black Panther* declared that, barring any unforeseen surprises, the Little team had succeeded in selecting a racially mixed jury who would "be sympathetic to Ms. Little's case."[229] In private Dees summed the defense's elation this way: jury consultants and lawyers "told themselves that the jury was so strongly disposed to Little . . . we couldn't lose."[230] "The voir dire," one courtroom observer said, "threw two different trial techniques against each other."[231]

The trial would end much like it began, with the prosecution and defense symbolizing the Janus face of the state. In closing his argument Wilkinson seized on the inconsistencies in the defense's argument and on the failure of two of Little's close friends, who the defense claimed were corroborating witnesses, to make an appearance on her behalf: "'Why aren't these two colored, Neg . . . black friends here?'" That blunder eclipsed a potentially plausible line of reasoning, wrote a *Raleigh News and Observer* court reporter. The anachronistic idiom of Wilkinson left nothing else to be said about Little's antagonists. Wilkinson, symptomatic of the litigants, town, and region he represented, personified a mindset attached to a bygone era.[232]

In his summation for the defense Paul seized the opportunity to remind jurors of the trial's broader social ramifications of sending a message to the entire nation and the world. He closed by encouraging the jury to revolt against provincialism and demonstrate that Wilkinson is "one of those rednecks they've been talking about. We're not rednecks. We're going to prove we're not by finding her not guilty."[233] While jurors may have disavowed the messenger, they subscribed to his message.[234] Jury foreman Nielsen commented publicly that the verdict was "a statement by the jury from which some women are going to take heart. It was time. I don't think it could have been otherwise."[235] "To me, it's a given right that a woman has a right to defend herself," he told reporters.[236]

Even expatriate Huey Newton, living in self-exile in Cuba (see chapter 5), praised "the just jury that acquitted JoAnne." Newton was confident that the jury's acquittal would have repercussions nationally. Their enlightened example, Newton added, "condemns the reactionary jury that convicted Inez [Garcia]" whose California rape-murder trial resembled Little's. "Inez will be set free because JoAnne is free."[237]

*   *   *

Daniel Joseph Singal has described a cosmopolitan thinker as possessing "the tendency to connect their dearest values with city life, while locating the source of the culture they detested in the countryside. To them, small town America constituted a hotbed of bigotry, political reaction, and anti-intellectualism; populism, both home and abroad."[238] This cosmopolitan disdain for the rural was fundamental to the defense, Little's sympathizers, and the media.

State cosmopolitanism in North Carolina, however, had little intersecting purpose with the identity articulated by Singal. The state was moved more by external stimuli than actually incorporating an enlightened corpus of values or guiding principles. This discord was readily apparent to Little supporters. Fearing that the state's nascent cosmopolitan image was jeopardized, stakeholders in this image—judges, officeholders, local print media, and ultimately a message-sending jury—acquiesced to public pressure and made Little's victory possible. Caught up in the rhetorical machinery of cosmopolitanism, the state moved to create operational space for Joan Little, deciding for a historic venue change that underscored a tacit expectation of the state's need to discharge duties in light of its membership in the larger nation. That cosmopolitanism was at least an expressed ideal was no doubt heartening to antiprovincialists. Conservative impulses remained, however, and in the coming years they would prevent both moderates and liberals from moving beyond the token triumph of cosmopolitanism. Reflecting the conservative streak that survived the Little case was the unwillingness of the courts to reverse the state statute regulating venue change or to rule the jury-selection process in Beaufort unconstitutional, thereby preventing a substantive legal precedent for future minority litigants facing trial in a reputedly hostile environment. As the next chapter shows, the dearest values of the cosmopolitan thinker eluded even Little's most fervent defenders, black nationalists.

Speaking Truth to Black Power
Cosmopolitan Black Nationalism and
Its Gendered Discontents

At the heart of the defense's strategy for Joan Little was a high-profile campaign that centered on publicly contesting the state's claim to southern cosmopolitanism.[1] Out front in exposing regional parochialism and in challenging Southern cosmopolitanism were black nationalists, enlisted by Little's legal defense team to serve as the official spokespersons and trustees of the Little Defense Committee.[2]

Initially the choice of black nationalists might seem strange, given that virtually all of them, whether racial, religious, or civic in their emphasis, embraced an ideology seemingly immersed in patriarchy, divisiveness, and provincialism. Yet in this campaign nationalists changed their rhetoric and adopted the cosmopolitan parlance of liberal universalism and human equality. In Raleigh a biracial jury acquitted Little in only seventy-eight minutes. Although it may not be plausible to attribute the venue change and legal victory entirely to black nationalists, their change in rhetoric is unmistakable and a likely contributor to the trial's outcome.[3] As Little's official spokespersons, North Carolina Black Panthers, along with other nationalists, contended that her story reflected a human experience accessible to anyone, regardless of race, gender, or nationality.

Even so, in many ways cosmopolitan nationalism remained inwardly conservative as it maintained a radical and progressive outlook. This is particularly notable on issues of gender, and especially evident during the defense of Little. In fact the nationalists most vocal in their sympathy and support for Little remained blind to the very issues that a cosmopolitan worldview was expected to confront.

Cosmopolitan Black Nationalism

Nationalist figures Elaine Brown and Huey Newton, along with local leader Larry Little and countless others, depicted Joan Little as the symbol of black womanhood. The Panthers made Joan Little their 1975 Woman of the Year, while Brown described her as "so delicate, so innocent, so naïve about what could possibly go on in that jail cell."[4] That nationalists depicted Little as a symbol of black womanhood (and in turn as a victim of racialized sexual violence) was significant but not unusual. Nationalism writ large, as others have previously argued, was an ideology most comfortable with reducing women to symbols.[5] In black nationalism in particular this trait was starkly reflected. What makes the black nationalist defense of Little noteworthy is that, publicly, it went beyond the deeply paternalist narratives of nation building. Instead, it was a defense ensconced in liberal universalist terms.

The fluidity with which the Panthers moved between the provincial and cosmopolitan was notable; they had to mobilize the grassroots, even as they developed a cogent global message.[6] Yet by trial's end, David G. Du Bois, stepson of cosmopolite incarnate W. E. B. Du Bois, praised the global theme that came together under the leadership of Larry Little. "It was this Chapter's efforts . . . particularly its leader," Du Bois wrote, that "made it possible for decent Americans, Black and White, to rally to JoAnne's defense."[7] The FBI grudgingly agreed, crediting Larry Little for the widespread support and success of the public campaign.[8]

Previous generations of race-conscious leaders may have dismissed sexism as peripheral.[9] But by taking on Joan Little the Panthers saw the necessity, first, of moving sexual oppression from the margins to the mainstream of their analysis, and then of expanding the scope of their analysis to include not only the black American experience but the entire human condition. Joining in this aim was Panther chairwoman Elaine Brown, whose July 18, 1975, speech, "JoAnne Little Acted for Us All," at a rally of perhaps five hundred at the Community Learning Center in East Oakland encapsulated the Panthers' new, broader agenda.[10]

Brown suggested that Little's rape (and the court's cavalier treatment of the alleged crime) was a story "transcending" race, one that resonated with all people. As Brown explained to the crowd, the jailer was "in pursuit of his fantasies of what Black women were all about." But, Brown continued, Little's actions went beyond protecting black womanhood, the black body politic, or the virtue of her "gender." In defending herself that night Little defended human dignity, said Brown. "All of us," in Brown's view, "Black and white, young and old, in all our various ways," were indebted to Joan Little. Little's story was not a racial experience exclusive to blacks but a story, of human suffering, understood immediately and intuitively by all people. In bringing a case against Little, then, the state showed its contempt for human dignity. In prosecuting her, they brought out "the major elements of what is wrong, unequal and unjust in our society." The Panther chairwoman elaborated: posing as interest-free arbiters, U.S. legal experts and policy makers, as well as their counterparts in other Western countries, "would like us to believe . . . that universal morality is always applied," without any prejudice or partiality based on race, class, or gender.[11] Yet in Brown's view, self-professed universalists were never universal enough.[12]

Theirs was a false universalism, Brown argued. Not simply were judges and others far from color blind, but by insisting on race-blind readings of law they ahistoricized the black experience. That is, when it came to law based on the Thirteenth, Fourteenth, and Fifteenth Amendments, status quo leaders blatantly disregarded the framers' original intent. In doing so they threatened the very people these reconstructed rights were designed to protect—the disempowered, especially African Americans.[13]

Brown charged that this came about because the state was ruled by plu-
tocrats whose elitist, antiegalitarian perspective led them to dismiss the individual and collective experiences of all but powerful white' men and their
agents.[14] Universalism should never be so exclusionary as to privilege a set
of rules and a way of life favoring a few individuals over the many—blacks,
women, and the poor. So-called arbiters of law revealed themselves to be
far from objective, however, when they or a member of the class to which
they belonged violated the law. In fact, they personified the moral relativism they ostensibly detested.[15]

Punctuating this moral relativism was Watergate and Richard Nixon,
who fashioned himself gatekeeper, along with J. Edgar Hoover, of the rule
of law and order. That Nixon promised an era of deference to law but
ultimately was alleged to be the nation's most notorious criminal was troubling enough. Emblematic of the favoritism that leaders conferred on one
another was that Ford and "those kind of people," as Brown referred to
Nixon's high-ranking advisers and defenders, refused to hold Nixon accountable to the high standard of justice implied by his own law-and-order
rhetoric, or even to any standard of justice. Brown suggested that Ford
acted as if laws did not apply in Nixon's case. Covering up the cover-up,
Ford erased with the stroke of a pen "all the offenses against the United
States which he, Richard Nixon, has committed" during his term of office.[16] Ford's pardon went beyond the Watergate affair to include Nixon's
exemption from other possible indictments, such as for bombing Cambodia and for escalating the Vietnam War without congressional consent.

Such relativism with respect to law enforcement defied any presupposition
that the society in which this had developed was true to the principles of
modern liberalism. The rigid caste system of the "middle of the hard core"
South, littered with racial and sexual brutality, made it an exceptional
place to make a stand and say "I am a human being," said Brown.[17] But
primitivism, she quickly pointed out, was not restricted to region or class.
To Brown there was a seamless web of barbarity meshing the interests and
values of the bucolic jailer—whom she reviled as a "low-grade and ill-bred
pig . . . a native son of America"—and those of the imperial president.
They were all primitivists in Brown's view. "I have no faith in barbarity. I
have no faith in the followers of Richard Nixon and whatever his name is
in the White House now," she said. Those kinds of people, Brown went on

to say, view the world through the subjective prism of their own political consciousness and motivations. From president to policeman, these public officials embodied an inherent power that afforded them the liberty of setting aside the Constitution at their personal convenience. The ability to control and manipulate law allowed them to satisfy their own self-interest. "It was only in the presence of such barbarity," Brown added, that the courts could begin "to say that JoAnne Little committed a crime."[18] From her modernist perch Brown condemned the courts' presumed fairness as a false objectivity indicative of premodern society—a society invested not in merit and earned reward but in presumed birthrights of racial and material privilege.

There exists another set of laws that is "always applied to the poor and to the people who suffer injustice and oppression throughout this world," according to Brown. Rules were skewed not essentially by race but in relation to the social standing of the parties involved. She argued that the legal system dealt unevenly with different societal groups, and that therefore the state ought to abandon its pretense of neutrality.[19]

Despite the appearance of objectivity and value-free ideology embedded in the legal truism about equality under the law, modern American jurisprudence was grounded in nothing more than political self-interest.[20] In the minds of Brown and Joan Little's defenders, justice and the judicial system were often at odds. This point was stressed at a posttrial discussion at the University of Cincinnati, titled "Justice vs. the Legal System" and featuring Joan Little and attorneys Karen Galloway and Jerry Paul.[21] Social justice required sensitivity to the broader social conditions giving rise to cultural heterogeneity and varying experiences. In contrast, the judicial system operated under a Hegelian sensibility steeped in legal realism, a philosophy of law where self-interest typically drove action. In the post–Warren Court days especially, self-interest for an appointed or elected judge translated into accepting the political reality that an unpopular but just decision might result in professional suicide, leading to threats of impeachment (à la Warren) and public ridicule (e.g., "Set 'em Loose Bruce" Wright) to threats of being voted out of office, as happened in the civil rights South where municipal and state judges were frequently elected officials. All were virtual career-killers for any judge. Judges' response to democratic will, however, was not in the cause of justice but its expense; it was a means of preserving their position in society.

Even so, Brown did not argue that objective truth should be totally rejected. Rather, she argued that truth must be judged from society's broad bottom and not in the sociolegal terms defined by and familiar to those at the narrow top.[22] She offered a competing vision of universalism. Like all universalist visions, hers was exclusionary and dismissed the prevailing standard of universality.[23] Her exclusion stemmed from intolerance for a political and legal authority that regularly dispensed arbitrary and uneven justice. It was a justice that, in Brown's words, allowed the Richard Nixons of America to "get $200,000 to retire on" after insulting democracy through the Watergate break-in and cover-up and after killing millions of Vietnamese people, and that at the same time advocated that the Joan Littles, who defended human dignity against rape, be given the death penalty. As Brown asked: "What would have happened had that been a Black man and had the same kind of circumstances existed? What . . . if . . . white? What . . . if . . . rich?" Freed from the almost Manichaean struggle between black and white, between good and evil, the Panthers now enjoyed the latitude to rationalize their own centrist move toward pragmatic politics. Indeed, by the time the trial ended in August 1975, the Panthers were willing to collude with their erstwhile adversaries, "mainstream" groups and interests—the Democratic Party, antiunion lobbies, the corporate-friendly policies of California Republicans. Speeches in which the Panthers' original animus toward black capitalism was softened underscored their moderating posture. Indeed, the Panthers frequently exhibited an abiding faith in the court system, as is evident in their civil litigation against the government and in their enthusiasm for a million-dollar civil suit filed by Joan Little. Perhaps the most blatant example of the Panthers' efforts to oblige the establishment was their willingness to appease a leading contributor to the Democratic Party by agreeing to the ouster of fellow Panther Erica Huggins as a delegate to the 1976 Democratic National Convention. Brown, and by extension the party, did not represent the dissenting voice of an individual or nihilist group so alienated from the establishment that it had no pragmatic bearings. Rather, throughout the mid-1970s the party increasingly pursued a participatory role in the established political culture. Politics made strange bedfellows, but, as Brown's continued rhetorical assault makes clear, it did not necessarily make enlightened ones.

Brown sought to expose the exclusionism of liberal universalism. In particular she criticized its presumption that it was egalitarian and color blind.

In challenging the courts and the state's threadbare claim to universalism, she called into question the state's assumed fairness. Preserving community remained a goal, but not at the expense of fairness.[24] The legitimacy of the state rested on its ability to protect against the violation of this belief.[25] To be sure, Brown never posited that universal truth was unworkable, nor did she withdraw to the isolationism of postmodernism, in which there was no higher authority than subjectivity.[26] She argued for a more inclusive, though not homogenizing, universalism, a universalism that not only legitimated elites but also validated the experience of the poor and women, both black and white, and the oppressed in general. By isolating what she termed "the political motivations and consciousness of men of power in the United States," Brown staked a nationalist claim to universalism—albeit not the prevailing version of it.

"I am certainly one of Joan Little's peers," Black Panther Party chairwoman Elaine Brown asserted in the course of her July 18 speech in East Oakland. A robed elite, however, ultimately controlled the case. Brown considered how the race, gender, social standing, and material values of those sitting in judgment might be different from Little's, and took exception to those who did not first acknowledge that they thereby might be cut off from disempowered parties, especially African Americans. Never denied the conventional routes to prestige and power, the privileged were not yet capable of navigating these differing and intersecting identities. Nor did they acknowledge that the multilayered identities and values of the privileged and the disempowered intertwined, reinforced one another on the way, and produced multiple loyalties. They consequently did not appreciate the racial and class-charged quality of the world and how differing social and racial orbits affected how people saw themselves and the world around them. Such were the "contextual elitist" obstacles, generally referred to by social theorist Patricia Hill Collins as both Eurocentric and masculine, which prevented white men in particular from impartially deciding Little's fate.[27] In contrast, Brown's speech mirrored a positivist discourse that allowed for scientific and objective descriptions, which enveloped (ostensibly without privileging) varying cultural assumptions, value judgments, experiences, emotions, and social realities.[28] Positive discourse meant, in essence, encouraging judges to view the case from the victims' perspective, and asserting Little's freedom to defend herself against Alligood by all means necessary.

Given that judges were unwilling to accept their own subjectivity and incapable of creating a safe and critical distance between themselves and the "objects" they studied—in this case, the oppositional actions of Joan Little—their own culture and personal experience influenced judges to organize and process information in a color- and class-conscious way.[29] Further undermining their legitimacy in Brown's eyes was their narrow claim to universalism. They preferred to assert that they were neutral and, by implication, capable of objectively judging Little's guilt or innocence. Without a willingness to acknowledge broader social contexts—for example, the experience of growing up poor, black, and female—self-described universalists could never adequately comprehend why Little did what she did; therefore they could never even broach the issue of whether Little acted in a justifiable and rational way.[30] One needed to be one of the people to truly understand what Brown meant when she pronounced that "Little defended us all." "All power to the people," Brown exclaimed, closing her speech with that mantra as a final reminder that it was the common, not the particular, that brought them together.

Brown's speech came during the mid-1970s, in a period when the nation's confidence in government was, according to Gallup public opinion polls at the time, at an all-time low and showed signs of plummeting even further.[31] Great expectations formed during a more idealistic period had begun to deteriorate into grand disillusionment, captured in newspaper reports that the FBI had long been spying on private citizens, including Martin Luther King Jr. and Robert Kennedy. The Senate and House, taking measures to arrest the erosion of public trust in government, introduced a sea change in government philosophy toward self-regulation by, for example, abolishing the House Committee on Internal Security and replacing it with senate and house government oversight committees.

Seeking ways to buoy public confidence, Congress enacted a series of amendments to the Freedom of Information Act. Likewise, house and senate committees continued with sweeping investigations that further documented abuses by the CIA as well as the FBI. Their exposure of covert activities escalated the climate of skepticism and suspicion.[32] Put simply, post-Watergate and post-Vietnam America produced a society gripped by mistrust of the U.S. government and its stewards. In her July 18 speech Brown reflected the public's growing skepticism toward politics and government.

A posttrial public message from Huey Newton, still in Cuba, can be seen as building on Brown's articulation of a nationalist claim to liberal universalism. This message, read aloud for Newton by David Du Bois, praised Joan Little for following the historic models of Harriet Tubman, Sojourner Truth, and, Newton added, George Jackson, a Panther organizer and murdered prisoner. Like them, "JoAnne set an example for people of today." Newton described Little's actions as a political act emerging from her particular circumstance but intended for the whole world. "She cried: No more abuse to humankind."[33] The Panthers' public position on the Little case appeared to be a logical outgrowth from their broader organizational commitment to liberal universalism and cosmopolitan nationalism.

Brown, Newton, and the entire BPP proposed an alternative universalist vision, a more democratic vision that offered, according to one political theorist, a "critique of universal standards [that] rested on the paradox that the state privileged certain individuals or groups of individuals. In other words, it is a critique of those standards for not being universalist enough!" What the party wondered aloud was why the state simply could not be all encompassing and more open. Consequently, rather than abandoning or opposing universalism, the "critique [was] itself based on an implicit universal valuation, albeit one that aims to be more inclusive than the ones critiqued."[34] Brown's universal appeal sat squarely with the Panthers' formal political commitment to the values of cosmopolitanism, which it embraced in the form of intercommunalism. Intercommunalism was a political philosophy that sought to balance openness to all with an operational commitment to black self-determination.

The most internationally oriented of all Black Power groups, the party had forged solidarity committees and coordinated activities in Denmark, Belgium, Britain, France, and West Germany. Relations were also fostered with the Pacific Rim countries of North Vietnam, Australia, North Korea, and China. Many of these nations' U.S. embassies regularly subscribed to the Panther newspaper. Theirs was a "people's diplomacy," leading Panthers would say, which believed in close cooperation across racial and cultural boundaries. The Panthers' organizational track record in the United States also lived up to the universalist ethos of inclusion. In fact, coining its relationship with peoples of color and progressive whites as the Rainbow Coalition, the party ceased referring in public to their white male enemies (e.g., Nixon) as "faggots" and "punks." It was also recognized as the first nongay black organization to address black homophobia by forging open alliances with the gay, lesbian, and women's movements.[35] By discarding a variety of rigid identity politics, they successfully wooed leading cosmopolitans, both foreign and domestic, including Leonard Bernstein, Jane Fonda, and Jean Genet. Panther experts Charles E. Jones and Judson L. Jeffries forcefully argue that the party "represented a model for genuine multiculturalism."[36]

The tenure of David Du Bois as the editor-in-chief of the *Black Panther Intercommunal Newspaper*, better known as simply *Black Panther*, from 1972 to 1976 sealed the party's institutional commitment to liberal universalism. Under Du Bois the paper reconfigured its coverage to include an ever-increasing number of subjects, even as the theme of "radical revolution now"—once the paper's main focus—virtually vanished. On Du Bois's watch the party organ grafted ideas and cited articles from mainstream international and national media, including the *New York Times*, the *Los Angeles Times*, and the *Washington Post*. He promoted a progressive ideology "that cuts across all color lines," claimed JoNina Abron, the paper's final editor. The party's embrace of this "aging bourgeois outsider," as Du Bois called himself, indicated its growing inclusiveness and tilt toward a markedly cosmopolitan worldview.[37]

Like those of other Panthers, his writings on Joan Little advanced a cosmopolitan nationalist perspective. "The JoAnne Little trial is making history," Du Bois wrote in a *Black Panther* editorial just prior to the verdict. "The people, through their enthusiastic nationwide support of JoAnne, have sternly warned would-be rapists, police departments and district attorney's offices across this country that we will not tolerate the chauvinistic and flippant attitude generally taken toward rape cases. . . . Elaine Brown has correctly stated that JoAnne Little acted for us all when she killed Clarence Alligood. The People realized that, and therefore the power of the people will set JoAnne Little free."[38] Du Bois later explained that "the people" meant all "humanity and dignity of all Black People, poor and oppressed humankind."[39] The Black Panthers were not exceptional in this view; rather, they were typical of many black nationalist groups who also supported Little.

Always on the cosmopolitan cusp of black nationalist thought and action, the BPP was poised to support Joan Little in liberal universalist language, and was destined to attract a broad cross section of supporters in the process.[40] Perhaps what is more instructive is that other nationalist groups, groups ostensibly less progressive, did the same. Cultural black nationalists of long standing expressed universalist sentiments, a striking change given their promotion of racial essentialism and of the preservation of traditional African customs and practices. Advocating a positive role for the state, the signature feature of New Deal and post–New Deal liberalism, had not generally been part of their agenda. That cultural nationalists as well as left nationalists like the Panthers coalesced over the Little case is indicative of the convergence of different strains of black nationalist ideology by the mid-1970s.

Ron Karenga (named "Maulana," Swahili for "Master teacher," by his fellow nationalists), titular head of cultural nationalism in America, deployed the most aggressive universalist language in support of Little. Appearing in the July/August 1975 issue of the *Black Scholar*, his essay "In Defense of Sis. Joanne: For Ourselves and History" was addressed largely to African Americans. Rather than repeat the classic "close ranks" nationalist bromide, he urged expanded dialogue, telling readers to grasp the broader human relevance of the case. The "issues involved have a human scope, significance and content," Karenga wrote. It was the obligation of fellow black nationalists, Karenga added, to "free ourselves intellectually and emotionally. . . . [The purpose is] to interpret . . . the world and this trial . . . in a rational and radical way."[41]

Like Brown, Karenga drew no substantive distinction between southern justice and justice outside the South. Southern justice was an outgrowth of the exploitative relations and broader prejudices equally present in national institutions and systems of government. "The jailer, and by extension, the town, were caught with their pants off," Karenga wrote. But so had the entire federal system of government, which Karenga found complicit in denying Little's "human need for freedom."[42]

There was nothing unusual in Karenga's condemnation of America or his defense of black women.[43] His exposition, however, was unique because of its cosmopolitan underpinning: it offered a theory of justice on the basis not so much of a gender or nationalist appraisal but of universal rights.[44] Coming from the leader of the nation's largest cultural nationalist organization, US, a more dramatic philosophical departure was unfathomable. Though long credited with assailing as the "devil's concept" the belief that women are equal to men, Karenga's essay indicated a clear ideological shift.[45] No longer a drum major for complementary gender-role theory, Karenga now trumpeted human value and human fullness: "The human value and social validity of anything can be measured by the kind of relations it creates, by how it supports and extends freedom and assists us in our struggle for human fullness. . . . No institution or system [of government] is self-validating, but must be judged by its contribution to the struggle for human freedom and fullness."[46]

Gone were preconceived gender roles for men and women. Gone too was the idea that men and women existed to function as parts of a whole. In place of that Karenga stressed to potential Little sympathizers the importance of a broader commitment to full human equality. Freedom and fullness as envisaged by Karenga meant neither the state treating citizens as equals nor the state's maintenance of a value-neutral posture toward individuals and their interactions with institutions such as laws and religion. Karenga continued pressing for enlightened state action that valued its obligation to a positive social environment where the polity's most vulnerable members would become full and active participants.[47] It was the state's responsibility to advance its citizenry's pursuit of full humanity. Justice required an activist political and judicial process, not one satisfied with a laissez-faire attitude. Anything less represented an abrogation of the state's social pact with its citizens. Through its political, social, and legal institutions, the state had an ongoing responsibility to presume that people were equal under the law and to promote the belief that they were. If the state's legitimacy and civic order were to be maintained, the state had to pursue the elusive ideal of the perfectibility of its citizens.[48] After all, Karenga wrote, the ultimate measure of any state should be its ability to "extend" and "assist" the struggle for human fullness.

Like Brown, Karenga muted the concept of the state as value free. The fact that Little had been the victim of racial, sexual, and class violence while in public custody—and was then indicted for defending herself—made plain that the state was an active participant in peoples' lives. Far from neutral, the state actually advanced racial and class prejudices while denying to others "the realization of human freedom in its fullest and most profound sense."[49] How did the state arrest this realization? Agents of the state, the courts in this instance, did it by intervening and legally denying Little's right of resistance. Karenga believed there were transcendent laws to be considered. In arguing for an expanded view of natural rights, he posited that the right of resistance was a natural law that eclipsed the scope of courts, legislatures, and even national boundaries. Resistance was a law with universal prerogative, he said: "It is everywhere valid, valuable and vital to human life and development." This instance of psychocultural violence against the defenseless Little captured the reality of the government's aggression toward any efforts to correcting human relations that were unequal, exploitative, and oppressive. Little not only became a victim of gender violence. She was made, as Karenga wrote, "a victim of [the state] and [its] restrictions on human freedom."[50]

Rather than express waning faith in building an international consensus, Karenga affirmed it. Racial solidarity was important to Karenga, but equally important was the business of drawing on a global perspective in order to expand what one author has termed "the circle of we."[51] As Karenga said, "let our people" but also "the world know the real reasons" that Little's pursuit of full humanity and freedom was arrested by the state.[52] As he continued to reject racial parochialism, Karenga stressed the universal theme of Little's plight.

Of course Joan Little was "a symbol of black womanhood," Karenga stated almost parenthetically. But she also personified, for men and women everywhere, resistance to "dehumanizing acts and assumptions negative to their freedom and human fullness." "All personal resistance," Karenga reiterated, is "connected . . . to the larger struggle for our freedom and human fullness." This true or "substantive freedom" went beyond providing the Joan Littles of the world basic political and civil rights.[53] True freedom viewed freedom as a means to economic opportunity, social opportunities, and protective security, not merely as an end in itself.[54] From the perspective of Karenga and other nationalists, however, "America" had failed to facilitate either human freedom or fullness and had actually warped and stunted it.[55] America had failed to provide for Little, and, by extension, for the masses of black Americans, the more complete human experience required by the cosmopolitanism that America claimed.

Because of their emphasis on cosmopolitanism, Black American and African nationalists are credited widely for the prominent rise and rapid acceptance of this new view, which was well received in the mid-to-late 1970s, especially among U.S. sociologists and other social scientists.[56] In proposing coalitions based on common principles and raising universalist calls for human fullness and gender equity, Karenga, the Black Panthers, and other nationalists were speaking the language of an enlightened black nationalism. Like other liberal nationalists they preached a message of accepting difference.[57] In a word, they were—or at least had the face and expression of—cosmopolitan nationalists.

Gendered Discontents

Although the rhetoric of black nationalists changed, their deeds, both before and during the trial, suggested values contrary to the enlightened nationalism that they now espoused.[58] With disturbing regularity, nationalists fell victim to the atavistic trappings of patriarchy and chauvinism, even as they publicly pronounced otherwise.[59] Little's official spokespersons, the Panthers, proved a classic example of this. It was the commonness of "macho attitudes" within its ranks, claimed Elaine Brown, that finally "destroyed the Black Panthers."[60] The dissonance between Panther rhetoric on gender and the abuse female members suffered at the hands of male cohorts was so pervasive, said one party confidant, Martin Kenner, that "it literally drove Black Panther women like Elaine Brown crazy."[61] Kenner's psychological assessment aside, it does hint at the stark difference between ideology and practice among many of the nationalist faithfuls supporting Little.

One telling scene was a tension-filled meeting between Nation of Islam (NOI) minister Louis Farrakhan and Huey Newton. Their respective groups met out of a desire to smooth out organizational differences and to advance black solidarity. As Elaine Brown remembered it, Newton sought common ground with the NOI minister by genuflecting to the group's concerns about the emasculation of the party. Eager to please, Newton suggested that Panther women dress in "long skirts and long sleeved blouses, befitting some ideal look of a Muslim woman." Brown, one of two women present at the meeting, added: "She was to serve tea; I was to take notes—appropriate roles for us as women, Huey joked." Not surprisingly, Brown, Newton's sometime girlfriend, mused by night's end: "Huey and Farrakhan looked . . . liked mirror images of each other."[62]

Newton appeared unwilling to confront male sexist attitudes inside the black community. Unlike Farrakhan, however, who offered no concessions to sexual equality, Newton bowed to NOI's conservative gender conventions *after* the 1971 publication of his watershed pamphlet, *The Women's Liberation and Gay Liberation Movement.* Admiring it as a landmark BPP statement marking its transition toward postchauvinist views regarding women and homosexuality, some even suggested Newton's tract had thrust the party into the vanguard of the entire New Left on gender issues. Despite this, Newton showed no qualms about sacrificing party principles to Farrakhan or about the patriarchal notions associated with his brand of nationalism. If Newton, the author of the nationalist movement's most forward-looking statement on women and gender, could so blithely retreat to the fail-safe measure of affirming gender roles in order to spare his macho image, then where did that leave others *not* touting such "enlightened" manifestos?

Underlying the actions of Newton and the apparent attitudes of the rank and file was the tacit belief in and search for black male redemption. Among some Black Power activists it was commonly believed that black men needed to assert their patriarchal identity to compensate for the emasculation they suffered as a result of slavery and its aftermath, and then in turn to restore order to the black family and society. At times, though, black men's expression of their masculinity was so far from benefiting the black family and society that black women in particular felt it as a weapon directed against them.[63] Few knew this better than Kathleen Cleaver, who told Julia Herve in a 1971 interview: "For black men . . . to regain a sense of manhood, they many times took out their resentment of their position against their own black women."[64] It also undoubtedly contributed to the male backlash against female leaders. This appeared to be the case both during and after 1971.

By 1971 women reportedly led half of all branches and chapters of the Black Panther Party.[65] Black women were the heads or high-ranking leaders of prominent affiliates in Los Angeles, Seattle, Chicago, East St. Louis, Cleveland, Boston, and Winston-Salem.[66] The ascendancy of women to leadership roles was the result not so much of Panther initiatives promoting equality and diversity in the workplace as of the attrition of male membership—a byproduct, largely, of law enforcement's war on the Panthers.[67] As one Panther summed up the men's grudging acceptance of female authority, they had no choice, since all the Panther men were imprisoned. According to party insider Masai Hewitt, when it came down to a choice between different women for the same position, often their physical attractiveness mattered as much as their ability and drive.[68]

Women at the local, state, and national levels of the party did not simply stave off organizational collapse after 1971, they were instrumental in planning and implementing the party's critical transition to mainstream electoral politics. Indeed, the growing number of women taking visible leadership roles headed a larger organizational shift, which came about through a series of evolving stands on electoral politics, armed revolution, and even capitalism. By the fall of 1974 the BPP had its first female chair, who told the media, "members aren't ris[ing] to overthrow [the] establishment" anymore.[69] Under Elaine Brown's leadership in the mid-1970s, the Panthers sent delegates to the Democratic National Convention and severed their storied relations with the generation's best-known black Red, Angela Davis. In publicly cutting ties with Davis the Panthers followed the pattern set a quarter century earlier by the NAACP and key Jewish groups, who were eager to prove their civic nationalist bona fides. Caught up in cold war currents, Panthers explicitly disparaged the Communist Party and singled out for particular rebuke those individual Communists who "shared their ethnic or racial background."[70] Similarly, Tracye Matthews writes that as Panther women increasingly held key leadership roles, the types of activities they focused on, often centering on nurturing, child care, and transmitting morals, compelled a rethinking of what is political.[71]

The composition of party membership continued to approach parity between the sexes—approximately 45 percent of party members in 1972 and 1973 were women. The presence of so many talented, college-educated women seemingly fueled a male Panther backlash.[72] This dynamic was noted by Angela D. LeBlanc-Ernest, historian and director of Stanford's Black Panther Party Research Project, who noted that "the proliferation of female leadership occurred in the midst of gender inequality" inside the party.[73] Belligerent attitudes and behavior persisted in part because party leadership did little to challenge the "baggage" male members brought into the organization. With respect to women, "I had the same attitude in the party as I had on the street," said one Panther who remained a member throughout the BPP's involvement in the Little movement. The women's movement of the 1960s and 1970s had no discernible influence on the Panthers of that period, member Bobby Bowen recollected.[74] Moreover, those speaking out against sexism were liable to face retribution from party superiors. One male member of the central committee, for example, was charged with insubordination and then demoted for speaking out about internal injustices against, as Newton called them, those "bitches and whores."[75] In the early and mid-1970s it "was not a fight against sexism," according to Hewitt, minister of education for the party at the time.[76] "What we [didn't] want is force and intimidation," which, however, is precisely what they got around the time of the Little trial.

The Little movement took place amid distressing stories of male Panther leaders, including Huey Newton, exploiting and abusing black women. In August 1974, just prior to the breaking of the Little story, Newton was the lead suspect for the murder of Kathleen Smith, a seventeen-year-old black teenager who was shot, allegedly for calling Newton "baby" in public.[77] Insisting that he had been framed, Newton fled to Cuba, from which he made pronouncements about the heroism of Joan Little. Following his repatriation in 1977, he was publicly accused of having raped and beaten Carol Rucker—a Panther coworker long respected for her dedication to the Sickle Cell Anemia Clinic—before he fled the country.[78] Around the same time, Newton also faced allegations that he attacked Hazel Mack, a Winston-Salem Panther, during her stay in Oakland. Mack had been a student at the University of North Carolina who left Chapel Hill to work for the BPP full-time in the late 1960s. News of her attack devastated the chapter's morale. After Newton's alleged assault, Mack left the party for good.[79] Not surprisingly, Elaine Brown, citing the "re-emergence" of chauvinist attitudes, promptly resigned as party chair when Newton returned to the United States in November 1977.[80]

The party at large was awash with accounts of sexual exploitation. Male Panthers spurned by a female party member might associate her rejection with reifying black emasculation: "Comrade sister. You do the same thing to me that the white man does. You're fucking with my manhood." Members of the central committee, especially prior to Brown's leadership, could extort sex from women by promising to promote them. At least one member of the committee argued that a woman's rejection of a party member's sexual advances was legitimate grounds for her expulsion. It was not uncommon to hear male members comment, as one Panther put it, "All the women in the party was walking p——," an attitude that eerily mirrored the offensive comments and threats jailers like Alligood regularly hurled at Little and other female captives.[81] In an effort to improve party finances during the time of the Little campaign, some female members were actually prostituted.[82] In sum, male-female relations within the party were defined by the assertion of the men that they could control the bodies and the sexuality of the women. By winter 1974, organizational policies instructed members on such issues as dating outside the party and the use of birth control. Still, one man felt that during his membership in the party, which included the Little case and its aftermath, "there was no attempt on the part of the leadership, or no educational attempt, to talk about oppression of women, the principal[ed] relationship that men and women should have."[83]

Du Bois's interview with Joan Little three weeks after her acquittal provides a case in point. Although the highly respected *Black Panther* editor had previously editorialized about the far-reaching effects of the Little trial on chauvinism and on flippant attitudes toward sexual violence, Du Bois was slow to grapple with or even discuss its presence within black America—let alone within the party itself. Domestic violence and other intraracial gender issues "faded to black" during Du Bois's posttrial interview with Little, when nearly every other subject—black communists, white feminists, organizing strategies, the prison rights movement, and so on—was explored. What had the potential to be a forum in which chauvinist attitudes within the black community could be examined ultimately degenerated into Du Bois pillorying Angela Davis, a black Communist. (Davis's essay "JoAnne Little: The Dialectics of Rape," appearing in the June 1975 issue of *Ms.*, concluded with a unity call, but not before asking about the problem of rape within the black community.)[84] Certainly the Black Panther Party had an interest in dramatizing its fundamental differences with Davis and Communists generally. Party officials considered Davis's and Communists' views generally to be highly damaging to the interests of black people, but Du Bois's focus on Davis and Communism occluded the issue of sexual exploitation, a subject more familiar to readers and central in freeing Little.[85]

Not once during his interview of Little did Du Bois broach the issues of intraracial sexual abuse or, more generally, of male-female relations among blacks. Given that *Black Panther* in its extensive reporting on Little featured her as representative of black womanhood and her case as representative of the black woman's troika of race, gender, and class, it is significant that Du Bois did not take the opportunity to plumb Little's views on these issues.

Flippant attitudes toward gender violence in the black community did not go completely unvisited. "The attitudes of black men . . . are put sharply into focus in this highly controversial case," wrote Evangeline Grant Redding, a North Carolina black woman activist and author who penned a 1976 pamphlet on the problems black women encountered with men within and beyond their race. Many of the black men she knew agreed, in effect, with their white male counterparts in seeing Little as "a nappy headed, evil, loud mouth Sapphire." Black discussants of a more dignified persuasion settled in for round-table discussions, each taking turns "describing, and enjoying, his impression of how the actual events took place in his mind," observed Redding. Still, some were ambivalent about what had transpired. Redding quoted one black man "consoling" his tearful wife: "Now, Baby, Alligood didn't actually rape the girl, he just made her suck his peter."[86]

Compounding the problem was the unwillingness of the legal system to take seriously the sexual vulnerability of black women, whether the assailant was white or black. Published in October 1975, a survey of sexual assault sentencing quantified the legal consequences for men convicted in crimes of intraracial sexual violence. The study revealed that 47 percent of all black men convicted for criminal assault on black women were immediately released on probation. The average sentence received by black men was 4.2 years if the victim was black, and 16.4 years if the victim was white.[87] If one judge's frightening response to such uneven dispensation of justice is taken at face value, the courts could not be counted on to provide equal protection for black women anytime soon: "With the Negro community, you really have to redefine rape. You never know about them."[88] Rather than address such concerns, Larry Little, as both the coordinator of the Winston-Salem chapter of the BPP and as national spokesman of the Joan Little Defense Committee, opted for obfuscation by trying to throw the spotlight on black male victimization. "If Joan Little had been a white woman and stabbed a Black man, she would have gotten the medal of honor," Little boldly told four hundred protestors in Richmond.[89] Evidence did suggest that, when compared to white men facing the same charges, black men were disproportionately threatened with prosecution and conviction, but that inequity did not obviate the need for a discussion of sexual abuse and violence in the black community, especially in light of the blatant coercion and conflict that appeared to exist.[90]

"Sisterhood" was a relative term. Despite the ubiquitous refrains to Little as "Sister" Joan and a "symbol of black womanhood," black women often had less standing when the aggressor was also black and a party member. One woman, a fifteen-year-old runaway who joined the Panthers just as the Little movement began to develop, later recounted the psychological abuse and physical threats she experienced in the party. These included a moment when the national spokesperson allegedly put a gun to her head. "Money was tight," she remembered. "He thought I should bring in more."[91] Episodes like the above did not deter Celine Chenier, an early devotee of the Little movement and a longtime state activist. "The Panthers have a way of dealing with women," said Chenier about the party, and about Little's spokesperson in particular.[92] Indeed, Chenier and others were probably taken aback less by the actual acts of violence than by Hewitt's assertion that the party's stance on sexism supported the eradication of intimidation and force.

When Larry Little praised black entertainers performing at a benefit concert for "putting Joanne Little's self-interest" ahead of their own material gain, some female party members found it brazen and offensive, as he resided in a lavish townhouse (complete with tennis court and swimming pool) while his party chapter and its community service projects were suffering financially.[93] "He was a grandstander," according to women ranging from the rank and file to party chair Elaine Brown. "There was no limelight for him," Brown said of the postacquittal phase, "If you think you're a star, and there's no limelight, what do you do?"[94] These comments would precipitate Larry Little's departure from the party in February 1976, a departure still shrouded in controversy.

Whether Larry Little was ousted because of his insubordination to Brown or quit to avoid corporal punishment remained a subject of internal debate. In either case his departure reveals how the party's culture of dissembling—members publicly cultivated behaviors that created an appearance of openness while shielding their inner lives and selves—cut both ways. Brown, whose authority was constantly questioned and threatened by men within the party, needed to show force in order to be respected and taken seriously. Real and perceived insubordination was handled swiftly. Like other male Panthers, Little appeared to have problems with Brown's leadership: "I saw some jealousy; some people thought that women had [their] place," a local party member and grassroots organizer of the Joan

Little movement recalled. "You [could] tell there was tension [between Brown and Larry Little]. If her name was mentioned, he'd say she's not doing what the chairman [Newton] wants."[95]

As for Larry Little, his exit suggests the degree to which black men were threatened and felt their masculinity circumscribed by the culture of dissemblance. Publicly, Larry Little resigned, according to the *Winston-Salem Sentinel*, for "political and personal reasons."[96] In private years later he explained that he left in fear of the extreme physical punishment ordered by Elaine Brown after she demanded that he fly to California to address questions of insubordination. Strong and fearless in public, male Panthers cowered, and rightly so, facing Brown's so-called "goon squad," a group whose purpose was to keep order and internal party discipline. The goon squad's presence, Brown claimed, was all the more necessary because male Panthers were hostile to female members, whose numbers and influence were growing. A man who admitted he feared Brown's power would incur the insult that he was soft, which may account for Little's long silence on the topic.[97] In sharp contrast, James Baldwin, whose open homosexuality made him among the least likely to engage in dissemblance, was admired by Charles Zollicoffer and others as Joan Little's most sincere supporter.[98] These examples of dissonance between men and women in the BPP are typical of the attitude and behavior that men in the party brought to issues relating to sex and sexism.

Simply isolating the Panthers as being the only Black Power group with such attitudes toward women would be unfair and misleading. In a broader sense the party was widely regarded as the black activist group most committed to gender equality. When compared to women in other organizations in the Black Power movement, recalled Assata Shakur, Black Panther women were at least "moderately liberated."[99] Any blanket indictment that the Panthers were sexist and misogynist would have to be qualified by, for example, their endorsement of Congresswoman Shirley Chisholm for president in 1972 and the particular contribution of Jean Genet, a noted French playwright and avowed homosexual, as a party emissary at more than a dozen universities during his four-month visit to the United States in February 1970.[100] "No black woman would report being raped by a white man to the police," one black female respondent told the questioners in a study of rape in Oakland during the early 1970s. Searching for justice, she added, they "might report it to the Panthers."[101] Where, though, would a woman turn if the man were a member of the party or of groups that espoused similarly enlightened views on gender equality?

Rumors regarding sexual harassment surrounded another of Joan Little's more visible defenders, the Rev. Benjamin F. Chavis Jr. of the Wilmington Ten.[102] To defenders of Little and of the Wilmington Ten, each trial reinforced the other as textbook cases of racial injustice and the struggle for human rights.[103] Activists targeted the state government, which they claimed willfully violated the civil and human rights of the defendants. Speeches, public demonstrations, and political essays were regularly interlaced with demands for the release of the Wilmington Ten and with exhortations to fight for Joan Little.[104]

Out of the Wilmington case emerged Chavis, whose leading role propelled him to the fore of the black nationalist struggle.[105] Young, black, and relatively obscure, this North Carolinian minister of the United Church of Christ became one of the most famous political prisoners in the world.[106] His politically inspired prosecution, combined with his tireless efforts for economic and social justice, would eventually earn for Chavis numerous international and human rights awards.[107] As a leading Black Power spokesperson and a coming figure on the world stage, Chavis lent his support to several causes célèbres and progressive social movements, including the women's movement. Some twenty years after Little, in fact, an embattled Chavis reminded critics of what he referred to as "my strong opposition and long history of defending victims of racial and sexual discrimination"; a history of militant advocacy that began at the national level with his support of Joan Little.[108]

Freed on bail, Chavis spoke at numerous protest rallies for Little throughout the spring and summer of 1975. From the steps of the nation's capitol to the courthouse steps in Raleigh, Chavis engaged in his steely rhetorical defense of Little against the abuse of power.[109] Ironically, it was amid concerns about his own abuse of power against women that Chavis spoke out in support of Little to defend herself by any means necessary. Even then, one prominent member of the Little team privately said, Chavis's inclination toward sexual impropriety was well known. Throughout his career Chavis would be the object of harassment reports that were contemporaneous with his public advocacy against sexual harassment and for women's rights.

Struggles with sexual opportunism and harassment, it appears, stemmed from his days as a member of the Wilmington Ten in the early 1970s. The specter of sexual impropriety shadowed his career. Despite the damage it did to his reputation, Chavis actually "savor[ed] this persona," according to Abiola Sinclair, editor and publisher of *Black History Magazine*.[110] His troubling pattern of behavior was not broken until decades later, when a lawsuit accusing him of sexual harassment and discrimination was filed after he attempted and failed to cover up reports that he "coerced a [subordinate employee] woman into having . . . sex" at a hotel in downtown Washington, D.C.[111]

Chavis's reply to the lawsuit invoked vivid imagery: "I'm a victim of a lynching." Chavis then urged that others, once again, judge him by his record of public service: "I have spent 34 years of my life . . . fighting against racial and sexual injustice."[112] Yet for most of that period his personal aggression against women went unaddressed publicly.[113] Apparently years of concealment had so emboldened Chavis that he made a remarkable confession to an audience at Columbia University on April 18, 2000. What he regretted most about the hotel incident, he told them, was not the harassment itself and his payoff to the woman to keep silent about it, nor was it the allegations of others that he was guilty of sexual discrimination. Rather, what he regretted most was that he did not inform the NAACP board, which appointed him executive director in 1993, about his sexual harassment settlement with complainant Mary Stansel. And why did he regret not telling them? Because he probably could have told them with impunity, since the "small number of Board members [who first] knew" about the private settlement of the sexual harassment charge had, according to Chavis, taken little if any action.[114]

Why were progressive black leaders, both female and male, silent about a leader whose career was littered with troubling accusations of sexual opportunism and negative treatment of female subordinates?[115] Perhaps they feared that questioning Chavis would expose them to the charge that they were "betrayers of the black nation," as Chavis reflexively branded Stansel's defenders. Perhaps loyalists were swayed by Chavis's all-too-familiar appeal to them to close ranks. It was a time not to succumb to the divisive forces threatening black America; it was a time for racial unity.[116] Just as likely, the failure of black leaders to challenge the track record of Chavis and of others reflected a longstanding willingness, as reporter Julianne Malveaux would write, to excuse "flawed judgments because black men have been denied leadership opportunities in other arenas."[117]

Decades-long reticence could also have stemmed from a deep-seated, tacit belief that black women *did* possess lax morals and a welfare mentality—a stereotype that Chavis's camp invoked during court proceedings, Stansel's law degree notwithstanding. Stansel was portrayed as "simply attempting to extract monies from the NAACP to avoid having to work." The highly suggestive imagery employed in Chavis's defense was even more damaging given the tenor of the ongoing political debate over national welfare reform.[118] Moreover, the excuses and the silence of Chavis's contemporaries added another baleful element to the story of his public fall, which came at the apogee of his personal success and at a propitious moment during the civil rights movement.[119]

The response of cultural nationalists to the Joan Little case was notable for their willingness to reappraise their traditional patriarchal views. Cultural nationalists had greatly evolved since groups like the Karenga-backed Committee for United Newark (CFUN) published pamphlets in the early 1970s that stated that "the value of men and women can be seen as in the value of gold and silver—they are not equal but both have great value."[120] By the time of the Little case the paladins of the cultural nationalist movement—most notably Amiri Baraka, Haki Madhubuti, and Maulana Karenga—had publicly denounced sexism within their organizations and the black community at large.[121] In fact their response to Little demonstrated "the degree to which cultural nationalists took seriously the issues raised by black women in the struggle" for gender and racial justice, according to historian Komozi Woodard.[122] But did it really?

Of the leading cultural nationalists, no one offered more aggressive commentary on and support for Little than Karenga. As is evidenced in an April 1975 interview published in *New York* magazine, Karenga brought his enlightened critiques to bear on modern cultural nationalism generally. Particularly chided by Karenga were fellow culturalists he considered less progressive, including Haki Madhubuti, "for mask[ing] contradictions among blacks." In retrospect Karenga himself appears to have benefited as much as anyone from the contradictions—between liberal, enlightened rhetoric and personal behavior—that characterized the black nationalist movement with respect to women's rights.[123]

"The first requirement," Karenga had told nationalists and the public at large in making his case for Little, "is to accept and support [Joan's Little's] account of what actually happened." On March 26, 1971, Karenga was convicted of assaulting two black women but demanded no comparable presumption of innocence for them as he did for Joan Little. Charged with sexual torture, he displayed not the slightest regret or compassion while his follower Imamu Clyde Halisi discredited the accusers and their account of events. Halisi was also dismissive about the court proceedings, which largely revolved around the story of two black women held hostage and sexually abused in Karenga's Southern California home—it was "a circus from beginning to end . . . [that] easily could have been put on by Barnum and Bailey." Just the thought of the Master Teacher engaged in any act, consensual or otherwise, with these two black women repulsed an apparently incredulous Halisi. "What could be more distasteful?" he asked *Black Scholar* readers.[124]

Almost as distasteful to Karenga's defenders was the continuing character "attack on black leaders" by the state and the media. The highly negative image of Karenga was the consequence of these attacks, Halisi argued. In "disassembling any positive projection" of him, the media and the state had successfully built "this myth of Maulana" and his "thuggish" followers. Now Halisi would reply with a character assault of his own. Halisi's first reaction was to win Karenga's freedom by publicly assailing female defendants and witnesses, questioning their trustworthiness and reliability by invoking caricatures of black females: one easily gulled, the other full of guile.[125] For testifying that she "heard screams coming from the garage where her [then] husband [Ron Karenga] and the codefendants were holding the women hostages," Haiba Karenga was discounted as a "frightened and intimidated" state witness.[126] Similarly, the testimony of the alleged victim was portrayed as a deceptive and manipulative female desperate to arrange a deal to escape her own criminal charge of theft. Halisi also raised questions about the victim's promiscuity. After all, he pointed out, Deborah Jones, erstwhile member of US, had leveled the same charges only a short while ago—and not, Halisi added, against just one man but "against a group of persons."[127]

Jones, Haiba Karenga, and those siding with them were labeled race traitors. The fact was that Maulana Karenga was being prosecuted for his seven years of nation building and "loyalty to black people and black values," Halisi maintained. In contrast the two black women codefendants and Karenga's estranged wife, as their speaking out proved, had no such racial loyalty or consciousness. Neither did the predominantly black jury, which convicted Karenga. Karenga partisans assumed that his record of public service nullified his alleged transgressions, that the jury would not "overlook . . . the impressive list of contributions Maulana has made" to black America. Shocked at the verdict, Halisi asked rhetorically: how serious could the crime of felonious sexual assault be? Karenga deserved probation at most, particularly given the parties involved. Not surprisingly, Halisi, national chairman of us, Black Power's most enduring institution of cultural nationalism, failed to read the events of March 1971 in light of the complex and contradictory sexual politics that underlay Karenga's behavior and his teaching.

What Halisi failed to acknowledge in his statement in the *Black Scholar* was that Karenga's abusive treatment of women, from the late 1960s through his conviction and ten-year sentence for sexual torture of a woman in 1971, had grown to almost legendary proportions. Also conspicuously absent from Halisi's statement was mention of the second female defendant, Gill Davis, whose account appeared to be devastating to Karenga's case.[128] According to Amiri Baraka, head of the Committee for United Newark, a group that "bore the mark of Ron Karenga's us Organization," Maulana's doctrine and social practices regarding women were "so far out I never attempted to bring it to Newark."[129] When details of Karenga's past abuses reached the East Coast, historians Robin Kelley and Betsy Esch tell us, it so revolted CFUN members that it threatened to break the group's relationship with him.[130] Not until Amina Baraka struggled with her husband, Amiri, over these views did he begin to reevaluate Maulanaism and CFUN's organizational relationship with us.[131]

That the *Black Scholar* threw its considerable weight behind Karenga without qualification may be even more telling. It was the intellectual organ of the broad-based Black Power movement. Beverly Guy-Sheftall rightly called the coverage of sexual politics by editors Robert Chrisman and Robert L. Allen "the most extensive and sober" of that period. For more than a decade, beginning with "Black Women's Liberation" in April 1973, the *Black Scholar* boldly treated the subject of sexual politics, particularly feminism, surpassing its peer publications (e.g., *Black World, Freedomways* and *Black Books Bulletin*) in the black community.[132] Editor Sara S. Whaley of the *Women Studies Abstract* (*WSA*) lavished yet higher praise on the *Black Scholar* in 1975, citing it as the only journal covered by the *WSA* that year to dedicate periodic special issues to women.[133] Nonetheless, absent from the journal was any discussion of the misogynist and sexual impropriety imputed to Karenga, a highly visible black nationalist leader.

The *Black Scholar*'s direct response to Karenga about the female complainants effectively perpetuated, though at times the journal went out of its way to denounce, the claim that controversy about sexual violence among black Americans was a nefarious plot advanced by whites with the ostensible cooperation of black women. In its prefatory note introducing Karenga's "In Defense of Sis. Joanne," the editors wrote that Karenga had been convicted of the "trumped-up charge of assault."[134] Moreover, in the months leading up to the Little trial and before Karenga's release, the editors gave space to him and Halisi to solicit funds for Karenga's legal defense, though they did not grant space for the defense of Karenga's alleged victims. Other publishing and media outlets were available, but the cachet of the *Black Scholar* among black intellectuals and activists was unrivaled.[135]

It was not that the *Black Scholar* and the black nationalism it represented simply privileged race over gender, but that they were complicit in silencing the voices of female victims of sexual exploitation. When the issue of sexual exploitation passed from the abstract to the specific, as in Karenga's case, the *Black Scholar* ignored it or glossed it over. The editors remained evasive in the face of evidence that *someone* had sexually abused black women with an electrical cord and baton. It appeared that the right of women everywhere "to be free from sexual abuse, oppression and exploitation," as Karenga phrased it, ended abruptly where the Brahmins of Black Power refused to acknowledge that they and their fellow nationalists exploited and abused women.[136] "Given the choice between being attentive to allegations of black male victimization and being attentive to claims of black female oppression," the *Black Scholar*, speaking for the nationalist establishment, opted for the former.[137]

Apologies from Karenga were not forthcoming—either to the defendants, defense witnesses in the Karenga trial, or to the numerous other black women whose lives he had apparently affected adversely. Instead, obfuscation and silence prevailed. Four months prior to his celebrated breakthrough paper on Little, Karenga still could not muster a forthright public apology or any expression of even faint concern for his abusive behavior. The best the reformed Karenga would do was utter a vague acknowledgment of the necessity to "be aware of and admit our shortcomings in our relations with each other."[138]

Many black feminists shared the sense of resignation expressed by Elaine Brown and activist-historian E. Frances White. White wrote that the post-prison Karenga deserved some credit for revising his public critiques on gender roles and relations. But, she quickly added, in an age when such overt sexism had largely become taboo, his newfound posture appeared to be as much for public consumption as it was genuine. Karenga knew all the right things to say publicly, "despite his continued hostility to feminists."[139] Elaine Brown agreed. His enlightened nationalism, manifest in his essay on Little, did nothing to change Brown's mind about Karenga. If the situation warranted, Brown asserted, he would still invoke "the name of Africa to justify the suppression of black women."[140] Karenga, in short, is a particularly illuminating guide for disciples of black nationalism.[141] Others appropriated Africa in similar fashion. The African Liberation Support Committee (ALSC), for example, a clearinghouse for Black Power groups, organized demonstrations for Little but failed to reprimand or correct members whose own attitudes and behavior toward women threatened to perpetuate abuse.[142] An essay by a key ALSC official published amid the Little frenzy is instructive:

> It was not until the colonial system introduced its shameful practices of oppression and exploitation that the role of women became distorted in its form and contents. . . .
>
> Under foreign rule the traditional patterns of African society were gradually supplanted by negative values; this process eventually resulted in the degradation of the position of women in our society, depriving them of their most sacred human rights. . . .
>
> However, colonialist examples of spoilation, arbitrary authority, oppression and exploitation brought about a reversal of the traditional social order, victimizing women most cruelly. Now, fortunately, the progress of decolonization and African unity which dominates Africa's political situation is tending to put the process of evolution of our people on quite a different path.[143]

Written by Guinean president Sekou Toure, this argument for a "traditional" and romanticized role for women elicited no comment from the African Liberation Support Committee, young radicals intellectually vested in consciousness raising and a Maoist style of self-criticism. Their acceptance of Toure's trouble-free reminiscence of what in reality were the complex gender relations of precolonial Africans had the effect of sanctioning violence against women. Toure's invocation of a golden age for women in precolonial Africa invited black nationalists to blame any sexism in their movement on the culturally damaging influences of Eurocentric patriarchy. It also discouraged an honest assessment of how difficult the task of advancing women's rights in contemporary Africa might be. Perhaps the most damaging element of Toure's argument was its notion of trickle-down gender equality, which disillusioned an entire generation of would-be nationalist loyalists, E. Frances White among them, who were repulsed as much by sexism as by racism. The ALSC, whose support for Joan Little paled in comparison to the energy it devoted to African foreign policy, opted for silence when faced with the difficult prospect of speaking truth about sexism to Black Power advocates.[144]

* * *

Some scholars have suggested that black nationalists contributed to the downfall of national liberation struggles when they began to embrace the cosmopolitan virtue of liberal universalism, which distracted them from "the subtlety of the real world" of oppressed and exploited peoples.[145] Whatever the truth to this claim, for Joan Little the move by nationalists to speak in broader terms and appeal to a broader audience possibly meant the difference between life and death. The judge dropped Little's death penalty charge based on a lack of prosecutorial evidence; yet without a nation and world watching, one wonders if the judge would have either lessened the charge or acceded to a venue change.[146] The argument has also been made that black nationalist activism on behalf of Joan Little was a decisive moment in the development of black nationalism, which, now enlightened, could recognize, address, and correct sexism and move beyond it.[147] I question this interpretation and point to my profiles of nationalists who, while most public in their rhetorical support for Little, were at the same time men who embodied the patriarchy and misogyny bound up with the Black Power movement. Complicit, too, were other prominent nationalists who substituted obfuscation and silence for speaking the truth about the sexual abuse and exploitation of black women. In fact the visible role of nationalists in the Little case and their strong language in her defense masked their own troubling records on intraracial gender relations.

These issues eventually led black women to form their own institutions. The National Black Feminist Organization and its offshoot, the Combahee River Collective, which were established near the same time as the Little campaign, emerged as institutional reminders to the black liberation movement "that sexism is destroying and crippling us from within."[148] "The only people who care enough about us to work consistently for our liberation," according to the authors of the Combahee River Collective Statement, "is us."[149]

Loyalty to black nationalism and loyalty to women's rights within the black community could easily be viewed as contradictory. The silence of many in the face of this unfortunate dilemma points to the agonizing choice that African Americans confronted and the decision that they made—and continue to make.

6 Federally Subsidized Black Nationalism
Soul City, Statist Liberalism, and the Rise of the New Right, 1968–1980

"They never give up," Robert F. Williams wrote to his publisher in November 1971. Exasperated by his anticipated extradition to North Carolina on a 1961 kidnapping charge, the Black Power fugitive continued: "The establishment is moving might and main to get me back . . . for a legal lynching." His North Carolina–based publisher, Floyd B. McKissick, had just recently purchased the rights to Williams's Black Power primer *Negroes with Guns*. McKissick, however, could hardly identify with his author.[1] In fact, he owed the existence and success of his business, McKissick Enterprises, to the powers responsible for Williams's political and criminal woes. "[I'm] sleeping with them right now," McKissick boasted, speaking of the same cabal whom Williams regarded as his state-sponsored tormentors.[2]

Indeed, Democratic Governor Bob Scott of North Carolina and former Democratic Governor Terry Sanford were key underwriters of the new project of Soul City—the signature holding of McKissick Enterprises. First announced in 1969, Soul City was designed to be a new, black-owned and operated town in Warren County, North Carolina. As a freestanding town located in the eastern Piedmont county bordering Virginia, Soul City's future would rest on its ability to bring in private industry, which would provide the town's tax base. Town founders believed that, in the long run, industrial investors would flock to Soul City because of the area's reservoir of low-wage labor—labor that was predominantly black and displaced by the collapse of the region's agricultural economy. Political investors, however, provided Soul City with its critical seed money. Governor Scott would eventually hand off the project to his Republican successor, James Holshouser, who would take up McKissick's cause even more vigorously. Through public and private investment, the North Carolina "establishment" would ultimately lend Soul City financial and technical support to the tune of more than $20 million. This support would, in turn, free monies for McKissick to create other business ventures, including Thunder and Lightning Publishing.[3]

Republican administrations, at the federal and state levels, contended that Soul City offered the nation a new growth pole—an emerging market that would attract trade, commerce, and manufacturing investment, and that would stimulate job growth. Nixon, Ford, and Holshouser predicted that employment opportunities at the site would not only help to stem the devastating tide of black out-migration from eastern North Carolina but would provide a safety valve for America's riot-plagued, socially roiled northern cities. Touting Soul City as a domestic Marshall Plan, state and federal sponsors made it the largest publicly financed project ever underwritten for an African American. "I can't imagine this administration doing anything as positive as Soul City," NAACP executive director Roy Wilkins wrote to McKissick, speaking of the Nixon administration.[4]

In exchange, McKissick promised to President Nixon, Governor Holshouser, GOP Chairman George H. W. Bush, and other Republican investors electoral dividends for the next twenty years, yielding returns that would grow the minority base of the GOP by bringing prodigal blacks back home to the party of Lincoln. McKissick was so central to Republican hopes in the early 1970s for expanding the party's base that the *New York*

Times and *Chicago Tribune* labeled McKissick the "chairman emeritus of President Nixon's campaign organization."[5] The pact between one of the early 1970s most recognizable black Republicans and Republican party leaders, however, proved to be more of a Faustian bargain than a quid pro quo. Despite McKissick's and other black nationalist leaders' accommodation of the Republican party, neither a viable Soul City nor a broad-based GOP would come to be. Indeed, their demise was intimately connected.

McKissick and Meme: How the Soul City Idea Traveled over Time and Place

Born in 1922, Floyd McKissick was raised in the western mountains of Jim Crow–era North Carolina. McKissick spent his youth during the Great Depression selling newspapers, hewing wood, and making fish and ice deliveries on his handmade wagon. Economic and racial hardships, coupled with an entrepreneurial spirit forged during the Depression, provided formidable experiences for a young McKissick, but not enough to make sense of the embryonic ideological and practical underpinnings of Soul City. For that, one must travel across the Atlantic Ocean.

Like the invention of nationalism itself, the model and motivation inspiring Soul City are found in Western Europe rather than in 1960s racial disillusionment or Third World anticolonialism. As a young Second World War army sergeant, McKissick watched and aided in rebuilding towns of war-torn northeastern France under a nascent Marshall Plan. For McKissick the popularity and success of rebuilding European societies held out the promise that American aid might be allocated to black America to help it achieve a greater measure of control over its collective destiny. His experiences showed McKissick that black self-determination did not necessarily preclude reliance on outside assistance. In fact McKissick thought that the Marshall Plan later proved that economic independence most likely necessitated outside aid as a stimulus to offset growing social dislocation, poverty, and dangerously explosive social turmoil.[6]

McKissick returned home in the late 1940s. For the next three decades the germ of the Soul City idea—that through capital investment, institutions of self-determination might stabilize problem regions insulating larger societies from potential revolt—gestated and traveled with McKissick: from joining the state NAACP and his first foray into national electoral politics, in 1948, as a Wallace Progressive; through a pioneering legal career as the first black law student at the University of North Carolina capped, in the 1950s, by his successful defense of a segregated black local of the Tobacco Workers International denied seniority by the AFL-CIO; then, through his rise through the Congress of Racial Equality (CORE) ranks, from organizer to General Counsel associate to national chairman to its national director in April 1966. By the late 1960s McKissick had made CORE the sole civil rights group among the so-called Big Four (which also included the NAACP, the National Urban League, and the SCLC) that questioned the usefulness of nonviolence while talking openly about blacks as comprising a nation within a nation.

Twice before Soul City McKissick had sought state and private aid to create programs similar to the institution-building ones he witnessed in Europe. First, prior to the popular call of Black Power, McKissick looked to a mix of state and private aid to establish trading posts in North Carolina. Second, as CORE head he launched economic cooperative initiatives in the South. Through his firsthand experiences he came to believe that there was no contradiction in accepting a substantial role for a liberal democratic state like America in the soul-making projects of Black Power. It was not until he left CORE during the winter of 1968, however, that McKissick dedicated his energies full-time to doing so.

After CORE, McKissick established Floyd B. McKissick Enterprises. Its mission was captured in the bottom right-hand corner of McKissick's letterhead: "Dedicated to Building Black Economic Power." His aim was to establish an economy owned and operated by black people. "Black America's struggle," McKissick wrote in the introductory message of the enterprise's brochure in 1968, was "for Economic Power and Self-determination. . . . These bring respect to those who gain them."[7] "The *only* hope for real progress" lay in black unity, said McKissick.[8] "We need not justify any demands for 'separatism' to anybody white," he told *Black Scholar* readers. "The real separatists moved to the suburbs long ago."[9] For too long black life had been dictated by the preconditions and circumstance of white America. McKissick argued that black control of institutions was a precondition of independence.[10]

Based in Harlem, McKissick Enterprises set in motion several subsidiary projects, including a restaurant, shopping center, publishing company, drama production company, a job training consortium for the perpetually unemployed, and the centerpiece of the organization: a freestanding new town called Soul City. While recognizing that much of the capital would come from white financial institutions and businesses, the enterprises' primary goal was black economic independence for equality, McKissick wrote in his introductory brochure, on "Black control of its own institutions." But the Soul City project showed in part that McKissick, whom, as historian Gareth Davies put it, struck "fear into the hearts of white liberals" as the sole civil rights leader among the Big Four to countenance political violence in the cause of Black Power, ultimately became accountable to them.[11]

The Edifice Complex: Bipartisanism and the Regulatory State in the Making of Soul City

Soul City was first officially announced a wintry Monday morning, January 13, 1969, one week before Richard Nixon's inauguration, in Washington, D.C., by the Johnson administration. McKissick initially looked to Democrats for support, pitching the new town project to officials under Lyndon Johnson, who opted not to run for reelection after the Tet Offensive in January 1968, then to New York Senator Robert Kennedy. The assassination of Kennedy in June 1968 not only deprived the Democratic Party of its most popular and sentimental candidate but nearly dashed any realistic hope for Soul City. Few gave Democrats a chance of keeping the White House, especially not with the nomination falling to Johnson's vice president, Hubert Humphrey, whose campaign suffered from its identification with an unpopular president running an unpopular war. While a lame-duck Johnson administration maintained support for Soul City, thanks in no small way to friends of McKissick's throughout various federal agencies, the new town founder surveyed the 1968 presidential landscape.

McKissick settled on Richard Nixon. McKissick easily navigated the two parties, which while disagreeing over war and other civil rights matters shared common ground on black capitalism. Liberals from Nelson Rockefeller to the editorial board of the *New York Times* put aside initial concerns that black capitalism promoted black segregation and endorsed Nixon's contention that federal aid be given to minority enterprises as a means of growing the black middle class. As Nixon, just days before his presidential oath, vowed to "do more for the Negro than any president has ever done," America's thirty-seventh president seemed to confirm McKissick's belief that he did the right thing by supporting a candidate who not only could win but would back Soul City.[12]

Nixon was not a liberal, and his conservative beliefs guided his thinking and political behavior before and while occupying 1600 Pennsylvania Avenue. Still, what Nixon hated more than liberalism was irrelevancy. So while tacking to the right helped Nixon the campaigner, it seemed a less effective governing strategy when confronted with a Democratic Congress. The result was a conservative presidency periodically experiencing paroxysms of progressivism—supporting or signing domestic bills that grew the regulatory state; that gave publicly financed radio, National Public Radio (NPR), to the nation; and that imposed Keynesian-style wage and price freezes. Indeed, historian James Patterson tells us that federal spending grew by some 30 percent during Nixon's tenure in the White House; meanwhile defense spending, adjusted for inflation, shrunk for the first time since 1945. It was in these lapsed moments of liberalism that McKissick imagined himself operating and institutionalizing Black Power.[13]

Despite being perhaps the best-known civil rights leader supporting Nixon in 1968, McKissick, like other blacks, held no measurable influence within the new Republican administration.[14] This lack of influence in Washington disheartened McKissick and other black leaders. By the close of President Nixon's first hundred days it had become clear that African Americans were not involved in any important decisions that Nixon or his staff made. This was particularly evident in the case of Nixon's flagship black capitalist initiative, Executive Order 11458. The order, issued on March 5, 1969, created the Office of Minority Business Enterprise (OMBE). Crafting the executive order with negligible input from Nixon's Black Kitchen Cabinet, Nixon placed the OMBE under the Department of Commerce with no budget of its own, thus forcing the ten-member staff to forage for funds from other agencies. "To my mind the Administration's actions have not reflected real concern for the concept of 'Black Economic Power,'" McKissick complained to Robert Brown, a long-time friend and the president's top black aide.[15] Other prominent black Republicans, notably Jackie Robinson and the Urban League's Whitney Young, who favored the program in principle, nonetheless criticized the process of its implementation.[16]

The inability of Soul City to shape its own destiny was glimpsed as early as June 1969, when the House Appropriations Committee and the Department of Housing and Urban Development (HUD) quashed any pretensions of Soul City as a separatist venture. HUD would not financially back "any community that was designed for one race or the other," Assistant Secretary Samuel C. Jackson told McKissick. He assured the House Committee on Appropriations of this as well, at a hearing on June 18, 1969. Soul City, like any other municipality in the United States, would not have the power to regulate its racial composition. Government subsidies would dictate an interracial Soul City.[17]

McKissick concealed the disappointment the regulatory reality imposed on his racial vision. McKissick preferred seeing it as a necessary trade-off for tapping into the near limitless bounty of the federal government, which he claimed was "as full as a Christmas turkey."[18] At a house subcommittee meeting on housing in June 1970, McKissick confessed that Soul City, "need[ed] funding from pretty nearly every federal agency that is involved in the building of cities."[19] Shaky credit status, with many of Soul City's subsidiaries like the Warren Regional Planning Corporation and Soul City Foundation already in crisis by January 1971, made securing industrial commitments or attracting private investors even more difficult. That Soul City had managed to fend off creditors throughout the winter and spring of 1972 was due mostly to modest but much-needed government aid and grants from white-owned corporations. Nixon would be up for reelection, however, before the administration finally settled on Floyd McKissick as the face of black capitalism and their point man on black republicanism.[20]

Soul City's inability to dictate who would make up its local citizenry, and thus shape its own destiny, resulted not because of conservatives in the Nixon administration but because of two of the most liberal power centers inside the federal government: a heavily Democratic Congress and HUD, which since its founding until the early 1980s was best known as the home for racial progressives in the executive branch, regardless of which party occupied the White House. Congress and HUD appeared inseparable on the acid issue that racial inclusion was the entry bar for receiving federal dollars. But there existed a broader, unmistakable message. In the best-case scenario, by accepting federal outlay, Soul City's destiny would rest with regulatory liberalism.

A Revolutionary Turns Republican: McKissick and the Committee to Re-elect the President (CREEP) in the 1972 Election

Within the Nixon administration some of the president's closest advisors, like White House chief counsel Charles Colson, expressed indignation over any public cajoling of blacks. "I realize we want to cool the race issue and . . . win Black support," Charles Colson wrote to appointment secretary Dwight Chapin, about a request from the newly founded Congressional Black Caucus (CBC) to meet with Nixon.[21] Colson added, however, that "We are not going to degrade the office of the President . . . [until] this group shows that they have a proper respect for the *office* of the President."[22] He was skeptical of the CBC, which presented itself as "representative at-large for 20 million black people," and he calculated little political risk in writing off blacks.[23] According to Colson, all blacks, even well-established middle-class blacks, "were irretrievably into the Democratic Party" anyway.[24]

More moderate and liberal Republicans pushed ahead with targeting the middle and upper strata of the black population through minority-enterprise programs, by May 1971 building their black vote program around loan recipients of the Small Business Administration and the Office of Minority Business Enterprise.[25] Continuing in this vein, Harry Dent, Nixon's southern strategist, spent the fall of 1971 meting out rewards and punishments in an effort to purge radicals and Democratic sympathizers before the campaign heated up. "I have . . . delayed the promotion of the Southeastern OEO man to the #3 spot in OEO until he demonstrates proof-positive that he is rechanneling money from Democrats to RN [Richard Nixon] blacks," Dent explained to the attorney general and the president's chief of staff. Though he coauthored the notorious 1968 southern strategy—candidate Nixon's opportunistic play for southern and suburban white Democrats by exploiting their mounting antipathy to perceived excesses of the civil rights movement—Dent had come to believe that certain inroads could be made with key black Republicans, particularly during the reelection effort. He worried, though, that too many administration officials and grant recipients were aligned against the president. For this reason he initiated a process by October 1971 "to identify and put our own blacks," mostly from the South, in bureaucratic-level jobs, on honorary committees, and in positions to acquire grants.[26]

Nixon told aides to narrow their focus to the black silent majority, the "probably 30% who are potentially on our side." That figure—comprising the "stable" elements of the black working class and growing black middle class—seemed attainable to party campaigners. A Gallup poll in January 1972 showed that while 45 percent of blacks favored busing, 47 percent opposed it. Nixon strategists saw black ambivalence about busing and the nurturing of black institutions as ways to appeal to blacks.[27] At this point, even critics of the black-vote plan—like Pat Buchanan, who had all but written off black voters in October—backtracked. "The idea—that the black middle class voter is reachable"—is a "good one," Buchanan told Nixon's chief of staff H. R. Haldeman.[28]

Former high-ranking black officials in Nixon's administration wanted more aggressive racial campaigning during the bid for reelection. Nixon was too modest, said James Farmer and Arthur Fletcher. They told the press that what hurt the president's standing among black voters were not his programs and policies, but his "not letting the people know what he has done."[29] He "should toot his own horn" more, they argued. McKissick agreed, elaborating that the Democratic party had "brainwashed Black people into believing that they are more liberal in philosophy, do more for Black people than [Republicans]."[30]

By the spring of 1972 a flourishing black middle class had not translated into significant support for Nixon. Like Fletcher and Farmer before him, McKissick explained that the problem was not the party's message, but its deployment. Marketing the message of "a government-sponsored framework within which black entrepreneurship and urban regeneration could be nurtured" was getting them nowhere because of Nixon's black managerial elite, McKissick told Brown. McKissick questioned the verve of this coronated class of black bureaucrats who, according to McKissick, lacked the experience in mobilizing blacks at the grassroots level. "They are good followers," the former CORE shock troop leader wrote of desk-bound blacks inside the party, "*but not the warriors we now need . . .* ahead of the masses" (original emphasis).[31]

Going into the summer the national party was growing frustrated as well, as it encountered problems strengthening the field organizations to court black voters for November. The leader of the Black Votes Division of the Committee to Re-elect the President (CREEP), Paul Jones, was too much of a political novice in recruiting and developing effective field operations. The result, White House staffer Fred Malek wrote to Nixon's campaign manager, John Mitchell, was that no field organization existed at all for the black vote division. "The Black team has not fully utilized the resources available to them through Government grants and loan programs," added Malek. Malek concluded that the campaign needed to publicize past grants, identify all blacks receiving money from the administration, and tap the most visible of those blacks "to reach voters in their areas of influence."[32]

Minority-run organizations that had received administration funds but that were not pulling their weight for the campaign were singled out to be sacked. The Opportunity Industrialization Centers (OIC), for instance, receiving 80 percent of its funds from the administration, were seen as a poor investment because they featured a steady diet of speeches by such Nixon critics as Ralph Abernathy, Vernon Jordan, and Roy Wilkins. Nixon's reelection team believed that an antiadministration streak stretched beyond OIC to a host of other government-sponsored and federal agencies, especially Model Cities, the Office of Economic Opportunity, and the Office of Minority Business Enterprise.[33] OMBE director John Jenkins personified the campaign's problem. Nixon considered the economic front his strongest area of accomplishment for black and Spanish-speaking communities.[34] The reelection team believed that Jenkins, by continuing to give grants to Democrats, was squandering the administration's best leverage for garnering black votes.[35]

The perceived mulishness of Jenkins and others was out of synch with the campaign Nixon-Agnew wanted to run. They expected unilateral support from federal agencies, which Nixon aides controlled and supported financially. CREEP dubbed this stealthy contribution of various agencies the Responsiveness Program.

The Responsiveness Program, originating as far back as March 1972, was established by Malek, with Haldeman's approval, "to ensure that politically beneficial grants are channeled into high payoff areas."[36] It saw to it that federal grants, contracts, loans, subsidies, procurement and/or construction projects were awarded based on recipients' active contributions to the reelection effort. This involved expediting the review process for cooperative applicants and making favorable grant decisions that might not otherwise have been made. All instruments of the executive branch—the departments of Treasury, Labor, Transportation, Interior, Justice, and HEW, the General Services Administration, and the Veterans Administration (now Veterans Affairs)—were "coordinated with campaign needs."[37] Not even the space shuttle program was sacrosanct, in that much of its early funding, Watergate records would show, came via a political payoff for heavy campaign contributions.[38]

More often than not the Responsiveness Program gave short shrift to black Americans when their interests conflicted with those of other potential voting blocs, including key ethnic groups (Poles, Italians, and Latinos), labor, and southern whites, all of whose votes were considered contestable and were concentrated in key electoral-college states.[39] It was in this climate that William Brown of the Equal Employment Opportunity Commission (EEOC) abruptly abandoned its racial discrimination suit against the University of Texas because it held "disastrous" possibilities for Nixon among white Texans. Judgments of merit in federal contract reviews were conditioned on support as well. In Cleveland a summer recreational center grant was halved, because, according to Malek, its design "to impact inner city residents" did "not fall within our political guidelines."[40] The responsiveness program did not eliminate support altogether, but it instituted a selective approach to "future grants, loans, contracts, and appointments" for black individuals, firms, and organizations that would "have a multiplier effect on black vote support for the President."[41]

With that strategy in place the White House began courting Jesse Jackson, hoping for his support or, at minimum, neutrality in the campaign. Indeed, federal support materialized for Jackson's recently formed Operation PUSH after he broke with the Democratic nominee, George McGovern, just prior to the general election. Similarly, James Farmer, Nixon's one-time assistant secretary of HEW—whom Jones and Brown allowed to remain publicly nonpartisan so as not to "harm his credibility"—received $150,000, but only following a final sign-off by Jones and Brown. Farmer repaid the administration by "speaking on the administration's behalf" and "also talk[ing] to key black leaders to gain their loyalties."[42]

Floyd McKissick, however, gave more to the 1972 reelection campaign than either Farmer or Jackson. Soul City was recognized by established civil rights leaders like Roy Wilkins as "the only definite accomplishment of the Nixon administration," which increased McKissick's stock as a possible Republican party spokesman.[43] The close chum of Malcolm X, McKissick capitalized on his robust civil rights record to contest the image of a race-baiting Republican party. As a once-discontented Democrat, McKissick explained the pragmatism behind his decision to switch parties: "The Republicans were fast becoming an all-white party, and that meant that when they were in power, blacks were isolated; they put all their eggs in one basket. I went in so blacks would have a voice—and I got a lot of heat."[44] McKissick's visible support for Nixon, it was hoped, would either swing a significant voting constituency or tip the scales with a few decisive votes.

Jackson, McKissick, and Farmer were all representative race leaders. They were homegrown black leaders, with a history of activism that was persuasive to blocs of black voters.[45] This was to the GOP's advantage, and white party leaders knew it. Later in the decade and in the 1980s, the GOP would court black leaders whose roots were in establishment networks, who had not come through the organic ranks of social protest and activism, and who thus offered no sizable black constituency.[46] Old Guard Republicans in the early 1970s, though, understood that winning over black voters was difficult work, and that they would have to go beyond the politics of racial tokenism. When racial tokenism did come into play in the campaign of 1972, it was often about procuring the votes of fence-sitting white moderates.

McKissick held symbolic political value for GOP consultants and image makers, seeking to allay the angst of moderate whites who were not yet comfortable with the racial undertones encoded in the presidential campaign's narrative of antidemonstration, anticrime, and pro–law and order rhetoric. As a civil rights veteran backing Nixon, McKissick also tempered the antiblack tone both for disillusioned Democrats and for moderate Republicans who found the GOP's southern strategy unsettling. Above all, McKissick furthered an image of a Republican Party that, publicly at least, presented itself as neither openly hostile to the principle of civil rights nor willing "to [be] held hostage" by the current strand of civil rights leaders.

The Republican National Convention was planned for mid-August in Miami Beach. During the months leading up to the convention and the general election, with each cabinet office cooperatively on board, CREEP intensified its strategy for recruiting black votes. CREEP's Black Vote Division turned to McKissick, Elaine Jenkins, and Berkley Burrell to develop an overall campaign strategy for the group.[47] More widely known and respected in black electoral circles than the others, McKissick became Nixon's chief black surrogate, standing in for the president in public appearances in Chicago and other cities across the United States.

Returning Blacks to the Party of Lincoln: The 1972 General Election, Blacks for Nixon, and Political Fluidity

By the time of the national convention, the browning of the Republican Party was evident. The convention in 1972 saw a 115 percent increase in representation by black delegates over the 1968 convention, the largest leap in black membership since the late 1800s. Fifteen states that had no black delegates in 1968 sent at least one black delegate each in 1972. Black delegates represented at least 10 percent of the total delegations of Arkansas, Delaware, Louisiana, Maryland, Michigan, Virginia, and the District of Columbia. In five states (Arizona, Delaware, Iowa, Michigan, and Nevada) the percentage of black delegates exceeded the percentage of blacks in each state's population.[48] Racial moderates and liberals credited McKissick for much of the change. Dick Behn, of the partisan but progressive-minded Ripon Society, told McKissick: "Republican leaders to whom I spoke repeatedly mention your support of Nixon this year" for the influx of black delegates.[49] At the convention McKissick was easy enough to identify. Conspicuous to reporters by his "'72 Self-Determination" lapel button, which featured a black GOP-style elephant, McKissick sported his new party proudly. *Newsweek* reported that McKissick was weighing an offer to lead the "Blacks for Nixon" drive down its postconvention stretch.[50]

In a calculated move to galvanize the black vote for the 1972 general election, Republicans created an organization called Blacks for Nixon, headed by and including high-profile blacks—officials in the Nixon administration, black GOP officials, athletes, actors, entertainers, and the so-called revolutionary-turned-Republican McKissick.[51] Despite the gains in African American participation in the Republican Convention, whoever headed

Blacks for Nixon would face a tough challenge for two reasons.[52] First, Nixon's overall appeal to many conservatives gave many progressives pause. The Nixon administration, for example, filed the first federal government amicus brief against school desegregation, and Nixon's appointments of William Rehnquist and Lewis Powell to the U.S. Supreme Court, some feared, might set back desegregation. On the other hand, some also blamed the Nixon administration for defeating racial conservatism. The White House's enforcement of civil rights policies, in particular refusing to nullify court-ordered busing, risked the "security and the safety of the children of our region and every other the region," warned Democrat and presidential hopeful George Wallace on the political talk show *Face the Nation.*[53]

Late 1960s and 1970s domestic politics hinged on more than race and civil rights, according to the scholarship of Matthew Lassiter, Richard Johnston, and Byron Shafer.[54] That appeared the case for McKissick, who in the 1972 campaign canvassed undecided moderates and black voters, reminding them of the Nixon administration's support for not only voting rights and school desegregation but nondefense government spending as well. Nixon may have been conservative, but his administration did have progressive moments. It was this progressive side that McKissick imagined himself tapping and advancing. In this way, Soul City's programmatic pursuit of federal dollars stayed consistent with McKissick's political rhetoric supporting an activist state—one in which state-sponsored Black Power Soul City might mesh with a national retreat from integrationist remedies.

Second, the George McGovern–Sargent Shriver Democratic team in 1972 was arguably the most left-liberal ticket any major party had ever sponsored.[55] Blacks for Nixon eschewed the strategy to present Nixon as a stark conservative alternative, however. Instead, under McKissick they attempted to blur the distinctions on issues ranging from immediate Vietnam withdrawal to defense spending cuts, welfare, and civil rights.

When opportunities did arise to distinguish Nixon favorably, Blacks for Nixon gladly drew distinctions. On August 29, 1972, less than a week after the Republican National Convention, in a speech to Wall Street financiers, McGovern introduced his would-be economic legislation and choices for top-level cabinet posts—most notably touting powerful House, Ways, and Means chairman Wilbur Mills as Treasury secretary. McKissick's spin to the press on this speech was that McGovern had just sold his core constituencies—the National Welfare Rights Organization, the Congressional Black Caucus, and the National Black Political Convention—"down the river" to "save the whole plantation." The Arkansan's voting record on civil rights, claimed McKissick, was virtually indistinguishable from James Eastland's. The McGovern ticket, Nixon's black campaigners argued, revealed the chameleon nature of liberal white Democrats—whose prairie radicalism in the primaries got homespun into unreconstructed Democratic politics once the nomination was sewn up.[56]

McGovern's Wall Street speech set the tone for the Blacks for Nixon fall campaign. From September until Election Day twenty-four black men and women championed the purported civil rights legacy of Nixon. They armed themselves with facts and figures comparing the conditions of blacks in the current year of Nixon's administration with those in the final year of Lyndon Johnson's presidency. Nixon's black surrogates went into the battleground states of California, Illinois, Michigan, Missouri, New York, Ohio, Oregon, Pennsylvania, and Wisconsin. In guest appearances on radio and television they framed the Nixon presidency as the most accomplished on behalf of black America of any administration since Reconstruction. Measuring their candidate against President Johnson's civil rights benchmarks, the surrogates highlighted Nixon's spending record: compared to Johnson's spending, Nixon doubled aid to black colleges, from $108 to $200 million; more than tripled assistance to minority business enterprises, from $200 million to $700 million; quadrupled the Fair Housing Enforcement Budget, from $2 million to $8.2 million; increased the EEOC's budget almost fourfold, from $8.2 million to $30.5 million; and directed more than eight times as much money, from $75 million to $602 million, to the enforcement of civil rights. Under Johnson aid to Minority Bank Deposit programs did not exist. Under Nixon it was funded to the tune of over $250 million. Nixon also appointed more blacks to top government posts than any other president in history. To those skeptics who questioned Nixon's nominations of right-leaning Haynesworth and race-baiting Carswell to the Supreme Court, Nixon's black supporters reminded them that the president appointed two more minority federal judges than the Johnson administration, and did so in roughly half the length of time.[57]

Black publications that advocated reelection were sympathetic to Nixon because, as the editorial board of the *Cleveland Call and Post* put it, the president had kept with the Keynesian themes of the Roosevelt and John-son administrations, while plotting his own new federalist variation.[58] Huge economic-development grants, high-paying government jobs, and federal programs designed to bolster minority-business ownership topped the list of why *Black Business Digest* preferred Nixon to McGovern in the November 1972 election.[59] The campaign literature about Soul City, pre-pared and distributed by the Blacks for Nixon committee, best represented the GOP's credentials and made it a viable, if not favorable, alternative: "The Democrats endorsed it! The Republicans supported it. That's action."[60]

The mushrooming Blacks for Nixon movement alarmed black Demo-crats like Louis Stokes and Julian Bond, who warned fellow Democrats about the formidable threat posed to their hegemony in black America. Bond reserved his most tart comments for blacks who advocated voter abstention, or worse, an outright vote for Nixon. Bond branded them all "political prostitutes" in an address to a National Urban League conven-tion. He urged Urban Leaguers to shun McKissick, Betty Shabazz, Wilt Chamberlain, and any others asking them to elect "a man who gave us Carswell and Haynesworth."[61]

Lifetime Republican Arthur Fletcher penned the leading corrective on behalf of black Republicans. Fletcher reminded *Wall Street Journal* read-ers that both labor and blacks had opposed Nixon's two Supreme Court nominees. The comparisons ended there. Labor—alert to the separation of powers, politically pragmatic, and free from Democratic party control—sided with the administration on matters of mutual progress, such as the Vietnam War, the Supersonic Transport aircraft project, and the family-assistance plan. "This was not the case [with] the black community," wrote Fletcher, who helped father the Philadelphia Plan for affirmative action.[62] "In fact," he continued, "the exact opposite was true" of black leaders. Their reflexive animus toward all things Nixon rendered blacks invisible to the White House precisely at the moment when crucial policies and important appointments were being decided. Unions, on the other hand, were consulted on every major presidential appointment in the Labor De-partment—"Including my own," said Fletcher, Nixon's one-time assistant labor secretary.[63]

Fletcher underscored the political fluidity that existed in the early 1970s among black Republicans, black Democrats, and black third-party orga-nizers, on policies and appointments. Rarely did black Nixonians become apologists for nominees deemed essentially hostile to collective racial interests, but Massachusetts Senator Edward Brooke, Fletcher, and now McKissick proposed that moderate and liberal blacks engage with the president and the GOP to help sway appointments and modify important civil rights legislation.

With the election just four weeks away and victory virtually sealed, Nixon took a rare moment to reflect with the Black Executive Advisory Committee, an ad hoc sounding board for the president, which he had consulted on black voters and the election and postelection agenda.[64] "This is going to go down in history as a big election," Nixon told the committee on October 6, 1972. Then, an appreciative president turned to McKissick, seated beside him, and thanked him and other black apparatchiks for "working night and day . . . for me." "We're changing the tide," predicted the president. "More decisive than just an additional 5 percent."[65]

A week later, with Nixon's victory in sight, McKissick shifted gears to think about the future beyond the 1972 campaign. With the aid of CREEP matching funds, he launched the National Committee for a Two-Party System.[66] His plan was to use the committee to make further inroads into the black community. Through positive press, and voter education and registration, the committee hoped to institutionalize efforts at expanding the party's base of black voters. "The ongoing significance this group will have" in "building the Republican party," McKissick promised, would yield handsome electoral returns for the GOP beyond 1972.[67]

In November 1972 Nixon won the general election overwhelmingly. For the first time since 1956 the Republican Party gained black voters over the previous presidential election. While the 13 percent of blacks who voted for Nixon disappointed supporters, it still represented a 3 percent increase from 1968; this bump was largely credited to the efforts of Brown, McKissick, and a reinvigorated black Republican leadership.[68]

Sharing the goal of bringing estranged black voters back home to the party of Lincoln was the new chairman of the Republican National Committee (RNC), George H. W. Bush. Bush had opposed the Civil Rights Act of 1964, rising to political prominence, partly by making it a 1964 campaign issue in his failed bid to unseat the Democratic senator from Texas, Ralph Yarborough, who voted for the bill. In his new post as RNC chairman, though, Bush expressed a desire to build a cross-racial coalition. He began by allocating $300,000 to the liberal-moderate National Council of Black Republicans. Even though the presidential race had not produced the number of black votes some had hoped, party leaders persisted in their commitment to increasing minority enrollment. "Things are in the process of change here at the National Committee," Bush said. He admired McKissick's work toward this goal. The examples set by you, he told McKissick, "will be discuss[ed] with Bob Rousek, our new Communications Chief, some way . . . these ideas can be spread across the country." Bush went on: "I do want to work closely in order to develop an emerging Republican Party, and I appreciate the initiative you have already taken in this area."[69]

With this grand design in mind, Bush and McKissick, in a strategy meeting on March 30, 1973, laid the groundwork for the Two-Party's agenda for the next two years, in preparation for the 1974 midterm elections.[70] "I am determined that out of this will emerge a Republican party with a sound record toward all Americans and with a much greater image of an open door," Bush assured McKissick.[71] Determined to swell black Republican ranks to rival those of black Democrats, the Two-Party system organized throughout 1973.[72] Chapters were organized in Alabama, New York, Texas, and North Carolina, before branching into Pennsylvania, Illinois, and Florida—"all of the states having significant populations of black people," in the words of Charles Hurst, executive director of the National Committee for a Two-Party System.[73] The committee hoped to engineer massive black Republican registration and support for minority candidates seeking office under the Republican banner.[74] Its board was interracial, and in North Carolina its members included former congressman Charles Jonas and state Republican minority leader Donald Pollock. Soul City figured into their partisan plans as well—not simply as a quid pro quo but, as McKissick explained to Bush, a national and international model for economic development.[75]

In hindsight some simply might consider McKissick's gambit of casting Soul City's lot with the GOP foolhardy or evidence of his newfound conservatism. But to do so is to read history backward, for in the 1960s and early 1970s, party identity was more fluid than it was in later years. Ideology was not tantamount to political party in the minds of Americans from the 1960s through early 1970s. For example, in 1974, while self-described conservatives outnumbered liberals three to one, according to polls fewer than one in four of respondents claimed to be Republicans.[76] Nationally it was the Democrats dominated by conservatives, not the GOP, which was populated by many nonsouthern moderates. At the congressional level more Republicans than Democrats voted for the Civil Rights Act. Similarly, in Congress, less than 10 percent of Republicans represented the South. In North Carolina the state's GOP establishment was widely considered to be "nonideological" and moderate.[77] McKissick counted heavily on Jim Holshouser, a pro–Equal Rights Amendment (ERA) and pro–affirmative action governor, who headed up the state's Republican establishment and who "mount[ed] a very aggressive national industrial promotion campaign" on Soul City's behalf, according to an internal HUD memo, literally paving industry's way into Soul City by developing Industrial Boulevard Road—the major thoroughfare leading industry to the industrial park.[78] Holshouser, similar to Virginia neighbor and fellow Republican governor Linwood Holton—who voluntarily placed his twelve-year-old daughter in a black elementary school to desegregate Richmond's public schools—represented a supposed new breed of southern politician. The political scientist William C. Havard identified such politicians as media savvy and, in the post–Voting Rights South, far more sympathetic to civil rights than predecessors. Whereas the establishment Holshouser was among Soul City's most unflinching boosters, neophyte conservative GOPers like Jesse Helms and his "Jessecrats" followers demonized Soul City as the social engineering outgrowth of the Great Society.[79]

McKissick had staked Soul City's success on the Republican Party. Now that the HUD contract had been approved, he was tethered to the party more than ever. Not surprisingly, he solidified his ties to the GOP and, like many black Democrats, shed his affiliations with members of the Black Power movement and other advocates of a black third party.

By 1974 relations had grown tense between mainstream black leaders, including McKissick, and the still powerful, radical wing of Black Power. Their political strategies had diverged to the point that unity was no longer possible. Unity had characterized the first National Black Political Assembly (NBPA) in Gary, Indiana, two years earlier in 1972. It was the most widely attended black political convention in history. The Gary convention crystallized the possibilities of an independent, third political force, constituted by a tenuous coalition of black elected officials, activists, and political operatives. Some delegates had feared that the NBPA would require single-party allegiance, but the architects of the convention allowed black

Democrats and Republicans to pursue dual-political membership, giving them the option to affiliate with one of the major parties and with the NBPA simultaneously. Conveners of the convention believed that they had found a "flexible response to the dilemma of cooptation in the political mainstream."[80]

By 1974, however, mainstream black leaders had grown fearful any involvement might elicit political sanction from the established parties. They also appeared worried that a popular black political forum, like the NBPA, might challenge their power to broker the black vote.[81] Detroit Democratic congressman John Conyers Jr., for example, advised that the nationalist overtones would hurt absent Congressional Black Caucus members hoping to curry political favor inside the party. Mayor Richard Hatcher of Gary, coconvener of the convention and one of the few elected officials present, saw still a constructive role for the "native" black ruling class: "We need Roy Wilkins now. We need Vernon Jordan now. We need Ed Brooke now. We need Charles Diggs and we need Floyd McKissick and we need Tom Bradley. We need Coleman Young and we need every black man and woman who has risen from the ranks. If our leaders abandon us, we are lost." Seasoned activists like Owusu Sadauki (Howard Fuller), however, chided Hatcher and others who mistook McKissick and other so-called neocolonialists for black leaders. Their alliances with white corporatists, though sincere, made them too beholden to corporate capitalism and a white power structure, said Sadauki. Sadauki, former president of the now-defunct Malcolm X Liberation University, added: "I'm tired of begging [them] to participate."[82] But McKissick, who had sent delegates to Gary in 1972, dismissed the next major NBPA convention two years later in Little Rock, as did other mainstream leaders who depended on the major political parties. Attendance was down from six thousand delegates in 1972 to 1,737 delegates in 1974.[83]

McKissick's congratulatory telegram to North Carolina senator-elect Jesse Helms on election night 1972 sealed Soul City's compromise with all flanks of the Republican order. McKissick's telegram read: "In spite of the fact that no two men think alike, there are many common things that we should work together on, and many common things we should work together for." Helms's reply to Soul City's compromise ominously foreshadowed the future: "At the appropriate time, I intend to request a careful independent examination of expenditures" into Soul City.[84] That moment came midway into the freshman senator's first term. By the end of his first term in 1978, Soul City would be the most closely watched of all new community programs and among the most investigated. When Helms-inspired investigations proved feckless, Helms turned to purifying his party, purging it of black nationalists, liberals, and moderates alike.

McKissickgate: Soul City and the Politics of Scandal

On March 5, 1975, North Carolina's freshman Senator Jesse Helms and Democratic Congressman L. H. Fountain requested a fiscal and program audit of Soul City. They were prompted by an investigative newspaper series by Tom Stith of the *Raleigh News and Observer*, who leveled thirty-three allegations ranging from political payoffs, interlocking directorships, conflicts of interests, and cronyism and nepotism to illegal expenditures and financial misappropriation. Helms made known his desire to end what he considered the bilking of American taxpayers by Soul City and its founder. Helms introduced an appropriations amendment that blocked HUD from providing further assistance to the project. Helms's colleague, Senator Edward Brooke of Massachusetts, raised objections, but HUD secretary Carla Hills froze Soul City funding until the audit was completed by the General Accounting Office (GAO).[85] The General Assembly of North Carolina similarly passed a resolution to withhold funds until a state probe of Soul City was completed.[86] Helms, himself a recent target of the *Raleigh News and Observer* concerning political quid pro quo, pontificated, nonetheless: Soul City is like that "New York City scandal, where somebody just walked off with a pile of money." After seven years and $19 million, Helms and the newspaper complained, Soul City still failed "to crank it up."[87]

It would take several months for the GAO to prepare its audit, leaving a cloud of uncertainty over Soul City throughout 1975. By June, however, the North Carolina State audit cleared Soul City of any wrongdoing. In light of this, a vindicated Governor James Holshouser unveiled the North Carolina Office of Minority Business Enterprise on July 21, 1975—an action that surely aggravated racial conservatives. Holshouser argued that state action was needed to make up for past racial wrongs and benign neglect. He wanted to open doors closed by past discrimination to racial minorities and others who, "because [of] a variety of circumstances, have not been able to fully take advantage of our American free enterprise system." Fostering minority-business enterprise was an appropriate state response to an "area that has especially suffered from neglect over a period of many years."[88]

Despite Governor Holshouser's vote of confidence, negative press about Soul City rocked the already shaky confidence of potential institutional investors. The investment economy was tight and it was a buyer's market; few financiers with the means of investing large-scale venture capital or corporate earnings would waste their time or money sorting between the rumors of wrongdoing and its substance. Even after the state audit cleared Soul City, for instance, the most promising leads soured. "I did not believe that a sincere prospect would be daunted by political allegations," Holshouser's stunned chief consultant on minority business wrote to Soul City's industrial recruiter. The federal government failed to meet its own August deadline for the audit, and so, in effect, nothing would change with investors until the GAO report was released in late December.[89] Only Soul City's federally guaranteed loan classification spared its AAA-bond rating from being downgraded by Moody's.

In mid-December the New Communities Administration at HUD announced a new $445,750 infrastructure grant to Soul City, one of fifteen new communities around the country.[90] The award foretold the direction of the GAO's finding and signaled Soul City's coming exoneration.[91] Until this moment Senator Helms and Congressman Fountain had shared supreme confidence in Congress's investigative arm, lauding the GAO's imperviousness to politics and glad-handing. "They call 'em right down the middle," Helms said admirably of the GAO.[92] When the office's ninety-eight-page report failed to recommend a criminal investigation, however, Helms changed his tune. While Fountain quietly withdrew his charges, Helms insisted that the Department of Justice review the GAO's review. "I am seeking a further review of the GAO on these and other points. Whatever the result," Helms told the Senate, "an obvious fact will remain—Soul City is suspected by many citizens of my state to be the greatest single waste of public money that anyone in North Carolina can remember."[93] HUD responded with greater regulatory stricture. At one point, it even refused McKissick photocopies until he coughed up a $1.10 check to cover the reproduction costs.[94]

The African American newspaper the *Carolinian* penned the fairest rendering of Soul City's in-house activities. James A. Shepard repeated in editorial after editorial that sloppy bookkeeping and accounting, nepotism, and overlapping and gross inefficiencies did not add up to the charges of "downright thefts."[95]

As for the destiny of Soul City, almost a full year after the GAO had given McKissick's project "a clean bill of health," more inquests were called for, this time by the state's junior senator, Robert Morgan. If it wasn't already, Soul City would become by October 1976 among the most closely watched of all new communities.[96] The project remained so throughout its brief life as a government project. Symbolizing the project's final descent from legitimacy into parody was the *National Enquirer*'s headline, "$19 Million Fleeced—And You Pay."[97]

Soul City's exoneration by the GAO did little to bring McKissick back within the national-party fold. "What appears to be lacking is a real and publicly articulated commitment to this project on the part of the Administration," McKissick told new Vice President Nelson Rockefeller.[98] In place of Nixon's support for Soul City, McKissick now had Rockefeller's ear, since the former New York governor and one-time Chase Bank chairman was Soul City's principal private backer. McKissick had no such rapprochement with the new president, however.

Within seven weeks of assuming office as president following Nixon's post-Watergate resignation, Gerald Ford had dropped his caretaker role of the Nixon White House. The Ford administration's urban policy was apathetic, if not contemptuous, of the New Communities program, McKissick complained to the new president's counsel, John Marsh. McKissick believed that Ford completely discounted the program's potential impact on black America, U.S. cities, and indeed the national economy.[99]

By early 1976 the pattern of not working to improve the civil rights image of the Republican Party upset McKissick enough to contact Rockefeller. McKissick impressed upon Rockefeller that in the minds of black voters, the image of the Republican party would be inextricably linked to the fate of Soul City. "In spite of this," closed McKissick, "We cannot even get the kind of access we need to decision makers when we need that access most." With Soul City's reputation as "the largest and most visible minority-owned project sponsored at least in part by the Federal government,"

McKissick believed the new town provided the Ford administration's best chance in growing GOP numbers among black voters. But these very reasons also explained why, with the conservative backlash underway in the Republican Party, the new administration neglected it.[100]

Certainly as much if not more than any southern state, North Carolina presented a window on to the national Republican Party. "Rooted in the historic economic ideology of the national Republican party," wrote political sociologist Paul Luebke, North Carolina republicanism had remained relatively strong throughout the post-1945 period compared to the GOP in other southern states. Voters had elected Congressman Charles Jonas in 1952, and Congressman James Broyhill ten years later.[101] Regarded as the dean of the state party, Broyhill underscored the race-moderate rhetoric of the North Carolina GOP. "I think that we have to show that we're appealing to all people, not just whites, but blacks and whites. . . . Unfortunately, over the years, we have had too many candidates in some places that get 100 percent of the [black] vote against them."[102] No Broyhill disciple rose more successfully through the party ranks than southern Appalachian native James Holshouser, who traced his Republican roots back to the Civil War. Yet this natural Republican son's support of voting and civil rights, affirmative action, and the ERA found him increasingly at odds with the conservative wing of his party. These differences came to a head in his public fallout with Senator Jesse Helms during the presidential primary campaign of 1976. Holshouser was chairing the southern campaign for Gerald Ford, and Helms was aggressively championing the maverick contender Ronald Reagan.[103]

The Unraveling: How the 1976 North Carolina Primary Helped Undo the Liberal–Black Power Entente and Power the New Right

Among modern conservatives the 1976 North Carolina presidential primary is often thought of as one of the two most important primaries in the rise of the modern conservative movement.[104] Its significance lay in what ensued following Reagan's upset of Ford. Reagan was expected to run well in North Carolina, his first southern primary, but no Ford or Reagan professionals believed Reagan might win the state.[105] What many pundits, as well as operatives inside Reagan's camp (including campaign manager

John Sears, who privately began exploring "the idea of joining forces with the Ford team"), mistakenly predicted would be Reagan's last bid for the presidential nomination actually augured the end of Holshouser and moderate Republicanism.[106]

With the March 23 North Carolina primary days away, Holshouser led a group of nine moderate Republican governors in a plan to put down the conservative insurgent; in a statement to the press they called on Reagan to get out of the race. Reagan was too polarizing a figure, both within the party and nationally, to win in November, the signatories declared. By remaining in the race the former fellow governor was doing irreparable harm to the party's presumptive nominee, driving up Ford's negatives and making the incumbent president vulnerable to the Democrats come fall.[107]

The press release was a political and public-relations disaster. The Republican governors' attempt to spirit Reagan out of the primary only engendered wider sympathies for the underdog. Reagan was seen as the quixotic GOP iconoclast, imbued with dogma immunizing him from the graft and vice many believed gripping politics in Washington. He has a "right to [enter] in each and every primary" went the common refrain from Republican regulars to the public at large.[108] One by one the governors who had signed the release tried to distance themselves from it. Even the statement's authors, Holshouser and Governor Daniel J. Evans of Washington, desperate to deflect the controversy from Ford, backpedaled.[109]

Holshouser soon came under fire from the then-powerful Congressional Club for his support of Soul City. Founded in North Carolina in 1972, the Congressional Club soon took hold as one of the nation's five leading political action committees for New Right candidates, targeting in particular contests where there were sharp ideological differences between candidates and where its fund-raising dollars might make a difference in a close race. That strategy received its first national exposure in the 1976 Republican primary.[110] According to the club, Soul City best symbolized the weakness of the Ford-Holshouser faction of the Republican Party. The Congressional Club believed that liberals and so-called candy-ass moderates like the governor were enabling a new black Republican menace. The club's attack was led by its chief strategist, Tom Ellis. His role in the attack came as a blow to McKissick, who as late as 1973 had hoped that Ellis might be the figure to bridge the divide between the philosophies represented by Holshouser and Helms.[111]

According to Helms, Reagan's campaign was at bottom a counterrevolution against the moral failings of liberalism. During Reagan's presidential run in 1976 he assailed Nixon-Ford's détente with the Soviet Union and open-door policy toward China as "appeasing Red[s]," thus recasting the cold war as a moral struggle between a city on the hill and empires of evil. Helms appropriated similar imagery in mobilizing "patriots" against the enemy within. That enemy within, according to Helms, was Soul City, which, like the nation-states of the Soviet Union and China, was "based upon concepts developed out of an intellectually and morally bankrupt doctrine." This doctrine, Helms argued over the years, was borne of a larger worldview "that suggests that enough money thrown at any problem will make it go away, or thrown at any proposal will make it happen."[112] His crusade against Soul City and other bloated public projects was not about depriving "the poor and needy," he insisted. "Any Senator . . . could take a switchblade knife and cut off 25 percent of [any federal project], and the poor would be better off if the proper utilization of the remaining money was effected." Nor, he added, was it an attack on "the idea that blacks needed to have a city all their own."[113]

Rather, Helms claimed to be alarmed by the liberalism behind Soul City. He believed that American liberalism's policy of engagement jeopardized national security abroad and nurtured, in Soul City, an American fifth column at home. Soul City posed a surreptitious threat: its overtures to bootstrap black capitalism and adherence to free-market principles cloaked its subversive agenda of expanding the welfare state. The enabling policies of liberals made it all possible. In Helms's mind North Carolina offered an alarming example of this liberalism, for its governor, James Holshouser, had literally created the space that brought the black chimera of Soul City into being. Helms certainly saw the groundbreaking speech for Soul City, delivered by Holshouser in 1973, as dramatic testament of that. In it, Holshouser told the gathering, Soul City signified "a new milestone in our nation's constant search for better human relations."[114] For Holshouser critics it was such moral obtuseness that ultimately transformed liberals from mere facilitators into state subversives themselves.

The Congressional Club saw no room for détente in this moral and political struggle.[115] Ellis viewed the primary as a referendum on the soul of the party, and defied both state-party leadership and Reagan's campaign chairman, John Sears, by waging a mass publicity campaign against the North Carolina governor. The centerpiece of his attack was a campaign flyer, mass mailed to North Carolina voters, that detailed Holshouser's unholy alliance with McKissick, complete with a caricature that depicted McKissick as a puppeteer pulling the strings of the Republican governor.

The Congressional Club followed the flyer with radio ads that falsely reported a backroom deal between President Ford and the Boston NAACP to select Edward Brooke as his running mate. Brooke was Soul City's staunchest supporter in the Senate, and in that sense the bane of Helms's political existence. The national press quickly picked up the inflammatory radio spots.[116] Mixing old myths with new political realities, the Congressional Club employed the tools of modern-era campaigns—the mass-mailed flyer and the electronic press—to tap into immemorial fears of debauched Negro-Republican rule. The fierce attack, led by Helms and the Congressional Club, successfully deposed progressive republicanism, black and white—and the repercussions went beyond North Carolina to the national level.

Reagan, skillfully connecting the dots, tapped into local tumult about Soul City by tying it to hemispheric and global politics, charging Ford with appeasing the Soviets and giving away the Panama Canal. "When Ford comes to North Carolina," Reagan told Tar Heel conservatives who were bristling about a series of so-called "federal giveaways," from the Panama Canal to Soul City, "the band won't know whether to play 'Hail to the Chief' or 'Santa Claus is Coming to Town.'"[117]

A resurrected Reagan, after his fourth consecutive presidential primary, upset Ford in the March 23 primary in North Carolina, 52 percent to 46 percent. Reagan's surprise victory led to a silencing of the diverse voices within the state party.[118] The national media put it all in perspective: *ABC Evening News* began its broadcast the next day by announcing that for the first time since 1952, when Harry Truman lost New Hampshire, a sitting president had lost a state primary.[119] No one could have predicted Reagan's victory in North Carolina, Walter Cronkite told CBS watchers.[120]

Holshouser scrambled to salvage the fractured pieces of centrist republicanism and beseeched members to put the party ahead of ideology. The "Senator [and I] have an obligation to unite the party . . . [at] the State convention," Holshouser stated, just days before the June 19 state convention.[121]

Helms and the Congressional Club greeted Holshouser's plea for unity, in the words of the North Carolina convention chairman, with "a gratuitous slap," denying the governor a delegate's seat at the Republican National Convention, a position to which he was entitled after winning statewide election in 1972.[122] In the aftermath of the primary coup by party neophytes, fear mounted that, as one long-time local Republican put it, "persons such as Mr. Helms" were out to "destroy our party."[123] Not satisfied with denying the chastened governor one of the state's two bonus seats, the state GOP junta blocked virtually every member from the Holshouser faction from serving as an official delegate at the national convention in Kansas City.[124] "I never wanted to leave a job so bad in my life," Robert G. Shaw, then the nominal state GOP chair, recalled.[125]

Nationally, the Ford team rewrote its strategy following the North Carolina debacle in an attempt to shore up the conservative grassroots constituency increasingly identified as the base of the GOP. This meant, in effect, writing out moderates like the once-promising Holshouser, not to mention moderate black Republicans like McKissick.[126] Early in the race Ford had hinted that he might invite Holshouser to be his running mate, but a governor incapable of delivering his home state in a primary was not welcome on the national ticket. Rumors of a cabinet appointment for Holshouser, who had been an almost-certain nominee prior to Reagan's success on March 23, ceased as well. Postprimary pollsters now debated what impact North Carolina's ideological realignment might have, at both the state and national levels.[127]

As a result of Reagan's surge in the primaries leading up to the National Republican Convention, Ford no longer had "the requisite delegates needed for the nomination." This forced the incumbent into intense bargaining with Reagan for individual delegates in order for Ford to secure his party's nomination. Summing up the weakness of Ford's position at the convention, his chief strategist, James Baker, admitted that there was not a single plank request—except maybe firing Henry Kissinger—that "the President would not swallow." (Even Kissinger believed he was expendable, keeping "semi-hidden throughout the convention.")[128] Reagan, Helms, and the Congressional Club had transformed the Republican Party in a few short months. In the years to come the Congressional Club's model for purifying the party would provide a template for toppling moderate state regimes.

In light of the Republican Party shakeup that only narrowly resulted in the president's nomination at the convention, one of the Ford administration's most visible symbols of black economic power, the New Communities Administration Development Board (NCADB), began to defer to Jesse Helms, rated America's number one senator by the John Birch Society.[129] To appease the senator the NCADB backed away from initial plans of an additional draw of debenture for Soul City. "This approach," as one NCADB official explained to another, "should enable the Board to put off the decision until after the November election, thereby avoiding perhaps (although I am not sure to what extent) the vigorous, adverse reaction from Senator Helms and the *Raleigh News and Observer*."[130] Ford's acquiescence to the Helms-Reagan faithful had important consequences when he faced Jimmy Carter in the general election. In retrospect it may well have been Ford's undoing, as he was defeated in what turned out to be the slimmest electoral margin since 1916.[131]

In the November election Ford garnered only 10 percent of the black vote—a declining GOP share from 1972 that reflected both the deleterious impact of Watergate and the GOP's abandonment of its black-vote infrastructure. Two factors suggest why demobilizing the Two-Party movement quite possibly cost Ford the election. First, while national voter turnout figures declined from 55.2 percent in 1972 to 53.5 percent in 1976, about six percent more blacks went to the polls in the latter year, and black voters provided Carter with narrow victory margins in thirteen states, nearly all of which were proposed targets of the Two-Party committee to get out the vote. Second, white voters, particularly in the South, had shifted to the Republican Party in large numbers in recent years, and yet, unlike the previous two elections, conservatives had no reasonable third-party alternative; it was Ford or bust.[132]

All the more ironic was that the use Ford's Republican opponents made of Soul City during the North Carolina primary campaign gave it a high visibility that was completely out of proportion to the meager support given it by the Ford White House.[133] Throughout his presidency Ford had all but ignored McKissick and the Soul City project. Still, Ford posters papered Soul Tech's office walls and cars parked on its lots for weeks after November 5. The reality of a Carter victory did not hasten their removal.[134] Perhaps more important, Ford's strategy of neglect in the fall of 1976 signaled the beginning of a more protracted battle to neutralize moderate and progressive black leadership within the GOP.

At minimum North Carolina in 1976 glimpsed a larger struggle for the soul of the Republican Party; at most the state changed the course of modern American politics. For the U.S. Right, if Reagan biographer Lou Cannon is to be believed, North Carolina signaled "the turning point in Reagan's pursuit of the presidency."[135] Reagan's primary upset over a sitting president triggered "a shoot-out" at the GOP convention, ending in Ford's political death at the general campaign. And Carter's victory over Ford ensured Reagan's position as his party's presumptive nominee in 1980. Before North Carolina, Reagan was a party crasher. "At all times after North Carolina," wrote one insider, Craig Shirley, "Reagan was a legitimate and full-fledged candidate."[136] Others, like James C. Roberts of *Human Events*, opined: "Without Reagan's victory in North Carolina, there would have been no Reagan presidency."[137]

For the Ford administration and campaign the setback in North Carolina triggered a full-run policy and campaign retreat, as Ford stopped using the language of détente almost altogether, taking a tougher stance toward the Soviet Union, and canceling plans to normalize relations with Cuba. Back home in North Carolina, retrenchment meant Ford abandoning McKissick's project, as the administration effectively backed away from a political fight and annexed Soul City's future to Jesse Helms.

Ending the Menace of Black Republicanism

The sacking of the nation's highest ranking black elected official, Senator Edward Brooke III of Massachusetts, was probably the capstone, marking the end of the menace of black Republicanism and fusion politics nationally. Since doing battle over Soul City on the senate floor in 1975, Brooke had been a ubiquitous though solitary foe of Helms's actions against the project. He regularly found himself "correcting" his North Carolina combatant for mischaracterizing the GAO audit.[138] Brooke's defense of Soul City and attack on Helms belonged to a larger pattern of taking on his party's march to the right. This pattern included his decision to break publicly with Nixon over his Supreme Court nomination of Judge Clement Haynsworth

Jr., which Brooke argued was "not in keeping with the historic movement toward equal justice."[139] As a prochoice Republican, Brooke had also advocated the government's responsibility to finance abortions for poor and indigent women.

Despite this, the lifelong Republican and former Massachusetts state attorney general stayed atop Nixon's list "as the best man for the 'black seat,'" when word surfaced that Thurgood Marshall might retire. "He's basically liberal," Nixon confessed to John Dean and John Mitchell. "But," the president continued in typical Nixon-speak, Brooke is "one of the few blacks who really talks in an intelligent way."[140] (Though years later a black Republican did replace Marshall, Marshall's successor, Clarence Thomas, was far from a prochoice, card-carrying member of the NAACP.) Careful not to conflate his personal racial bigotry with pragmatic politics, Nixon's consideration was also, no doubt, a political thank-you to Brooke, who, in fall 1968, put aside his deep political differences with the Republican candidate to stump for the nominee. Brooke's sacrifice would later be called among the most unifying acts of any Republican during the election. Hoping to capture an image of party, national, and racial unity, Nixon kept the progressive senator "close by his side in his travels through the country," historian Stephen Ambrose wrote.[141] Republican cannibalism in post-Watergate America, however, would overwhelm independent-minded moderate Republicans like Brooke.

Brooke's independence began to cost him politically by 1978. With no strong Democratic challengers in sight, fellow state Republicans opted to challenge the incumbent's renomination.[142] Mortally wounded, as Brooke put it, on "the firing line" of his own party during the primary season, an anemic Brooke lost the November 7 general election.[143] Not surprisingly, the number of Republican black candidates and voters identifying with the party had begun to decline by then.[144]

That same year, 1978, McKissick returned to the Democratic Party. McKissick's switch in party identification—backing Democrat Luther H. Hodges Jr. in his battle to unseat Senator Jesse Helms—did not represent a shift in McKissick's ideology. Rather, Hodges's campaign rhetoric was consistent with the best of Keynesianism: offering a budget that would boost public-employment programs, strengthen Social Security financing, and tackle other economic woes through spending rather than cutbacks. Conservatives can complain about social problems all day, Hodges told the Chapel Hill press, but they will not go away until the private economy becomes more productive.[145] Hodges's campaign literature summed the meaning behind the senate choices: "North Carolina used to be at the forefront of the New South. . . . There was a spirit of progress and a feeling that we were going in the right direction. But somehow we've lost the momentum we had. We've lost that direction."[146] Hodges lost.

Soul City and the Myth of Black Capitalism

Black capitalism offered no solace for Soul City. While major black trade groups of the order of the National Business League and National Association of Black Manufacturers publicly endorsed Soul City, only the Minority Enterprise Small Business Investment Corporation (MESBICS) backed such gestures with funding, a modest million dollar pledge that barely caused a ripple in recruitment.[147] "Three years ago sixty million dollars was considered a passable start," the *Carolina Financial Times* noted.[148]

Not only was black capital and technical expertise insufficient to bridge the resource gap but, in the absence of white private backers, black enterprise also appeared headed in the opposite direction—both financially and strategically.[149] Coinciding with Soul City's inception in 1969, black-owned enterprises suffered from prolonged stagnation and retrogression more acute than what the nation-at-large was experiencing.[150] Black business failed at a rate of over 13 percent or more during the first half of the decade. Black-owned businesses watched potential markets vanish, destroyed largely by inflation and black unemployment at crisis levels—as high as 30 to 45 percent in many areas.[151]

After 1975 black-owned firms had to get out of the ghetto and away from serving a minority clientele in order to succeed.[152] This was especially true for black America's financial sector. The black-banking graveyard of the late 1970s and 1980s, economist Andrew Brimmer wrote, was littered with race-conscious black lenders supplying credit to black-owned businesses (most of whom had high rates of bankruptcy). "The more they try to respond positively, the greater is the probability that they will fail."[153]

Brimmer and others watched black-to-black business continue to tumble throughout the remaining decade. The infrastructures within the black community, created in the early 1970s to stimulate and study black investment and economic expansion, came unhinged. The National Association of Black Manufacturers (NABM), in the throes of an institutional life-and-death struggle, was emblematic. Known since its 1971 founding as the "Voice of Minority Industry," association chairman Norman Hodges listed saving the "creditability of NABM" as the organization's number one priority by decade's end. Meanwhile, the New York–based Black Economic Research Center, established in 1969 to study and nurture economic and business maturation by black businesses, folded after financial resources dried up in 1978.[154] Unfortunately, the NABM, BERC, and moribund groups like them were oftentimes more albatross than asset for Soul City.

Desperate to entice industry McKissick, an erstwhile labor attorney, would openly play up state right-to-work laws in his promotional literature. Such antilabor appeals elicited a sharp reprimand from Bayard Rustin. Rustin warned McKissick that closing the city to unions would be anathema to the late A. Philip Randolph, whose name had been affixed to the Industrial Park in Soul City from the project's early days. In what can be considered a riposte to Rustin, McKissick dropped the name "A. Philip Randolph" from the industrial park, hoping that doing so might lure industrial suitors put off by the name honoring Randolph and his legacy of worker activism.[155]

Soul City on Ice

In its last five years Soul City struggled to gain its footing. From 1976 through 1978 residential sales achieved only 35 percent of projected targets; commercial and industrial land sales hit 50 percent and 16 percent, respectively.[156] Shortly after the midterm elections in November 1978, William White of HUD stated that Soul City was not worth the risk of the remaining $4 million in guaranteed assistance McKissick requested from HUD.[157] Though White retracted his statement before the new year, he prophesized Soul City's ill-fated last six months. By January 1979 HUD refused to accept Soul City's budget for the year, instead establishing a special task force to review the project's future viability.

From February till June the task force met twice a month, but the Carter administration, at least publicly, sided with the project.[158] Privately, more than a dozen congressmen pressured HUD to stop the funding.[159] Town boosters John Stewart and Billy Carmichael, having failed to persuade the Carter administration over the years to support the project, concluded that "Government will back away from any appearances of a new city that appears to represent any policy of racial separation."[160] McKissick, a veteran of such reviews, was unfazed and still operated with self-assurance. He told the task force members that "we can win" key Democrats "Senator Morgan and Congressman Fountain over if we use the 'proper strokes.'"[161] The need for such declarations was about to end. On that same day, the HUD task force recommended to Secretary Patricia Roberts Harris that support for Soul City be discontinued. "The General Partners of The Soul City Company were shocked and surprised," McKissick wrote to Harris. After twelve years and four presidential administrations, "We had absolutely no forewarning of this action and have no Defaults on record to warrant this extreme remedy."[162]

The task force took pains not to attribute the failure of Soul City to deficient management. Rather, they wrote that "economic conditions, site location and the projected growth were overwhelming obstacles beyond the control of the Developer." By the mid-1970s, three in four whites polled preferred color-blind approaches over reparative and distributive race-centered state action.[163] In such an environment a new town with a race-conscious name also deserved blame, according to the report: "The term 'soul' is a tired expression established of the 1960s. Today, the term alienates many businessmen and residents who might consider a move to the area."[164]

Legal wrangling between McKissick and HUD filled the months between July 1979 and March 1980, when the two groups finally reached a settlement.[165] HUD would take over by June 1, 1980, at which time McKissick reflected upon the "significant" accomplishments of Soul City: two hundred on-site jobs, eighty industrial acres prepared, two housing subdivisions completed, a two-county health-care center, and the construction of a regional water system. He spoke of his continuing faith in the New Town concept, with one crucial difference: the entrepreneur has decision-making authority. "This," McKissick said one last time, "we did not have."[166] The government forced a study "every time we did anything."[167] There was also no mistaking how McKissick and acolytes read the tea leaves of modern political currents: "It is unfortunate that the government seeks to renege on its contractual commitments because political sentiments have changed since the law was originally passed in the '60's, he continued."[168] McKissick's loss of influence had less to do with a new party in the White House than with a narrowing of national political parameters.

* * *

For McKissick, his experiences as the visionary town founder limned something arguably more important than the mere muting of economic black nationalism and his project. What it suggests is Black Power's willingness to make trade-offs, the first and perhaps most auspicious of which was McKissick's quid pro quo of an all-black Soul City in exchange for federal succor. Of course with federal overlay came oversight. Second, McKissick's next trade-off came shortly thereafter, in 1972, when he, like prominent elected and appointed figures climbing the ranks of both major parties, distanced himself from the National Black Political Convention movement, as he looked to curry personal favor inside the GOP by broadening the Republican base. But McKissick looked to grow the base while staying largely consistent with the liberal value of advocating statist solutions in rooting out poverty. For example, he lobbied the White House to strengthen its support for OMBE and the controversial OEO.[169] McKissick stayed steadfast on state interventionism in the face of Gallup indicating more Americans preferred the label conservative to liberal.[170] Third, McKissick's olive-branch telegram to Senator-elect Helms suggests the sacrifices the town founder was willing to make, swallowing personal pride, to a mortal critic of both McKissick and of the new town project, if doing so meant possibly staving off any future investigations into Soul City. He lost little by seeking to open a dialogue with Helms—something liberals consistently call for with enemies, especially those abroad. Indeed, in the best-case scenario, the telegram could have mollified Helms. The fourth major trade-off made in an effort to instantiate Black Power was promoting the state's right-to-work laws and eviscerating Randolph's name from the industrial park. From the progressive's perspective, appealing to the state's right-to-work laws was arguably the most troubling concession made by McKissick—for if successful it well could have consigned a new generation to low-wage and benefit suppression. From McKissick's perspective, however, it was a desperate measure by a desperate man. A longtime labor activist, McKissick had withstood previous pressuring from labor and industrial recruiters, acceding only while facing the collapse of the project. Moreover, had

McKissick been ambivalent on unionism one doubts if Randolph's name ever would have been etched on city signs.

As for the particular political query: whatever happened to black republicanism? How did the Republican strategy of the early 1970s to broaden its existing base to encompass a burgeoning black middle class not only fail to diversify the GOP but, within black America, solidify the party of Lincoln as, effectively, the "white man's party"? Floyd McKissick and Soul City shed some light on these oft-asked questions. Soul City encapsulated the agency and accommodation of the age. At the apogee of the Black Power movement Soul City appeared destined, as Nixon put it, to be a shining showcase of black capitalism. Such rhetoric became the public rationale behind making Soul City the largest federally funded project ever underwritten for an African American.

In response to the space created by liberalism, McKissick—the nationalist who, in the words of historian Harvard Sitkoff, had moved 1960s radicals to regard nonviolence as a dying and useless philosophy—would modify his politics over and beyond any of his 1970s Black Power contemporaries, as he repudiated the black third party and labor struggles, relinquished his near life-long association with the Democratic Party, and emerged as the leading voice of the new fusion politics within the Republican Party. Despite McKissick's accommodation to Republican leadership, however, the Soul City initiative would help fuel a backlash led by conservative insurgents within the GOP.

Conclusion

This book aims to intervene in two dominant schools in the writing of modern American history. The first is that of the Black Power specialists, who often isolate liberalism from Black Power. The second is the principal school of thought in the profession, along with the public writ large, which recognizes the liberal–Black Power interplay, but which nonetheless misinterprets the consequence of this interplay and assumes that black nationalism ran amok over liberalism. Thus far I have approached the rewriting of these two conflicting narratives by way of an archivally driven, close-up examination into the liberal–Black Power relations in one state. In this way readers have hopefully discovered the interaction behind the headlines. Still, it would be a misreading of this book to see North Carolina as an exceptional or catalyst case. While MXLU, the Black Panther Party, the Joan Little case and movement, and Soul City certainly made important contributions to the Black Power movement, rarely, if ever, did these respective Black Power initiatives blaze a trail as the first or sole institutional expression. What makes Black Power in North Carolina relevant to the isolationist and unraveling schools discussed in the introduction is not its uniqueness but its ubiquity. An observation of the broader landscape reveals how North Carolina demonstrates, rather than cordons off, how liberalism created an operational space for Black Power, and the effect liberal engagement had on black nationalism during the late 1960s and 1970s.

Let us begin where history is often said to arrive first: California. The shoot-out on the UCLA campus between the Black Panther Party and the cultural nationalist US organization signaled a point of departure in Black Power history. A turf war between two leading nationalist factions climaxed over control of black studies on the UCLA campus, ending in a bloody shoot-out and murders of two Panthers in 1969. Scholars including David Garrow, Clayborne Carson, and Van Deburg use this conflagration as a broader illustration of how ideological disputes turned deadly, disrupting unity inside the movement.[1] Certainly the more familiar account of the US-BPP shoot-out details the disruptive role played by FBI and law enforcement, who were out to shatter working alliances between the Black Power groups in Southern California. Yet lost in this well-worn internecine epic is the relatively hidden transcript of liberal–Black Power dialogue, without which this nadir in Black Power history might never have occurred.[2]

In authorizing the creation of black studies at the University of California's largest campus, UCLA chancellor Charles E. Young sided with black nationalists, overriding the objections of then-governor Ronald Reagan and university regents.[3] Young's decision to back black studies earned him the ire of the right, as he adhered to the advice of UCLA graduate student Maulana Karenga. Young named Karenga's selected candidate, Dr. Charles Thomas, to run the new program.[4] Backing Black Power was a brazen move, particularly for the inexperienced Young, who began that academic year as the youngest chancellor at a major university at age thirty-six.

By creating space Young also reduced the administration's visible opposition to black studies, setting the stage for Black Power's self-immolation. With the administration no longer the shared object of obstinacy, long-rooted tensions between cultural and political nationalists—two complementary but historically natural ideological rivals—turned inward. An internal power struggle ensued between Panther-backed black student union critics of Karenga, who effectively blamed Karenga and US cultural nationalists for being kept out of the decision-making loop about the future direction of black studies on campus and broader Black Power struggles. Tensions culminated two days later when, after a follow-up meeting of the black student union about the program, the shoot-out occurred.[5]

Instead of stopping there, Young looked to create more space. In the summer of 1969 he took on Sacramento full bore, attempting to block Governor Reagan and the board of regents; they had ordered the firing of a newly hired, largely unknown black woman assistant professor after stories surfaced of her close ties to a UC San Diego professor who was an alleged Communist Party member. To those wanting Angela Davis removed, the chancellor reportedly replied, "So what?" Young went on: "We were trying to establish the point that she ought to be judged on what she does as a professor and not what party she's a member of." While acknowledging that Davis was indeed subsequently removed, Young added, "That principle was established even though the regents voted to terminate her." "It was the most intense ten months I've ever spent," Young declared about these early days.[6]

When not creating space for Black Power's self-immolation, liberal integrationists like Martin Luther King Jr. were engaged to diffuse Black Power's embrace of political violence as a liberating force.[7] Migrating to the mid-South, the Memphis-based Invaders, a group patterned after the Black Panther Party, promulgated black nationalism even as its critics claimed the war on poverty rented office space to its members and kept many on the antipoverty employees' payroll. While some black ministers, including Andrew Young, isolated the Invaders, denouncing the fatigue-jacketed, amulet-attired activists as too violent and separatist, Martin Luther King Jr. took a slightly different tact. On April 4, 1968, King met and agreed to help the Invaders secure funding for community programs. Unfortunately for all, by evening's end he lay dead. As for the Invaders, though unsuccessful in securing a $50,000 National Council of Churches grant, it did get funding to manage some community programs later, thanks partly to local Jewish human rights advocates like Herschel Feibelman.[8] New Orleans, often called a last outpost of Bohemia where gay people found refuge and interracial couples escaped neighboring miscegenation laws, was also a Black Power harbor. New Orleans groups bore the classic mark of the era's political incorporation. Belying the ratcheting-up of revolution suggested in the eponym of organizational acronyms—SOUL, BOLD, and COUP—their trajectories followed a decidedly predictable path: absorption into the city's electoral body politic, with each group jockeying for board appointments, patronage, and jobs at city hall.[9]

In Pennsylvania during the mid-1970s, the outreach efforts of two Rockefeller Republican senate hopefuls, Arlen Specter and John Heinz, was a desultory but effective wedge inside the largest black nationalist political organization, the National Black Political Assembly. Pittsburgh NBPA urged that Specter and Heinz be endorsed and supported—a position the Philadelphia chapter strongly opposed.[10] Pennsylvania's split was a window into the trending away from black political autonomy, symptomatic of a larger brain drain that posed a protracted problem for future liberation struggle. As national NBPA chair Ronald Daniels lamented to the local press, while one-time committed nationalists like Pittsburgh's Phil Carter once made "substantial contributions to black politics," now center-to-left Democratic and progressive GOP poachers were stealing the "pretty good political crops" raised by the NBPA. "The parties come along," Daniels added, "and say, 'This is a good one.' And they take them into the party structure—never to be heard from again."[11] The historical record of the Philadelphia and Pittsburgh chapters of the NBPA reveal that as late as the 1970s, the splintering of black unity and self-determination was often a bipartisan action.

On Pittsburgh's cultural front the *Thrust* newspaper, published by a founding member of the regional NBPA, frequently echoed nationalists elsewhere. Editorials blasted Planned Parenthood and other exponents of "black genocidal policies," whose policy outcomes could surreptitiously abort black nationhood. According to the paper's masthead, *Thrust* editorials reached readers "around the world." That message was delivered partly because of the local Community Action Program office where the paper, its critics complained, was typed, printed, and distributed. Also contributing, despite the paper's radical alternative positioning relative to the staid *Pittsburgh Courier*, was a mélange of multiethnic and government advertisers purchasing ad space. Such spaces of commercial exchange indebted black press radicals to its clients as well as core readers: "Support Our Advertisers," went the *Thrust*'s pitch to readers.[12] Such politics of engagement—ranging from seed monies to office and advertising space—have been manifest in creating operational space for Black Power.

The agitprop entertainment of Stax Records, a Memphis-based recording label, appeared to offer yet another site for the interplay of liberalism and Black Power.[13] Dubbed Soulsville, U.S.A., Stax was known for its raw style vis-à-vis Motown or Atlantic. Whites were no strangers in Soulsville; in fact, whites Jim Stewart and Estelle Axton founded it, using the first two letters of their names for their company's name. "We had an open door policy," said Axton, a schoolteacher turned music mogul, "let people come in and let us hear them." That open-door policy gave the movement music classics of black liberation, including hits like "Midnight Hour," along with the black musical Moses, Isaac Hayes. Stax planned what the *Guardian* newspaper described as the biggest, baddest musical event of the Black Power era. The August 20, 1972, Wattstax concert opened to a crowd of over a hundred thousand at the Los Angeles Coliseum, with a clenched-fist salute from Jesse Jackson and Stax black executive Al Bell during the singing of the Black National Anthem, "Lift Every Voice and Sing." Black pride anthems like "Respect Yourself" and lyrics including lines like "No nationality could . . . survive like the black people" were performed. Most attributed the large turnout not only to Stax performers like Hayes but to discount tickets made possible by concert subsidizer Schlitz Beer Company, which allowed event planners to trim prices to one dollar.[14] As music historian Craig Werner saw it, Wattstax mirrored Black Power's half-mythic dream of self-determination.[15]

The contemporary view of Wattstax represented a milestone for black autonomy. According to *Soul* magazine's Judy Speigelman, it marked "the first all-black entertainment event of its size and scope ever to be completely black controlled!" Politicians embraced the musical event as well. For example, Los Angeles's maverick mayor, Sam Yorty, relapsing momentarily to his bygone progressive past, declared August 20 Wattstax Day. Once assured that the concert was not a pretext for another Watts uprising, California Senator Alan Cranston, a Democrat, joined in as well, valorizing the event to colleagues in the Senate as an inspirational model "of good citizenship to all Americans of every race, creed, and national origin."[16] Wattstax may well have been, as organizer Al Bell remembered it at the close of the 1970s, "an intellectual, social, and emotional rebellion taking place among a people . . . manifested . . . in the music."[17] Still, Cranston and other California liberals exhaled when, compared to the 1965 Watts uprising that the concert was created to commemorate, Wattstax was a quiet riot.

So endemic, in fact, was concern about liberalism's undue influence over black institution building that the Twenty-first Century Foundation was started in 1971. The foundation stated its raison d'être as "break[ing] the dependency on white philanthropy." Blacks' collective destiny, declared a founding document, should exist "entirely under black direction." Yet the New York–based foundation itself relied on a million-dollar seed endowment from the DJB Foundation, a progressive social change philanthropy established in 1948 by left-liberal stockbroker Daniel J. Bernstein. By 1971 DJB was run by his widow, Carol Bernstein Ferry, who after her husband's death married the long-time number two man at the Ford Foundation, W. H. "Ping" Ferry. Together the Ferrys set out to back controversial and unconventional projects like the Twenty-first Century Foundation. Throughout the decade the foundation's board members reinvested parts of the endowment to extend the value of the donation, and selectively applied the rest to underwrite and influence a bevy of institution-building initiatives, generally to the modest tune of $3,000 to $5,000 per community group. Board members targeted grantees, starting mostly in the South and then almost exclusively in northern cities by the mid-1970s, in the areas of education and economic development.[18] Despite this, Black Power specialists persist in covering up this evidentiary interchange by their creative avoidance of, to appropriate the parlance of the period, following the money.

Take the think-tank Institute of the Black World, for example. Based in Atlanta, IBW was the intellectual glue for black nation building, gathering theorists, strategists, and policy planners essential especially in the modern era. Its centrality to the civic religion of black nationalism can be gleaned from apostates and adherents alike who, in either reviling or revering IBW, christened it the Black Studies Vatican. Historian Stephen Ward, lifting an excerpt from an opening program, asserts that the institute, "as its name suggests, is by, of, for, and about the black peoples of the world." IBW, added Ward, was consistent with Black Power's call for independent institutions in the service of the black world.[19] Echoing this, another prominent Black Power specialist, Peniel Joseph, writes that IBW "originated out of conversations between professors" in 1967.[20] But the empirical evidence swims against the Black Power specialists' interpretive tide of IBW, for when conversations shifted to operational costs, IBW officials—like those at MXLU and the Center for Black Education, nationalist institutions with which IBW had "fraternal relationships"—turned to corporations and foundations. In fact IBW owed much of its institutional existence to seed money from the Wesleyan University Board of Trustees, which unanimously approved a $95,000 appropriation directly to IBW, along with $109,000 to its own campus-based Afro-American Institute, in each group's first year of operation.[21] IBW split with the King Memorial Center, where it was briefly housed until September 1970, parting primarily over nonviolence and IBW's commitment to total black philosophy, which excluded white students and scholars from participating in programs. However, this did not mean separating itself from corporate and foundational funding. Rather, IBW took other grant monies, for example from the National Endowment for the Humanities (NEH) and the Southern Education Foundation, in the service of black liberation by supporting staff, conferences, publications, visiting lectures, fellows, travel, and old building repairs.[22] If IBW "embodied the political imperatives, cultural sensibilities and ideological commitments of the era," as Ward writes, it also epitomized the engagement of Black Power's world with liberalism.[23] Yet the writing-out of liberalism from the narrative is commonplace among specialists chronicling the institutional rise of contemporary black nationalism. The exception that evinces this unwritten rule of Black Power historiography is Noliwe Rooks, who in addressing the absence of white money in current Black Power scholarship pondered what it meant when a usable past came at the cost of burying parts deemed inconvenient by some: "What, they asked, could possibly be gained by exploring a relationship between the development of the [black studies] field and a white philanthropic organization. . . . I began to think that perhaps historical memory should not be tampered with."[24]

To its credit, Black Power scholarship has taken up the Rankean task of researching the movement on its own terms. Yet if one insists that fellow historians "craft a fuller view of this period," as one Black Power studies scholar desires, perhaps specialists themselves might lead the way.[25] This begins not with digging deeper but with looking wider. While Black Power studies have extended its analysis—by, for example, dating Black Power's origins decades prior to the 1960s or relating the American Black Power movement to anticolonial struggles among people of color in Asia, Africa, and Latin America—the consequence (if not intent), generally though not always, seems to broaden the frame rather than change the interpretive landscape. For example, how might Garveyism, among the largest mass movements in America during the interwar years, change what historians know about the rise of global progressivism? Or, more recently, how does the Black Power project compel us to rethink Benedict Anderson's imaginary community or soft-power politics internationally? Metahistorically, in what ways might the current trend of deperiodizing Black Power be taken beyond the mere erasure of enclosing dates to clue in scholars—as East Asian historian Prasenjit Duara has done by inviting a rethinking of the way history is represented in China, Japan, and the United States—about the possible heuristic practices and hegemonic gains benefiting the state from such dating?[26]

These elemental elisions by specialists have epistemological consequences. First, the inability to acknowledge funding sources invites critics, whether from mainstream historians or nonscholars harboring some ideological motive, to be dismissive of Black Power specialist literature. For critics the implications behind Black Power scholars obviation is obvious: these specialists—willing even to silence or contort facts dictated by some ideologically driven end and more interested in jury-rigging the past than in moving our understanding to a closer historical truth—cloak a political agenda in scholarship. At times the walling-off of history leads to innocuous slips, like Gary Gerstle's reference in *American Crucible* to the US organization as "United Slaves," not the first-person plural pronoun, Us (as opposed to Them).[27] More substantively, at other times it is one event that yields two incongruent histories, as in the aftermath of King's murder, which the Black Power literature suggests is indicative of the bankruptcy of liberal democracy.[28] Compare the specialist view with the historiographic main, which often depicts liberals' response to the assassination as a kick-up in funding for black studies programs, nascent affirmative action, and recycled calls for a domestic Marshall Plan.

Second, epistemologically speaking, the very nature of the isolationist enterprise wards off interpretive engagement, since their methodology rewards digging in popular archival spots. Thus foundational records, government funding agencies, and personal interviews and correspondence with exogamous backers of Black Power have been largely neglected. The end result is a scholarly publication that reinforces insularity—both in the respective subfield and, given it is never explicitly engaged and thus rarely directly disturbed, in the dominant narrative itself. Because of this inward-looking orientation, the conclusions of specialists tend to inform few beyond its subfield, truncating the fuller potential of modern black nationalism's explanatory power. The isolationist scholar then wonders why, to borrow historian Peniel Joseph's soliloquy in a special issue of the *Black Scholar*, "the Black Power era has not been taken seriously by mainstream scholars" who don't respond to and address Black Power literature.[29]

The irony here is that the less inclined mainstream historians are to engage this specialist literature, the more it reifies the "master narrative" that specialists deem so problematic. One would be hard-pressed to identify another field of subresearch in which the gap in perception between specialists and the general academic audience—let alone the broader public— varies more widely. With this perception gap comes a gap in the credibility of specialists. On the rare occasion of a generalist appraisal, mainstream historians use their limited space in flagship disciplinary journals to raise questions about the specialists' commitment to scholarly standards of fairness and objectivity. As reviewer Michael Flamm writes of *American Babylon*, a book otherwise a product of careful research, its prizewinning author, Robert Self, "eschews balance and nuance" when the interpretive moment comes to explain how nonradical whites responded to black activism. Instead, Flamm suggests that not only are facts "selectively" chosen or elided but that a double standard in interpreting events is applied. Regarding the concerns swirling around Black Power, like crime and urban renewal, Flamm writes that *American Babylon* patiently limns the "complex actions and motivations" of blacks, like mayoral candidate Lionel Wilson who made public safety central to his successful run in Oakland. Yet, Flamm concluded, when the subject turned to why whites reacted to similar social issues, the book instinctively fell back on "sweeping assertions," seeing only purely racial motives.[30] Such interpretive divergences have not escaped some students of the nation-state like Thomas Bender, who acknowledges the innovations of recent scholarship in U.S. history especially in nationalism and race, while concluding that, nonetheless, "it has not changed the dominant narrative structure." "Too often," Bender explains, "new scholarship is bracketed (literally so in textbooks) rather than integrated. Much is added, but the basic narrative stays the same."[31] By definition the isolationist thesis, if unwittingly, serves to reify the master narrative it wishes to revise.

Third, the ghettoization that animates recent historiography suggests that Americanists and Black Power specialists, like the clustering of millions of like-minded Americans since the 1970s, are participant-observers in the current trending of American segregation, what journalists and sociologists dub "gated" communications communities, where communities of interest choose to inform, read, and hear only the things that bolster their worldview. More important, these gated communications communities, according to Bill Bishop and Robert G. Cushing, authors of *The Big Sort: Why the Clustering of Like-Minded America Is Tearing Us Apart*, have literally, physically segregated themselves. The result has been that, in 1976, only 38 percent of counties had a partisan spread larger than 20 percentage points; in the astonishingly close election of 2004, more than 60 percent of U.S. counties saw landslides. Americans spend their daily lives with people who think just like they do. Such self-selected migration, though not necessarily conscious, nonetheless may have real-life consequences, "the worst of which," authors conclude, "is an ideological inbreeding that is creating a dangerous distance between Americans who hold opposing worldviews."[32]

Fourth, by walling off history, the historiographic main continues to miss the big picture, one that reveals implications of this interplay. Indeed, as is described in the introduction to this book, the notion of America's unraveling is not simply the default interpretation. It is the gold standard by which contemporary works on post-1965 America by prizewinning authors like James Patterson and Nick Kotz are measured. Let me illustrate how a closer evidentiary reading of the sources, one limited neither by region nor programmatic expression, makes the case for how liberal engagement contributed not to the making of an American dystopia but, depending on one's perspective, to the moderating of black nationalism.

I begin by expounding on two black nationalist projects, NBPA and IBW, before introducing the Organization of Black American Culture and the Black Economic Research Center, two projects in which the outcome of the liberal–Black Power interplay is equally palpable.

Liberal engagement undermined the main thrust of black nationalist political organizing at the time, the National Black Political Assembly. For the NBPA the primary question confronted was whether to build a third party within America's existing political framework. Yet even that option was undone by an engaging liberalism, particularly among moderates and progressive Democrats, both northern and southern, who looked to peel off NBPA blacks. According to one NBPA historian, the greatest threat to the foremost black political nationalist organization during the 1970s was the Democratic Party.[33]

At stake for the Democrats was their survival as a national party. Since at least the late 1870s, southern Democrats at the state and federal levels had represented the largest bulwark against black advancement, scholars like Ira Katznelson and Robert Lieberman write, almost single-handedly dismantling black franchisement and full citizenship.[34] That political calculus changed by the 1960s in the aftermath of the civil rights movement and mid-1960s legislation. Southern white flight from the national Democratic Party coincided with hundreds of thousands of black voters moving into the party. As southern political experts Earl and Merle Black explain, "Most conservative Democrats did not blame their Democratic representatives, whose careers had ordinarily been devoted to maintaining racial segregation, for the passage of civil rights and voting-rights legislation."[35] They did, however, hold the national party accountable. Presidential scholar William Leuchtenberg notes that despite being the first southern elected official to be president since Andrew Johnson, Lyndon Johnson won with the smallest proportion of southern votes of any Democratic candidate since Reconstruction.[36] Aside from briefly flirting with Carter in 1976, southern whites continued to move away from the party during the late 1960s and 1970s. A bleak outlook for Democrats, then, blanketed future presidential, and increasingly congressional, campaigns—save for discrete progressive pockets in the South, like the metro Piedmont counties of Durham where Hubert Humphrey won in 1968; and Orange, where Democratic nominees got a majority both in 1968 and 1972, even without massive black voter support and turnout. Democrats calculated that the mass exodus of white southerners would only add value to newly enfranchised black voters, making them the likely key constituency within a reconstituted Democratic party—assuming Democrats desired to sustain its political hegemony in the South and viability as a national party.[37] In sum, if pre–civil rights southern Democratic politics revolved around the position of the Negro, as V. O. Key concluded in his 1949 classic, the position of blacks seemed to have improved inestimably after the civil and voting rights acts.[38]

Here amid the dissolution of the one-party South is the nub of the question: how did black political nationalists play their racial hand, given black America's putative newfound electoral leverage? Why would one expert of the foremost black political power organization conclude that the greatest threat to its membership and radical character lay with the Democratic Party? That answer is largely found in the National Black Political Assembly, for whom Democrats' engagement did less to embolden than to trigger an identity crisis. Such questions and facts complicate the impressionistic view so often presented by general political and southern historians of neatly "herding blacks," to quote one historian of the South, to go quietly and "cohesively" into the Democratic fold. Such unreconstructed readings of blacks' jejune faith in a political party is as much a lingering Dunning artifact, based on century-long working assumptions about a bovine-minded black bloc, than a postmortem of post-1960s black politics driven by NBPA (or comparable) primary sources.[39]

Democratic engagement helped split black nationalist politics because the NBPA was torn strategically over its direction. As demonstrated previously in Pennsylvania, the NBPA chapters in small and large U.S. cities spent much of the 1970s grappling with the tug of the party system in its membership and platform. For example, northeastern and midwestern delegates generally leaned toward building a third party and fielding third-party candidates, whereas southern delegates tended toward using the NBPA as a protopolitical action committee, backing candidates who reflected the assembly's policy positions without actually running candidates under a new, third-party label.[40] Whichever path these competing visions preferred, neither seriously pursued a politics of isolation. Instead, each ensconced itself further in the nation's electoral process. Even Left nationalists inside the NBPA, often considered most skeptical about the promise of the two-party system, understood strategic alliances with black elected officials could mean access to antipoverty programs and funds, which had become essential to so many black nationalist efforts.[41]

The currency of this argument is found not simply in institutions but also in individuals like Left nationalist Amiri Baraka. As arguably the best-known and most visible NBPA member, Baraka was active in electing the first African American big-city mayor in the Northeast. Canvassing for Newark's Kenneth Gibson and others, Baraka believed, might help him secure public funding for community projects. But Baraka soured on this approach by February 1975, when Gibson, along with black city council members, sided with party regulars and blocked Baraka's obtainment of antipoverty funds in the form of a tax abatement and federal and state loan guarantees for the realization of NJR-32, a community and housing development plan in the city's central ward. Disillusioned, Baraka concluded that black public officials were more accountable to political parties and corporate contributors than to local black constituents, which eroded their legitimacy within the black convention movement and thus fed the breakdown of the united black front.[42] By 1976 the NBPA political director questioned if the organization "still has a strong nationalist feel."[43]

In resigning as national treasurer of NBPA, Oklahoma's Hannah Atkins, a state legislator and one-time law instructor, described another way that constitutional liberalism contaminated black nationalist thinking. Atkins explained her departure by employing classic civil liberties language, stating that she left because her critics inside NBPA were enemies of free speech, "shouting down disruptions, capturing microphones, bypassing or ignoring those wishing to speak." Yet taking her case to the court of public opinion, obviating criticism inside NBPA and appealing to media outside it, made sense only if the NBPA took free-speech rights and open debate seriously, and if Atkins believed its members would be shamed by exposing the group's efforts to curb free speech. Others, notably *Black Scholar* magazine's founder Nathan Hare, echoed Atkins's concerns. Nonetheless, Atkins added, the black nation still needed a "blacks-only" party if it could be located within the boundaries of liberal democratic notions of openness and freedom of speech and association.[44]

To then-chairman of NBPA Amiri Baraka, Atkins was part of a larger exodus of nationalist-minded elected officials who, despite nationalist leanings, left the assembly behind for the ostensibly broader tent of the Democratic Party. They could join "George Wallace," Baraka noted, pondering aloud why blacks, instead of supporting him, backed the former party of the archsegregationist Alabama governor, yet "[they] can't be here with me."[45] A backlash against Baraka's alienating tactics ensued, resulting in his ouster by 1975; with his departure went the organizational apparatus he had set up. Whether pushed out because of repressed liberties or pulled out because of putative political rewards inside the Democratic Party, liberalism's DNA was all over the NBPA's disintegration.

In some instances, liberal engagement had the unintended consequence of only spurring black nationalism to greater militancy, as many conservatives and not a few Black Power proponents argued. In Detroit, for example, Heather Thompson has written, liberal efforts of engagement with Black Power militants may well have backfired. According to Thompson, made frustrated and angry by liberals, Detroit's Black Power movement grew more militant and activist in its political orientation. As black activists in Detroit happily took money from liberals, Thompson notes, the movement there grew more, not less, hostile to liberalism over time.

But Detroit seems more the exception than the rule. The preponderance of evidence suggests otherwise. While political scientists Adolph Reed and Robert C. Smith may differ over the rationale of Black Power decision making, they nonetheless agree on the results: the political incorporation of Black Power across the ideological spectrum into the larger electoral process. Likewise, in his Philadelphia study, historian Matthew Countryman identifies a movement driven less by frustration and anger than strategic logic. That logic, he concludes, is central to understanding Black Power's ultimate incorporation, as militant groups (e.g., Philadelphia's Black Political Forum) deduced that they could most likely achieve their goal of community control by way of electoral participation. Liberalism figured prominently in the political calculus of Philadelphia activists regardless of where Black Power practitioners might be found on the ideological continuum—from moderate activists, like future Mayor Wilson Goode, to more militant ones like future state legislator David Richardson. Indeed, Countryman asserts that Black Power victories in Philadelphia "depended *entirely* on the goodwill of government officials and the ability of those officials to remain in power. When more racially conservative politicians replaced the Black Power activists' liberal allies, first on the national level and then in local elections, the structures of community control that had been so laboriously established quickly disappeared" (emphasis added).[46] In sum, strategic logic invariably brought and kept Black Power militants in the liberal orbit.

Philadelphia Black Panther Barbara Easley Cox personifies Countryman's political analysis. Starting in the 1970s, Cox went to work for one of Philadelphia's oldest antipoverty organizations, the Advocate Community Development Corporation. By the 1980s she was elected to its board, and by the 1990s she chaired it. This was in addition to her government job with the Pennsylvania Department of Public Welfare, where she worked for twenty-seven years. As fellow Panther Dr. Yvonne King feted Cox at a 2004 dinner in her honor, "Barbara's work with the Advocate Community Development Corporation is an example of her ongoing efforts to implement the Black Panther Party's Ten-Point Platform and Program, which states in Point no. 4: We want decent housing fit for the shelter of human beings."[47] Symbiosis, at least as much as repulsion, captured the personal experiences of Cox's engagement with one of the city's most lasting liberal institutions of the era.

Even if Black Power had no oppositional state to overcome, nation builders averred the need to inculcate diasporic blacks with a greater collective awareness of personal and cultural belonging to a nation. That disconnect between the people and nationalism's architects troubled Baraka, who posed the challenge to a gathering of Pan-Africanists in 1970: "We are a people . . . with no means of relaying what our brain has conceived to our arms and legs and our muscles. We are a body whose muscles do not even know they belong to the body that the head belongs to."[48] Here, too, liberalism often functioned heuristically as a sort of central nervous system in the black body politic, the connective tissue facilitating the nation building of the black intelligentsia's outreach efforts. Liberals did so by underwriting schools, newspapers, building projects, think tanks, commercial enterprises, political campaigns, songs, and books. But liberalism filtered messages as much as it funneled resources. Again, IBW offers a classic example of how policies of engagement effectively mediated and moderated Black Power.

The IBW's main challenge, fellow Lerone Bennett contended, was "giving [blackness] visible body and form so that black people can plug into it and absorb the energy we need to fulfill our purpose." IBW found a cooperative partner in mass corporate media.[49] Responding to black consumer demands in the nation's capital, station officials at WMAL-TV in Washington, D.C., turned to black university proponent and Howard University English professor Stephen Henderson, who in turn contacted IBW's Vincent Harding. By January 1973, WMAL hired Harding to author a book on black struggle as the basis of a television series. "Under the arrangement," Harding recalled, "WMAL would provide funding for the research and writing of the book and would also take the major responsibility for seeking out a commercial broadcast outlet and one or more sponsors for the series." Harding went on: "It was their intention to begin at the network level, and to drop back to their local grouping only if the larger goal proved impossible to achieve." Harding and others were "very excited" about the visual medium possibility.[50] But access came at a cost for the institute. The IBW geared the book around the television schedule, planning a 1976 release and retitling the book *The Other American Revolution*—largely in an effort to maximize the country's bicentennial viewing audience.

More importantly, filtering transmogrified the IBW in another way. It challenged what some historians claimed was IBW's radical critique of capitalism. The IBW would cozy up to corporate-owned media at the time of their regulatory battles against the Federal Communications Commission. The IBW looked to air its program on WMAL, whose parent company, the Washington Star, was under FCC investigation for violating federal monopoly laws. The FCC forced WMAL to divest its local radio and television outlets in Washington, D.C. One way that WMAL pared down its operations, in hopes of avoiding legal action, was canceling the IBW program.[51] IBW did not fall victim to media consolidation as much as antimonopoly regulation. Instead, the commodification of dissent, as much as a radical capitalist critique, seemed the upshot of this engagement.[52] WMAL represented neither the first (CBS in 1969) nor last (PBS from 1975 to 1977) time that IBW sought common ground with corporate media. In the instance of WMAL, though, the revolution was not televised because regulatory forces arrayed against concentrated capital, which had partnered with the IBW.

In this way Black Power spread its message like other subnationalities in late-twentieth-century Europe where, according to Benedict Anderson, they attempted to change their subordinate status by firmly breaking into print and, increasingly, into electronic media.[53] Black nationalism hoped broadcast capitalism might do what print capitalism had been doing since the mid-sixteenth century: forge an imagined community by way of a usable past, but spread this time through the opiate of modern technology—television, which could share blackness and spread nationalism into the living rooms of black Americans far faster than print media.[54] That message was often mediated and moderated by policies of engagement.

As the IBW also reveals, funding Black Power was not about charitable giving. It was, at times, a commercial choice. As Theodor Adorno wryly opined, the rich man will sell you the rope used to hang him if he sees he can profit from it. This greed motive allowed dissenters to exploit the system to their own ends. Corporate capitalism, driven by material returns, responded to consumer demands within an alienation market. This mutuality of commercial choice and Black Power need spawned working relations, like that of the WMAL and the IBW, as well as the most famous ritual borne out of the black nationalist years: Kwanzaa.[55] As historian Nell Painter wrote of the holiday, "In 30 years Kwanzaa had gone from a new, separatist black nationalist observation to a corporate celebration of American multicultural marketing."[56]

A desire to mediate the public messages partly explains why the family name synonymous with twentieth-century corporate capitalism was in the business of underwriting various local Black Power projects. In funding the Misseduc Foundation, National Black United Fund, Karamau Foundation, Arts for Racial Identity, and Black Theatre Alliance, among others, Rockefeller foundations took the so-called "contrarian" donor approach—a term used in the philanthropy world to denote grantors who target gifts for unpopular causes or marginalized groups. Like the Ford Foundation, Rockefeller grant-making agencies supported some of the leading local men and women of the Black Power years and disseminated the black worldview in communities across the country in ways that Rockefeller could shape, influence, and control.[57]

The contrarian approach helps to explain the Rockefeller's sponsorship of the National Black Theater (NBT), and by extension the foundation's efforts to redirect the larger cultural thrust of Black Power. Founded in Harlem in 1968 by director, actor, and dancer Barbara Ann Teer, NBT imagined itself the "theater for the black nation." Despite such nationalist imagery, Rockefeller Foundation grant administrators believed it might serve as a cultural counterweight to the mantras of more militant theaters. As the assistant art director for Rockefeller grants awards, Herbert Klein, saw it, NBT plays and workshops celebrated the possibility of change and human renewal, which could ultimately lead to reconciliation.

NBT's production and performance of *A Ritual* was a pivotal moment in the Rockefeller's funding decision. "A Ritual," wrote Klein in an internal field report for those who were still ambivalent, opened with "some dashiki-clad, others in black leather jackets, three 'tough' girls . . . [all of whom] seemed visibly to soften as they joined in the affirmations and finally the group dancing. . . . It had a resounding impact on the predominantly black audience." Don't be misled by NBT exhortations of "It's Nation-time," Rockefeller's gatekeeper of the arts allayed administrators at the foundation. The thirty-six-member NBT presented the Rockefeller with an alternative to supporting other guerrilla black theater houses whose favorite sport, Klein felt, appeared to be attacking whites as a means to coalesce blacks.[58] Two factors in particular gave the contrarian Rockefeller Foundation even greater control over NBT. First were the recessionary years of the 1970s into the early 1980s, which led to the contraction of philanthropic dollars. The foundation responded partly by establishing stricter benchmarks on how funding should be spent, and often required accountants to scrutinize the books of grantees. The drying up of grant moneys ramped up competition between outlaw artists and troupes for an ever-shrinking pot.[59] The second point was what political scientist Jacob Hacker labeled as the great risk shift. The great risk shift of the late 1970s looked to reallocate responsibilities and liabilities from institutions to individuals. Government and corporations often colluded to privatize risk—whether health care, auto insurance, student loans, or employee pensions—fragmenting groups of Americans into smaller and smaller risk pools, reducing the ability of these groups to bargain collectively against concentrated capital interests.[60] The cultural counterpart of this great risk shift is found, in microcosm, in the Rockefeller. Through the 1970s the granting emphasis of the Rockefeller Foundation increasingly shifted from funding institutions (e.g., playhouses) to directly awarding grants to individuals (e.g., playwrights), thus vesting the foundation with even more direct control over artists and the cultural production of recipients. "We don't support any theaters at this point, our playwright-in-residence program being our only program," Klein informed Teer by 1980, when any NBT pretension toward nationalism had been safely and securely neutered.[61]

A decade prior NBT spoke the naturalist language of cultural nationalism—"We start from the premise [that] black people are energy people, feeling people . . . that is true black identity."[62] By the late 1970s its statement of purpose had undergone a dramatic transformation to read: "mind expansion and trans-personal growth. The institution is organized around the concept of . . . 'I Amness.'" How much the Rockefeller Foundation influenced NBT's conversion to privileging the personal is difficult to ascertain, but it is hard to believe that NBT's interactions with the foundation was a nonfactor.[63]

The contrarian approach was also employed to contain the white ethnic movement, which had a small but growing following in the 1970s. While aiding various all-black initiatives, grant administrators balked at funding white ethnic centers—borne of the revival in European ethnic consciousness inspired partly by Black Power. "Too much emphasis on ethnic origins can ultimately be devisive [sic], don't you think?" wrote one Rockefeller grantor to a fellow colleague. "If we dwell on ethnic groups, the humanities would have them be viewed as part of mankind as a whole. Which goes to say that MN's [Michael Novack's] version of ethnicity was okay for starters, but beyond that lies world culture . . . 'interdependent' world culture, which is the greater RF emphasis."[64] Rightly fearing that an exclusive focus on European immigrant ethnics would doom funding, one director of a regional ethnic heritage studies center acceded—assuring those at the foundation that, if funded, the Michigan-based ethnic center he was running would "not confine itself to white ethnics." Instead, a high priority would be placed on the experiences of Hispanics, Arab Americans, Asian Americans, African Americans, and Native Americans.[65] Among the largest philanthropies, and one specializing in making national awards, the Rockefeller foundations collectively served as a bellwether and catalyst for the smaller grant-making world.

Some cultural histories of the postwar United States remain silent on leading cultural black nationalist outfits like the Organization of Black American Culture, and its role in America's road to recovery. Typifying this is Andreas Killen's recent psychoanalysis of the 1960s, which implicates Black Power in the nation's "nervous breakdown." Indeed, in the mid-1970s, when Killen contends that "Americans began to rewrite the national story line," one finds the leading literary cultural nationalists of the late 1960s insinuating themselves into a formulaic plot, characterized by literary patronage and big-city brokerage politics, rather than proffering their own script.

Take, for example, a midwestern group regarded among Black Power specialists as the literary vanguard of black nationalism, the Chicago-based Organization of Black American Culture.[66] Founded in 1967, OBAC (pronounced *Oba-see*) was regarded, in the apt summation of scholar James Smethurst, as "far more nationalistic" than member organizations in giving life to the expressive vernacular and visual flourishing known as the Black Arts Movement. Although it did not pursue much if any grant monies, OBAC's trajectory nonetheless illustrates the seductive influence and effect of incorporation that went beyond simple subvention.[67] Rent parties for the Chicago-based group covered operational expenses, but rent parties and similar fund-raising activities were insufficient to support the personal and career aspirations of many OBAC artists.

Conflicting visions beset OBAC during its earliest days. Within the first year or so, several co-organizers left OBAC, unsettled in part by what they considered the entrepreneurial and increasingly individualistic path that writers inside the organization were following. Erstwhile members, particularly those trained in the social sciences, grew concerned that OBAC's most talented members were drifting toward climbing personal ladders of success and the parvenu associated with publishing, instead of sublimating their artist's ego to the obscurity of organizing that so often accompanies collective uplift and liberation politics.[68] (Even those departing agreed that OBAC writers' desire for public recognition was not simply understandable but late in coming, given that they and other black artists had long been shut out of the large publishing market and therefore denied access to a wider reading audience.)[69]

Some of OBAC's most gifted members, like star poet Carolyn Rodgers, were wooed away from Chicago's four black publishing houses by mainstream publishers.[70] OBAC cofounder Conrad Kent Rivers offers a stark example. Playwright and poet, Rivers turned to the London-based Heritage Press partly because of racism in the U.S. publishing industry but also partly because, if Rivers's British publisher and good friend Paul Breman is to be believed, the representative of black consciousness assumed that the cachet of an international press would lead to more and better reviews, boosting book sales and thereby heightening his personal prestige in the literary world.[71] Under Breman, Heritage Press published twenty-seven volumes of black consciousness poetry over a dozen years, placing it along-side important black presses like Third World Press and Path Press. There is an argument to be made that the individual achievements of Rodgers and Rivers actually complemented the general claims of black nationhood made by OBAC.[72] Some scholars of liberal nationalism, for instance, contend that individual achievements contributed to the national endeavor. The painter working, the poet writing, and the athlete competing transcend their particular function, becoming "a source of national pride [which] is one of the most appealing aspects of nationalism."[73]

Nonetheless, by the late 1970s and early 1980s, OBAC's most visible and vested mainstays had also embarked on an instrumentalist path, ostensibly sublimating their nationalist agendas to the reformist multiethnic coali-tion building of politician Harold Washington.[74] OBAC's Bennett Johnson and Haki Madhubuti did significant electioneering for Washington, whose rainbow coalition—79 percent of the Puerto Rican vote, 68 percent of the Mexican vote, and 38 percent of the Jewish vote—in the general campaign proved vital in getting him elected in 1983 as Chicago's first black mayor.[75] Madhubuti's involvement was particularly noteworthy since he was a late-comer to coalition-building politics. As government professor Dianne Pin-derhughes writes of the poet's steadfast nationalism, fellow Black Power travelers had already begun to soften their stances on interracial alliances, "but Madhubuti continued to emphasize black nationalism." Yet Mad-hubuti set aside differences and worked with what was a broader base than Washington's mayoral team had ever expected. In a sense, OBAC's char-ismatic leader personified the institutional trajectory of Black Power to-ward normative politics, one in which, Johnson recalls, nearly every OBAC member canvassed for pedigreed career politician Washington. Son of a precinct captain who was groomed by the South Side's political elite for the state senate and later the U.S. Congress, Washington ran as a reformist mayor eager to end entrenched and corrosive patronage while advocating a (usurpless) government jobs program—partly by muting criticisms and partly by joining with Latinos, progressive whites, and other blacks to se-cure victory.[76]

Whereas Killen implicates Black Power as a causative agent in the United States' putative nervous breakdown yet stays silent about Black Power's role in the national road to recovery, Elisabeth Lasch-Quinn in *Race Ex-perts* finds Black Power tightly woven into the fabric of America's new-age therapeutic culture. But Lasch-Quinn shares Killens's dystopian diagnosis of Black Power practitioners. Opening her book with Black Power and its codependency on liberalism, saying the former "was a politics of posture that relied on an integrated audience," Lasch-Quinn argues that the liberal–Black Power interplay epitomizes how the application of psychotherapeutic approaches to contemporary social problems like race relations essentially made them worse. In her view "black assertion, white submission" pushed American race relations closer toward racial dystopia because they papered over the political, social, and structural causes for racial tensions.[77]

The posturing point is evinced by Baraka himself, who explained that black militants, having built up false expectations among whites, could not live up to their own advanced racial killing billing: "Negroes have sold white people wolf tickets for the last decade. . . . now he believes that we mean to kill him; we have convinced him for ten years that we want to kill him and now he believes it." Despite this, the hyperbolic "hijacking" language employed by Lasch-Quinn may generate more heat than it sheds light on the subject of liberalism's impact on Black Power.[78]

Paradoxically, liberalism's success has helped Lasch-Quinn overlook the forgotten alternatives posed by black nationalism. Black radicals became race experts, Lasch-Quinn tells us, providing innocuous therapy on matters of larger personal growth and self-esteem movements. By the end of the 1970s, these erstwhile framers of revolution would spend much of their time counseling in classrooms and corporate boardrooms, as liberals helped to channel Black Power into what was a nascent self-help industry, designed to shed pathologies and spread positive thinking. Liberals did so over growing conservative opposition, which objected to any efforts to aid diversity programming. If the hyperbolic language of "hijack," used in the subtitle of Lasch-Quinn's book, has any explanatory function in illuminating race relations in America, it seems more accurate to employ it toward the conclusion that liberals hijacked Black Power—given liberalism's role in detouring black nationalism's revolution to what Lasch-Quinn sees as the "rituals" of new-age therapy, a far cry from the new day in Babylon envisaged by black nationalists.[79]

Like others, Tommie Shelby's promising work, *We Who Are Dark: The Philosophical Foundations of Black Solidarity*, seems to have assumed such silence to mean an absence of engagement. Describing the aim of his book as "a research agenda that extends beyond the abstract concerns of philosophy," Shelby contends that, in theory, black nationalism overlaps with liberalism's core values, defined mostly by its commitment to equal citizenship, cultural tolerance, and freedom of association and expression. Black nationalism, he correctly insists, should not be considered a radical break from liberal political philosophy. Yet despite his keen intellectual instincts, the ontological shortcomings of his work undermine the power of the thesis. Indeed, he addresses the basic ontological question—what actually existed, in this case, between liberals and Black Power—by concluding that liberals dismissed or feared black nationalists. Not even in a chapter titled "Black Power Nationalism" does the author acknowledge or detect the quotidian relations extant between liberals and Black Power adherents. This oversight is a byproduct of two things: sources and assumptions. Despite promising "a more historically informed approach than is typical of philosophy," the argument relies almost exclusively on black nationalist doctrines, readings, and social and political thought.[80] Banking a case on dogma to the near exclusion of decisions and deeds seems a thin methodological reed—especially considering the centrality of pragmatism to the book's premise. That said, even these limited sources could have explicated the liberal–Black Power interplay. Black power theoreticians dropped enough rhetorical hints—in both speeches (evinced in Malcolm X's "it's like coffee" political reasoning to the "wolf ticket" cultural recitations of Baraka) and writings (for instance, separatist Robert Browne's rethinking of the role liberals could play in theorizing black economic liberation)—for those attentive to the intersectionality thesis.

It is not that Shelby fails to link claims to verifiable practices. Indeed, his consideration of the Congressional Black Caucus offers a good example, demonstrating his larger point about how solidarity might function institutionally. He also connects claims to practices individually by interrogating black thinkers, particularly regarding questions of class and gender. Yet when it came to the arguments on which the thesis hinges—liberalism— he accepts nationalists' rhetorical statements at face value. The "focus of attention on historically specific examples," designed to ground the study, never materializes regarding Black Power figures or Black Power institutions.[81] Perhaps if it had, we would have seen not just the philosophical overlap, where wolf tickets might be mistaken for the actual show, but rather the interplay during the 1960s and 1970s between individuals and institutions, between Black Power adherents and liberals. The evidence of liberal contamination of black nationalism is much more prevalent than Shelby imagines. The sources selected, however, are an extension of his working assumptions about black nationalism. Second, Shelby's oversight apparently results from his acceptance of the isolationists' canard that black nationalism operated sans liberalism. Such assumptions are belied by the reality that for many moderate and liberal politicians, as Komozi Woodard has written about a key pet project of Baraka's, "silence was the wisest policy, because it could be documented easily that they had worked for the development of Kawaida Towers."[82]

Shelby mentor Kwame Anthony Appiah, in making a case for cultural contamination (by which he means the importance of intermingling and the transformation that comes of new and unexpected combinations), underestimates not simply the soft persuasive powers of liberalism but also the level of openness of nationalism, even in its thickest forms like cultural Black Power. The traits shared by contaminants, traits that define and distinguish them from other competing universalisms, number at least six: (1) having experienced travel, trade, or conquest; (2) appeal to the enlightened across the world, rather than being blinded by "narrow nationalist" loyalties like kith and kin; (3) appropriation of such liberal democratic values as equality and freedom of expression and association; (4) an exhibited intolerance typically reserved for radical intolerance—the kind, Appiah says, that so often leads to authoritarianism or, worse, murder and violence; (5) a recognition that knowledge is imperfect, provisional, and hence, in the face of new evidence, always subject to revision; (6) a curiosity about and desire to communicate across cultures—not to gain friends or influence people, though that is obviously a wished-for effect, but to further an exchange of perspectives. Such a dialogue goes to the ideal of the cosmopolitan enterprise, what Appiah calls his golden rule: celebrating the dialectic manifest in the transformation that comes from new and unexpected combinations. One should rejoice in "mongrelisation," adds Appiah, quoting Salman Rushdie. Finally, the right approach to understanding cosmopolitanism, Appiah argues, is not by studying nations, tribes, or people. Rather, cosmopolitanism begins with and should be embodied in individuals; it is thus to the individual, black nationalist Robert S. Browne, that we shall turn.[83]

Few individuals fit Appiah's cosmopolitan profile better than Browne, whose reputation of being among the most radical black separatists of the time masks his own liberal democratic DNA. By 1953 Browne had traveled to three continents and well over twenty countries. Dedicated to promoting development and trade, from 1954 to 1958 Browne worked for the U.S. International Cooperation Administration, now known as the U.S. Agency for International Development, whose central aim was to use trade and other forms of economic development to promote American-style democracy. As an American liaison, Browne prepared annual requests for aid on behalf of Cambodia and Vietnam. Travels to Indochina not only introduced Browne to the consequences of America's conquests, but also to personal journeys such as meeting his future wife, Huoi Nguyen, a woman of mixed Vietnamese and Chinese ancestry residing in Cambodia.[84]

The future black separatist continued living the example of Appiah's cosmopolitan composite once he returned to the States in 1961. An appeal to enlightened, liberal democratic values and intolerance for extremism were all folded into Browne's famous tract, "Case for Black Separatism," written partly for the 1967 Black Power conference in Newark, New Jersey. The tract was designed to appeal to lay learners of history with "Jeffersonian" mindsets, whom Browne averred placed "a decent respect of the opinions of mankind" above "intense emotionalism." As Browne explained, he wrote the separatist tract to rescue the issue "from the deadly embrace of extremists," whether black or white. Browne looked to reach across ethnic, ideological, and cultural divides in hopes of avoiding "the classic error of ignoring the pleas of the moderate center . . . to the terror of the irresponsibles on the two extremes." In keeping with this view, Browne's writings appeared in *Cross Currents* and the *New York Times*; he personally reached out to open-minded civic organizations like the National Jewish Community Relations Council. But what ultimately drove Browne to call for separatism was not his advocacy of violence but his disdain for and desire to avoid it.[85]

Browne raised the partition question precisely because of his travels. It was an outgrowth of the cosmopolitan's contamination, not his expressed desire to be immune from it. An international aid worker in the 1950s, Browne personally witnessed the human costs exacted when long-simmering identity strife triggered sudden and largely unplanned partitioning as in Pakistan and India, resulting in the dislocation of millions of peoples and protracted violence along the shared border. Browne's position on violence placed him among the early opposition to the Vietnam War and made him a prominent member of SANE (Committe for a Sane Nuclear Policy), which called for unilateral nuclear disarmament.

Browne conceded that his knowledge regarding the fallout from partitioning was "imperfect." Still, he thought the alternative, rash partitioning, would almost certainly lead to protracted race war. Browne hoped that, at minimum, the tract might start an exchange of perspectives, or what Browne called "encouraging a national dialogue," over black secession. That conversation appeared partly in print, repackaged as a dialogic pamphlet that Browne coauthored with the faithful integrationist Bayard Rustin, debating an all-black state. It also put Browne, synonymous with black separatism in white minds, in conversation with the Vanderbilt Business School dean, who was also eager for cross-cultural dialogue, and prompted the Quakers' American Service Committee, with whom Browne had previous relations, to offer him a summer faculty position. His case for separatism provided added value in Black Power circles as well. Browne both underscores Appiah's case for contamination even as his case militates against Appiah acolytes who, in extrapolating from their mentor's thesis, might underestimate the openness of Black Power theorists and practitioners. Finally, for the sense that his knowledge was provisional and thus subject to revision, one need only be reminded of the sea change Browne made regarding the *Review of Black Political Economy*, where the evidence of more intellectually rigorous essays by nonblack contributors persuaded Browne to rethink publicly the notion that the national liberation struggle should necessarily exclude the contributive insights of whites.[86]

On paper the New York–based Black Economic Research Center, founded in October 1969, and its quarterly organ the *Review of Black Political Economy* appear to be institutional extensions of one of black nationalism's most polarizing architects: Robert Browne himself. The facts, as Browne later acknowledged, played themselves out somewhat differently. Although an ascendant black nationalism may have provided inspiration for BERC, both the center and the *Review* owed their institutional livelihoods, in large part, to the time, money, and human capital provided by liberals. For example, the provost of Fairleigh Dickinson University acceded to Browne's countless requests for open-ended teaching leaves, usually with full health and other fringe benefits for the husband and father of two. It was a remarkable accommodation to Browne, a gifted graduate student who nonetheless was still more than a decade away from completing his dissertation. Thus free to apply for grants that allowed him to build the Black Economic Research Center, Browne secured his major source of funding from the Ford Foundation. With patronage came concerns about quid pro quo, namely in the form of a potential loss of institutional autonomy. The Ford "placed considerable pressure on me to affiliate BERC with a university, arguing such an affiliation would mean a substantial expansion of the types of human and physical resources available to us," Browne recalled. He stood steadfast, however, and the Ford Foundation ultimately relented.[87]

Publishing the *Review of Black Political Economy* forced new realities on Browne. By the time he had assembled the magazine's inaugural issue, the dearth of qualified blacks prepared to write about their ideas for a black economy compelled Browne to rethink his policy of publishing solely black contributors. "It rather quickly became apparent," Browne reflected years later, "that the vast majority of the manuscripts were being submitted from whites—in fact, that the bulk of the really good manuscripts were from whites—and that the number of publishable manuscripts coming from blacks would not be sufficient to permit the magazine to continue. . . . It had not been my intention to include a white author so early on." Showing himself "contaminated" by the social science value, girded by the notion that methodological rigor matters, the *Review* publisher went on: "How optimistic I was to think that a journal of this type could rely mainly on black writers for its substance!" For Browne, sound social science proved more useful in the service of black nation building than racial purity or symbolic victories of black agency. Dean Robinson tells us that Browne also played a key role in the Republic of New Africa (1968–74). Browne provided "the basic ideological framework around which [these territorial nationalists] formulated its politics."[88]

In these ways Browne was not atypical of cosmopolitan scholars of the postwar generation. These U.S. academics, though mostly historians and American Studies practitioners, had their conceptual horizons (re)shaped while studying and teaching abroad or serving in U.S. foreign affairs, often with the military, Office of Strategic Services, and the World War II–era Office of War Information. But for historian Richard Pells and others, Browne appears an anomaly, for his postwar pedigree was supposed to militate against producing race-conscious academics: "It was precisely their involvement that helped to enlarge their knowledge of foreign cultures, and to make their work cosmopolitan." As Pells writes: "The necessity of having to explain the United States to foreigners was intellectually invigorating. It made Americanists more alert to cultural differences than they might have been had they never left the United States. And, in answering often challenging questions, they were forced to look at America in new ways, reevaluating those characteristics of life in the United States that they had taken for granted."[89]

These new ways of looking at America often meant recognizing American exceptionalism. With Richard Hofstadter, Louis Hartz, Oscar Handlin, and other scholars taking up academic residence abroad, Browne's ambition and cosmopolitanism, not a sense of parochialism, likely informed him about what made the history and culture of America distinctive.[90] Consistent with his contemporaries in cold war diplomacy, Browne too bought into the notion of American exceptionalism. That said, Browne's take on American exceptionalism hardly fit the cold war consensus stereotype erected by Pells and others. To Browne, America was exceptional not in the sense of the superiority of its expressive values, but in its purveyance of violence—both at home and in the world. Violence in the United States was hegemonic, seeping into and permeating the country's identity, both external (rising military expenditures) and internal (domestic consumer purchasing, where violent toys are, ironically, among the most popular sold, when celebrating the birth of the prince of peace). Within the country's broader culture of violence black America had no free social space. "Among all the major ethno-cultural groups in the world," Browne stated, blacks were "unique in this respect."[91] Black America's rootlessness necessitated the creation of a homeland, for without it blacks would remain restive about their fate in white America. Even progressive paragons like Lyndon Johnson who, in the aftermath of the 1966 urban uprisings, reminded blacks that riots beget pogroms and that they were just 10 percent of the nation's population, made clear the limits of liberal loyalties.

Although Browne's commitment to various nationalist causes ate away at his research and writing time, it is equally hard to square him with the stereotypes of Christopher Lasch, who saw in black nationalism efforts at "legitimizing . . . new erosions of standards in the name of pedagogical creativity."[92] Indeed, as already mentioned, Browne ensured that although the *Review* started as a race-first journal, it conformed to the disciplinary principles of the economics profession, adhering to systematic methods of data gathering and analysis as well as academic mathematical standards and styles—even if it meant that most articles were authored by whites.

Similarly, the Institute of the Black World, with faculty associates whom black studies programs measured themselves against or aspired to emulate, bore little resemblance to the quarrels with Black Power raised by public intellectuals like Christopher Lasch. Lasch described Black Power spokespeople in the educational world as "eager to exploit white liberal guilt . . . demanding separate programs of black studies, an end to the tyranny of the written word, instruction in English as a second language." A quick glance at IBW alumni does not, as Lasch (and Alan Bloom also) contends, show these scholars settling for separate programs of black studies as much as planting a foot in both black studies and in mainstream academic departments, most typically as joint-appointed professors. Similarly, Lasch's prediction that black studies promised to usher out "the tyranny of the written word" seems equally inaccurate.[93] Can one conclude that the pioneering generation of black studies in the 1970s did not leave behind a substantial paper trail of scholarly production? At the IBW, Lasch's coup to overtake the written word was led by Vincent Harding, Margaret Walker, Manning Marable, Joyce Ladner, and David Levering Lewis, whose collective productivity resulted in books running into third and fourth editions, a National Book Award lifetime achievement, a Pulitzer Prize, and a MacArthur Fellowship. The IBW examples are amplified by a 1974 U.S. Department of Health, Education, and Welfare commissioned report of twenty-nine representative black studies programs, which described black studies' move toward the vital academic center in this way: "As the programs emerged . . . it became obvious that their acceptance as [a] respectable academic [field] would depend on the extent to which their structures, purposes and course offerings approximated traditional programs."[94]

At times it appears that contemporary mainstream historians raised the bar far higher for entry into the imagined community than did either Benedict Anderson or Uncle Sam. Take as but one vivid example a photograph, widely distributed, of a black American soldier in Vietnam, saluting the camera with a submachine gun in his left hand while raising a Black Power fist with his right. As the historian Gary Gerstle queries readers, in his award-winning study of U.S. nationalism: "How much this soldier on patrol in Vietnam sympathized with Black Power ideology cannot be known, but his pose suggests how much he internalized the Black Power style."[95] Yet Gerstle, who cites in his introduction Benedict Anderson's own award-winning *Imagined Communities* as the driving inspiration of *American Crucible*, seems to forget Anderson's axiomatic chapter on race and patriotism. "Dying for one's country," Anderson wrote, remarking on the state's power of persuasion, "which usually one does not choose, assumes a moral grandeur which dying for the Labour Party, the American Medical Association, or perhaps even Amnesty International can not rival, for these are all bodies one can join or leave at easy will." To lay down one's life was the ultimate sacrifice for the nation idea.[96] Similarly, Uncle Sam, if only for recruitment's sake, came around to reconciling Black Power's coexistence with civic nationalism. As one 1972 navy poster, featuring two dashiki-clad black male twentysomethings, eyes glaring at white America, promised in its caption: "You Can Be Black, and Navy Too." Domestic pressure to end the draft for the most unpopular war of the century, along with well-publicized racial riots aboard the *Kitty Hawk* aircraft carrier, compelled Uncle Sam to stretch his civic nationalism imaginings to lure black candidates who then represented a microscopic 0.67 percent of naval officers.[97] Though he never lived up to his avuncular rhetoric, Uncle Sam's public message of mutuality remains significant: so long as black militants agreed to pick up the gun for America, there was no need to put down Black Power, for in the imagined community Black Power drew not simply on racial nationalism but on civic nationalism as well.

Perhaps to better conceptualize the history of liberalism and black nationalism in the United States, historians living and writing on America should, as Ian Tyrell has urged, "study the history of other countries more than they do, and possibly as much as they study their own national past."[98] Indeed, a brief survey of liberal democracies on both sides of the Atlantic suggests them to be breeding grounds for ethnic and regional movements of self-determination during the 1960s and 1970s. Mirroring the advance of Black Power in America, indigenous subnationalist movements sprouted up in virtually every postwar Western European country. During the 1960s and 1970s not a single country in Western Europe escaped unscathed from ethnic and regional nationalism inside its liberal democratic borders. In the United Kingdom, for example, the Plaid Cymru of Wales, Scots, and the Northern Irish all rose up against the supranation-state of

Britain. In France the Bretons and Alsatians—the latter 1.2 million German speakers living in the south—had their own separatist visions from which nationalists charted their own courses of political independence. In Belgium, Wallon and Flemish breathed new life into their respective century-old nationalisms, gaining such cultural concessions as special schools and academic programming from the Belgium government. In Spain national self-determination sprang from Basque and Catalan separatists who fought for political autonomy.[99] Post-Salazar Portugal confronted similar longings of autonomy from the Galicians. The shared national fate of Galicia—which may well have been less a regional than a consciousness-raising project—had as its romanticized purpose restoring its glorious past, though it is doubtful that this meant the literal restoration of the actual physical kingdom that had once stretched to Eastern Europe and Asia Minor. In Italy the South Tyrol, a German-speaking minority of Austrians living in present-day northern Italy, mobilized for nationhood from the 1950s through 1970s against Italy's mainly coalition governments. Likewise, in the Federal Republic of Germany (West Germany), Bavarians and Prussians waged nationalist if not secessionist struggles. The United States' neighbor to the north, Canada, is home to the hemisphere's most robust liberal democracy yet still has an unresolved regional and ethnic subnationalist question of Quebecois independence and sovereignty. As Robert Browne observed, for separatists in other liberal democratic nations "dialogue proceeds at a leisurely pace" within "racially white and culturally Western countries" like Belgium, Canada, and Spain, but black American separatists are "considered lunatic fringe."[100]

These concurrent nationalist movements share four significant traits with Black Power. First, all were region-based or ethnic nationalist movements. Second, all came out of imaginings by an indigenous people with a shared ancestry and a shared destiny to live on sacred lands (like the Galicians of Portugal or in the U.S. example, the Republic of New Africa, which predicated its nationalist claims largely on black Americans' centuries-long ties to the South) as opposed to newly arrived immigrant populations like southern Italians and Turks in Germany, or the Pakistanis and Indians in Great Britain.[101] Third, almost all looked for recognition and political and economic renegotiation of the terms of their relationship in the nation-state, rather than, as liberation struggles did elsewhere, forging united fronts on the dual state-making agendas of full-blown state autonomy and severing of economic and political ties with the existing sovereign federal state.[102] Fourth, all emerged within contemporaneous liberal democracies.

In sharp contrast, comparable ethnic or regional nationalism movements did not take hold within the totalizing systems of postwar Eastern Europe. Hungary, Czechoslovakia, Romania, and other Communist-bloc countries, despite their multiethnic makeup and the historic continuities of their cultures, failed to produce or yield comparable nationalist struggles. The geopolitical spaces of liberal democracies, modern history tells us, proved to be the breeding ground for nationalist movements of self-determination, not totalitarian ones. Totalitarianism seemed less hospitable to the marketplace of ideas, it gave little room for competing voices, and it left no berth for the rhetoric of independence, let alone its actual program. Put another way, the characters and settings of the nationalist-liberal interplay may invariably change, but the play's structure and form stay surprisingly familiar: the rise of indigenous ethnic or regional nationalist movements within Western liberal democracies who call for self-determination. Black Power in America is no exception to this leitmotif.

Like coffee, nationalisms are known to take the shapes of their container, and in the United States that container was a liberal democracy.

NOTES

Introduction

1. Although the authorship of this particular greeting card remains unclear, through its newspaper especially, the BPP at the time (ca. 1969–70) was not shy about displaying images that advocated armed struggle. For more, see "'Guerrilla Warfare in the US'—FBI Report," *US News and World Report*, 9 Nov. 1970, 53–55.

2. "The FBI: Happy Birthday," *Newsweek*, 12 Jan. 1970, 20; *Supplementary Detailed Staff Reports of Intelligence Activities and the Rights of Americans*, book 3, *Final Report of the Select Committee to Study Governmental Operations with Respect to Intelligence Activities*, U.S. Senate, 23 April 1976; see also Black Panther Intercommunal News Service (BPINS) on microfilm ca. 1968–70; Allen Matusow, *The Unraveling of America: A History of Liberalism in the 1960s* (New York: Harper & Row, 1984).

3. "Malcolm X Speech, London School of Economics," 11 Feb. 1965, in Malcolm X, *February 1965: The Final Speeches* (New York: Pathfinder, 1992).

4. With historical sensibilities in mind, I use the term "rapist" to be consistent with the term Little herself used.

5. Nelson Malloy, interview with the author.

6. William L. Van Deburg, *New Day in Babylon: The Black Power Movement and American Culture, 1965–1975* (Chicago: University of Chicago Press, 1992); Robert O. Self, *American Babylon: Race and the Struggle for Postwar Oakland* (Princeton, N.J.: Princeton University Press, 2003); Komozi Woodard, *A Nation within a Nation: Amiri Baraka (LeRoi Jones) and Black Power Politics* (Chapel Hill: University of North Carolina Press, 1999); and Timothy B. Tyson, *Radio Free Dixie: Robert F. Williams and the Roots of Black Power* (Chapel Hill: University of North Carolina Press, 1999). Other scholars include Scot Brown, Rod Bush, Peniel Joseph, James Smethurst, Heather Ann Thompson, and Fanon Wilkins.

7. Self, *American Babylon*, 226.

8. See, for example, the works of Scot Brown, *Fighting for US: Maulana Karenga, the US Organization, and Black Cultural Nationalism* (New York: New York University Press, 2003); Peniel E. Joseph, *Waiting 'Til the Midnight Hour: A Narrative History of Black Power in America* (New York: Owl Books, Henry Holt, 2006); and James Smethurst, *The Black Arts Movement: Literary Nationalism in the 1960s and 1970s* (Chapel Hill: University of North Carolina Press, 2005).

9. Matusow, *Unraveling of America*; Steven Gillon, *Boomer Nation: The Largest and Richest Generation Ever and How It Changed America* (New York: Free Press, 2004); Gareth Davies, *From Opportunity to Entitlement: The Transformation and Decline of Great Society Liberalism* (Lawrence: University Press of Kansas, 1996).

10. William L. O'Neill, *Coming Apart: An Informal History of America in the 1960's* (Chicago: Ivan R. Dee, 2005); Gary Gerstle, "The Collapse of the Rooseveltian Nation" and "The Spread of Anti-Americanism," *American Crucible: Race and Nation in the Twentieth Century* (Princeton, N.J.: Princeton University Press, 2002); David Farber, "The Liberal Dream and Its Nightmare" and "The War Within," *The Age of Great Dreams: America in the 1960s* (New York: Hill & Wang, 1994); Maurice Isserman and Michael Kazin, *America Divided: The Civil War of the 1960s* (New York: Oxford University Press, 2000); and Richard Polenberg, *One Nation Divisible: Class, Race, and Ethnicity in the United States since 1938* (Harmondsworth, Eng., and New York: Penguin, 1980).

11. Samuel Huntington, *Clash of Civilizations and the Remaking of World Order* (New York: Simon & Schuster, 1996); Michael Heale, *The Sixties in America: History, Politics, and Protest* (Edinburgh: Edinburgh University Press, 2001).

12. Lizabeth Cohen's *Consumer's Republic: The Politics of Mass Consumption in Postwar America* (New York: Knopf, 2003; Pulitzer finalist) and James Patterson's *Grand Expectations: The United States, 1945–1974* (New York: Oxford University Press, 1996; Bancroft winner), as well as works by prominent scholars such as Gary Gerstle and Elisabeth Lasch-Quinn.

13. Matthew Dallek, *The Right Moment: Ronald Reagan's First Victory and the Decisive Turning Point in American Politics* (New York: Free Press, 2000); Lisa McGirr, *Suburban Warriors: The Origins of the New American Right* (Princeton, N.J.: Princeton University Press, 2001); Kevin M. Kruse, *White Flight: Atlanta and the Making of Modern Conservatism* (Princeton, N.J.: Princeton University Press, 2005).

14. Michael Flamm, *Law and Order: Street Crime, Civil Unrest, and the Crisis of Liberalism in the 1960s* (New York: Columbia University Press, 2005); Byron Shafer and Richard Johnston, *The End of Southern Exceptionalism: Class, Race, and Partisan Change in the Postwar South* (Cambridge, Mass.: Harvard University Press, 2006).

15. Panel conversation between Sean Wilentz and George F. Will, "The Left Starts to Rethink Reagan," *Newsweek*, 12 May 2008, 38.

16. "Malcolm X Speech, London School of Economics."

17. See iPOLL "Black Power," Science Resources Statistics Amalgam Survey [April 1968], National Opinion Research Center, University of Chicago.

18. See iPOLL "Racial Violence," Gallup/Newsweek Poll, August 1969.

19. Carmichael quoted in Joseph, *Waiting 'Til the Midnight Hour*, 240; Jeffrey O. G. Ogbar, *Black Power: Radical Politics and African American Identity* (Baltimore: John Hopkins University Press, 2004), 2.

20. Tom Wolfe, *Radical Chic and Mau-Mauing the Flak Catchers* (New York: Farrar, Straus & Giroux, 1970), 56, 57, 66.

21. Arthur Schlesinger, *Robert Kennedy and His Times* (New York: Houghton Mifflin, 2002), 781.

22. William E. Leuchtenberg, *The White House Looks South: Franklin D. Roosevelt, Harry S. Truman, and Lyndon B. Johnson* (Baton Rouge: Louisiana State University Press, 2005), 330.

23. Mark Hamilton Lytle, *America's Uncivil Wars: The Sixties Era from Elvis to the Fall of Richard Nixon* (New York: Oxford University Press, 2006), see esp. chaps. 10 and 11.

24. Wolfe, *Radical Chic and Mau-Mauing the Flak Catchers*, 56.

Chapter 1. Hidden Histories of Remittance

1. Paul Wellstone, "Black Militants in the Ghetto: Why They Believe in Violence" (PhD diss., University of North Carolina, 1969); Bill Lofy, *Paul Wellstone: The Life of a Passionate Progressive* (Ann Arbor: University of Michigan Press, 2005); Jim Stimson (a classmate of Wellstone's), interviews by the author, 30 June and 1 July 2005.

2. "United States: After Wellstone," *Economist* 365 (2 Nov. 2002): 56.

3. This has been suggested in the best-known interpretations of the participation of Black Power advocates in antipoverty programs, notably Nicholas Lemann, *The Promised Land: The Great Migration and How It Changed America* (New York: Vintage Books, 1992), 180–81; Gareth Davies, *From Opportunity to Entitlement: The Transformation and Decline of Great Society Liberalism* (Lawrence: University Press of Kansas, 1996), chap. 5; and Allen Matusow, *The Unraveling of America: A History of Liberalism in the 1960s* (New York: Harper, 1984), 259. See also Komozi Woodard, *A Nation within a Nation: Amiri Baraka (LeRoi Jones) and Black Power Politics* (Chapel Hill: University of North Carolina Press, 1999); Rod Bush, *We Are Not What We Seem: Black Nationalism and Class Struggle in the American Century* (New York: New York University Press, 1999); Harvard Sitkoff, *The Struggle for Black Equality, 1954–1980* (New York: Hill & Wang, 1981); and Jack M. Bloom, *Class, Race, and the Civil Rights Movement* (Bloomington: Indiana University Press, 1987).

4. Lemann, *Promised Land*, 179.

5. See ibid., 152.

6. *History of Operation Breakthrough*, "A Case Study in Community Action: Durham's Operation Breakthrough," n.d., folder 4351, North Carolina Fund Papers, Southern Historical Collection, University of North Carolina at Chapel Hill (hereafter cited as NCF Papers).

7. Christina Greene, *Our Separate Ways: Women and the Black Freedom Movement in Durham, North Carolina* (Chapel Hill: University of North Carolina, 2005), 109–10.

8. Howard Covington and Marion Ellis, *Terry Sanford: Politics, Progress, and Outrageous Ambitions* (Durham, N.C.: Duke University Press, 1999), 302–3.

9. Peter Bell, "The Ford Foundation as Transnational Actor," *International Organization* 25 (summer 1971): 472.

10. Ibid.; Samuel Huntington, "Transnational Organizations in World Politics," *World Politics* 25 (April 1973): 334.

11. Quoted in Bell, "Ford Foundation as Transnational Actor," 469.

12. Louis Hartz, *The Liberal Tradition in America: An Interpretation of American Political Thought since the Revolution* (1955; rpt. San Diego: Harcourt Brace Jovanovich, 1991), 78.

13. See Robert R. Korstad and James L. Leloudis, "Student Volunteers, the North Carolina Fund, and the Meanings of Citizenship," author's collection; see also Emily Herring Wilson, *For the People of North Carolina: The Z. Smith Reynolds Foundation at Half-Century, 1936–1986* (Chapel Hill: University of North Carolina Press, 1988), 65–83; Covington and Ellis, *Terry Sanford*, 328–32.

14. History of Operation Breakthrough, 2.

15. See Korstad and Leloudis, "Student Volunteers, the North Carolina Fund, and the Meanings of Citizenship"; see also "No Easy Walk: Race, Poverty, and the North Carolina Fund Project," Southern Historical Collection, University of North Carolina at Chapel Hill. For an important study about place in postwar politics and social environs, see William Leuchtenberg, *The White House Looks South: Franklin D. Roosevelt, Harry S. Truman, Lyndon B. Johnson* (Baton Rouge: Louisiana State University Press, 2005), intro., though he downplays geopolitical differences within states.

16. These areas, which consist of over five hundred square miles, are known as the Eastern Piedmont and Coastal Plains. Whereas in post–World War II era the state has been approximately 22 percent African American, Eastern Piedmont counties are 34 percent black and the Coastal Plains total 32 percent black. The postwar black population throughout the state was 22 percent. In all but one of the twelve counties comprising the Eastern Piedmont, blacks have been at or above the black population average. With a heavy black population came the need for mechanisms of social control. Its economic and social conservatism stemmed in part from the heavy dependence on slave labor in the area, long an agricultural stronghold of tobacco and textile farmers. Both the Eastern Piedmont and the Coastal Plains are known for small towns, rural values, low incomes, and high unemployment, see Paul Luebke, *Tar Heel Politics 2000* (Chapel Hill: University of North Carolina Press, 1998), 59–61.

17. In *Along Freedom Road*, a study of school desegregation in one eastern county, David Cecelski counters Jack Bass and Walter De Vries' point that eastern North Carolina protests were anemic or absent altogether. On the issue of racial resiliency vis-à-vis more urban spaces, Cecelski acknowledges that because rural blacks held little political power, "patterns of racism in the process of integration were more pronounced" in the black belt. See Cecelski, *Along Freedom Road: Hyde County, North Carolina and the Fate of Black Schools in the South* (Chapel Hill: University of North Carolina Press, 1994), 12; Lisa Hazirjian, "Negotiating Poverty" (PhD diss., Duke University, 2003); Charles McKinney, "Our People Began to Press for Greater Freedom" (PhD diss., Duke University, 2003); and Jack Bass and Walter De Vries, *Transformation of Southern Politics: Social Change and Political Consequence since 1945* (Athens: University of Georgia Press, 1995), 242.

18. Luebke, *Tar Heel Politics 2000*, 73.

19. *Congressional Quarterly Almanac* (Washington, D.C.: CQ News Features), 1964–

70, on Party Unity, Conservative Coalition, and Bipartisan Support. Similarly, both labor's Committee for Political Education and cold war liberals at the Americans for Democratic Action gave Fountain a zero (*Congressional Quarterly Almanac* is hereafter cited as *CQA*). Wilmington congressman Alton Lennon also earned a zero; see *Almanac of American Politics*, North Carolina, 1968.

20. 1965 *CQA*, 1083–99; see also 1966 *CQA*, 1020–31.

21. Edward Berkowitz, "The Great Society," in *American Congress: The Building of Democracy*, ed. Julian E. Zelizer (Boston: Houghton Mifflin, 2004), 567.

22. For more on NEED, see Lisa Hazirjian, "Combating NEED: Urban Conflict and the Transformations of the War on Poverty and the African American Freedom Struggle in Rocky Mount, North Carolina," unpublished manuscript, author's collection.

23. David Henderson to Sargent Shriver, 14 Sept. 1966, folder 318, NCF Papers.

24. Hugh Sawyer to Daniel K. Moore, 2 March 1966; J. O. Bishop to Dan Moore, 3 March 1966, NCF folder, box 112, General Correspondence Series 1966, Governor Daniel K. Moore Papers, North Carolina State Archives, Raleigh (hereafter cited as GCS 1966, Moore Papers).

25. Tim Brinn to L. H. Fountain, 21 July 1967, Gardner file, NCF Papers.

26. Robert Gould to R. Tim Brinn, 22 June 1966, folder 313, NCF Papers.

27. Ibid.

28. Robert Gould to Tim Brinn, Political Activity and the North Carolina Fund, 8, folder 313, NCF Papers.

29. Gould to Brinn, 22 June 1966; "Brief Summary of Mr. [Robert] Monte's Position on the North Carolina Fund as Stated to the Governor on 13 October 1966," NCF Papers.

30. "Political Activity and the North Carolina Fund," press release by Congressman Jim Gardner, 25 July 1967, folder 318, NCF Papers.

31. Fuller was a friend of McDonald's from their organizing days for the Milwaukee Urban League.

32. "United Organization for Community Improvement: Black Political Power in Durham," 1968, 6, folder 4563, NCF Papers.

33. "City Hall Marchers Laugh, Sing, Shout, 'Black Power,'" *Durham Morning Herald*, 20 March 1967, notebook 1 of 2, folder 337, NCF Papers.

34. "Black Power Weak in N.C.," *Raleigh News and Observer*, n.d., NCF Papers. Of course Coltrane and Alexander's view completely ignored the homegrown Robert F. Williams who, as Timothy Tyson has written at length, actually helped pioneer the Black Power movement, not simply in North Carolina but across the nation.

35. Timothy B. Tyson, *Radio Free Dixie: Robert F. Williams and the Roots of Black Power* (Chapel Hill: University of North Carolina Press, 1999).

36. Howard Fuller's activism was, in the view of historian Christina Greene, "indispensable to Durham's freedom struggle." But the charge of outside agitator leveled by opportunistic critics is not without credence: Fuller had never lived in North Carolina before 1965, coming to the state hoping to mobilize Durham's poor, see Greene, *Our Separate Ways*, 5.

37. Fuller was one of several speakers at this event, which was organized by the People's Program on Poverty and funded by an NCF grant. Some speakers, like Jim MacDonald, were asked not to speak on Black Power; see *Rich Square (N.C.) Times-News*, 3 Aug. 1967.

38. See Fuller's speech, 30 July 1966, folders 3378 and 4932, NCF Papers; see also Osha Gray Davidson, *The Best of Enemies: Race and Redemption in the New South* (New York: Scribner, 1996), 177.

39. Fuller's speech.

40. Ibid.

41. Ibid.

42. See *Durham Morning Herald*, 2 Aug. 1966, NCF Papers; folders 3378 and 4932, ibid.

43. See *Durham Morning Herald*/Response to Woodland Speech, folders 3378, 4862, and 4932, NCF Papers.

44. Ibid.

45. Passed in 1938, the Hatch Act was extended in 1940 to include city and state officials salaried by the federal government.

46. Flowers to Burt, 2 Aug. 1966, folder 313, NCF Papers; Burt to Flowers, 4 Aug. 1966, ibid.; Garrett to Esser, 23 Aug. 1966, ibid.

47. Monte to Henderson, 13 Sept. 1966, folder 316, NCF Papers.

48. Ibid.

49. Henderson to Shriver, 14 Sept. 1966, folder 316, NCF Papers.

50. Shriver to Monte, 20 Sept. 1966, ibid.

51. "Brief Summary of Mr. Monte's Position on the North Carolina Fund as Stated to the Governor on October 13, 1966," NCF folder, box 112, GCS 1966, Moore Papers; Monte to Henderson, 13 Sept. 1966; Henderson to Shriver, 14 Sept. 1966, NCF Papers; Esser to Monte, 20 Sept. 1966, folder 316, box 31, NCF Papers; Esser to Henderson, 20 Sept. 1966, ibid.; Monte to Esser, 23 Sept. 1966, ibid.

52. Esser to Sanford, memo, 27 Sept. 1966, folder 316, NCF Papers; Esser to Shaw, 15 Dec. 1966, ibid.; "Brief Summary of Mr. Monte's Position."

53. "Brief Summary of Mr. Monte's Position."

54. See "UOCI" [United Organization for Community Improvement], folder 4563, 21, NCF Papers.

55. W. E. B. Du Bois, "The Upbuilding of Black Durham: The Success of the Negroes and Their Value to a Tolerant and Helpful Southern City," *World's Work* 23 (January 1912), electronic edition, North Carolina Collection, Wilson Library, University of North Carolina at Chapel Hill (hereafter cited as NCC/UNC).

56. Ibid.

57. For more on black Durham since 1945, see Walter Weare, *Black Business in the New South: A Social History of the North Carolina Mutual Life Insurance Company* (Urbana: University of Illinois Press, 1973), 265–87; Leslie Brown, "Common Space, Separate Lives: Gender and Racial Conflict in the Capital of the Black Middle Class" (PhD diss., Duke University, 1997); Greene, *Our Separate Ways*, 128.

58. Greene, *Our Separate Ways*, 128.

59. The desired changes included housing code and ordinance enforcement and greater involvement in decisions like urban renewal. Ibid., 12, 18, 128.

60. Transcript of Question-Answer Portion of News Conference Held by Congressman James Gardner, Voyager Inn, Raleigh, N.C., 25 July 1967, Gardner file, NCF Papers.

61. "N.C. Fund Leaders Brand Gardner Charges 'Untrue,'" folder 337, NCF Papers.

62. Quoted in Emily H. Wilson, *For the People of North Carolina: The Z. Smith Reynolds Foundation at Half-Century, 1936–1986* (Chapel Hill: University of North Carolina Press, 1988), 81.

63. "N.C. Fund Leaders Brand Gardner Charges 'Untrue.'"

64. *Durham Morning Herald*, 21 July 1967; Charles Clay, "Sanford—Will He or Won't He Take on Ervin?" *North Carolina Anvil*, 11 Nov. 1967, 3.

65. Grady Jeffreys and Charles Heatherly, *Jim Gardner: A Question of Character* (Raleigh: Patriot Press, 1992), 55, 59; Esser to Galifianakis and Gardner, telegram, 24 July 1967, folder 318, NCF Papers; *Durham Morning Herald*, 21 July 1967.

66. Jeffreys and Heatherly, *Jim Gardner*, 51; "The Governor's Race," *North Carolina Anvil*, 26 Oct. 1968, 1.

67. Shriver shared his deep reservations with Whitney Young of the National Urban League; see Otis A. Singletary Jr., Oral History Collection, Lyndon B. Johnson Library, General Service Administration, National Archives and Record Service, University of Texas, Austin, 2–3 (hereafter cited as OHC-LBJ); Davies, *From Opportunity to Entitlement*, 50.

68. Lemann, *Promised Land*, 152–54.

69. See Kenneth O'Reilly, *Nixon's Piano: Presidents and Racial Politics from Washington to Clinton* (New York: Free Press, 1995), 266; Lemann, *Promised Land*, 327.

70. See Singletary, OHC-LBJ, 10–11, 13, 18; Davies, *From Opportunity to Entitlement*, 195; see also Devin Fergus, "Liberalism and Black Nationalism in an American Southern State, 1965–1980" (PhD diss., Columbia University, 2002), chap. 1.

71. Particularly bitter struggles between OEO organizers and public officials occurred in Chicago, Philadelphia, San Francisco, Detroit, Syracuse, and elsewhere. See James T. Patterson, *America's Struggle against Poverty in the Twentieth Century* (Cambridge, Mass.: Harvard University Press, 2000), chap. 9. Robert Weisbrot, *Freedom Bound: A History of the Civil Rights Movement* (1990; New York: Plume, 1991), 165.

72. Lemann, *Promised Land*, 165.

73. See Mike Manatos, interview I, 41, OHC-LBJ.

74. Califano would ultimately become secretary of HUD; Lemann, *Promised Land*, 165.

75. Davies, *From Opportunity to Entitlement*, 196.

76. Maximum feasible participation encouraged poorer members of the community to serve as representatives. For its part, Congress enacted a series of legislative amendments that shifted funds to "safe" programs like Head Start, authorized local and state governments to design and approve future agencies, and watered down the

poor's representation on local boards from at least one-third in February 1965 to no more than one-third by 1967. It also dropped the controversial words "maximum feasible participation." See Patterson, *America's Struggle against Poverty*, 143; Lemann, *Promised Land*, 168.

77. John Strange to George Esser, memo, 26 Sept. 1967, folder 322, NCF Papers.

78. "Press Release by Congressman James Gardner, 25 July 1967, Political Activity and the North Carolina Fund in Point No. 12," folder 318, NCF Papers. "Fuller's salary, when he first joined the Fund, was paid entirely by that organization until Fuller began to teach in a federally-funded tutorial program. At that time 15 percent of his salary was taken over by federal funds." See *Durham Morning Herald*, 21 July 1967.

79. Neither Fuller nor faculty members at the University of North Carolina, and clearly not NCF employees like Esser and John Strange, seemed interested in cajoling Fuller's most acerbic rivals. At times, it almost appeared they enjoyed chafing them. John Strange to Esser, memo, 29 Sept. 1967, NCF Papers.

80. "Press Release by Congressman James Gardner."

81. "Official of N.C. Fund Denies Causing Violence," *Winston-Salem Journal*, 27 July 1967, folder 337, NCF Papers.

82. *Greensboro Daily News*, 7 Oct. 1967.

83. This regulation, passed in 1963 and overturned in 1968, was known as the communist speaker ban. Daniel K. Moore, *Messages, Addresses, and Public Papers of Daniel K. Moore, Governor of North Carolina, 1965–1969*, ed. Memory Mitchell (Raleigh: North Carolina Department of Archives and History, 1971), 228.

84. See William Link, *William Friday: Power, Purpose, and American Higher Education* (Chapel Hill: University of North Carolina Press, 1995), 112–13; see also "Viewpoint No. 1693," *Greensboro Daily News*, 5 Oct. 1967; *Greensboro Daily News*, 7 Oct. 1969.

85. "Viewpoint No. 1693"; *Greensboro Daily News*, 7 Oct. 1969.

86. Transcript of Q&A held by Gardner, 25 July 1967, see folders 318–21, as well as T-4710/244 G22, NCF Papers.

87. Winston-Salem's *Twin City Sentinel*, though far from sympathetic to Fuller, questioned why Gardner had no evidence of partisan activities; see *Twin City Sentinel*, 17 Aug. 1967, folder 338, NCF Papers; *Raleigh News and Observer*, 23 July 1967, ibid.; *Charlotte Observer*, 23 July 1967, ibid.; *Greensboro Daily News*, 5 Aug. 1967, ibid.; and *Winston-Salem Journal*, 28 July 1967, ibid.

88. See Black Response Letters, in "Letters in Support of Howard Fuller, July 1967" file, folder 4482, NCF Papers.

89. See Greene, *Our Separate Ways*, 129.

90. In February 1968 Fuller resigned following his participation and arrest in a sympathy demonstration for three blacks killed in Orangeburg, S.C. See *Raleigh News and Observer*, 17 Feb. 1968; Ed Martin, "Windows Broken; Fuller and Two Others Arrested," *Durham Herald*, n.d., folder 333, NCF Papers; "White Establishment Encouraging Racism," *North Carolina Anvil*, n.d., folder 918, ibid. For further information,

see "Appeals Order," n.d., ibid.; Wayne Hurder, "Fuller May Violate UNC Court Order," folder 338, NCF Papers.

91. "Appeals Order"; Hurder, "Fuller May Violate UNC Court Order."

92. Howard Fuller, "Radish Interview with Howard Fuller," *Radish*, 28 July–10 Aug. 1969, folder 916, NCF Papers.

93. Davies, *From Opportunity to Entitlement*, 194–97.

94. Speech by Howard Fuller, Durham Council on Human Relations Committee Meeting, 25 Nov. 1968, tape 3, side 1, Nathaniel White Oral History Collection, Center for the Study of Black History, Hayti Heritage Center, Durham, N.C.; proposal for MXLU, 1, MXLU Structure/Background folder, ibid.

95. Fuller, Durham Council on Human Relations Committee Meeting. The "they" Fuller was referring to included members of the city council, increasingly the mayor, and members of the business establishment, such as the Durham Chamber of Commerce and Durham Merchants Association.

96. Ibid.

97. Fuller, "Radish Interview with Howard Fuller."

98. Fuller, Durham Council on Human Relations Committee Meeting.

99. Ibid.

100. Ibid.

101. Chuck Hopkins, "Malcolm X Liberation University," *Negro Digest* (March 1970): 40; proposal for MXLU, 20 June 1969, to Board of Directors of the Foundation for Community Development, 2, folder 903, NCF Papers.

102. "Opportunities Beyond the Classroom," *Information for Prospective Students* (Durham, N.C.: Duke University, 1970).

103. Duke Divinity School desegregated in 1960, the graduate and professional schools in 1961. See Don Yanella, "Race Relations at Duke University and the Allen Building Takeover" (honors thesis, Duke University, 1985), 1–3; *New York Times*, 17 Feb. 1969; "History Worth Saving," Duke Online Edition 3 (winter 2004).

104. Yanella, "Race Relations at Duke University," 6.

105. Fuller, "Radish Interview with Howard Fuller."

106. Yanella, "Race Relations at Duke University," 14.

107. Ibid., 23.

108. Ibid.; *North Carolina Anvil*, 15 Feb. 1969.

109. Quoted by Bertie Howard, tape-recorded interview by the author, Durham, N.C., 28 Jan. 1994; *North Carolina Anvil*, 15 Feb. 1969.

110. *North Carolina Anvil*, 15 Feb. 1969.

111. Many black students such as Chuck Hopkins were disappointed that while the purpose of the Black Is Beautiful event week was to educate the campus, the only events well attended by whites were the entertaining ones; see Yanella, "Race Relations at Duke University," 25.

112. See also Kara Miles Turner, "Malcolm X Liberation University: Institution Building during the Black Power Era," graduate seminar paper written for History

310s, Prof. Raymond Gavins, Duke University, 3 May 1993, author's collection. See also Yanella, "Race Relations at Duke University," 26–33, 35.

113. *North Carolina Anvil*, 15 Feb. 1969; Yanella, "Race Relations at Duke University," 40.

114. Yanella, "Race Relations at Duke University," 51.

115. Ibid.

116. Ibid., 62–67; *North Carolina Anvil*, 22 Feb. 1969.

117. *North Carolina Anvil*; according to the *Duke News Bureau*, attendance was close to normal, see Yanella, "Race Relations at Duke University," 65–67.

118. Yanella, "Race Relations at Duke University," 68.

119. Ibid., 67.

120. For Knight's account see Douglas M. Knight, *Street of Dreams: The Nature and Legacy of the 1960s* (Durham, N.C.: Duke University Press, 1989), 95–142.

121. Yanella, "Race Relations at Duke University," 68.

122. *North Carolina Anvil*, 22 Feb. 1969.

123. *New York Times*, 17 Feb. 1969.

124. "A Black Scholar Special: Student Strikes, 1968–1969," *Black Scholar* (Jan.–Feb. 1970): 65–75.

125. Ibid.

126. Ibid.; see also Noliwe Rooks, *White Money/Black Power: The Surprising History of African American Studies and the Crisis of Race in Higher Education* (Boston: Beacon Press, 2006).

127. Turner, "Malcolm X Liberation University."

128. *Malcolm X Liberation University*, brochure (hereafter cited as *MXLU* brochure), NCC/UNC; *Raleigh News and Observer*, 5 Oct. 1969.

129. *North Carolina Anvil*, 15 March 1969. Duke students actually thought up the name MXLU a year prior at a sit-in in the president's office, largely because the sit-in occurred around the slain black nationalist's birthday.

130. Nonacademic employees at Duke were apparently disappointed at the vacillation of black Duke students, who often encouraged workers to "stay off your job" and "take a chance on losing your livelihood" but were unwilling to continue the withdrawal themselves; see Fuller, "Radish Interview with Howard Fuller"; *North Carolina Anvil*, 22 March 1969.

131. Bertie Howard, interview by Kara Miles Turner, 13 March 1993.

132. Ibid.

133. Howard L. Fuller, interview by the author, Milwaukee, 14 Dec. 1998.

134. Federal City College was later renamed the University of the District of Columbia. See Howard, interview by Turner, 13 March 1993; Chuck Hopkins, "Interim Report: Malcolm X Liberation University," *Negro Digest* (March 1970): 41, 44–48; and *Negro Digest* (March 1970): 39.

135. *Malcolm X Liberation University: African Peoples' Ideological and Technical Institute* (student handbook, hereafter cited as *MXLU* handbook), 2, Howard Fuller

personal papers, Milwaukee; *Durham Morning Herald*, 26 Oct. 1969; Hopkins, "Malcolm X Liberation University," 41.

136. *Durham Morning Herald*, 3 Oct. 1969; *Duke Chronicle*, n.d., Duke University Archives, Durham, N.C.

137. Howard Fuller and Watts Hill Jr., interview by Buie Shuell, "Where Is Black Studies Going in North Carolina: Discussing the Status of Education in Black America," 24 Oct. 1969, NCC/UNC; *Durham Morning Herald*, 3 Oct. 1969, ibid.

138. MXLU officially closed on 23 June 1973; see *Charlotte Observer*, 1 Dec. 1969.

139. MXLU raised the minimum age next year. See "Background Information on the Malcolm X Liberation University," March 1969, folder 903, NCF Papers.

140. From the Interim Committee of Malcolm X Liberation University to the Board of Directors of the Foundation for Community Development, "Proposal for Malcolm X Liberation University, 5 June 1967," 20 June 1967, folder 903, NCF Papers.

141. *Durham Morning Herald*, 19 Oct. 1969.

142. Greene, *Our Separate Ways*, 303.

143. From Malcolm X University North Carolina Episcopal Collection, n.d., Episcopal Diocese of North Carolina archives, Raleigh (hereafter cited as EDNC archives).

144. See *African Warrior*, a bimonthly student paper, and *MXLU* handbook, 20; Proposal for Malcolm X Liberation University, 1972–1973, 18 Oct. 1972, 2, 5, Fuller personal papers.

145. Proposal for Malcolm X Liberation University, Fuller personal papers.

146. *MXLU* brochure; *MXLU* handbook; Proposal for MXLU, Budget April–September 1972; Proposal for Malcolm X Liberation University, Fuller personal papers.

147. *New York Times*, n.d., private collection of Kara Miles Turner. Howard Fuller adopted the name Owusu ("one who clears the way for others"—Ghanaian) and Sadaukai ("one who gathers strength from ancestors to lead his people"—Hausa/Nigeria). Fuller changed his name back years later. See *MXLU* handbook, 38.

148. Stokely Carmichael, "We Are All Africans: A Speech by Stokely Carmichael to Malcolm X Liberation University," *Black Scholar* (May 1970): 15–19.

149. Ibid., 17–18.

150. *Raleigh News and Observer*, 3 Nov. 1969. While British historian Eric Hobsbawm acknowledges that communism and socialism do not strongly affect traditions whose main aims are inculcating values and beliefs, they do hold up another overlapping type of invented tradition observed by Hobsbawm: that is, those invented traditions set to establish or symbolize "social cohesion or the memberships of groups, real or artificial communities." At minimum, MXLU, and black nationalism more broadly, fit this latter description. See Eric Hobsbawm and Terence Ranger, eds., *The Invention of Tradition* (1983; rpt. Cambridge and New York: Cambridge University Press, 1992), 8–9; Prys Morgan, "The Hunt for the Welsh Past in the Romantic Period," in ibid., chap. 3.

151. *Raleigh News and Observer*, 3 Nov. 1969.

152. *MXLU* handbook, 13.

153. *Raleigh News and Observer*, 3 Nov. 1969.

154. Dean M. Kelley, *Why Conservative Churches Are Growing: A Study in Sociology of Religion* (New York: Harper & Row, 1972), 168.

155. Proposal for Malcolm X Liberation University, 1, Fuller personal papers.

156. Judy Mathe Foley, "Diary of a Grant," *Episcopalian* (July 1970): 17; Fuller interview by the author, Milwaukee, 15 Dec. 1998; Proposal for MXLU, NCF Papers, 15.

157. Proposal for MXLU, NCF Papers, 15; Fuller interview by the author, 15 Dec. 1998; *Carolina Times*, 19 Oct. 1969; James T. Wooten, "Malcolm X University to Open," *New York Times*, 28 Oct. 1969.

158. 1970 Address of the Bishop, 74, EDNC archives; *Durham Morning Herald*, 10 Oct. 1969; Mason P. Thomas Jr., "Urban Crisis Body Lists '70 Goals," *NC Churchman* (February 1970): 6.

159. *Raleigh News and Observer*, 1 Nov. 1969.

160. Sarah M. Lemmon, "Liberal-Conservative Showdown Averted at Diocesan Convention," *NC Churchman* (April 1970): 12.

161. Foley, "Diary of a Grant," 17.

162. Harold T. Parker, *A History of St. Philip's Episcopal Church, 1878–1994* (Durham, N.C.: [St. Philip's Episcopal] Church, 1996), 215.

163. Foley, "Diary of a Grant," 18; *Raleigh News and Observer*, 31 Oct. 1969.

164. Foley, "Diary of a Grant."

165. *Durham Morning Herald*, 10 Oct. 1969.

166. *Chapel Hill Weekly*, 22 Oct. 1969. Also see *Raleigh News and Observer*, 31 Oct. 1969.

167. Foley, "Diary of a Grant," 24.

168. Ibid.

169. Ibid.

170. Ibid.

171. 1970 Address of the Bishop, 75.

172. *Raleigh News and Observer*, 22 Oct. 1969; "N.C. Episcopals May Quit U.S. Group," *Raleigh News and Observer*, 22 Jan. 1970.

173. *Raleigh News and Observer*, 22 Oct. 1969.

174. Parker, *History of St. Philip's Episcopal Church*, 211.

175. Foley, "Diary of a Grant," 26; Parker, *History of St. Philip's Episcopal Church*, 211; Rev. Canon Edwin E. Smith to Viola Plummer, 3 Feb. 1970, EDNC archives; *Raleigh News and Observer*, 22 Jan. 1970.

176. Parker, *History of St. Philip's Episcopal Church*, 211.

177. Foley, "Diary of a Grant," 26.

178. *NC Churchman* (April 1970): 12; Foley, "Diary of a Grant," 26.

179. Minutes of the Meeting of the Diocesan Council, 23–24 Nov. 1969, EDNC archives; Fraser to Rectors and Wardens [of St. Philip's Episcopal Church], 25 Nov. 1970, ibid.

180. *Journal of the General Convention* (1969), 131, EDNC archives; William L. Van Deburg, *New Day in Babylon: The Black Power Movement and American Culture, 1965–1975* (Chicago: University of Chicago Press, 1992), 246, 295.

181. Foley, "Diary of a Grant," 18.

182. Heather Thompson, *Whose Detroit? Politics, Labor, and Race in a Modern American City* (Ithaca, N.Y.: Cornell University Press, 2001), 116–19; John Morton Blum, *Years of Discord: American Politics and Society, 1961–1974* (New York: Norton, 1991), 310–11; Lisa McGirr, *Suburban Warriors: The Origins of the New American Right* (Princeton, N.J.: Princeton University Press, 2001), 211.

183. Dan T. Carter, *The Politics of Rage: George Wallace, the Origins of the New Conservatism, and the Transformation of American Politics* (1995; 2nd ed. Baton Rouge: Louisiana State University Press, 2000), 472.

184. Ibid., 351.

185. Thompson, *Whose Detroit?*, 79–81. To examine the racialized attitudes of white Detroit before Black Power, see Kevin Boyle, *The Arc of Justice: A Saga of Race, Civil Rights, and Murder in the Jazz Age* (New York: Henry Holt, 2004); and Thomas Sugrue, *The Origins of the Urban Crisis: Race and Inequality in Postwar Detroit* (Princeton, N.J.: Princeton University Press, 1996).

186. Jonathan Schoenwald, *Time for Choosing: The Rise of Modern American Conservatism* (New York: Oxford, 2001), 305; F. Clifton White and William J. Gill, *Why Reagan Won: A Narrative History of the Conservative Movement 1964–1981* (Chicago: Regnery Gateway, 1981), 139.

187. Michael Flamm, *Law and Order: Street Crime, Civil Unrest, and the Crisis of Liberalism in the 1960s* (New York: Columbia University Press, 2004), 8; Michael Flamm, "Law and Order at Large," *Historian* 64 (2002): 643–65.

188. Carter, *Politics of Rage*, 30–31.

189. *Chapel Hill Weekly*, 22 Oct. 1969.

190. Parker, *History of St. Philip's Episcopal Church*, 195.

191. McGirr, *Suburban Warriors*, 256; Martin Marty, "The Revival of Evangelicalism and Southern Religion," in *Varieties of Southern Evangelicalism*, ed. David Edwin Harrell Jr. (Macon, Ga.: Mercer University Press, 1991).

192. Gardiner H. Shattuck Jr., *Episcopalians and Race: Civil War to Civil Rights* (Lexington: University of Kentucky Press, 2000).

193. Foley, "Diary of a Grant," 16.

194. James F. Findlay Jr., *Church People in the Struggle: The National Council of Churches and the Black Freedom Movement, 1950–1970* (New York: Oxford University Press, 1993), 206–7.

195. Oran P. Smith, *The Rise of Baptist Republicanism* (New York: New York University Press, 1997), 69.

196. Anthony D. Smith, *Nationalism and Modernism: A Critical Survey of Recent Theories of Nations and Nationalism* (London and New York: Routledge, 1998), 178.

197. Tommie Shelby, speech, Labyrinth Bookstore, New Haven, Conn., 8 Jan. 2006, C-SPAN broadcast.

198. Tommie Shelby, *We Who Are Dark: The Philosophical Foundations of Black Solidarity* (Cambridge, Mass.: Harvard University Press, Belknap Press, 2005).

199. Shelby writes that "there is a strand of black nationalism that is compatible

with the core values of liberalism" (ibid., 6–7). From what Shelby gives us as his working definition, that strand does not appear to include thick expressions of Black Power like cultural nationalism.

200. Peniel Joseph, "Dashikis and Democracy," *Journal of African-American History* 88 (spring 2003): 193.

201. At UCLA, for example, the university chancellor spent his political capital, almost at the cost of his ouster by then-governor Ronald Reagan, by first backing the hire of Angela Davis, a black socialist organizer and Marcuse sociologist by training, and second, by drumming up financial aid for a black studies program, run initially by Kwanzaa founder Maulana Karenga. San Francisco State University President Robert R. Smith ignored conservative critics within the Reagan administration, allying himself instead with campus progressives in the historic decision to hire Nathan Hare as the country's first black studies chairperson, though Smith was forced out that same fall. See Rooks, *White Money/Black Power*, 44–56; also, for a somewhat different view about the UC system campus fallout, see White and Gill, *Why Reagan Won*, 89, 138, 194. Even the Institute of the Black World, which critics resented as a Black Studies Vatican for their desired hegemony "to determine the content . . . of a highly pluralistic field," was far from sovereign. Indeed, the institute owed its start-up funds to trustees at Wesleyan University and their unanimous approval; see Board of Trustee Minutes, 12 April 1969, University Archives, Wesleyan University; Robert H. Wiebe, *Who We Are: A History of Popular Nationalism* (Princeton, N.J.: Princeton University Press, 2002), 6.

202. *New York Times*, 9 Oct. 2000.

Chapter 2. "We Had a Beautiful Thing"

1. Kalamu Ya Salaam, "Tell No Lies, Claim No Easy Victories," *Black World* (October 1974): 23.

2. Manning Marable, *Race, Reform, and Rebellion: The Second Reconstruction in Black America, 1845–1990*, rev. 2d ed. (Jackson: University Press of Mississippi, 1991), 134–35.

3. Neal R. Peirce, "A City's Courageous Crusader," *National Journal* 27 (5 Aug. 1995).

4. Position Statement of Owusu Sadaukai, *African World* 4 (July 1974): 11.

5. For black nationalism in particular, such popular memories often means reducing the Black Power movement to its celebrities rather than a grounding of blacks, collectively, in their own history and culture. In so doing, scholars risk removing human agency—defined by Frances Fox Piven as the "idea that reflective and purposeful people matter in the patterning of social life"—from the analysis. See Frances Fox Piven, "Deviant Behavior and the Making of the World," *Social Problems* 28 (June 1981): 489–508.

6. The number of registered black voters in Durham by decade's end contrasted sharply with the state's average of 49.8 percent. It was also distinct from the abject political disfranchisement of blacks in the Deep South during the early and mid-1960s in Alabama counties like Dallas, Wilkes, and Lowndes, where the number of black regis-

tered voters in Alabama totaled only two-thirds of that of Durham blacks. See Harvard Sitkoff, *The Struggle for Black Equality, 1954–1980* (New York: Hill & Wang, 1981), 168–70; and U.S. Department of Commerce, *Statistical Abstract of the United States, 1975*, 96th ed. (Washington, D.C.: Government Printing Office, 1975), 449, 554.

7. In his 1962 lamentation of old-fashioned virtues gone awry in the new black bourgeoisie in larger northern metropolises like Chicago and Detroit, sociologist E. Franklin Frazier found intellectual and moral solace in "the younger generations of Negro businessmen in Durham" as "still influenced by the older traditions that had grown up in the Negro community." See E. Franklin Frazier, *Black Bourgeoisie* (New York: Collier Books, 1962), 107–11; E. Franklin Frazier, "Durham: Capital of the Black Middle Class," in *The New Negro*, ed. Alain Locke, with a new preface by Robert Hayden (New York: Atheneum, 1970), 333–40; and Jeffrey J. Crow, Paul D. Escott, and Flora J. Hatley, *A History of African Americans in North Carolina* (Raleigh: North Carolina Department of Cultural Resources, 1992), 117–20.

8. *History of Operation Breakthrough*, 24, folder 4351, North Carolina Fund Papers, Southern Historical Collection, University of North Carolina at Chapel Hill (hereafter cited as NCF Papers).

9. "The Negro and Community Action," 6:18–19, *History of Operation Breakthrough*.

10. Ibid., 23.

11. Richard Critchfield, "OEO Grant to Durham Negroes Is Protested," *Washington, D.C., Evening Star*, 26 May 1969. Ultimately this grant was delayed for a year and reduced to $300,000.

12. Ibid.

13. *Evening Star*, 26 May 1969; Cornelia Olive, "Most City Councilmen Question Role of FCD in OEO Grant," *Durham Morning Herald*, 13 June 1969; "Black Capitalism in Durham," *Greensboro Daily News*, 1 May 1969; and Ed Martin, "OEO Explains Grant to Durham-based Agency," *Durham Morning Herald*, 30 April 1969.

14. "OEO Explains Grant to Durham-based Agency."

15. *Durham Morning Herald*, 24 Feb. 1969; *Durham Morning Herald*, 6 May 1969.

16. *Durham Morning Herald*, 16 July 1969.

17. See "Indecision in Durham," *Greensboro Daily News*, 12 May 1969; "OEO Grant Withdrawal Asked by Durham GOP," *Raleigh News and Observer*, 25 April 1969; "GOP Head Opposes OEO Grant," *Durham Morning Herald*, 24 April 1969.

18. *Durham Morning Herald*, 24 April 1969.

19. *History of Operation Breakthrough*, 25.

20. Bertie Howard and Steven Redburn, "UOCI: Black Political Power in Durham, 1968," 15 July 1968, revised 7 Aug. 1968, folder 4563, NCF Papers.

21. Emily Herring Wilson, *For the People of North Carolina: The Z. Smith Reynolds Foundation at Half-Century, 1936–1986* (Chapel Hill: University of North Carolina Press, 1988), 78.

22. "OEO Head Given FCD Probe Data," *Durham Morning Herald*, 14 June 1969.

23. Osha G. Davidson, *Best of Enemies: Race and Redemption in the New South* (New York: Scribner, 1996), 175–76.

24. *North Carolina Anvil*, 30 March 1969, 5.

25. Davidson, *Best of Enemies*, 175. Angered and humiliated, Stith ordered his handyman to hose down demonstrators.

26. Ibid., 176.

27. "oEO Head Given FCD Probe Data."

28. "Officials Denies oEO Released Inquiry Results," *Durham Morning Herald*, 18 June 1969.

29. uoci Mass Meeting, 6 July 1969, tape 12, sides 1–2, Nathaniel White Oral History Collection, Center for the Study of Black History, Hayti Heritage Center, Durham, N.C. (hereafter cited as White Collection).

30. Ibid.

31. Ibid.

32. "Fuller Granted FCD Leave to Push Malcolm X Work," *Durham Morning Herald*, 23 July 1969; "Durham Poverty Unit Expects Aid Despite Southern GOP Protests," *Raleigh News and Observer*, 23 July 1969; and Bertie Howard, interview by Kara Miles Turner, 3 March 1993, interview 2, 3, transcript, private collection of Kara Miles Turner.

33. "Final Report to oEO: Summer Intern and Curriculum Development Programs, 30–32," folder 3222, NCF Papers; "uoci," 3, 50, folder 4563, ibid.

34. "uoci Mass Meeting," 6 July 1969, tape 12, sides 1–2, White Collection.

35. A 1969 evaluation of Durham government saved its harshest criticism for the predominantly white housing authority: "There is little evidence that the Authority is willing to accept any responsibility for solving the social problems of its tenants or to permit tenant councils to have a voice in the policy-making process." Davidson, *Best of Enemies*, 235.

36. Ibid., 211.

37. Alexander Barnes, "'Bull City' Scene of Meeting," *Carolinian*, 20 Sept. 1969.

38. "A. Barnes Clarifies Position," ibid., 11 Oct. 1969.

39. "'Bull City' Scene of Meeting," ibid., 20 Sept. 1969.

40. DCNA, see Davidson, *Best of Enemies*, 51, 90, 134. For Black Ministerial Alliance, also see Davidson, *Best of Enemies*, 89, 134; See also *North Carolina Anvil*, 26 Feb. 1972; "Abandoning the Poor in Durham," *North Carolina Anvil*, 8 Nov. 1969; Walter B. Weare, *Black Business in the New South: A Social History of the North Carolina Mutual Life Insurance Company* (Urbana: University of Illinois Press, 1973), 240–50. For more on Austin and the impact of low-income blacks on the black freedom struggle in Durham, see Christina Greene, *Our Separate Ways: Women and the Black Freedom Movement in Durham, North Carolina* (Chapel Hill: University of North Carolina Press, 2007).

41. See "Can Stith Win?" *North Carolina Anvil*, 30 March 1968.

42. Christina Greene, "In the Best Interest of the Total Community?" *Frontiers* (1996): 190–217.

43. Ralph Goldman, "Politics of Political Integration," *Journal of Negro Education* (winter 1964): 26–34.

44. Lewis Bowman and G. R. Boynton, "Coalition as Party in a One-Party

Southern Area: A Theoretical and Case Analysis," *Midwest Journal of Political Science* (1964): 277–97.

45. Ibid.

46. Benjamin S. Abram, "A Case Study in Urban Policy: Durham, North Carolina." 16 Dec. 2005, at http://abram.pratt.duke.edu/research/abramDURHAM.pdf, accessed 7 Sept. 2008.

47. "Abandoning the Poor in Durham," *North Carolina Anvil*, 8 Nov. 1969.

48. Marv Zommick to Dick First, 10 Feb. 1966, Meeting of Durham Committee on Negro Affairs, folder 4401, NCF Papers; and Edward McConville, "The Prophetic Voice of C. P. Ellis," *Nation*, 15 Oct. 1973, 364; "Abandoning the Poor in Durham," *North Carolina Anvil*, 8 Nov. 1969.

49. Quoted in Davidson, *Best of Enemies*, 181.

50. "Is This Dream a Nightmare?" *Durham Carolina Times*, 1 Nov. 1969.

51. Quoted in ibid.; *History of Operation Breakthrough*; and Devin Fergus, "Liberalism and Black Nationalism in an American Southern State, 1965–1980" (PhD diss., Columbia University, 2002), 81.

52. UOCI Mass Meeting, 6 July 1969, tape 12, sides 1–2, White Collection.

53. Ibid.

54. Ibid.

55. Richard D. Lyons, "President Names Phase 2 Panels," *New York Times*, 11 Nov. 1971, Politics and Government: Committee on State and Local Government Cooperation, November 1971, box 66, Asa and Elna Spaulding Papers, Special Collections, Perkins Library, Duke University (hereafter cited as Spaulding Papers).

56. Weare, *Black Business in the New South*, 163–66.

57. *Baltimore Evening Sun*, 20 March 1967.

58. Asa T. Spaulding, interview by Walter B. Weare, Durham, N.C., 16 April 1979, tape 8:1, 14–15, transcript by Dorothy M. Casey, Southern Oral History Program, Louis Round Wilson Library, University of North Carolina.

59. Patricia Wallace, "Minority Groups and the Poor: Their Role in the Community Action Process," 5 May 1967, "Participation of the Poor in Durham," folder 4433, 9, NCF Papers.

60. See Ruffin to Spaulding, 4 March 1969, Civil Rights Series: United Durham Inc., 1961–69, box 55, Spaulding Papers; see also Community Development Corporation Oral History Project (UDI/CDC) Web site at http://www.picced.org/advocacy/udicdc.htm.

61. Spaulding to Shriver; Esser, 25 July 1967, folder 319, NCF Papers.

62. "Durham Labor Endorses," *Labor News*, 3 May 1968; "Precinct Breakdown on Durham County," *Durham Sun*, 6 Nov. 1968.

63. Howard Fuller (speaker), Durham Council on Human Relations Committee Meeting, 25 Nov. 1968, tape 3, White Collection.

64. "Precinct Breakdown on Durham County Voting."

65. Ibid.; "Durham Labor Endorses," *Labor News*, 3 May 1968; and "While the State Cops Out, New Politics People Deliver," *North Carolina Anvil*, 9 Nov. 1969.

66. Fuller, DCHRC Meeting, White Collection.

67. Howard Fuller, "Radish Interview with Howard Fuller," *Radish*, 28 July–10 Aug. 1969, folder 916, NCF Papers.

68. Spaulding to Fuller, 7 May 1968, Politics and Government: Durham County Commission, 1968, box 67, Spaulding Papers.

69. Victory Statement, 5 Nov. 1968, ibid.

70. Committee for Spaulding for County Commissioner, 15 Oct. 1970, Politics and Government: Durham County Commission, January–April 1971, box 68, Spaulding Papers.

71. In the 1980s Virginia's Douglas Wilder may have been the most successful at this, see Manning Marable, "Black Politics and the Challenges for the Left," *Monthly Review* (April 1990): 22–32.

72. Easley's less-hostile attitude toward labor was the one notable exception. See *Durham Sun*, 3 July 1972; *Labor News*, 3 May 1968; *North Carolina Anvil*, 4 May 1974; see also folder 4351, NCF Papers.

73. "Change Needed on Durham Board," *North Carolina Anvil*, 4 May 1974; "Spaulding, Scarborough Best," ibid.; Spaulding to John H. Wheeler, 30 Oct. 1970, Politics and Government: Durham County Commission, January–April 1971, box 68, Spaulding Papers; *North Carolina Anvil*, 26 Oct. 1968; and Spaulding to Edwin Clements, Spaulding to Stauber, Spaulding to Scarboro, Politics and Government: Mayor of Durham, Public Statements, 6 March 1971, box 71, Spaulding Papers.

74. J. Edgar Hoover to Spaulding, 15 May 1958, White Rock Baptist Church, April 1958–1959, box 293, Spaulding Papers; "A Statement by Asa T. Spaulding before HUAC," 25 Oct. 1967, Spaulding Papers; "Result of Riots 'Debatable' Spaulding Tells House Group," *Rochester Times-Union*, 26 Oct. 1967, Politics and Government: HUAC, 1967 folder, box 70, Spaulding Papers; Alonzo Hamby, *Liberalism and Its Challengers: From F. D. R. to Bush*, 2nd ed. (New York: Oxford University Press, 1992), 149–50.

75. Richard D. Lyons, "President Names Phase 2 Panels," *New York Times*, 11 Nov. 1971; Spaulding to Hon. George H. Boldt, 22 Nov. 1971, Politics and Government: Committee on State and Local Government Cooperation, January 1972, box 66, Spaulding Papers.

76. Charles Bartlett, "Black Power Stripped of Hostility Spells Pride," *Washington, D.C., Evening Star*, 11 July 1968, clippings 1956–1971 folder, box 47, Spaulding Papers; Spaulding to L. M. Quinn, 26 Oct. 1972, Spaulding Papers; Spaulding to Vivian Henderson, 30 Jan. 1973, Civil Rights: Urban National Corporation, October–December 1972, January–March 1973, box 57, Spaulding Papers.

77. Asa T. Spaulding, interview by Walter B. Weare, interview 2, 7.

78. Fergus, "Liberalism and Black Nationalism in an American Southern State," 88.

79. In future years, NNBPC annual donations were expected to far exceed $1 million; see "Wealthy Negroes Buoy Rights Drive by Pledging Funds," *New York Times*, 30 April 1967.

80. "Wealthy Negroes Buoy Rights Drive by Pledging Funds."

81. NAACP, LDF-NNBPC North Carolina State Meeting official minutes, 3, Civil Rights: NAACP, July–September 1967, box 43, Spaulding Papers.

82. *Durham Morning Herald*, 22 March 1967.

83. "Wealthy Negroes Buoy Rights Drive by Pledging Funds."

84. "Quiet Rights Champion," *New York Times*, 20 March 1967; and "Quiet Champion of Civil Rights," *Rochester Times-Union*, 3 April 1967.

85. Annual Report of the A. Philip Randolph Institute, January–December 1972, A. Philip Randolph Institute, 1969–1972 folder, box 38, Spaulding Papers.

86. For example, "Spaulding Uses Quiet, Effective Approach," *Baltimore Evening Sun*, 20 March 1967.

87. James A. Finley to Spaulding, 30 March 1967, Spaulding Papers; Spaulding to Finley, 3 April 1967, Civil Rights: NAACP, April 1967, box 42, Spaulding Papers.

88. Roy Wilkins to Spaulding, 20 Feb. 1968, Civil Rights: NAACP, January–April 1968, box 43, Spaulding Papers.

89. Minutes of an Organization Meeting of NNBPC of LDF, 23 April 1967, in Spaulding to Julian, 9 May 1967, Civil Rights: NAACP, May 1967, box 42, Spaulding Papers; LDF Press Release, 5 July 1967; and North Carolina State Meeting Minutes, 25 June 1967, Memorandum John S. Stewart to Members of the North Carolina Committee, 8 Sept. 1967, Civil Rights: NAACP, July–September 1967, box 43, Spaulding Papers.

90. One of the few legal challenges privileging the pocketbook issues of the poor was the tenants rights case *Joyce Thorpe v. Durham Housing Authority* (1967), see *Thorpe v. Housing Authority*, 386 U.S. 670 (1967).

91. Press release, 5 July 1967, Spaulding Papers; 26 Aug. 1967, July–September 1967 folder, box 43, ibid.; Legal Defense Fund to W. Rory Coker, 18 Oct. 1968, Civil Rights Series: NAACP, May–December 1968 folder, box 43, ibid.

92. NAACP-LDEF North Carolina Docket Report, April 1967, Civil Rights Series: NAACP, January–April, box 43, Spaulding Papers.

93. "Spaulding Advocates More Black Representation on Boards of Directors," Politics and Government: Durham County Commission, January–April [1970], box 68, ibid.

94. Davis was charged in 1970 and later exonerated as an accomplice to conspiracy, kidnapping, and murder. Memorandum from LDEF Law Interns to Board of Directors, 10 Nov. 1970, ibid.; Francis E. Rivers to Staff, memo, 16 Nov. 1970, ibid.; and Jack Greenberg to NAACP-LDEF Board of Directors, memo, 16 Nov. 1970, Civil Rights: NAACP, 1969–1972, box 43, ibid.

95. LDEF Law Interns to Board of Directors, memo, 10 Nov. 1970, Civil Rights: NAACP, 1969–1972, box 43, Spaulding Papers.

96. People do not make decisions based on rational choice or self-interest, according to *Choices, Values, and Frames*, ed. Amos Tversky and Daniel Kahneman (Cambridge: Cambridge University Press, 2000).

97. See Asa T. Spaulding, "The People Have a Right to Know," 18 May 1971, Politics and Government: Mayor of Durham: Public Statements, box 71, Spaulding Papers. Also see "Durham Vote Patterns Saturday," *Durham Morning Herald*, editorial, 18 May

1971; "Hawkins Wins Durham Race," *Raleigh News and Observer*, 16 May 1971; Voting Results by Precincts," *Durham Sun*, 17 May 1971; John Myers, "Interview with Jim Hawkins," *Durham Carolina Times*, 19 June 1971; *Durham Morning Herald*, 13 May 1971; and Ed Cottingham to Spaulding, 17 May 1971, Mayor of Durham, Miscellany, 1970–1971, box 71, Spaulding Papers.

98. Spaulding, "People Have a Right to Know"; Ed Cottingham, WDNC-TV News Director, to Spaulding, 17 May 1971, Spaulding Papers; Spaulding to Cottingham, 18 May 1971, ibid.; Cottingham to Spaulding, 24 May 1971, Mayor of Durham, Miscellany, 1970–1971, box 71, ibid.

99. Chuck Hopkins, interview by Kara Miles Turner, October 1996, interview 1, 6, transcript, private collection of Kara Miles Turner.

100. "Fuller Chastises Students," *Raleigh News and Observer*, 5 Oct. 1967.

101. "The Africanization of the Cracker," part 3, *North Carolina Anvil*, 22 June 1968.

102. Ibid., part 1, 8 June 1968.

103. Ibid., part 2, 15 June 1968.

104. Ibid., part 3.

105. Howard Fuller, tape-recorded interview by the author, 15 Dec. 1998, Milwaukee.

106. *North Carolina Anvil*, 22 June 1968; Fuller, interview by author; and Faculty List in "Background Information of the Malcolm X Liberation University," March 1969, 8, folder 903, NCF Papers.

107. David Cooper, "Non-violence Is Out," *Chapel Hill Weekly*, 28 Feb. 1968.

108. "Where Do We Go from Here? Fuller Speaks Out," *North Carolina Anvil*, 24 Feb. 1968.

109. Supervisor H. R. Starling to State Bureau of Investigation Director, 18 April 1967, State Bureau of Investigation Reports folder, 1967, box 208, Governor Daniel K. Moore Papers, North Carolina State Archives, Raleigh; and Cooper, "Non-violence Is Out"; Speech by Howard Fuller, UOCI Mass Meeting, 6 July 1969, tape 12, sides 1–2, White Collection.

110. Richard Daw, "MXLU Having Woes," *Durham Sun*, 5 Feb. 1970.

111. Dean C. L. Patterson to Bishop Thomas Fraser, 9 June 1972, Episcopal Diocese of North Carolina archives, Raleigh (hereafter cited as EDNC archives).

112. "MXLU Move Considered," *Durham Morning Herald*, 18 Feb. 1970.

113. "Liberation School Moves Operation," *Raleigh News and Observer*, 21 Aug. 1970; Wayne Hurder, "Malcolm X University May Move," n.d., private collection of Kara Miles Turner.

114. FCD, MXLU, and Cummins Engine Foundation grant notes and materials, private collection of Karen Miles Turner.

115. Jack White, "Black University Survives in N.C.," *Race Relations Reporter*, 6 July 1971, Interreligious Foundation for Community Organization (IFCO) Records, box 30, folder 37, Schomburg Center for Research in Black Culture, New York Public Library.

116. To see the historic intraorganizational relationship between the North Carolina NAACP leaders and grassroots workers, see William Powell Jones, "The NAACP, the Cold War, and the Making of the Civil Rights Movement in North Carolina, 1943–1960" (M.A. thesis, University of North Carolina at Chapel Hill, 1996); and William H. Chafe, *Civilities and Civil Rights: Greensboro, North Carolina, and the Black Struggle for Freedom* (Oxford: Oxford University Press, 1981), 178.

117. Chafe, *Civilities and Civil Rights*.

118. Bertie Howard, interview by Kara Miles Turner, 13 March 1993, interview 2, 1, 5, private collection of Kara Miles Turner; and "Report on An Analysis of Community Development in Some Selected Communities in North Carolina, August 11–September 1, 1968," Evaluation: Summer 1968, folder 3272, NCF Papers. Chafe, *Civilities and Civil Rights*, 178–83.

119. Chafe, *Civilities and Civil Rights*, 181; Howard, interview with Turner, 1; and "Liberation School Moves Operations," n.d., private collection of Kara Miles Turner. North Carolina College became North Carolina Central University in 1969.

120. See Marable, *Race, Reform, Rebellion*, 134; Chafe, *Civilities and Civil Rights*, 220; and "Malcolm X Said Moving to Greensboro," *NC Churchman* (October 1970): 10–11.

121. Chafe, *Civilities and Civil Rights*, 219.

122. See Richard H. Leach, "The Politics of Elementary and Secondary Education in North Carolina," in *Politics and Policy in North Carolina*, ed. Thad L. Beyle and Merle Black (New York: MSS Information Corporation, 1975), 178–97.

123. Chafe, *Civilities and Civil Rights*, 221.

124. For more on busing in Charlotte and beyond, see Stephen S. Smith, *Boom for Whom? Education, Desegregation, and Development in Charlotte* (New York: SUNY Press, 2004); Davison M. Douglas, *Reading, Writing, and Race: The Desegregation of the Charlotte Schools* (Chapel Hill: University of North Carolina Press, 1995); Lee Hubbard, "The End of Busing," *Jacksonville Free Press*, 20 Oct. 1999; *Addresses and Public Papers of Robert Walter Scott, Governor of North Carolina, 1969–1973*, ed. Memory F. Mitchell (Raleigh: Department of Cultural Resources, 1974), 560–61.

125. See A. B. Cochran, "Desegregating Public Education in North Carolina," in Beyle and Black, *Politics and Policy in North Carolina*, 210.

126. Chafe, *Civilities and Civil Rights*, 222–23, 223–29.

127. "Understanding the African Struggle: A Series of Essays by the Ideological Research Staff of Malcolm X Liberation University," 26, private collection of Howard Fuller.

128. Chafe, *Civilities and Civil Rights*, 229; See also Peter Skerry, "The Strange Politics of Affirmative Action," in *Race and Ethnic Relations 98/99* (Guilford, Conn.: Dushkin, 1998), 28.

129. Stevenson's editorial was critical of integration's failure to consider "the black teachers fired . . . fighting on behalf of integration. . . . [And] the common laborers who . . . guard[ed] . . . homes assaulted by white opponents of desegregation." Chafe, *Civilities and Civil Rights*, 230.

130. Chafe, *Civilities and Civil Rights*, 230.

131. Howard interview with Turner.

132. "Black Separatist University May Purchase Defunct School," *Durham Morning Herald*, 1 Sept. 1971.

133. See Sandra Smith and Earle H. West, "Charlotte Hawkins Brown," *Journal of Negro Education* 51 (summer 1982): 191–206; Charles Wadelington and Richard Knapp, *Charlotte Hawkins Brown and Palmer Memorial Institute: What One Young African American Woman Could Do* (Chapel Hill: University of North Carolina Press, 1999); and Tera Hunter, "'The Correct Thing': Charles H. Brown and the Palmer Memorial Institute," *Southern Exposure* 11 (Sept./Oct. 1983): 37–43.

134. "Malcolm X University Seeks a Campus," *Asheville Citizen*, 2 Sept. 1971.

135. "Crushing a Black University's Advance," *North Carolina Anvil*, 30 Oct. 1971.

136. Ibid.

137. *Durham Morning Herald*, 1 Sept. 1971.

138. Fergus, "Liberalism and Black Nationalism in an American Southern State," 103.

139. Many of these rumors were linked to the FBI, see Davidson, *Best of Enemies*, 293; Elizabeth Wheaton, *Codename GREENKIL: The 1979 Greensboro Killings* (Athens: University of Georgia Press, 1987), 28–31, 295–96; and "Crushing a Black University's Advance."

140. "Crushing a Black University's Advance."

141. MXLU did have outside endorsements from activist and former SNCC leader Julian Bond, Shaw University President J. Archie Hargraves, and others. Yet local opposition was hard to overcome. See Meeting of Local Committee of Rectors and Senior Wardens in Greensboro, 13 June 1972, EDNC archives.

142. Christopher Strain, "Soul City, North Carolina," *Journal of African-American History* 89 (winter 2004): 60.

143. Anthony Richmond, "Ethnic Nationalism and Post-Industrialism," in *Nationalism*, ed. John Hutchinson and Anthony D. Smith (New York: Oxford University Press, 1994), 298.

144. Harry Johnson, "Economic Nationalism in New States," in ibid., 237.

145. Weare, *Black Business*, 280–87.

146. Diary of Howard Fuller, 13–14, circa 28 Aug. 1971, in the author's collection (hereafter cited as Fuller Diary).

147. Most of conceptual framing is molded by growing up in a particular culture, one's own identity and values, and even things taken for granted in an individual's everyday life. To be accepted, the facts or logic of an argument must fit a person's frame. Otherwise, as cognitive linguist George Lakoff puts it, arguments "are not heard, or they are not accepted as facts, or they mystify us." Lakoff, *Don't Think of an Elephant! Know Your Values and Frame the Debate: The Essential Guide for Progressives* (White River Junction, Vt.: Chelsea Green, 2004), 17, 52, 60, 73.

148. Fuller Diary, 15–16.

149. Ibid., 16; see also 80.

150. Of the four schools affiliated with the Federation of Pan-African Institutions grant proposal, the largest allocation, $75,000, was proposed for Malcolm X Liberation University.

151. Carl F. Herman to Members of the Standing Committee, 16 June 1972, EDNC archives.

152. Ibid.

153. Howard Fuller, interview by author; Dean C. L. Patterson to the Right Rev. Thomas Fraser, 9 June 1972, EDNC archives; and Davidson, *Best of Enemies*, 294.

154. See also Presiding Bishop John E. Hines to the Rt. Rev. Thomas A. Fraser, 25 May 1972, EDNC archives; "Bishop Reports on MX Matter," *NC Churchman* (October 1972): 4; Thomas A. Fraser to the Rt. Rev. John E. Hines, 21 June 1972, EDNC archives.

155. The Local Committee of Rectors and Senior Wardens meeting at the Church of the Redeemer, 9 June 1972, EDNC archives.

156. Ibid.

157. Ibid., 12 June 1972.

158. Ibid.

159. Ibid.

160. Bishop Fraser to Rectors and Wardens, 25 Nov. 1970, EDNC archives; Ben F. Park, "Council Urges Tightening Up of Grant Screening Process Utilized by National Church," *NC Churchmen* (November 1969): 2–3.

161. Patterson to Fraser, 9 June 1972, EDNC archives.

162. Thomas A. Fraser to Rt. Rev. John E. Hines, 21 June 1972, ibid.

163. Unable to secure a second grant, MXLU pursued black sources, but with little success.

164. "New Malcolm X School," *Chicago Defender*, 4 Nov. 1969.

165. Ibid.

166. Fuller's time with IFCO would be short-lived, however. George Dugan, "Black Action Unit Takes Aim at Bias," *New York Times*, 19 March 1972.

167. Paul DeLaney, "Southern University Students Restive," *New York Times*, 28 Nov. 1972. This did not mean that Fuller did not still demonstrate sympathy toward armed revolutionary struggle elsewhere, particularly causes outside the country, as was the case in his lead role in organizing sympathy demonstrations for African guerrilla movements. But this hardly distinguished Fuller from mainstream civil rights organizations and black elected officials—for both the SCLC and the Congressional Black Caucus participated in these events, see for example Ivan Brandon, "Rallies Set for African Guerrillas," *Washington Post*, 21 March 1972.

168. Critics of the WCC charged that its Programme to Combat Racism helped finance groups engaged in terrorism and military tactics against apartheid regimes in Africa. First, most if not all of the incidents of violence cited by PCR detractors (e.g., $85,000 to the Zimbabwean Patriotic Front in 1978; days after the grant announcement it was implicated in shooting down a civilian aircraft) actually occurred outside of liberal democracies and in colonial and apartheid regimes (e.g., Rhodesia and South

Africa); they also occurred after the PCR-MXLU funding relationship was already over, and when MXLU was in the process of closing its doors altogether. Second, beyond MXLU, the past use of violence by liberation movements did not preclude the PCR from offering grant money. That said, once funded PCR emphasized nonviolent methods for social change. Third, by 1973, the PCR restated its mission to follow the nonviolent values set forth by Mohandas Gandhi and Martin Luther King Jr. Policywise, this meant allocating monies primarily toward groups focused on disinvestment in South Africa while pressuring banks to cease making loans. Fourth, PCR detractors rarely consider the South African government's active political and media campaign to discredit the WCC, which was public about its aim to end apartheid in that country. Last, some critics are more fair-minded than others. Steenkemp's work makes this clear. In one of the most critical scholarly pieces on the work and applied philosophy of the WCC, Steenkemp nonetheless stops short of stating WCC sanctioned or participated in violence. See Programme to Combat Racism Microfilm, Grants, 1970–1980, 6, Malcolm X Liberation University, USA (reel 34), World Council of Churches Archives, microfilm (Boston: IDC Publishers, 2004); Baldwin Sjollema, "Combating Racism: A Chapter in Ecumenical History," *Ecumenical Review* (October 2004): 470–79; Claude Welch, "Mobilizing Morality," *Human Rights Quarterly* 23 (2001): 863–910. While it is true that Howard Fuller held demonstrations of support for small liberation armies, so did other well-established institutions like the CBC and SCLC, *Washington Post*, 21 March 1972. On domestic issues, however, Fuller was less inclined to support or advocate violent exchange than verbal exchange. In Fuller's birthplace of Louisiana, for example, after the shooting deaths of two Southern University students by Baton Rouge law enforcement, Fuller led a contingent discussing the disciplining of police and local reform measures with Governor Edwin Edwards.

169. David E. Anderson, "Religion in America," *Chicago Defender*, 20 July 1974.

170. "Position Statement of Owusu Sadaukai," *African World* 4 (July 1974): 11.

171. I have taken some creative license with the term "soft power." My intent is not to broaden its application. I use "soft power" interchangeably with "liberalism" and a bit differently from its original meaning in the early 1990s, when Joseph Nye coined it. For Nye soft power meant "the ability to get what you want through attraction rather than coercion and payment." Soft power practitioners persuaded others, according to Nye, through American culture, political ideals, and policies, see Joseph S. Nye Jr., *Soft Power: The Means to Success in World Politics* (New York: Public Affairs, 2004), preface.

Chapter 3. From Rebellion to Reform

1. For the definitive study on earlier black electoralism in Winston-Salem and how its relations with left-liberal politics led to the election of Kenneth Williams in 1947, the first black elected official in the twentieth-century South to defeat a white opponent, see Robert Korstad, *Civil Rights Unionism: Tobacco Workers and the Struggle for Democracy in the Mid-Twentieth-Century South* (Chapel Hill: University of North Carolina Press, 2003), chap. 3, 306–10; and Nelson Lichtenstein, "Opportunities Found

and Lost: Labor, Radicals, and the Early Civil Rights Movement," *Journal of American History* (December 1988): 786–811; and Benjamin R. Friedman, "Fighting Back: The North Carolina Chapter of the Black Panther Party" (MA thesis, George Washington University, 1994), 92–93.

2. Opting not to seek reelection, Little selected a local NAACP member to run.

3. Little, ranked eighteenth, was one position ahead of his minister, the Rev. Jerry Drayton of New Bethel Baptist Church. See *Winston-Salem Journal*, 7 March 1982; *Winston-Salem Sentinel*, 7 July 1977. *Winston-Salem Chronicle* editor (confidential source), telephone interview by the author, 22 July 1999; *Winston-Salem Chronicle*, 6 Jan. 1983; Winston-Salem State University archivist Carter Cue, telephone interview by the author, 22 July 1999.

4. Among others, the following works describe in varying degrees the public's association of Black Power with criminality: Richard Polenberg, *One Nation Divisible: Class, Race, Ethnicity in the United States Since 1938* (New York: Penguin Books, 1980), 234–35; Kenneth O'Reilly, *Nixon's Piano: Presidents and Racial Politics from Washington to Clinton* (New York: Free Press, 1995), 269–70, 272, 288; Hugh Pearson, *The Shadow of the Panther: Huey Newton and the Price of Black Power* (Reading, Mass.: Addison-Wesley, 1994), 95–96; Chris Booker, "Lumpenization: A Critical Error of the Black Panther Party," in *Black Panther Party Reconsidered*, ed. Charles E. Jones (1998; rpt. Baltimore: Black Classic Press, 2005), 337–62. Charles Jones and Judson L. Jeffries, in an effort to debunk overgeneralizations, present a cogent counterthesis in "'Don't Believe the Hype:' Debunking the Panther Mythology," in ibid., 25–56.

5. For a small sampling suggesting this hypercritical view of Black Power, particularly within the broader critique of liberalism, see Allen Matusow, *The Unraveling of America: A History of Liberalism in the 1960s* (New York: Harper Torchbooks, 1984), 345–75; Gareth Davies, *From Opportunity to Entitlement: The Transformation and Decline of Great Society Liberalism*, chap. 5; and Hugh Davis Graham, *Civil Rights and the Presidency: Race and Gender in American Politics, 1960–1972* (New York: Oxford University Press, 1992), chap. 5.

6. Jim Gallagher to Honorable Congressman John Ashbrook, confidential memo, "Committee on Internal Security," preliminary review of *Gun-Barrel Politics: The Black Panther Party, 1966–1971*, 28 June 1971, folder 4, box 65, vertical file series, *The Black Panther Report*, 1971, Joseph Brown Matthews Papers, Special Collections Library, Duke University (hereafter cited as J. B. Matthews Papers).

7. U.S. House of Representatives Committee on Internal Security, "Separate Minority Views," in *Gun-Barrel Politics: The Black Panther Party, 1966–1971*. A Report by the Committee on Internal Security House of Representatives Ninety-second Congress First Session. Together with Minority Views and a Summation by Honorable Richardson Preyer, Subcommittee Chairman (Washington, D.C.: U.S. Government Printing Office, 1971), 141 (hereafter cited as HCIS, *Gun-Barrel Politics*).

8. Of course elsewhere, notably in Oakland in 1973, Panthers were running for elected office. See Huey Newton as quoted in the *North Carolina Anvil*, n.d.

9. Nelson Malloy, interview with the author.

10. Rhone Fraser, "The Black Panthers, a Photo Journey: Interview with Bobby Seale," *WBAI Arts Magazine*, n.d., http://www.wbai.org/index.php?option=com_content&task=view&id=9458&Itemid=2, accessed 18 Sept. 2008

11. "Winston-Salem Free Ambulance Service Opens," *Black Panther*, 16 Feb. 1974.

12. "Law and Order? Phrase Riles Tar Heel Negroes," *Charlotte Observer*, 23 Aug. 1968, 17A.

13. "Charlotte's Murder Rate Worst in State," *Charlotte Observer*, 27 Aug. 1968, 1.

14. Nixon was able to appeal to probusiness economic conservatives who had already begun to migrate South, see John B. Boles, *The South through Time: A History of an American Region*, 2nd ed. (Upper Saddle River, N.J.: Prentice Hall, 1999), 560; and William Chafe, *The Unfinished Journey: America since World War II*, 2nd ed. (New York: Oxford University Press, 1991), 381.

15. Gardner lost the November 1968 gubernatorial election to Democrat Bob Scott, see Jack Bass and Walter De Vries, *Transformation of Southern Politics: Social Change and Political Consequence since 1945* (Athens: University of Georgia Press, 1995), 232; "Despite Stock Speech, Nixon Made Net Gain in Visit Here," *Charlotte Observer*, 23 Aug. 1968; and "Gardner Outlines Law and Order Plan," ibid., 13 Sept. 1968.

16. Nixon won North Carolina and all southern border states except Texas and Arkansas. See Charles Roland, *The Improbable Era: The South since World War II* (Lexington: University Press of Kentucky, 1976), 87.

17. "Violence Swings U.S. to Right. Militants Defeat Selves by Rousing Masses' Fear of Anarchy," *Charlotte Observer*, 30 May 1969, 12; "Violent Crime Rate Shames North Carolina, Charlotte," *Charlotte Observer*, 16 Aug. 1969.

18. J. Christopher Schutz, "The Burning of America: Race, Radicalism, and the 'Charlotte Three' Trial in 1970s North Carolina," *North Carolina Historical Review* (January 1999): 645–65; Wayne Grimsley, *James B. Hunt: A North Carolina Progressive* (Jefferson, N.C.: McFarland & Co, 2003).

19. According to Little the Panthers did not like the way Chavis went about organizing. See Friedman, "Fighting Back," 49–50. See also John W. Larner, ed., *Guide to the Microfilm Edition of the FBI File on the Black Panther Party, North Carolina* [microfilm E 185.615 F35] (Wilmington, Del.: Scholarly Resources, 1986), sec. 1, p. 3.

20. See Friedman, "Fighting Back," 45–46; Devin Fergus, "The Early Years of the Black Panther Party, North Carolina" (MA thesis, North Carolina State University, 1994), 49–50.

21. *FBI File on the Black Panther Party, North Carolina*, microfilm version, 1:97 (Wilmington, Del.: Scholarly Resources, 1986); hereafter cited as *FBI File*.

22. Friedman, "Fighting Back," 46.

23. According to FBI reports, the group was plotting the bombing of a science building at nearby Belmont Abbey College, see Friedman, "Fighting Back," 46–7.

24. Friedman, "Fighting Back," 47.

25. "Jackanape" was a term used by party members to describe someone who is fearless but dangerous. See Bobby Seale, *Seize the Time: The Story of the Black Panther Party*

and Huey P. Newton (Baltimore, Md.: Black Classic Press, 1991), 373–93; Louis Heath, ed., *Off the Pigs! The History and Literature of the Black Panther Party* (Metuchen, N.J.: Scarecrow Press, 1976), 92; Chuck Moore, *I Was a Black Panther* (Garden City, New York: Doubleday & Co., 1970), typifies the malevolence of jackanapes; see also "U.S. Agents Raid Black Panthers," *Charlotte Observer*, 28 May 1969.

26. "U.S. Agents Raid Black Panthers."

27. "Chief Places Top Priority on Panther Probe," *Charlotte Observer*, 29 May 1969, 10A.

28. "Black Panthers Reclaim 3 Guns," ibid., 30 May 1969, 1B.

29. "Chief Places Top Priority on Panther Probe."

30. "2 Men Charged After Shoot-Out," *Charlotte Observer*, 17 May 1969, 1D; Friedman, "Fighting Back," 48.

31. Michael B. Richardson, "'Not Gradually . . . but Now': Reginald Hawkins, Black Leadership, and Desegregation in Charlotte, North Carolina," *North Carolina Historical Review* (July 2005).

32. Davison Douglas, *Reading, Writing, and Race: The Desegregation of the Charlotte Schools* (Chapel Hill: University of North Carolina Press, 1995).

33. One of MRPP's first initiatives was a formal protest of the Democrat Party's exclusion of black and women delegates from its state and national conventions, see Richardson, "'Not Gradually . . . but Now,'" 377.

34. Fergus, "Early Years of the Black Panther Party," 58.

35. *FBI File*, 3A: 70, 82; Friedman, "Fighting Back," 49.

36. Friedman, "Fighting Back," 48.

37. The college campus has traditionally been considered a tinder box for igniting social change. See Jeffrey Crow, Paul D. Escott, and Flora Hatley, *A History of African Americans in North Carolina* (Raleigh: North Carolina Department of Cultural Resources, Division of Archives and History, 1992), 123, 125–26, 161.

38. See 1970 U.S. Census.

39. The discussion of a chapter on Bennett and A&T campuses should by no means suggest this was the origin of activism at these colleges. See William Chafe, *Civilities and Civil Rights: Greensboro, North Carolina, and the Black Struggle for Freedom* (New York: Oxford University Press, 1980), 257; Friedman, "Fighting Back," 40.

40. *FBI File*, 1:125.

41. *FBI File*, 2B:14.

42. Greensboro's list included Lillian Smith, *Killers of the Dream*; William Greer and Price Cobbs, *Black Rage*; and Mao Tse Tung, *Red Book*; see *FBI File* 2B:64. See Fergus, "Early Years of the Black Panther Party," 66; Philip Foner, *Black Panthers Speak* (Philadelphia: J. B. Lippincott Co., 1970), 6. Heath, *Off the Pigs!* 92.

43. Fergus, "Early Years of the Black Panther Party," 68.

44. Much of the intelligence marshaled to show putative Panther activity in the area, however, was later discovered to be largely misinformed tips supplied by FBI informants.

45. By December 1968 Carmichael had already grown estranged from the party,

resigning in 1969; see Jones, *Black Panther Party Reconsidered*, 230; 369–70; The FBI frequently embellished stories prior to sending the information to Greensboro police; see Friedman, "Fighting Back," 43.

46. Elizabeth Wheaton, *Codename GREENKIL: The 1979 Greensboro Killings* (Athens: University of Georgia Press, 1987), 27–28.

47. Name withheld, interview by the author, 28 Jan. 1994; *FBI File*, 2B: 15, 17.

48. Bertie Howard, interview by the author, 28 Jan. 1994.

49. For a detailed discussion of the FBI-agent provocateur in Greensboro, see Chafe, *Civilities and Civil Rights*, 265.

50. Chafe, *Civilities and Civil Rights*, 273, 284, 406–8, 194, 201, 265–66; *FBI File*, parts 2A and 2B.

51. For example, see *FBI File*, parts 2A and 2B.

52. Chafe, *Civilities and Civil Rights*, 265.

53. A few suspected Brown as well because of his ties to Avent, but Brown's harsh sentence persuaded cynics he was not a provocateur.

54. Chafe, *Civilities and Civil Rights*, 266.

55. According to FBI surveillance, there were at least five informants in the North Carolina area; see Fergus, "Early Years of the Black Panther Party," 132; see also *FBI File*, 4A:42–5B, notes 20 and 116.

56. HCIS, *Gun-Barrel Politics*, 77–78. For an alternative view of Detroit, see also 72.

57. Michael Newton, *Bitter Grain* (Los Angeles: Holloway House, 1980), 199.

58. The BPP newspaper repeatedly ran articles denouncing not only informants but also "jackanapes"—those who were dangerous and careless about violence, using the gun to steal rather than as a tool of self-defense. "Panthers, Pigs, and Fools," which condemned the disruptive and criminal elements in North Carolina who endorsed the party only as convenient cover for criminal wrongdoing is but one example.

59. "Confidential Listing of the Winston-Salem Black Panther Party: Known Members and Sympathizers," 13 July 1970, "For Police Use Only" (stamp), author's collection.

60. Fergus, "Early Years of the Black Panther Party," 133.

61. See "A Word about Personnel and Standards," *Winston-Salem Journal*, 14 May 1971; for more about the general objectives of such orientations, see Masai Hewitt, interview by Ron Grele and Bret Eynon, interview 2, Los Angeles, 7 April 1984, 105, Oral History Research Office, Columbia University.

62. Larry Little, interview by the author, 5 March 1994.

63. Fergus, "Early Years of the Black Panther Party," 109.

64. *Winston-Salem Journal*, 12, 15, and 16 Nov. 1969.

65. By this time Robert Greer had left the party.

66. "A Change in Leadership Caused Change in Attitudes," *Winston-Salem Journal*, 10 May 1971; "Time to Remember," *Winston-Salem Journal*, 24 July 1994; Key Figure in Eviction Is Buried"; Friedman, "Fighting Back," 58.

67. "Key Figure in Eviction Is Buried"; *Winston-Salem Journal*, 24 July 1994.

68. Pauline Greer is the mother of Robert Greer, then the NCCF leader. Robert Greer, interview by the author, 26 March 1994, 3. See "Key Figure in Eviction Is Buried," *Winston-Salem Sentinel*, 19 Aug. 1971.

69. The Panthers' armed showdown in the State House in Sacramento during the late 1960s, for example, resulted in a spike in its membership rolls where chapters existed and inquiries about starting chapters where they did not.

70. *Winston Salem Journal*, 22 and 23 Sept. 1969.

71. See Dr. H. Rembert Malloy, interview by the author, 12 Aug. 1994.

72. For more on armed self-defense in North Carolina, see Timothy B. Tyson, *Radio Free Dixie: Robert F. Williams and the Roots of Black Power* (Chapel Hill: University of North Carolina Press, 1999); and Marcellus Barksdale, "Robert F. Williams and the Indigenous Civil Rights Movement in Monroe, North Carolina, 1961," *Journal of Negro History* 79 (spring 1984): 73–89. For a broader discussion of the psychological value of self-defense as essential to physical and group liberation, see Huey P. Newton, *Revolutionary Suicide* (New York: Harcourt Brace Jovanovich, 1973); Frantz Fanon, *Wretched of the Earth*, trans. Constance Farrington (New York: Grove Press, 1996); and Amilcar Cabral, *Return to the Source: Selected Speeches* (New York: Monthly Review Press, 1974).

73. Adam Fairclough notes that "historians have often defined resistance and protest too narrowly. Instead of confining their purview to membership in organizations and to formal political activity, they should recognize that blacks resisted white supremacy in a variety of informal, indirect, and individual ways. A black passenger might dispute a streetcar conductor but never dream of joining the NAACP. A black worker might subtly resist his or her white employer without ever belonging to a union. In the context of the rural South, even the most innocuous act—reading the *Pittsburgh Courier*, driving a fancy car, failing to yield the sidewalk—represented a subversion of white authority and an assertion of equality." See *Race and Democracy: The Civil Rights Struggle in Louisiana, 1913–1971* (Athens: University of Georgia Press, 1995).

74. "Newton Speaks Out," *Winston-Salem Sentinel*, 8 March 1969.

75. Ibid.

76. Bobby Seale was awaiting trial in Connecticut for murder.

77. Dhoruba Bin Wahad of New York was in the area along with Kathy Harrison to assist the branch's orientation; see Friedman, "Fighting Back," 57–58; Fergus, "Early Years of the Black Panther Party," 85.

78. "Black People of Winston-Salem, N.C., Boycott Avaricious A&P Grocery," *Black Panther*, 20 June 1970; "Carver Community Wants Changes at Food Store," *Winston-Salem Journal*, 2 June 1970.

79. "James Cato of Winston-Salem Subjected to Fascist Frame-Up," *Black Panther*, 5 Sept. 1970; *FBI File*, 8B: 1, 4; Friedman, "Fighting Back," 64–65.

80. *FBI File*, 7B:8.

81. Nelson Malloy, interview by the author, 5 March 1994.

82. Little was picked by Robert Greer to attend the Oakland training session; see Roy Thompson, "A Word About Personnel and Standards," *Winston-Salem Journal*, 14 May 1971; Little, interview by the author.

83. Regarding the *Black Panther* paper, it is nearly impossible to determine the cause of low paper sales as either law enforcement or would-be Panthers. For example, on the one hand the lack of Panther paper sales may be indicative of a lack of community support, crucial for the survival of any local branch. On the other hand it is also indicative that the FBI may well be the chief source in suppressing paper sales in the town. In other words, if the conclusion is elliptical it is because the evidence is.

84. Friedman, "Fighting Back," 77.

85. *Winston-Salem Sentinel*, 9 March 1971.

86. Ibid.

87. Ibid., 24 Feb. 1971, 8 March 1971, and 9 March 1971.

88. *Winston-Salem Journal*, 13 May 1971, and *Twin City Sentinel*, 13 May 1971.

89. See *Winston-Salem Journal*, 15 Nov. 1969, 10 May 1971, and 14 May 1971; see also Special Agent-in-Charge Charlotte to Director, *FBI File*, 11B:46; Friedman, "Fighting Back," 69.

90. *Winston-Salem Journal* and *Twin City Sentinel*, 13 May 1971.

91. *Winston-Salem Journal*, 9 March 1971.

92. "Personal Notes of Norman B. Smith," Little, Larry D. (In the matter of imprisonment of), folder 2, box B-55, Records of the General Counsel, Cases Closed, 1975–1980, NCCLU Papers, Special Collections, Duke University.

93. Renn Drum to Norman Smith, memo, 14 March 1971, ibid.

94. "Panthers Cry 'Harassment,'" *Winston-Salem Sentinel*, 31 October 1969.

95. Greer, interview by the author.

96. John Moore, interview by the author, 5 March 1994.

97. Manning Marable, *Race, Reform, and Rebellion: The Second Reconstruction in Black America, 1945–1982* (Oxford: University Press of Mississippi, 1984), 143.

98. "Confidential Listing of the Winston-Salem Black Panther Party."

99. Ward Churchill and Jim Vander Wall, eds., *The COINTELPRO Papers: Documents from the FBI's Secret Wars against Domestic Dissent* (Boston: South End Press, 1990), 144; Larry Little, interview by the author, 26 Oct. 1993. Little learned of the FBI's newspaper campaign through a Freedom of Information Act request. For more about problems encountered selling the *Black Panther*, see *State v. McDonald* (North Carolina, 1972) and "Freedom of Expression Cases," NCCLU Papers.

100. Friedman, "Fighting Back," 68.

101. See Jones, *Black Panther Party Reconsidered*, 374; "FBI Conducted Smear Campaign against Black Panthers," *Winston-Salem Journal*, 26 Aug. 1977; "Anonymous Panther Letter Has Blacks Here in a Swivel," *Winston-Salem Journal*, 14 Feb. 1971.

102. Such tactics effectively neutralized programs in Omaha and Des Moines, among other cities across the country; see Jones, *Black Panther Party Reconsidered*, 185.

103. "FBI Conducted Smear Campaign."

104. "Winston-Salem Police Informer Confesses," *FBI File*, 1464–65; see also Friedman, "Fighting Back," 85.

105. Jones, *Black Panther Party Reconsidered*, 375.

106. Ibid., 375–76.

107. Kenneth O'Reilly, *Racial Matters: The FBI's Secret File on Black America, 1960–1972* (New York: Free Press, 1989), 318; "City Is Caught in Panther Rivalry," *Winston-Salem Journal*, 14 May 1971; "A Word about Personnel and Standards," ibid.

108. Churchill and Vander Wall, *COINTELPRO Papers*, 123–64, esp. 142.

109. *FBI File*, 1504.

110. O'Reilly, *Racial Matters*, 310–18.

111. See "Fire at Headquarters Gave Panthers a Platform," *Winston-Salem Journal*, 11 May 1971.

112. Ibid.

113. See Friedman, "Fighting Back," 66.

114. "Firemen Deny Taking Files," *Winston-Salem Journal*, n.d., author's collection.

115. "Judge Rules against Panthers and Police," *Winston-Salem Journal*, n.d., author's collection.

116. Quoted in Norman B. Smith, personal notes.

117. "7 Pretrial Motions Filed for Panthers Held in Theft," *Winston-Salem Journal*, 4 May 1971.

118. "Police Raid on Panther House Brings Questions," ibid., 17 Jan. 1971; "Confiscated Items Labeled as Stolen," ibid., 13 Jan. 1971.

119. Both Little and Cornell pleaded no contest to a misdemeanor larceny charge. Neither would be sentenced. See Friedman, "Fighting Back," 79.

120. "Time to Remember."

121. See O'Reilly, *Racial Matters*, 321–24. For state repression of political prisoners, see Jones, *Black Panther Party Reconsidered*, 363–90; For the Waddell case specifically, refer to Herman Schwartz, ACLU–Prisoners Rights Project, to Norman B. Smith, General Counsel ACLU of North Carolina, 12 July 1972, Black Panthers, box B-1, folder 12, Records of the General Counsel, Cases Closed, 1971–1974, NCCLU Papers; Norman B. Smith to Herman Schwartz, 20 July 1972, ibid.; and *FBI File*, 9A:59.

122. Robert V. N. Brown, "Black Panther Dies in Central Prison," *North Carolina Anvil*, 8 July 1972, 1.

123. Smith to Herman Schwartz, 20 July 1972.

124. "Black Panther Rally Emphasizes Unity," *Winston-Salem Journal*, 20 Sept. 1971; "Black Panther Dies in Central Prison"; Schwartz, ACLU–Prisoners Rights Project, to Smith, General Counsel ACLU of North Carolina, July 12, 1972, and Schwartz to Smith, July 12, 1972; W. W. Finlator, "Report on Visit to Black Panthers at Central Prison," n.d., Black Panthers, folder 12, box B-1, Records of the Counsel, 1971–1974, NCCLU Papers.

125. SAC Charlotte to Director, *FBI File*, 18 Jan. 1971, document 105-165706-8-389; Friedman, "Fighting Back," 65. In addition, also see the extension of remarks by Ohio

Congressman John M. Ashbrook, "Keep the Radicals Away from the Prisoners," in *Congressional Record*, 16 Sept. 1971, 117 92d Cong., 1st sess. (1971), 32251.

126. *Winston-Salem Journal*, 26 Aug. 1977.

127. Allegations of drug peddling were later disproved. For more, see *FBI File*, 1465–66.

128. *Winston Salem Sentinel*, 3 Oct. 1980.

129. "Little Calls on Students to Help Fight Oppression," ibid., 26 Oct. 1979.

130. Martin Kenner, interview by Ron Grele, 112, Oral History Research Office, Columbia University.

131. Jim Gallagher to John Ashbrook, 28 June 1971, J. B. Matthews Papers.

132. Ibid.

133. Separate Minority View, HCIS, *Gun-Barrel Politics*, 141.

134. HCIS, *Gun-Barrel Politics*, 142. Ashbrook and other minority members were most likely unaware that 61 percent of African Americans under the age of twenty-one saw the Panthers with community and personal pride, according to a *Time* magazine Harris poll in April that same year.

135. HCIS, *Gun-Barrel Politics*, 143.

136. Preyer went on to say that for "what remains of the Panther Party," its lawlessness and revolutionary paramilitary posturing, had undermined the party's effectiveness—though much of that largely mythical—among fascinated white liberals, idealists, and moderate blacks.

137. Martin Kenner, interview by Ron Grele, 111, Oral History Research Office, Columbia University.

138. For the BPP's evolving program, see Ross Baker, "The Transformation of the Panthers," *Washington Post*, 13 Feb. 1971; Huey Newton, "On the Defection of Eldridge Cleaver from the Black Community," *Black Panther*, 17 April 1971; Joel Dreyfuss, "An Analysis of the Shifting Images of Huey Newton," *North Carolina Anvil*, 1 June 1975. Charles Hopkins, "The De-radicalization of the Black Panther Party" (PhD diss., University of North Carolina, 1978), 15–16, 141; Earl Anthony, *Picking Up the Gun: A Report on the Black Panthers* (New York: Dial Press, 1970), 120.

139. *Winston-Salem Journal*, 26 Aug. 1977.

140. Friedman, "Fighting Back," 80.

141. Fergus, "Early Years of the Black Panther Party," 154.

142. Huey P. Newton, "Black Capitalism Re-Analyzed," *Black Panther*, 5 June 1971.

143. *North Carolina Anvil*, 20 July 1974.

144. *Winston-Salem Chronicle*, 6 Jan. 1983.

145. Fergus, "Early Years of the Black Panther Party," 108–9.

146. SAC Charlotte to Director, *FBI File*, 21 Aug. 1972, document 105-165706-8-671; *FBI File*, 14A:86.

147. SAC Charlotte to Acting Director, *FBI File*, 1 Aug. 1972, document 105-165-706-8-669.

148. Friedman, "Fighting Back," 77.

149. *Winston-Salem Sentinel*, 1973, author's collection.

150. Bishop L. Moultrie Moore to Rectors and Senior Wardens, memo, 27 April 1973, Episcopal Diocese of North Carolina archives, Raleigh (hereafter cited as EDNC archives).

151. Committee Members to the Rev. Robert N. Davis, 14 March 1973, ibid.; Lloyd H. Abbott to Hazel Mack and Nelson Malloy, 15 March 1973, ibid.; Margaret L. Sharpe to Nelson Malloy, 17 March 1973, ibid.; Winston-Salem Branch of the Black Panther Party, "Amendment to Prior Proposal for (Free Ambulance Program) to the General Convention for Special Programs" (received 5 April 1973), ibid.

152. Friedman, "Fighting Back," 81; Little remained "skeptical of the commitment among whites—both the general public and government officials—toward the black community." See *North Carolina Anvil*, 20 July 1974.

153. Thomas Fraser to Viola Plummer, 19 March 1973, EDNC archives.

154. Friedman, "Fighting Back," 81.

155. "Free Service—Panther Vision," *North Carolina Anvil*, 13 Oct. 1973; local Panthers working to improve community relations also conforms to FBI reports, see *FBI File*, 14A:92–97.

156. *FBI File*, 1442; *NBC Nightly News*, 25 Feb. 1974, TV News Archive, Vanderbilt University, Nashville, Tenn.

157. GCSP application, 20 Jan. 1975, 2, EDNC archives.

158. For an example of how Panthers and supporters claimed government abdicated this responsibility, see "Panthers to Start Ambulance Service," *North Carolina Anvil*, 3 July 1971.

159. Greer, interview by the author.

160. Ralph Bennet, "The Terrorists among Us: An Intelligence Report," *Reader's Digest* (Oct 1971).

161. For more on the survival programs, see Tracye Matthews, "No One Ever Asks What a Man's Role in the Revolution Is," in *Sisters in the Struggle: African-American Women in the Civil Rights–Black Power Movement*, ed. Bettye Collier-Thomas and V. P. Franklin (New York: New York University Press, 2001), 230–56.

162. *Winston-Salem Journal*, 2 Aug. 1977.

163. Nelson Malloy, interview with the author.

164. See Fergus, "Early Years of the Black Panther Party," 105.

165. *FBI File*, 1521; *State v. McDonald* and "Freedom of Expression Cases."

166. David Hilliard, interview by the author, 3 Nov. 1993.

167. In suggesting liberalism was strengthened via social democracy is to recognize there is strength in numbers. Liberalism stood to benefit—expanding its network, for example, to incorporate potential allies like the Panthers—from the web of mutuality it spun with social democracy. For more on the ways in which social democracy informs and enriches liberalism, see Robert Kuttner, "Liberalism, Socialism, and Democracy," in *The American Prospect Reader in American Politics*, ed. Walter Dean Burnham

(Chatham, N.J.: Chatham House, 1995), 52–60; "News Release Issued by the American Civil Liberties Union, December 29, 1969," in *The Black Panthers Speak*, ed. Philip S. Foner (New York: Da Capo Press, 1995), 265.

168. *Winston-Salem Journal*, 23 Jan. 1971. Whenever possible the NCCLU took up the Panther legal cause. *Winston-Salem Journal*, 15 Jan., 4 May, 9 May, and 11 May 1971; also see Fergus, "Early Years of the Black Panther Party," 162.

169. Joseph Tieger to James Yates, Forsyth County District Court, 2 March 1971, folder 1, box B-55, Records of the General Counsel, NCCLU Papers; *Winston-Salem Journal*, 9 March 1971.

170. "In the Matter of Larry Little, Petitioner," U.S. Supreme Court Reports—U.S. 30 L Ed 2d 708, 92 S Ct [no. 71-244] 24 Jan. 1972, Larry D. Little (In the Matter of the Imprisonment of), folder 1, box B-55, Records of the General Counsel, Closed Cases 1975–1980, NCCLU Papers.

171. *Winston-Salem Journal*, 19 March 1971.

172. In upholding the original decision, state courts essentially ruled that "Little's claim of being a political prisoner and his charge . . . [of] bias . . . constituted direct criminal contempt within the meaning of North Carolina law"; see *Winston-Salem Journal*, 19 March 1971.

173. *Winston-Salem Journal*, 17 June 1971.

174. Ibid., 6 Feb., 17 March, 19 March, 28 April, 29 April, 5 May, 18 May, and 17 June 1971, and 25 Jan. 1972.

175. Justice Louis B. Heller, Supreme Court of the State of New York, to Norman B. Smith, 9 March 1972, in Little (In the matter of the imprisonment of), folder 1, box B-55, Records of the General Counsel, Closed Cases, 1975–1980, NCCLU Papers; Smith to Heller, 16 March 1972, ibid.; Smith to Heller, 30 March 1972, ibid.; Alan Scheflin to Norman B. Smith, 7 Dec. 1971, ibid.; Daniel H. Pollitt to Norman B. Smith, 26 Jan. 1972, ibid.

176. *Winston-Salem Journal*, 20 March 1971.

177. Few attorneys willingly chanced a Panther case in state court. North Carolina state courts, except on rare occasion—as in the controversial state superior court jury peer decision that was subsequently overturned—displayed little tolerance for unpopular litigants like the Panthers. Accordingly, the NCCLU wisely pursued legal remedy through federal courts. *Wall Street Journal*, 21 March 1971.

178. While the ACLU's motion for a preliminary injunction prohibiting the police from interfering with Panther activity was denied, more damaging was U.S. District Court Judge Eugene Gordon's denial to the defense. Citing *First Citizen v. Camp*, Gordon stated it was standard procedure not to issue a preliminary injunction if parties can comply—like the police had done—without court interference. *Winston-Salem Journal*, 6 July 1971; see "Brief in Support of the Defense of the Lack of Jurisdiction Over the Subject Matter," NCCLU Papers, 1973–1983.

179. *Winston-Salem Journal*, 24 Sept. 1971.

180. *Winston-Salem Chapter of the National Committee to Combat Fascism v. Justus*

Tucker, Chief of Police, Winston-Salem, et al. (1974), Records of the General Counsel, NCCLU Papers.

181. Larry Little and Hazel Mack to Smith, Patterson, Follin & Curtis, 14 March 1973, Cases Closed, 1975–1980, box B73, Records of the General Counsel, Cases Closed, NCCLU Papers; Michael K. Curtis to John L. W. Garrou, 17 April 1973, ibid.; Garrou to Curtis, 14 June 1973, ibid.; Curtis to Mack, Deloris Wright, and Little, 18 June 1973, ibid.; Curtis to Garrou, 1 Oct. 1973; Curtis to Little, 21 Sept. 1973, ibid.; Little to Harkavay, 30 Oct. 1973 (and memo of said document from Harkavay to Smith, 11 Nov. 1973), ibid.; Garrou to Smith, 1 Feb. 1974, ibid.; Smith to Little, 6 Feb. 1974; Smith to Little, 20 Sept. 1974, ibid.; *Winston-Salem Chapter of the NCCF et al. v. Justus Tucker et al. (1974)*.

182. Larry Little to Mark Harkavay, 30 Oct. 1973, NCCLU Papers.

183. *Winston-Salem Journal*, 23 Sept. 1971.

184. Efforts to build a prosecutorial case against the Panthers under the Smith (or Alien Registration) Act; see O'Reilly, *Racial Matters*, 264–65, 298–99; Jones, *Black Panther Party Reconsidered*, 365–89. Also see Churchill and Vander Wall, *COINTELPRO Papers*, 23.

185. *Winston-Salem Journal*, 21 and 23 Sept. 1971, 17 Jan. 1971, and 24 July 1994.

186. Elaine Brown and Bobby Seale had already prepared campaigns by the spring of 1972; see Elaine Brown, *A Taste of Power: A Black Woman's Story* (New York: Anchor Books, 1992), 321–27.

187. *North Carolina Anvil*, 20 July 1974.

188. *FBI File*, 1442.

189. One or more of the following infractions were said to have occurred: (1) oaths may not have been administered; (2) third persons, rather than the official registrar, may have actually done the registering; and (3) proper identification may not have been procured from the registrants.

190. *Larry D. Little v. North Carolina State Board of Elections*, Supreme Court of North Carolina (1975); hereafter cited as *LDL v. NCSBE* (1975). In *Larry D. Little v. North Carolina State Board of Elections*, General Court of Justice, Superior Court Division (1974), folder 3, box B-55, Record of the General Counsel, Cases Closed, 1975–1980, NCCLU Papers; hereafter cited as *LDL v. NCSBE* (1974).

191. See *LDL v. NCSBE* (1975).

192. *LDL v. NCSBE* (1975); *LDL v. NCSBE* (1974).

193. *LDL v. NCSBE* (1975).

194. *Winston-Salem Journal*, 14 June 1974; see also Friedman, "Fighting Back," 86.

195. Meeting of Rectors and Wardens, 7 June 1976, EDNC archives.

196. *Winston-Salem Chronicle* editor (confidential source), interview by the author; Cue, interview by the author.

197. Dan Chapman, "Questioning by Law Board Went Well, Little Says," *Winston-Salem Journal*, 28 Oct. 1988.

198. Kenner, interview by Grele.

199. Bishop L. Moultrie Moore to Rectors and Senior Wardens, memo, EDNC archives.

200. *Black Panther*, 12 April 1975 and 28 Feb. 1976.

201. See, for example, Chicago BPP, *NBC Nightly News*, 8 Dec. 1969, Television News Archives; Alan Brisbort, "The Night of the Panthers," *Hartford Courant*, 30 Nov. 2003; D.C. BPP, Bar Report.

202. Michael Schudson, *Good Citizen: A History of American Civic Life* (Cambridge, Mass.: Harvard University Press, 1998), chap. 6 and concl.

203. See "News Release Issued by the American Civil Liberties Union," 263.

204. Stanley I. Kutler, *The Wars of Watergate: The Last Crisis of Richard Nixon* (New York: Knopf, 1990), 316. Other scholars also identify Watergate as one of the nation's most significant constitutional crises including Gladys E. Lang and Kurt Lang, *The Battle for Public Opinion: The President, the Press, and the Polls during Watergate* (New York: Columbia University Press, 1983); Howard Ball, *"We Have A Duty": The Supreme Court and the Watergate Litigation* (Westport, Conn.: Greenwood Press, 1990); Philip Kurland, *Watergate and the Constitution* (Chicago: University of Chicago Press, 1978); Rexford Tugwell and Thomas Cronin, eds., *The Presidency Reappraised* (New York: Praeger, 1974); see, for example, Thomas De Frank, "Watergate Was an Ominous, Spooky, and Nasty Time," *Knight Ridder Tribune News Service*, 3 June 2005.

205. Max Holland, "After Thirty Years: Making Sense of the Assassination," *Reviews in American History* 22 (1994): 204; see also Alan M. Levin's 1988 documentary film, *The Secret Government: The Constitution in Crisis*.

Chapter 4. In Defense of Sister Joan

1. Wayne King, "Killing of North Carolina Jailer," *New York Times*, 1 Dec. 1974.

2. By 1975 North Carolina already had sixty-nine people on death row (seventy-five according to the *Progressive*), the highest number by far of any state, and reportedly nearly a third of all death-row inmates in the country; see "Joanne Little Wins New Trial Site," *Off Our Backs* (May–June 1975): 8; "JoAnne Little Defense Fund," *Northwest Passage* 12 (3 March 1975): 20. See Morris Dees in *A Season for Justice: The Life and Times of Civil Rights Lawyer Morris Dees* (New York: Charles Scribner's Sons, 1991), 165. This, its critics said, explained why over 50 percent of death-row inmates were either black or Native Americans; see Mark Pinsky, "North Carolina's Tarnished Image," *Progressive* 39 (August 1975): 32–33. This included the famous conviction of the Tarboro Three, black men sentenced to death for the rape of a white woman, *Black Panther*, 8 Jan. 1975. See James E. Holshouser, *Addresses and Public Papers of James Eubert Holshouser, Jr., Governor of North Carolina, 1973–1977*, ed. Memory F. Mitchell (Raleigh, N.C.: Department of Cultural Resources, 1978), 533.

3. Angela Davis, "JoAnne Little," *Ms.* (June 1975): 76.

4. Fred Harwell, *A True Deliverance* (New York: Alfred A. Knopf, 1980), 117.

5. *North Carolina Anvil*, 18 Jan. 1975.

6. Dees, *Season for Justice*, 165.

7. Some representative works include Genna Rae McNeil, "Joanne Is You, Joanne Is Me: A Consideration of African American Women and the 'Free Joan Little' Movement, 1974–75," in *Sisters in the Struggle: African American Women in the Civil Rights–Black Power Movement*, ed. Bettye Collier-Thomas and V. P. Franklin (New York: New York University Press, 2001), 259–79; also see McNeil's upcoming book-length monograph on the Little movement. In addition to McNeil, see the forthcoming studies of Waldo Martin and Christina Greene on the Little case and movement.

8. Cosmopolitanism privileges centralization and process, both of which were judged to be safeguards against mistrust and intolerance of provincial wisdom.

9. Jack Bass and Walter De Vries, *The Transformation of Southern Politics: Social Change and Political Consequence since 1945* (New York: New American Library, 1977), 242. The title for this section is drawn from Daniel Bell, "The Revolt against Modernity," *Public Interest* 81 (1985): 42–63.

10. James Reston Jr. "The Joanne Little Case," *New York Times*, n.d., James Reston Collection of Joan Little Trial Materials, Southern Historical Collection, University of North Carolina at Chapel Hill (hereafter cited as Reston Collection).

11. In cultural and social character, it was like much of America's heartland, as described by Daniel Joseph Singal in "Beyond Consensus: Richard Hofstadter and American Historiography," *American Historical Review* 89 (October–December 1984): 991.

12. Harwell, *True Deliverance*, 73.

13. Singal, "Beyond Consensus," 989.

14. *Washington Daily News*, 3 June 1974; James Reston Jr., *The Innocence of Joan Little: A Southern Mystery* (New York: Times Books, 1977), 127–28; see also Jerry Paul, in Joan Little interview by James Reston, James Reston Collection; see also Singal, "Beyond Consensus," 992. This is not to imply that fundamentalism is exclusive to religion, see Alan Brinkley, *Liberalism and Its Discontents* (Cambridge, Mass.: Harvard University Press, 1999), 292.

15. Studies going back as far as 1965 have shared this view; see J. David Singer, "Cosmopolitan Attitudes and International Relation Courses: Some Tentative Correlations," *Journal of Politics* 27 (1965): 318–38.

16. Rick Nichols, "Attitudes on Trial in Joanne Little Case," *Raleigh News and Observer*, 20 April 1975, 6.

17. *North Carolina Anvil*, 4 Oct. 1975; "Lee Won't Lead Rally for Little," *Raleigh News and Observer*, 10 March 1975, 6. William Geimer, interview by the author, Lexington, Virginia, 10 April 2001. Geimer was a North Carolina Civil Liberties Union board member and later head of North Carolinians against the Death Penalty.

18. Bass and De Vries, *Transformation of Southern Politics*, 238.

19. Ronnie Vetter, "Can a Black Woman Convict Persuade a North Carolina Jury Jailer-Killing was Self Defense?" *Majority Report* 4 (8 Feb. 1975): 3.

20. Editor Ashley Futrell later claimed to be unaware of the details surrounding the Little-Alligood event; Rick Nichols, "National Issues Engulf Unlikely N.C. Celebrity,"

Raleigh News and Observer, 13 July 1975, 1; Cindy Jaquith, "Joan Little Wins New Trial Site," *Militant* (16 May 1975): 28.

21. Michael Bane, "State of North Carolina v. Joanne Little," *Win* 11 (2 Feb. 1975): 13.

22. Douglas Watson, "The Joanne Little Case," *Washington Post*, 5 May 1975; Jackie MacMillan, "Interview: Joanne Little, No Escape," *Off Our Backs* (January 1975): 4.

23. Carl T. Rowan quoted in Nichols, "National Issues Engulf Unlikely N.C. Celebrity."

24. Richard Kluger, Review of *The Innocence of Joanne Little*, by James Reston Jr., *New York Times*, 18 Dec. 1977, 12. "A stranger doesn't have to be in town long to hear racial slurs," observed an out-of-town beat reporter for the Little trial; see Watson, "Joanne Little Case."

25. See Cindy Jaquith, "Joanne Little Trial: Prosecution Case Based on Racism, Not on Evidence," *Militant* (15 Aug. 1975): 8; Vetter, "Can a Black Woman Convict Persuade a North Carolina Jury?"; "Doctor Supports Defense Charge of JoAnne Little Rape," *Black Panther*, 11 Aug. 1975, 7.

26. Martha Pettit, "Joanne Little: 'Symbol for Blacks and Women,'" *Militant* 39 (18 July 1975): 28.

27. Jaquith, "Joanne Little Trial."

28. "State Oks Joanne Little Trial Change," *Black Panther*, 5 May 1975, 7.

29. Jaquith, "Joanne Little Trial."

30. Harwell, *True Deliverance*, 98.

31. Paul, in Little interview by Reston.

32. William Geimer, interview by the author.

33. Jackie MacMillan, "Interview: Joanne Little," *Off Our Backs* (January 1975): 4; Harwell, *True Deliverance*, 124.

34. Dees, *Season for Justice*, 165.

35. Courtney Mullin, interview by James Reston, Reston Collection; Harwell, *True Deliverance*, 148–50.

36. Pettit, "Joanne Little."

37. "Joanne Little Wins New Trial Site"; Edward Tivnan, "Jury by Trial," *New York Times*, 16 Nov. 1975, 31. Other questions asked in the survey, Little attorney Marvin Miller noted, included "Do you think people on welfare get too much money?" and "Do you feel Black people are more dishonest?"

38. Mullin, interview by Reston; Harwell, *True Deliverance*, 148–50; Nichols, "Attitudes on Trial in Joanne Little Case." Eastern North Carolina may have been known in the minds of some for the legendary story of the "son who shot and killed his father on the steps of the church during a dispute over a Bible passage"; see William J. Cooper, *The American South* (New York: McGraw-Hill, 1990–91), 750.

39. Harwell, *True Deliverance*, 153.

40. See Reston, *Innocence of Joan Little*, 176–77; James Reston, "The Joan Little Case; In a Small Southern Town," *New York Times*, 6 April 1975, 39–41.

41. Louis Randolph, interview by James Reston, Reston Collection.

42. Jim Grant, "Little Trial Moved to Raleigh," *Southern Patriot* (March 1975): 1, 8.

43. Bass and De Vries, *Transformation of Southern Politics*, 242.

44. Bernard E. Garnett, "Black Woman's Trial in NC Splits Rights Groups," *Wall Street Journal*, 18 April 1975, 1. See also Jaquith, "Joan Little Wins New Trial Site"; Randolph, interview by Reston.

45. Grant, "Little Trial Moved," *Southern Patriot*, 1.

46. Bane, "State of North Carolina v. Joanne Little."

47. Paul, in Little interview by Reston.

48. *Statistical Abstract of the United States* (Washington, D.C.: U.S. Dept. of Commerce, 1975), 151.

49. *Statistical Abstract*, 151.

50. See *Sourcebook of Criminal Justice Statistics, 1976* (Washington, D.C.: U.S. Dept. of Justice), 68; see also *Statistical Abstracts*, 12.

51. *Sourcebook, 1976*, 58.

52. Oliver Williams and Richard J. Richardson, "The Impact of Criminal Justice Policy on Blacks in North Carolina Trial Courts," in *Politics and Policy in North Carolina*, ed. Thad L. Beyle and Merle Black (New York: MSS Information, 1975), 274–77.

53. By 31 December 1974, North Carolina had 65 of the 254 national prisoners under the sentence of death. Out those 65, 39 were black and 5 Native Americans. While raw total numbers in North Carolina grew to 177 by July 1976, their national share dropped from 25 to 20 percent. See *Sourcebook, 1976*, 763, 764, 776.

54. The other state was Louisiana. See Hugo Adam Bedau, ed., *The Death Penalty in America*, 3d ed. (New York: Oxford University Press, 1982), 300.

55. Ibid., 300.

56. Ibid., 289.

57. In *Woodson v. North Carolina* (1976), the U.S. Supreme Court overturned the state's mandatory death provision. Paul Knepper, *North Carolina's Criminal Justice System* (Durham, N.C.: Carolina Academic Press, 1999), 171.

58. Bedau, *Death Penalty in America*, 289–90.

59. Claude Sitton, "Editorial: The Making of State's Cause Celebre," *Raleigh News and Observer*, 6 July 1975, sec. 4, 4; see also Harwell, *True Deliverance*, 5.

60. Laurence French, "The Incarcerated Black Female: The Case of Social Double Jeopardy," in *The Black Woman Cross-Culturally*, ed. Filomena Chioma (Rochester, Vt.: Schenkman Books, 1985), 371.

61. *New York Times*, 24 April 1975.

62. Paul, in Little interview by Reston.

63. "Woman Loses Bid in Staying at Jail," *New York Times*, 24 April 1975; D. J. Hill, "Biased Grand Jury Seen in Little Case," *Washington Post*, 15 April 1975.

64. "Woman Loses Bid in Staying at Jail."

65. For a partial list of defense motions denied, see "Joan Little Defense Denied Removal of Special Prosecutor," *Black Panther*, 12 May 1975, 5.

66. Grant, "Little Trial Moved."

67. Cathy Steele Roche, "Judge Shifts Little Trial in Interests of Justice," *Washington Post*, 2 May 1975.

68. Singal, "Beyond Consensus," 991.

69. Judge Henry McKinnon, interview by James Reston, Reston Collection.

70. Courtney Mullin contends that in his oral announcement McKinnon did mention the high level of racism in eastern counties, though it was not mentioned in the written order; see John B. McConahay, Courtney Mullin, Jeffrey Frederick, "The Uses of Social Science in Trials with Political and Racial Overtones: The Trial of Joan Little," *Law and Contemporary Problems* 41 (winter 1977): 213; Mullin, interview by Reston.

71. Some say McKinnon came to Beaufort already considering relocating to Raleigh, see Harwell, *True Deliverance*, 150.

72. Even though Futrell was a longtime political adversary of John Wilkinson, he was hired by the Alligood family to aid the prosecution; Harwell, *True Deliverance*, 152–53.

73. Ginny Carroll, "Court Acts Quickly, Upholds Move," *Raleigh News and Observer*, 16 May 1975, 29.

74. Roche, "Judge Shifts Little Trial."

75. Judge Henry McKinnon, interview by James Reston, Reston Collection.

76. Charles Zollicoffer, telephone interview by the author, 30 March 2000.

77. Singal, "Beyond Consensus," 993.

78. See McKinnon, interview by Reston. Also see "McKinnon Relieved Hearing Is Over," *Raleigh News and Observer*, 4 May 1975, 10.

79. "Joan Little's Trial Will Be in Raleigh," *Raleigh News and Observer*, 2 May 1975, 1.

80. "Joanne Little—The Struggle Must Continue," *Workers' Power* (3–23 July 1975): 11.

81. Julio Ghigliotty, "KKK Lawyer Prosecutes Joann Little," *Workers World* (25 July 1975): 4.

82. Quoted in Cathy Steele Roche, "US Action Asked in Joan Little Case," *Washington Post*, 16 April 1975, A3.

83. "Jail Abuse of Women Becomes Issue in State," *Raleigh News and Observer*, 20 April 1975, 118; Bob McMahon, "Support for Joann Little Grows," *Guardian* 27 (30 April 1975): 4; Robert Weisbrot, *Freedom Bound: A History of the Civil Rights Movement* (New York: Plume, 1990), 273–75.

84. "Joanne Little Wins New Trial Site."

85. Ibid.

86. McKinnon, interview by Reston.

87. "Joanne Little Wins New Trial Site."

88. See Candy Lee Metz Beal, *Raleigh, The First Two-Hundred Years: A Brief Look at People, Places, and Events in the History of Raleigh* (Raleigh, N.C.: Bicentennial Task Force, 1991), 35.

89. The black population in Raleigh totaled 30,800, 22 percent of the 140,000 total population. No Piedmont city in North Carolina had a smaller percentage of African

Americans; see Douglas Watson, "Raleigh Taking Little Trial in Stride," *Washington Post*, 25 July 1975, A3.

90. "White Vote Gives Raleigh Its First Black Mayor," *North Carolina Anvil*, 24 Nov. 1973. Bass and De Vries, *Transformation of Southern Politics*, 50–52.

91. Economic and nonracial factors contributed to white flight since the late 1940s, as Kenneth Jackson, Kevin Kruse, Thomas Sugrue among others have shown. The election of black mayors likely made the white exodus worse. For example, see Heather Thompson, *Whose Detroit? Politics, Labor, and Race in a Modern American City* (New York: Cornell University Press, 2001), 206; Bryant Rollins, "White Fear of Black Mayors," *New York Times*, 30 Jan. 1977.

92. Watson, "Raleigh Taking Little Trial in Stride."

93. Bass and De Vries, *Transformation of Southern Politics*, 243.

94. This included a police force that was 20 percent black.

95. Paul Luebke, *Tar Heel Politics 2000* (Chapel Hill: University of North Carolina Press, 1998), 67; Wilmoth A. Carter, *The Urban Negro in the South* (New York: Russell & Russell, 1973), 37.

96. Devin Fergus, "Liberalism and Black Nationalism in an American Southern State, 1965–1980" (PhD diss., Columbia University, 2002), 202, 243.

97. Watson, "Raleigh Taking Little Trial in Stride."

98. John Llewellyn, "Swimming Uphill: A Decade in Politics and Government," *American Communication Journal* 2 (January 2000).

99. Douglas Watson, "8 Women, 4 Men to Try Joanne Little," *Raleigh News and Observer*, 24 July 1975, A8.

100. Douglas Watson, "Raleigh Taking Little Trial in Stride: Two Alternate Jurors Picked for Little Trial," *Washington Post*, 25 July 1975.

101. Watson, "Joanne Little Case."

102. Those supporting Little were primarily local activists who often faced stiff rebuke, even among presumed progressive institutions in the urban Piedmont area. Celine Chenier, hired as a teacher by the Carolina Friends School near Chapel Hill in early September, was asked to resign shortly after her involvement with the Little camp became known. Chenier had taken the position in part because she expected her political activism would not be problematic at the Quaker institution—popular in the early and mid-1970s for its stance against southern corporate militarism, the Vietnam War, and other rearguard activities—but she believed her participation in the Little Movement contributed to her dismissal. Whether actual or not, fear of reprisals probably contributed to Little's lack of support. Celine Chenier, interview by James Reston, Reston Collection; Mark Pinsky, "The Innocence of James Reston, Jr.," *Southern Exposure* 6 (1977): 41; see also Jeral Monneyham, "Southern Corporate Militarism," *North Carolina Anvil*, 13 Oct. 1973, 1.

103. Paul's behavior typified what Gunnar Myrdal and V. O. Key regard as the core features of southern liberalism—namely, southern liberals' influence is frequently derived from and dependent on northern philanthropy and liberal foundations.

104. "Joanne Little: No Escape Yet," *Off Our Backs* (January 1975): 5.

105. Pinsky, "North Carolina's Tarnished Image."

106. Nichols, "National Issues Engulf Unlikely N.C. Celebrity."

107. Wayne King, "Killing of Carolina Jailer," *New York Times*, 1 Dec. 1974.

108. James Reston, "The Innocence of Joan Little," *Southern Exposure* 6, no. 1 (1978): 30–47.

109. R. Brown, "State's Case Lacking in Little Trial," *North Carolina Anvil*, 2 Aug. 1975, 1.

110. "College Group Plans Aid to Joan Little," *Raleigh News and Observer*, 2 Feb. 1975, 6; Harwell, *True Deliverance*, 135–36.

111. There were, of course, black efforts to garner support for Little, which I discuss in the next chapter. Some included Angela Davis's influential piece in *Ms.* Magazine; the black press, the national Black Panther Party, and black women's church groups. Nichols, "National Issues Engulf Unlikely N.C. Celebrity."

112. "We Have a Long Way to Go Before We're Free," *Black Panther*, 1 Sept. 1975, 14–15; "Defense Fund Seeks $20,000 for Ms. Little," *North Carolina Anvil*, 5 Oct. 1974; "Abuse of Inmates Challenged," ibid., 18 Jan. 1975; "Little Released on Bail," *Black Panther*, 8 March 1975.

113. Additional monies were raised by the SPLC.

114. Frinks responded with his own charges about the misallocation of resources by the board of directors of the Joan Little Defense Fund and their decision to renege on a working agreement with him. "Directors Deny Misuse of Fund for Joanne Little," *Raleigh News and Observer*, 28 March 1975, 2. See also Diane Sechrest and Jerry Allegood, "Dispute Erupts among Little Supporters," ibid., 14 March 1975, 1; Jerry Allegood, "Suit Filed to Block Joan Little Fund Use," ibid., 21 March 1975, 1.

115. Randolph, interview by Reston.

116. Reston, *Innocence of Joan Little*, 64–65.

117. From March on, the Little defense team was organized into two parts. Attorneys Karen Galloway, Paul, and Dees conducted legal matters; the public defense arm of the Little team, led by the Black Panther Party and other activist groups, led fundraisings, publicity, and educating the community about the case. Zollicoffer, interview by the author.

118. *Chicago Daily News*, quoted in Open letter from Julian Bond of the Southern Poverty Law Center to Contributors, James Holshouser Governor's Papers, North Carolina State Archives, Raleigh (hereafter cited as Holshouser Papers).

119. James Reston Jr., "The Trial of Joan Little: Cause Celebre or Curse," *Chicago Tribune*, 6 April 1975.

120. Muriel B. Fielo, Clerk to the Board of Chosen Freeholders, to James E. Holshouser, 21 March 1975, Holshouser Papers.

121. Bane, "State of North Carolina v. Joanne Little"; see also Melynn Glusman, "Remembering Joan Little: The Rise and Fall of a Mythical Black Woman" (MA thesis, University of North Carolina, 1997), 18–29.

122. The original bill, which had passed both the House and Senate but was pocket vetoed by President Ford while Congress was adjourned, was eventually enacted into

law over presidential veto on 29 July 1975; see *Congressional Record*, 31 Jan. 1975, 2008; *Congressional Record*, 24 Feb. 1975, 4034; *Congressional Record*, 17 July 1975, 23478; *Congressional Record*, 22 Oct. 1975, 33726.

123. *Congressional Record*, 29 Jan. 1975, 1703.

124. Open Letter from Julian Bond.

125. The center also sponsored protests; see "Winston-Salem B.P.P. Holds Rally for Jo Ann Little," *Black Panther*, 28 April 1975, 8.

126. Laurence French, "The Incarcerated Black Female," in *The Black Woman Cross-Culturally*, ed. Filomina Chioma Steady (Rochester, Vt.: Schenkman Books, 1981), 369–82.

127. "Black Women Organize in Support of Joanne Little," *Southern Patriot* (April 1975): 3; "Three U.S. Congressmen Urge U.S. Action," *Washington Post*, 16 April 1975, 3; "Joan Little Addresses D.C. Rally on Defense Aid," *Washington Post*, 28 April 1975.

128. Similarly, for an April rally sponsored by Frinks that expected 1,000 to 1,500 people, only 150 people showed. The poor showing was the result of Frinks's damaged reputation; see Randolph, interview by Reston.

129. Sitton, "Making of State's Cause Celebre," *Raleigh News and Observer*, 4.

130. David DuBouisson, "Editorial: Moving Little Trial to Raleigh Justified, Despite Cost," ibid., 1 June 1975, 3.

131. Carroll, "Court Acts Quickly," ibid., 29.

132. For the role of practical politicians, as opposed to symbolic politicians or those with fundamentalist views, see Singal, "Beyond Consensus," 992. For the failed "garrison mentality" in fighting the national government, see William C. Havard, "Intransigence to Tradition," *Virginia Quarterly Review* (autumn 1975): 514–15.

133. Watson, "8 Women, 4 Men to Try Joanne Little."

134. "Joanne Little—the Struggle Must Continue."

135. Little received black southern church support, most notably in the formation of the Concerned Women for Justice and Fairness for Joan Little, a group of black churchwomen. This group later became the Concerned Women for Justice.

136. Her ordeal at Beaufort County Jail was no aberration, Little intoned. Rather, she said it was an all-too-common experience for North Carolina's female prison population. "Support Rally Held for Joanne Little, Inez Garcia," *Workers' Power* (3–23 July 1975): 5; see also "Joanne Little's Address to Oakland Victory Rally," *Black Panther*, 1 Sept. 1975, 14.

137. Cindy Jaquith, "Eyes of Cindy Jaquith: Eyes of Nation Turn to Raleigh as Joanne Little Faces Trial for Her Life," *Militant*, 25 July 1975, 3; Stephen J. Lynton, "1,000 Rally Here, Protest Conviction of Wilmington 10," *Washington Post*, 1 June 1975; Tom Gardner, "2,000 Demand Freedom for Wilmington 10/Joan Little," *Workers World*, 6 June 1975.

138. "Dellums' Corner," *Black Panther*, 22 Feb. 1975, 9; also Open Letter from Julian Bond.

139. McMahon, "Support for Little Grows."

140. Essex County Board of Chosen Freeholders Resolution Number 32982, Holshouser Papers.

141. Approximate number from Holshouser Papers; see also Bass and De Vries, *Transformation of Southern Politics*, 238–39.

142. Kathy Love, "Joanne Little—The Victim, Not the Criminal," *Militant* 39 (8 Aug. 1975): 23.

143. The Little trial, the story went, was an extension of North Carolina's persecution of the Wilmington Ten and Charlotte Three. All were "part of a pattern of harassment by North Carolina's legal machinery," argued Congressman John Conyers of Michigan, "in a state that ironically boasts of its New South image." See *Congressional Record*, Extension of Remarks, 20 June 1975, 20613–20164, and 2 Oct. 1975, 31309; also see Pinsky, "North Carolina's Tarnished Image"; Tom Gardner, "Freedom for Wilmington 10/Joanne Little," *Workers World* 17 (6 June 1975), 4.

144. Harwell, *True Deliverance*, 154–57.

145. R. Brown, "A Test of Conscience," *North Carolina Anvil*, 26 July 1975, 4.

146. "Lawyer Hired to Aid Prosecution," *Raleigh News and Observer*, 13 March 1975, 41.

147. "Bar States No Ethical Conflict in Wilkinson's Prosecution of Her," ibid., 19 July 1975, 19; "Group Protests Chalmer's Role," ibid., 22 July 1975, 17; "Joan Little Denied Removal of Special Prosecutor," *Black Panther*, 12 May 1975, 5.

148. "Support Rally Held for Joanne Little, Inez Garcia," *Workers' Power* (3–23 July 1975): 5.

149. Glusman, "Remembering Joan Little," 16.

150. Ibid., 11, 59–60.

151. Ibid., 17, 59–86.

152. Rufus Edmisten, interview by the author, 5 Jan. 2001.

153. Harwell, *True Deliverance*, 150. Edmisten's election was aided measurably by the black caucus of the state Democratic Executive Committee, which provided the margin of victory; see Bass and De Vries, *Transformation of Southern Politics*, 242. Supporters also mobilized a petition drive and open letter campaign. See "Free Joann Little! Folder Third World Women and 'Justice,'" box 10, Atlanta Lesbian Feminist Alliance Archives, Rare Book, Manuscript, and Special Collections Library, Duke University, Durham, North Carolina.

154. Grant, "Little Trial Moved"; see Luebke, *Tar Heel Politics 2000*, 196–97.

155. Edmisten, interview by the author. It was widely believed that state attorney general Rufus Edmisten was holding secret reports detailing numerous sexual allegations against Alligood and other Beaufort County law enforcement officials. See Paul, in Little interview by Reston.

156. Resolutions included House Joint Resolutions 181, 212, and 213. *Congressional Record*, 19 Feb. 1975, 3668.

157. Forcible rape was the fastest growing crime of violence in the United States; see *Congressional Record*, 17 July 1975, 23478; *Congressional Record*, 22 Oct. 1975, 33726.

158. Ghigliotty, "KKK Lawyer Prosecutes Joann Little."

159. "Judge Curbs Little Support," *Guardian* 27 (9 July 1975): 2.

160. Unlike Washington, Raleigh possessed a sizable law enforcement force, including a ready national guard, which would swiftly and, if necessary, forcibly quell demonstrations. Randolph, interview by Reston, and Zollicoffer, interview by the author.

161. Raleigh's city manager was also leery of the additional cost, which he tried unsuccessfully to recoup. See Phillip J. Kirk to L. P. Zachary, 31 March 1976, Holshouser Papers; S. Kenneth Howard to Phillip J. Kirk, memo, 29 March 1976, ibid.; L. P. Zachary to James E. Holshouser, 1 Oct. 1974, ibid.; L. P. Zachary to Holshouser, 9 Dec. 1975, ibid.

162. Peter Rossi, "The Middle-sized American City at Mid-Century," *Library Quarterly* 33 (1963): 3–13.

163. Havard, "Intransigence to Tradition," 518–19.

164. In addition to Carter, gubernatorial contemporaries included Democrats Dale Bumpers (Arkansas), Reuben Askew (Florida), Edwin Edwards (Louisiana), and John West (Virginia); and Republicans Linwood Holton (Virginia) and Winfield Dunn (Tennessee); see Havard, "Intransigence to Tradition," 519.

165. Edmisten, interview by the author.

166. McMahon, "Little Trial Begins," *Guardian* 27 (23 July 1975): 5.

167. Protest cities included Atlanta, Boston, Cincinnati, Houston, Los Angeles, New York, Oakland, San Diego, St. Louis, Washington, D.C., and Madison, Wisconsin. Cliff Conner, "N.Y. Rally Demands: 'Free Joanne Little!'" *Militant* 39 (25 July 1975), 4.

168. Ibid.

169. Pettit, "Joanne Little."

170. Reston, "Innocence of Joan Little."

171. Nichols, "National Issues Engulf Unlikely N.C. Celebrity."

172. Cindy Jaquith, "Reporter's Notebook: Court Officials Frown at Ivan's Cartoon," *Militant* (15 Aug. 1975): 3; see also Reston, *Innocence of Joan Little*, 174.

173. "Black Women: Internationalizing the Struggle," *Freedomways* 15 (1975): 5–6; "Editorial: Women's Year," *Crisis* 82 (May 1975).

174. *North Carolina Anvil*, 27 Sept. 1975.

175. Holshouser, *Addresses and Public Papers*, xx–xxx, 380.

176. "Free Joanne!" *Red Tide* 19 (August 1975): 1.

177. "JoAnne Little: 'The Time for Us to Seize Our Freedom Is Now,'" *Black Panther*, 1 Sept.1975, 7; "Editorial: JoAnne Little in Oakland," *Black Panther*, 1 Sept. 1975, 2.

178. "Solidarity Meeting in Rochester," *Workers World* 17 (11 July 1975): 3.

179. Clyde Haberman, "Attica," *New York Times*, 9 Jan. 2000, 3

180. "Free Joann Little!" Atlanta Lesbian Feminist Alliance Archives.

181. *Atlanta Journal*, editorial, Holshouser Papers.

182. "Peaceful Courthouse Rally Marks Eve of Trial," *Raleigh News and Observer*, 14 July 1975, 1; Holshouser, *Addresses and Public Papers*, 17.

183. "History of Struggle in Song," *Southern Patriot* (June–July 1975): 4.

184. Jaquith, "Reporter's Notebook: Ivan's Cartoon."

185. "Free Joanne!" *Red Tide* 19 (August 1975): 1.

186. Richard Kluger, review of *The Innocence of Joan Little*, by James Reston Jr., *New York Times*, 18 Dec. 1977, 12.

187. Nichols, "National Issues Engulf Unlikely N.C. Celebrity."; see also Fergus, "Liberalism and Black Nationalism in an American Southern State," chap. 4.

188. Jaquith, "Eyes of Cindy Jaquith: Eyes of Nation"; McMahon, "Little Trial Begins."

189. Zollicoffer, interview by the author.

190. Love, "Joanne Little—The Victim."

191. "Editorial: Wider Exposure for Joan Little Trial," *Raleigh News and Observer*, 9 July 1975, 4.

192. Jaquith, "Reporter's Notebook: Ivan's Cartoon."

193. *Raleigh News and Observer*, 15 Aug. 1975, 5B.

194. "The Case May Be Dropped If Jury Can't Agree," *Raleigh News and Observer*.

195. "Wider Exposure," *Raleigh News and Observer*, 9 July 1975.

196. According to a previous study, television tends to be more national in outlook, as opposed to the local and community orientation of newspapers. Interest in viewing national and international events on television—as opposed to pure entertainment programs—increases with income and education; see Leo Bogart, "Newspapers in the Age of Television," *Daedalus* 92 (1963): 116–27.

197. "Wider Exposure," *Raleigh News and Observer*, 9 July 1975.

198. Sitton, "Making of State's Cause Celebre," *Raleigh News and Observer*, 6 July 1975; "Court on Trial in Joan Little Case," editorial, ibid., 17 July 1975.

199. *North Carolina Anvil*, 26 July 1975. For more on North Carolina's progressivism as myth, see William Chafe, *Civilities and Civil Rights: Greensboro, North Carolina, and the Black struggle for Freedom* (New York: Oxford University Press, 1981).

200. Some have estimated a thousand demonstrators. Little press secretary and speechwriter Charles Zollicoffer, however, claims as many as ten thousand. Zollicoffer, interview by the author; "Free Joanne!" *Red Tide* 19 (August 1975): 1.

201. "Judge Hobgood to Preside in Little trial," *Raleigh News and Observer*, 10 June 1975, 17; "Joan Little Loses Defense Lawyer," *New York Times*, 30 July 1975; Dees, *Season for Justice*, 179.

202. Michael Coakley, "Kunstler Enters Little Trial; Goes Directly to Jail," *Chicago Tribune*, 5 Aug. 1975, 1.

203. *Washington Post*, 16 Aug. 1975, A4; Dees, *Season for Justice*, 182. For Dees, a suborning perjury conviction meant a ruined career, family disgraced, and a possible ten-year prison sentence.

204. See Jaquith, "Reporter's Notebook: Ivan's Cartoon"; Dees, *Season for Justice*, 185.

205. Dees, *Season for Justice*, 186.

206. Ibid.

207. Ibid.

208. McKinnon, interview by Reston.

209. Jaquith, "Eyes of Cindy Jaquith: Eyes of Nation."

210. "Picking the Jury—A Study in Courtroom Psychology," *Raleigh News and Observer*, 20 July 1975, 1.

211. Paul, in Little interview by Reston. Also see Donald Freed, interview by Ronald Grele, Oral History Research Office, Columbia University, 88. Also see "Tar Heel Editors Speak," Other Opinions, *Fayetteville Times* in *Raleigh News and Observer*, n.d.

212. Rick Nichols, "Six Now Seated on Jury in Joan Little Murder Case," *Raleigh News and Observer*, 18 July 1975, 27.

213. Paul, in Little interview by Reston.

214. A prospective juror's worldview was paramount to the defense, who asked questions regarding Watergate and magazine subscriptions, compared to the prosecution whose interview questions asked predominantly about preconceived notions about the trial and relationships to witnesses. See Rick Nichols, "Trial Judge Is Challenged," *Raleigh News and Observer*, 16 July 1975, 1.

215. "Jurors Fair, Joanne Little Attorneys Say," *Washington Post*, 22 July 1975.

216. See "Joan Little Trial Gets 12th Juror," *New York Times*, 24 July 1975; "Joan Little Loses a Key Trial Point," *New York Times*, 22 July 1975; "Jurors Fair"; Rick Nichols, "Joan Little Trial Jury Seated," *Raleigh News and Observer*, 24 July 1975, 1.

217. See also Dees, *Season for Justice*, 167.

218. "Jurors Fair,"; Nichols, "Joan Little Trial Jury Seated"; Douglas Watson, "Lack of Evidence Surprised Jurors," *Washington Post*, 16 Aug. 1975, A4.

219. "Joan Little Trial Gets 12th Juror," *New York Times*, 24 July 1975; Rick Nichols, "Jury Selection Begins in Joan Little Trial," *Raleigh News and Observer*, 15 July 1975, 1; Rick Nichols, "2nd Café Employe[e] Is on Little's Jury," ibid., 22 July 1975.

220. Rick Nichols, "3rd, 4th Jurors Seated as Little Trial Continues," ibid., 17 July 1975, 27.

221. Nichols, "Six Now Seated on Jury."

222. Personal opposition to the death penalty was not enough to automatically strike a juror. See "Picking the Jury—A Study in Courtroom Psychology."

223. "Jurors Fair."

224. A black man and a white woman were the final two alternates; see "Miss Little Denied Co-Counsel Status," *New York Times*, 26 July 1975; Rick Nichols, "2 Alternate Jurors Chosen in Joan Little Murder Trial," *Raleigh News and Observer*, 25 July 1975, 25.

225. During the trial one white female juror was replaced with the first alternate juror, a black male. The replacement changed the gender ratio (eight women/four men to seven women/five men), and racial balance, which became six blacks, six whites. Watson, "Lack of Evidence Surprised Jurors."

226. Ages of white jurors were twenty, twenty-one, twenty-three, twenty-five, twenty-six, and thirty-two.

227. Rick Nichols, "Jury Selection Slows as 11th Person Seated," *Raleigh News and Observer*, 23 July 1975, 37.

228. Watson, "8 Women, 4 Men to Try Joanne Little."

229. "Five Blacks Selected for JoAnne Little Trial," *Black Panther*, 24 Aug. 1975, 3.

230. Dees, *Season for Justice*, 169.

231. Harwell, *True Deliverance*, 201. Following the jury selection, the first-degree murder charge was reduced to voluntary manslaughter and second-degree murder, or murder with "no premeditation or deliberation," which in North Carolina carries a maximum of life in prison. Average sentences, however, were said to range from five to twenty years. See *Black Panther*, 4 Aug. 1975, 3.

232. "Case Goes to Jury Today," *Raleigh News and Observer*, 15 Aug. 1975, 1.

233. Reston, "Innocence of Joan Little."

234. People on the streets of Raleigh, Durham, and Chapel Hill revealed that the trial's broader symbolism was self-evident. "The Man on the Street Says," *North Carolina Anvil*, 2 Aug. 1975.

235. "Jury Jottings," *Pittsburgh Courier*, 23 Aug. 1975, 1. "Now for the first time, proclaimed a statement from the National Organization of Women, legal precedence has been set for women and their right of self-defense . . . against sexual attack" (ibid.).

236. Juror Donnell Livingston seemed to suggest Little's personal guilt or innocence was germane but not the sole or even the primary determinant. Rather, the case had to be understood in the context of historical and contemporary racial and sexual oppression. "I know damn well that it's happening all over the nation . . . that young women, Black and white, are being taken advantage of by jailers and police." Whether jurors were willing to admit it or not, the defense and Little supporters had successfully made jurors think about the case's broader social significance. A third juror, Cornelia Howell, told the *Militant*: "I believe what she said. . . . I do not believe she committed a crime. I think she acted in self-defense"; see Cindy Jaquith quoted in Willie Mae Reid, ed., *Black Women's Struggle for Equality* (New York: Pathfinder Press, 1976), 12; "Jury Jottings."

237. Huey Newton, "A Revolutionary Born in Jail," *Black Panther*, 1 Sept. 1975.

238. Singal, "Beyond Consensus," 980.

Chapter 5. Speaking Truth to Black Power

1. According to Alan Brinkley, a southern cosmopolitanism worldview maintained a tacit understanding that future development rested largely on a public disavowal of ethnic, religious, and regional provincialism; see Brinkley, *Liberalism and Its Discontents* (Cambridge, Mass.: Harvard University Press, 1998).

2. "Miss Little Appears on the Coast and Thanks the Black Panthers," *New York Times*, 28 Aug. 1975, 14.

3. The imagery invoked on behalf of Little was, by and large, constructed to engender broad support. Thus, while Power to the Pick may have been a mantra heard by maybe a thousand or so, millions of American television viewers saw and heard a far more sympathetic construction of Little. It is hard to be persuaded that "Power to the Ice Pick" was the dominant or desired mantra of the Little defense team, since it neither comports with Little's mien nor her attorney's exchanges with media. They

preferred to emphasize the defendant's defenselessness, carefully eschewing any militant imagery. "I was so frightened," Little told the CBS reporter; it was "self-defense and [she] ran," Galloway told America. Other placards—typically reading "We Support Joann Little," "Save Joann Little Rally," "Joanne Is Our Sister"—seem more reflective of how the Little attorneys and the "Free Joan Little" movement generally sought to frame the issue, and how the cause célèbre case was publicly consumed, than the more bellicose "Power to the Ice Pick." The Panther newspaper did not provide any print space to the "Power to the Ice Pick" mantra; rather, they framed Little as someone looking to avoid a fight, not spoiling for one. See, for example, *CBS Evening News*, 25 Feb. 1975; "1000 Rally," *Black Panther*, 28 July 1975; Genna Rae McNeil, "Joanne Is You and Joanne Is Me: A Consideration of African American Women and the 'Free Joan Little' Movement, 1974–75," in *Sisters in the Struggle: African American Women in the Civil Rights–Black Power Movement*, ed. Bettye Collier-Thomas and V. P. Franklin (New York: New York University Press, 2001), 259–79.

4. Little made her first posttrial public appearance at a Black Panther press conference in Oakland, where she expressed commitment to the Black Panther party and the cause of black liberation; see "JoAnne Little: The Time for Us to Seize Freedom Is Now," *Black Panther*, 1 Sept. 1975, 7. See also "JoAnne Little," *Black Panther*, 21 July 1975, 3.

5. See, for example, Nira Yuval-Davis, *Gender and Nation* (London: Sage, 1997); Celia O'Leary, *To Die For: The Paradox of American Patriotism* (Princeton, N.J.: Princeton University Press, 1999); Gary Gerstle, *American Crucible: Race and Nation in the Twentieth Century* (Princeton, N.J.: Princeton University Press, 2001).

6. Rooted cosmopolitanism, as such dual loyalties are called, is discussed more substantively in Mitchell Cohen, "Rooted Cosmopolitanism: Thoughts on the Left, Nationalism, and Multiculturalism," *Dissent* (fall 1992): 478–83; David Hollinger, "Nationalism, Cosmopolitanism, and the United States," in *Immigration and Citizenship in the Twenty-first Century*, ed. Noah M. J. Pickus (Lanham, Md.: Rowman & Littlefield, 1998), 85–106; For how this played itself out in Little, see Reston, "Innocence of Joanne Little," *Southern Exposure* 6, no. 1 (1978): 36; Jim Harlow, "400 at Richmond Rally for Joan," *Workers World*, 11 July 1975.

7. David Du Bois, in *Black Panther*, 1 Sept. 1975.

8. *FBI File on the Black Panther Party, North Carolina*, microfilm version, (Wilmington, Del.: Scholarly Resources, 1986), 1307; hereafter cited as *FBI File*.

9. Racialized sexual violence was not a new concern, though, regrettably, it may not have been a primary one for male-dominated black leadership. For representative interpretive views of sexism or racialized sexual violence, see the works of Darlene Clark Hine, *Hine Sight: Black Women and the Re-construction of American History* (Brooklyn, N.Y.: Carlson Publ., 1994); Deborah K. King, "Multiple Jeopardy, Multiple Consciousness: The Context of Black Feminist Ideology," *Signs: Journal of Women in Culture and Society* (autumn 1988): 88–111; Danielle McGuire, "'It Was Like All of Us Had Been Raped': Sexual Violence, Community Mobilization, and the African American Freedom Struggle," *Journal of American History* (December 2004): 906–31; see also

Manning Marable, *Race, Reform, and Rebellion: The Second Reconstruction in Black America, 1945–1990*, 2nd ed. (Jackson: University Press of Mississippi, 1991), 163–64.

10. Elaine Brown, "JoAnne Little Acted for Us All," *Black Panther*, 21 July 1975, 3.

11. Ibid.

12. For a legal argument defending universalism, see Randall Kennedy, "Racial Critique of Legal Academia," 102 *Harvard Law Review* 1745 (1989). Kennedy is particularly critical of three legal theorists: Derrick Bell, Richard Delgado, and Mari Matsuda. For an alternative discussion centering on whether the Supreme Court's color-blind jurisprudence has actually served to perpetuate white supremacy, see Neil Gotanda, "A Critique of 'Our Constitution Is Color-blind,'" 44 *Starr Law Review* 1 (1991), and Derrick Bell, *And We Are Not Saved: The Elusive Quest for Racial Justice* (New York: Basic Books, 1987), 26–50, 140–61.

13. For a secondary reading supporting this view, see Anthony E. Cook, "The Temptation and Fall of Original Understanding, 1990," *Duke Law Journal* 1163 (reviewing Robert H. Bork, *The Tempting of America: The Political Seduction of the Law* [1990]).

14. In contrast to this view Delgado claims that the broader perspective of critical legal theory remedies the exclusionist "defects" of liberalism; see Delgado and Stefancic, "Norms and Narratives: Can Judges Avoid Serious Moral Error?" 69 *Texas Law Review* 1929 (1991). Taking an opposing view is Leslie Espinoza, who criticizes narrower terms, like "race-consciousness," "feminist," and "class-centered" for reducing the perceived value of legal ideas outside of traditional or mechanic jurisprudence. See Leslie G. Espinoza, "Labeling Scholarship: Recognition or Barrier to Legitimacy," 10 *St. Louis University Public Law Review* 197 (1991).

15. See, for example, Milner S. Ball, "Stories of Origin and Constitutional Possibilities," 87 *Michigan Law Review* 2280 (1989); and Taunya L. Banks, "Teaching Laws with Flaws: Adopting a Pluralist Approach to Torts," 57 *Missouri Law Review* 443 (1992).

16. E. Brown, "JoAnne Little Acted for Us All."

17. *Black Panther*, 1 Sept. 1975.

18. E. Brown, "JoAnne Little Acted for Us All."

19. For more legal assertions of neutrality, see the work by Jerome McCristal Culp, "Firing Legal Canons and Shooting Blanks: Finding a Neutral Way in the Law," 10 *St. Louis University Public Law Review* 185 (1991).

20. This idea is traceable to pre–World War II legal scholarship, perhaps expressed best by Thurman Arnold in *The Folklore of Capitalism* (New Haven, Conn.: Yale University Press, 1937); see Paul D. Escott, ed., *W. J. Cash and the Mind of the South* (Baton Rouge: Louisiana State University Press, 1992), 71. Contemporary theorists using medical informed consent, cigarette warnings, and date rape as examples contend that objective rules favor empowered practices because they had their meanings and preferences inscribed in the culture long ago so that they now appear objectively true. See Richard Delgado, "Shadowboxing: An Essay on Power," 77 *Cornell Law Review* 813 (1992).

21. For more, see Derrick Bell, "The Dilemma of the Responsible Law Reform Lawyer in the Post–Free Enterprise Era," 4 *Law and Inequality Journal* 231 (1986), who

posits that court resistance to racial justice might spark civil disorder or revolution; "Joan Little to Speak in Ohio," *Washington Post*, n.d.

22. For current literature exploring the shared meanings of identity, truth, and law, see Jerome Culp, "Voice, Perspective, Truth, and Justice: Race and the Mountain in the Legal Academy," 38 *Loyola Law Review* 61 (1992), who makes a case for judging ideas and works on their own terms.

23. A universal vision, as defined by Jeffrey Reiman, "is based on excluding alternative possible interpretations [labeling] what doesn't fit by defining it as 'other,' 'lesser,' lower,' 'bad,' 'crazy,' 'primitive'"; see Jeffrey Reiman, *Critical Moral Liberalism: Theory and Practice* (Lanham, Md.: Rowman & Littlefield, 1997), 54.

24. For readings explaining elastic application and legitimacy of law in creating community, see Anthony E. Cook, "Foreword: The Postmodern Quest for Community: An Introduction to a Symposium on Republicanism and Voting Rights," 41 *Florida Law Review* 409 (1989).

25. Reiman, *Critical Moral Liberalism*, 64.

26. See Harvie Ferguson, *Modernity and Subjectivity: Body, Soul, Spirit* (Charlottesville: University Press of Virginia, 2000), 1–19.

27. Stephen L. Carter in *Reflections of an Affirmative Action Baby* (New York: Basic Books, 1991) argues against the excesses of this paradigm. Countering this is Peggy C. Davis, "Contextual Legal Criticism: A Demonstration Exploring Hierarchy and 'Feminine' Style," 66 *NYU Law Review* 1635 (1991).

28. For the values of the researcher (e.g., courts) theoretically affect conclusions, see Patricia Hill Collins, *Black Feminist Thought: Knowledge, Consciousness, and the Politics of Empowerment*, rev. 10th ann. ed. (New York: Routledge, 2000).

29. For a later argument on how judges are influenced by personal and social background, see T. Alexander Aleinikoff, "A Case for Race-Consciousness," 91 *Columbia Law Review* 1060 (1991).

30. For a contemporary debate, see Randall Kennedy. Kennedy argues that by elevating race into a positive credential to be factored, sociolegal theorists have mistakenly replaced merit as a mark of achievement with the author's perspective and experience; see Kennedy, "Racial Critiques of Legal Academia," 102 *Harvard Law Review* 1745 (1989).

31. *The Gallup Poll: Public Opinion*, vol. 1 (Wilmington, Del.: Scholarly Resources, 1972–77), 257; Devin Fergus, "Black Panther Party in the Disunited States of America: Constitutionalism, Watergate, and the Closing of the Americanists' Mind," in *Liberated Territory: Untold Local Perspectives on the Black Panther Party*, ed. Yohuru Williams and Jama Lazerow (Durham, N.C.: Duke University Press, 2008), 380.

32. The Church Committee was particularly effective in exposing these abuses.

33. Huey Newton, "A Revolutionary Born in Jail," *Black Panther*, 1 Sept. 1975.

34. Reiman, *Critical Moral Liberalism*, 54–55.

35. See Charles Jones, ed., *The Black Panther Party Reconsidered* (Baltimore: Black Classic Press, 1998), 35; Edmund White, *Genet: A Biography* (New York: Alfred A. Knopf, 1993), 521–40; Jean Genet, *Prisoner of Love*, trans. by Barbara Bray (New York:

New York Review Books, 2003), and his *Letter to American Intellectuals* (brochure), reprinted as *Here and Now for Bobby Seale*; see Jeanette L. Savona, *Jean Genet* (New York: Grove Press, 1984), 5–6, 99.

36. Charles Jones and Judson Jeffries, in Jones, *Black Panther Party Reconsidered*, 25–56.

37. Quoted in JoNina Abron, "'Raising the Consciousness of the People': The Black Intercommunal News Service, 1967–1980," in *Voices from the Underground*, ed. Ken Wachsberger (Tempe, Ariz.: Mica, 1993), 343–60; Christian A. Davenport, "Reading the 'Voice of the Vanguard': A Content Analysis of the Black Panther Intercommunal News Service, 1969–1973," in Jones, *Black Panther Party Reconsidered*, 193–210.

38. Editorial, *Black Panther*, 18 Aug. 1975.

39. Ibid.

40. The party remained frustrated that the establishment media supposedly downplayed Little and the Panthers' role in supporting her, however; see *Black Panther*, 8 Sept. 1975.

41. Maulana Karenga, "In Defense of Sis. Joanne: For Ourselves and History," *Black Scholar* 6 (July/August 1975): 37–42.

42. Ibid.

43. Early black nationalists David Walker, Alexander Crummell, and Henry Turner argued similarly.

44. Wilson J. Moses points out that an appeal to racial cosmopolitanism has been a trademark of black self-determination since at least the revolutionary era, though, as Moses rightly notes, these blacks were protonationalists articulating no national destiny or intention of creating a nation-state with a distinctive national culture. See Wilson Jeremiah Moses, ed., *Classical Black Nationalism: From the American Revolution to Marcus Garvey* (New York: New York University Press, 1996), 8–10.

45. Maulana Karenga, *The Quotable Karenga*, ed. Clyde Halisi (Los Angeles: US Organization, 1967).

46. Karenga, "In Defense of Sis. Joanne."

47. Desmond S. King, *In the Name of Liberalism: Illiberal Social Policy in the USA and Britain* (Oxford and New York: Oxford University Press, 1999), 16–17.

48. In this I mean, for example, Joseph Raz's understanding and development of "perfectionist liberalism" that endorses state action and toward that end promotes the cause of human fullness. Liberal neutrality, on the other hand, particularly in its extreme form of libertarian theory, "leaves individuals free to use their resources in whatever way they find most valuable." Perfectionism is especially pronounced among current American liberal thinkers; see Patrick Neal, *Liberalism and Its Discontents* (New York: New York University Press, 1997), 135–37.

49. Karenga, "In Defense of Sis. Joanne."

50. Ibid.

51. For a larger discussion of the "circle of we," see Hollinger, "Nationalism, Cosmopolitanism, and the United States," and response essays in Pickus, *Immigration and Citizenship*.

52. Karenga, "In Defense of Sis. Joanne."

53. Ibid.

54. In recent times the case for a substantive freedom has been most provocatively and cogently stated by Amartya Sen, 1998 Nobel Prize winner for economics. In addition Sen argues that true democratic government—as opposed to measuring quality of life by, for instance, income per capita—is an end of itself because it furthers human freedom. Nowhere is this more evident than with American black males. In Sen's view black men illustrate the shortcomings of American democracy as an agent for helping members of its body politic exercise their full human capacities. He "points out that many places with lower per capita incomes . . . have achieved higher life expectancies and literacy rates than much richer lands like Brazil, South Africa and Namibia." People in these "poor countries can expect to live longer than some groups in industrial countries, like American black men, who in monetary terms are richer"; see also Fareed Zakaria, "Beyond Money," review of *Development as Freedom*, by Amartya Sen, *New York Times Book Review* (28 Nov. 1999). For more on positive and negative freedoms, see Sir Isaiah Berlin, *Two Conceptions of Liberty* (Oxford, UK: Clarendon Press, 1958).

55. For Joan Little and countless other women, sexual assault and abuse proved psychologically damaging, Karenga concluded. He later added that in fact the abuse at the hands of state power was deforming to the human character and personality of its victim.

56. Charles McKelvey, *Beyond Ethnocentrism: A Reconstruction of Marx's Concept of Science* (Westport, Conn.: Greenwood Press, 1991), 173, 175.

57. For more on civic nation-states embracing ethnodiversity, as opposed to genocide and ethnic cleansing, see Geoff Eley and Ronald G. Suny, ed., *Becoming National: A Reader* (New York: Oxford University Press, 1996), intro.; also see Hollinger, "Nationalism, Cosmopolitanism, and the United States," 89–90.

58. David Hollinger, "Ethnic Diversity, Cosmopolitanism and the Emergence of the American Liberal Intelligentsia," *American Quarterly* 27 (1975): 148–49.

59. That chauvinism was not simply gendered but, at times, ethnic. While living in Cuba Newton expressed no interest in learning Spanish. The ethnic chauvinism harbored by Newton was perhaps most apparent in his bitter complaints that host Cubans should adopt and speak English as their first language. Newton's wife and children, however, had no problem in learning and speaking fluent Spanish. BPP minister of education Masai Hewitt remembered, "His attitude [was that] the whole world ought to learn English." See Ray "Masai" Hewitt, interview by Ron Grele, Oral History Research Office, Columbia University, 92.

60. See Deborah Gray White, *Too Heavy a Load: Black Women in Defense of Themselves, 1894–1994* (New York: W. W. Norton, 1999), 176–211, 219; Samuel Farber, "Social Decay and Class Struggle in African-American Struggle: The Black Panthers Reconsidered," *Against the Current* (September/October 1996): 23.

61. Though not a party member, Kenner was a supporter of numerous Panther causes. Martin Kenner, interview by Ron Grele, Oral History Research Office, Columbia University, 167.

62. Elaine Brown, *A Taste of Power: A Black Woman's Story* (New York: Anchor Books, 1992), 287, 288.

63. Donald Freed, interview by Ron Grele, Oral History Research Office, Columbia University, 73–74.

64. Kathleen Cleaver, "Black Scholar Interview: Kathleen Cleaver," *Black Scholar* (December 1971): 54–59.

65. Hewitt, interview by Grele, 5.

66. Leathers interview by author; Kenner, interview by Grele; Angela D. LeBlanc-Ernest, "'The Most Qualified Person to Handle the Job': Black Panther Party Women, 1966–1982," in Jones, *Black Panther Party Reconsidered*, 305–36.

67. Though formal gender titles were retired with the Panther-Pantherette corps in 1968, assumed gender responsibilities still applied; Charles E. Jones and Judson L. Jeffries, "Don't Believe the Hype: Debunking the Panther Mythology," in Jones, *Black Panther Party Reconsidered*, 32–33.

68. Hewitt, interview by Grele, 3.

69. "Headline: Black Panthers/Newton," *ABC Evening News*, 19 July 1977, TV News Archives.

70. David Du Bois, "JoAnne Little Talks with the Black Press," *Black Panther*, 8 Sept. 1975; Gerstle, *American Crucible*, 262.

71. Tracye Matthews, "No One Ever Asks What a Man's Place in the Revolution Is," in Jones, *Black Panther Party Reconsidered*, 291–92; for the impact the feminization of the party had on liberalizing the Panthers' position on abortion, arguably the most politically divisive issue in the modern electoral era, see Jennifer Nelson, *Women of Color* (New York: New York University Press, 2003), 108–10.

72. Hewitt interview by Grele, 6; LeBlanc-Ernest, "'Most Qualified Person to Handle the Job,'" 318.

73. LeBlanc-Ernest, "'Most Qualified Person to Handle the Job,'" 311.

74. Bobby Bowen, interview by Ron Grele, interview I-III, transcript, Oral History Research Office, Columbia University.

75. Hewitt, interview by Grele, II-138–140; see also Bowen, interview by Grele, I-113.

76. Hewitt, interview by Grele, 5.

77. Less than fourteen days later Newton reportedly pistol-whipped his tailor, Preston Callins, who had also innocently referred to Newton as "baby." Newton's call for the end of abuse to humankind apparently did not extend to those encountering Newton. Smith died three months after being shot. See Ollie A. Johnson III, "Explaining the Demise of the Black Panther Party: The Role of Internal Factors," in Jones, *Black Panther Party Reconsidered*, 406–7.

78. See Abron, "'Raising the Consciousness of the People,'" 356; Freed, interview by Grele, I-24; see also Michele Wallace, *Black Macho and the Myth of Superwoman* (New York: Dial, 1990), 51; Carol Rucker, interview by Lewis Cole, in *Black Thought and Culture* (Alexandria, Va.: Alexander Street Press, 2005), I–105.

79. *FBI File*, 1373–74, 1382.

80. LeBlanc-Ernest, "'Most Qualified Person to Handle the Job,'" 324.

81. Bowen, interview by Grele, 1-111.

82. See also Bowen, interview by Grele, 1-99, but here Bowen is an indirect source.

83. Ibid., 1-114; LeBlanc-Ernest, "'Most Qualified Person to Handle the Job'"; Assata Shakur and Joanne Chesimard, "Women in Prison: How We Are," *Black Scholar* (April 1978): 14.

84. Angela Davis, "JoAnne Little: The Dialectics of Rape," *Ms.* (June 1975): 74.

85. Only after Little branded Davis an opportunist and liar—urging that "Black people [should] stay away from them [communists] because I don't feel they have anything to offer Black people except deceit"—did Du Bois change the subject. He did not follow the same dogged pursuit of gender violence or anything remotely similar. Du Bois, *Black Panther*, 8 Sept. 1975.

86. Evangeline Grant Redding, *Nothing: The Mentality of the Black Woman* (Tillery, N.C.: A Heritage of Hope Book, 1976), 54–71.

87. Comparative figures on sentencing are exclusive of cases involving life imprisonment or death; see Joseph C. Howard, "Racial Discrimination in Sentencing," 59 *Judicature* (1975): 121, 123.

88. Carol Bohmer, "Judicial Attitudes towards Rape," 57 *Judicature* (1974): 303.

89. *Workers World*, 11 July 1975.

90. Jennifer Wriggins, "Rape, Racism, and the Law," 6 *Harvard Women's Law Journal* (1983): 103–41.

91. Rayyah Leathers, interview by the author, 19 July 2000.

92. Celine Chenier, interview by James Reston Jr., Southern Historical Collection, University of North Carolina, Chapel Hill.

93. Leathers, interview by the author; Charles Zollicoffer, interview by the author, 30 March 2000; Howard Carr, "National Panther Chairman Says Local Leader Fired," *Winston-Salem Sentinel*, n.d., Episcopal Diocese of North Carolina archives, Raleigh (hereafter cited as EDNC archives).

94. *Winston-Salem Sentinel*, n.d., EDNC archives.

95. Rayah Leathers, confidential interview by the author, 19 July 2000; Bowen, interview by Grele.

96. Howard Carr, "National Panther Chairman Says Local Leader Fired," *Winston-Salem Sentinel*, n.d., EDNC archives; Art Eisenstadt, "Panther Chief Calls for Unity," *Winston-Salem Sentinel*, 12 July 1976, ibid.

97. LeBlanc-Ernest, "'Most Qualified Person to Handle the Job'"; Brown, *Taste of Power*.

98. Zollicoffer, interview by the author.

99. Shakur, "Women in Prison," 14.

100. Charles Hopkins, "The Deradicalization of the Black Panther Party" (PhD diss., University of North Carolina, 1978), 165. Nikhil P. Singh, "The Black Panthers and the Undeveloped Country of the Left," in Jones, *Black Panther Party Reconsidered*, 57–108; White, *Genet*, 521–40.

101. Wriggins, "Rape, Racism, and the Law," 123.

102. The Wilmington Ten—consisting of Chavis, eight black male high school students, and a white woman, all civil rights workers—were charged with firebombing a white-owned grocery store in Wilmington, North Carolina. The case became an international cause célèbre as the widespread view was that Chavis and others were largely convicted for holding dissenting political beliefs. Amnesty International took up the cause in 1976, placing nine members on its list of political prisoners. With the case becoming an increasing embarrassment to state and federal officials, the convictions were overturned on a technicality by 1980. For more about the Ten, see John L. Godwin, *Black Wilmington and the North Carolina Way: Portrait of a Community in the Era of Civil Rights Protest* (Lanham, Md.: University Press of America, 2000); "Who Bombed Mike's Grocery?" *Time*, 23 May 1977.

103. Clarence Lusane, *African-Americans at the Crossroad: The Restructuring of Black Leadership and the 1992 Elections* (Boston: South End Press, 1994), 28.

104. For an example, see Angela Y. Davis, "The Struggle of Ben Chavis and the Wilmington 10," *Black Scholar* (April 1975): 30–31.

105. Godwin, *Black Wilmington and the North Carolina Way*.

106. It also helped launch the legal careers of African Americans like Lani Guinier; see Lusane, *African-Americans at the Crossroad*, 28.

107. Jeffrey Elliott, ed. *Black Voices in American Politics* (San Diego: Harcourt Brace Jovanovich, 1986), 297.

108. Ben Chavis, "Speaking Out on Sexual Harassment," *Washington Informer*, 17 Aug. 1994, 14. Apparently Ben Chavis introduced Angela Davis to the Little Case in 1974, see Genna Rae McNeil, "Joanne Is You and Joanne Is Me: A Consideration of African-American Women and the 'Free Joan Little' Movement, 1974–1975," draft in author's collection.

109. Cindy Jaquith, "Eyes of Cynthia Jaquith: Eyes of Nation Turn to Raleigh as Joanne Little Faces Trial for Her Life," *Militant*, 25 July 1975; Stephen J. Lynton, "1,000 Rally Here, Protest Conviction of Wilmington 10," *Washington Post*, 1 June 1975; Tom Gardner, "2,000 Demand freedom for Wilmington 10/Joan Little," *Workers World*, 6 June 1975.

110. Abiola Sinclair, "Betrayal—The Case against Ben Chavis," *New York Amsterdam News*, 8 Oct. 1994. This perhaps explains the absence of public feminists, gays, and lesbians in the 1994 Summit of African-American Leadership; see Manning Marable, *Beyond Black and White: Transforming African-American Politics* (New York: Verso, 1995), 162.

111. Mary E. Stansel, a lawyer and former U.S. Senate aide, agreed to a secret settlement with Chavis after her employment of only five weeks with the NAACP. In exchange for not taking her sexual harassment complaint to the NAACP board or the Equal Employment Opportunity Commission, Chavis privately paid Stansel $320,000 out of NAACP funds along with a promise to find her another job with a minimum salary of $80,000. Stansel filed a lawsuit after Chavis missed an installment. The Stansel payoff hastened a budgetary crisis for the national NAACP. For more on the impact Chavis's scandal and subsequent lawsuit had on the NAACP fiscal crisis, see Clarence Lusane and

James Steele, "A Fatal Attraction: The Firing of Ben Chavis by the NAACP," *Black Political Agenda* 2 (1994): 1, 10–13; Peter Kilborn, "Financial Problems Hinder the Work of the NAACP," *New York Times*, 4 Nov. 1994; Steven Holmes, "NAACP Plans to Rehire Most of Its Staff in Early '95," *New York Times*, 31 Dec. 1994; and Robert C. Smith, *We Have No Leaders: African Americans in the Post-Civil Rights Era* (Albany: State University of New York Press, 1996), 94, 312–13.

112. From Chavis's perspective the problem was that Stansel had adopted "an inflated view [of her] own importance." See also "Benjamin Chavis: Speaking out on sexual harassment," *Washington Informer*, 17 Aug. 1994.

113. Sinclair, *Amsterdam News*; Delvin Etienne, *Weekly Journal*, 25 Aug. 1994; Clarence Lusane, *Race in the Global Era: African Americans at the Millennium* (Boston: South End Press, 1997), 188; Devin Fergus, "Liberalism and Black Nationalism in an American Southern State, 1965–1980" (PhD diss., Columbia University, 2002), chap. 5.

114. "Discussion with Minister Benjamin Muhammad," Columbia University, author's collection.

115. See Abiola Sinclair, "Media Watch: Ben Chavis Bites the Dust, Blacks Blame Mary," *New York Amsterdam News*, 27 Aug. 1994.

116. "Benjamin Chavis: As He Sees It," *YSB* [Young Sisters and Brothers], 31 Jan. 1995.

117. Julianne Malveaux, "Malveaux-at-large: Women's Silence Is Indefensible," *Sun Reporter*, 11 Aug. 1994.

118. Delvin Etienne, *Weekly Journal*, 25 Aug. 1994; James D. Williams, "Court Orders BC," *Baltimore Afro-American*, 25 Nov. 1995.

119. The timing was significant not only because Chavis was considered the most progressive leader out of the national office since W. E. B. Du Bois, but also because it looked as if he might make a measurable difference in public policy. In addition to backing from the Congressional Black Caucus, Chavis's Oval Office support, according to one author, appeared to be growing in spite of his controversial relationship with the Nation of Islam. The Clinton administration was supportive in large measure because it did not like the presumed alternative: Jesse Jackson. Moreover, Vice President Al Gore shared deep mutual concerns about the environment. The vice president looked likely to press for funding environmental projects that Chavis, an early champion of environmental antiracism initiatives, helped make public issues.

120. Mumininas of Committee for United Newark, Mwanamke Mwananchi (Nationalist Woman) (Newark, N.J.: Jihad Productions, 1971), 4–5.

121. Komozi Woodard, *A Nation within a Nation: Amiri Baraka (LeRoi Jones) and Black Power Politics* (Chapel Hill: University of North Carolina Press, 1998), 183; for insights into the preternaturalist predilections girding Baraka's gender politics and writings from late 1960s to early 1970s, see Daniel Maitlin, "Lift Up Yr Self!" *Journal of American History* 93 (June 2006). Maitlin writes that Baraka's 1960s sexism was "inextricable from his understanding of the black race as a construct of nature rather than of society" (94).

122. Woodard, *Nation within a Nation*, 184.

123. Karenga was released from prison just prior to the actual Little trial. Charlayne Hunter, "Black Intellectuals Divided Over Ideological Direction," *New York Times*, 28 April 1975. For the definitive study of Karenga's US organization, see Scot Brown, *Fighting for US: Maulana Karenga, the US Organization, and Black Cultural Nationalism* (New York: New York University Press, 2003).

124. Imamu Clyde Halisi, "Maulana Ron Karenga: Black Leader in Captivity," *Black Scholar* (May 1972): 29; H. Greenwood Johnson, "Ron Karenga Convicted, Gets Ten Year Sentence," *Herald Dispatch*, 3 June 1971; Muhammad Ahmad, "We Are All Prisoners," *Black Scholar* (October 1972): 3.

125. Halisi, "Karenga," 28–29.

126. Ibid.; Woodard, *Nation within a Nation*, 166.

127. Halisi, 28–29; Patricia H. Collins, *Black Feminist Thought: Knowledge, Consciousness, and the Politics of Empowerment* (New York: Routledge, 1990), 70.

128. Johnson, "Ron Karenga Convicted."

129. Amiri Baraka, *Autobiography of LeRoi Jones* (Chicago: Lawrence Hill, 1997), 418.

130. Robin D. G. Kelley and Betsy Esch, "Black Like Mao: Red China and Black Revolution," *Souls* 1 (fall 1999): 28–29.

131. By 1970 CFUN's name would be changed to the Congress of African Peoples (CAP). At its founding convention it formally severed organizational ties with US. See Baraka, *Autobiography*, 417–18, 424–25.

132. Beverly Guy-Sheftall, ed., *Words of Fire: An Anthology of African-American Feminist Thought* (New York: New Press, 1995), 1–23.

133. Sara S. Whaley, *Black Scholar*, in *Women Studies Abstract* (1975): 401A.

134. Karenga, "In Defense of Sis. Joanne."

135. Conspicuous, too, in their silence were many black elected officials in California who quietly won parole for Karenga in May 1975. *Ebony* (September 1975); Johnson, "Ron Karenga Convicted."

136. Karenga, "In Defense of Sis. Joanne."

137. Comparable examples include Clarence Thomas–Anita Hill and Mike Tyson–Desiree Coleman. For detail see literary and cultural critic Michael Awkward's "'You're Turning Me On': The Boxer, the Beauty Queen, and the Rituals of Gender," in *Black Men on Race, Gender, and Sexuality: A Critical Reader*, ed. Devon W. Carbado (New York: New York University Press, 1999), 128–46.

138. Maulana Karenga, "In Love and Struggle: Toward A Greater Togetherness," *Black Scholar* (March 1975): 17.

139. See E. Frances White, "Africa on My Mind: Gender, Counterdiscourse, and African American Nationalism," in Guy-Sheftall, *Words of Fire*, 504, 519; Kimberlé Crenshaw's essay, "Demarginalizing the Intersection of Race and Sex: A Black Feminist Critique of Antidiscrimination Doctrine, Feminist Theory and Antiracist Politics," in *Black Feminist Reader*, ed. Joy James and T. Denean-Sharpley Whiting (Malden, Mass.: Blackwell Publishers, 2000), 224; see as well Gloria Joseph, "Black Feminist Pedagogy and Schooling in Capitalist White America," in Guy-Sheftall, *Words of Fire*,

462–72, and Adolph Reed, *Class Notes: Posing as Politics and Other Thoughts on the American Scene* (New York: New Press, 2000), 25.

140. Brown, *Taste of Power*, 368.

141. Karenga's misogyny should not be claimed as representative of black nationalism as a whole—just as it would be wrong to essentialize the mendacity of Jim Baker as representative of the faithful viewers of his 700 Club during the 1970s and 1980s; rather, each fall from proverbial grace is a primer for their followers, as well as the master teachers to come, about the ongoing didactic value of group self-scrutiny. The word "Karenga" means "nationalist," that is, "master teacher of nationalists"; Baraka, *Autobiography*, 357.

142. "African Liberation Day, May 24, 1975," *Southern Patriot* (March 1975): 5.

143. Sekou Toure, "The Role of Women in the Revolution," *Black Scholar* (March 1975): 33.

144. Key ALSC members included Stokely Carmichael, Howard Fuller, and Cleveland Sellers. Woodard, *Nation within a Nation*, 173–80; Whaley, 401A; White, "Africa on My Mind," 504–19; Rod Bush, *We Are Not What We Seem: Black Nationalism and Class Struggle in the American Century* (New York: New York University Press, 1999), 211–12; Marable, *Race, Reform, and Rebellion*, 134.

145. See, for example, Bush, *We Are Not What We Seem*.

146. Mike Coakley, "Judge Alters Charge in Joan Little Case; Death Penalty Out," *Chicago Tribune*, 7 Aug. 1975.

147. See, for example, Woodard, *Nation within a Nation*, 182–84.

148. Black feminist institutional responses to black nationalist sexism existed prior to the 1970s; see Kimberly Springer's *Living for the Revolution: Black Feminist Organizations, 1968–1980* (Durham, N.C.: Duke University Press, 2006). The NBFO did not take a public stand but joined other women's groups (e.g., Women's Legal Defense Fund, the Feminist Alliance against Rape, the Rape Crisis Center) in fundraising for Little. The Combahee River Collective was "not doing political work as a group" at the time of the Little trial. See Melynn Glusman, "Remembering Joan Little: The Rise and Fall of a Mythical Black Woman," (MA thesis, University of North Carolina, 1997), 82; Combahee River Collective, "A Black Feminist Statement," in Guy-Sheftall, *Words of Fire*, 238; James Reston, "The Joan Little Case," *New York Times*, n.d.

149. See "The Combahee River Collective Statement," 231–40, esp. 234; see also "But Some of Us Are Brave: A History of Black Women in the U.S.," 9, www.mit.edu:8001/activities/thistle/v9/9.01/6blackf.html; Jane Mansbridge and Barbara Smith, "'How Did Feminism Get to Be All White'? A Conversation between Jane Mansbridge and Barbara Smith," *American Prospect Online* 11, no. 9 (13 March 2000).

Chapter 6. Federally Subsidized Black Nationalism

1. Robert F. Williams to Floyd B. McKissick (hereafter cited as FBM), 4 Nov. 1971, folder 6740, Floyd B. McKissick Papers, Southern Historical Collection, University of North Carolina at Chapel Hill (hereafter cited as FBM Papers); FBM to Williams, 10 Nov. 1971, ibid.

2. "Soul City" conference transcript, Howard University, Washington, D.C., 21 Feb. 1969, folder 6571, FBM Papers.

3. To date no monographic literature exists on Soul City. For journal-length scholarly treatises on the new town, see Christopher Strain, "Soul City, North Carolina: Black Power, Utopia, and the African American Dream," *Journal of African American History* 89 (winter 2004): 57–74; and Timothy Minchin's "A Brand New Shining City: Floyd B. McKissick and the Struggle to Build Soul City" *North Carolina Historical Review* 82 (April 2005): 1–31. Offering a more critical view is Sundiata Cha Jua, "Selling Soul City: Floyd B. McKissick Sr., Black Capitalism, and the Origins of Contemporary Black Conservatism" presented at the Association for the Study of African American Life and History Conference, Milwaukee, Wisc., 10–19 Oct. 2003. For an interpretation in between, see Roger Biles, "Rise and Fall of Soul City: Planning, Politics, and Race in Recent America," *Journal of Planning History* 4 (2005): 52–72.

4. Roy Wilkins to FBM, 5 Nov. 1973, Soul City [2 of 3], subject files White House Central Files, Staff Member and Office Files, Patterson, Nixon Presidential Materials (NPM), National Archives and Records Administration, College Park, Md. (hereafter cited as WHCF-SMOF).

5. Wayne King, "McKissick Is Succeeding Although Not 'Supposed To'; A Spur to Country," *New York Times*, 22 Dec. 1974, 29; "North Carolina's Soul City Builds on Ability—Not Color," *Chicago Tribune*, 29 Dec. 1974, 26.

6. "Floyd B. McKissick: Making Black Capitalism Work," in *Black Voices in American Politics*, ed. Jeffrey M. Elliott (San Diego: Harcourt Brace Jovanovich, 1986), 281–96.

7. Floyd B. McKissick, "Black Business Development with Social Commitment to Black Communities," in *Black Nationalism in America*, ed. John H. Bracey, August Meier, and Elliot Rudwick (Indianapolis and New York: Bobbs-Merrill, 1970), 492–503.

8. "Black people must liberate themselves," he challenged blacks and cautioned sympathetic white students on the Raleigh campus of North Carolina State University in November 1969. "'Liberate Selves—McKissick,'" *Carolinian*, November 1969, FBM Papers.

9. McKissick, "Black Business Development," 492; see also Robert O. Self, *American Babylon: Race and the Struggle for Postwar Oakland* (Princeton, N.J.: Princeton University Press, 2003).

10. McKissick, "Black Business Development."

11. Gareth Davies, *From Opportunity to Entitlement: The Transformation and Decline of Great Society Liberalism* (Lawrence: University Press of Kansas, 1996), 191.

12. Dean Kotlowski, *Nixon's Civil Rights: Politics, Principle, and Policy* (Cambridge, Mass.: Harvard University Press, 2001), 131–33.

13. Unlike the argument above, there are other scholars who actually posit a Nixon-as-liberal thesis, locating him within New Deal liberalism. For example, as historian Manning Marable, in *Race, Reform, and Rebellion*, has written: Nixon was "part of the great 'centrist social liberalism' tendency" that existed from Roosevelt (1932) until

Reagan (1980). I cite *Race, Reform, and Rebellion: The Second Reconstruction and Beyond in Black America, 1945–2006* because Marable presented this thesis as far back as 1984, a full decade before the best-known book on the subject, Joan Hoff, *Nixon Reconsidered* (New York: Basic Books, 1994). In addition, see Dean Kotlowski, *Nixon's Civil Rights* and Stephen Ambrose, *Nixon* (New York: Simon & Schuster, 1987)

14. The state's seizure of Soul City's decision-making apparatuses threatened to completely remove chief architect and town planner Harvey Gantt. John T. Sun to Ronald F. Scott, memo, 3 June 1971, series Office of Policy and Planning, box 32, New Community Program folder, James Holshouser Governor's Papers, North Carolina State Archives, Raleigh (hereafter cited as Holshouser Papers); John T. Sun to Ronald F. Scott, memo, 6 July 1971, series Office of Policy and Planning, box 32, Intra-Division or Department folder, ibid.

15. See FBM to Robert Brown, Assistant to the President, 4 April 1969, folder 6201, FBM Papers. For more on Brown's position, see Paul Frymer and John David Skrentny, "Coalition Building and the Politics of Electoral Capture during the Nixon Administration: African Americans, Labor, Latinos," *Studies in American Political Development* 12 (1998): 145; see also Melvin Small, *The Presidency of Richard Nixon* (Lawrence: University Press of Kansas, 1999), 131–61.

16. Kotlowski, "Black Power-Nixon Style," *Business History Review* 72 (1998): 422.

17. "HUD Won't Give Funds to Build One-Race Towns," *Washington Evening Star*, 19 June 1969.

18. The next eleven months proved more disheartening for McKissick. "We all know where Richard Nixon stands—and" like Johnson, wrote McKissick in the *Black Scholar*, "if [Nixon] thought Black Power was a real threat to the status quo, he would hardly be for it." McKissick, "The Way to a Black Ideology," *Black Scholar* (December 1969): 17.

19. "Soul City" conference transcript, Howard University, 21 Feb. 1969, folder 6571, FBM Papers; HUD Legislation—1970, Hearings before the Subcommittee on Housing of the Committee on Banking and Currency, House of Representatives, 91st Cong., 2nd sess., part 2, 8 June 1970, 664, *Congressional Record*. No non–Soul City investiture, including T&L Publishing, survived beyond 1972.

20. John R. Brown to Harry Dent, memo, 25 March 1970, Dent, Presidential Memos—1971, Staff Secretary (box 83), WHSF-SMOF.

21. Colson objected especially to the CBC boycott of Nixon's 1970 State of the Union, for Nixon's opposition to the Voting Rights Act, legal aid, the Job Corps program, health and Manpower programs, and cuts in educational aid; CBC to the president, 21 Jan. 1971, Clark MacGregor folder (February 1971), H. R. Haldeman, WHCF-SMOF; see also CBC statement in *Black Politician* 3 (1971): 4–12.

22. Charles Colson to Dwight Chapin, memo, 18 Feb. 1971, Clark MacGregor folder (February 1971), H. R. Haldeman, WHCF-SMOF.

23. Nixon met the CBC but only after fourteen months. Marguerite Barnett, "The Congressional Black Caucus," *Black Scholar* (January/February 1977), 20; Frymer and Skrentny, "Coalition Building and the Politics of Electoral Capture," 143.

24. Colson later urged exploiting latent tensions. We "need to remind . . . Spanish groups of the Democrats' commitment to blacks at their expense," Colson advised Ehrlichman, see ibid., 159; Small, *Nixon*, 48.

25. Jeb B. Magruder to Mr. Marik [*sic*], memo 6 May 1971, record group (RG) 460, Records of the Watergate Special Prosecution Force (WSPF), Plumbers Task Force, Responsiveness Program Investigation, NPM.

26. Harry Dent to Bob Brown, memo, 21 Oct. 1971, and Dent to Attorney General and H. R. Haldeman, memo, 26 Oct. 1971, Harry Dent (October 1971), H. R. Haldeman, WHCF-SMOF.

27. Kotlowski, *Nixon's Civil Rights*, 155. Despite the southern strategy, Nixon more than doubled Goldwater's share of nonwhite voters.

28. Pat Buchanan to H. R. Haldeman, 25 Jan. 1972; Kenneth L. Khachigian, 24 Jan. 1972, P. Buchanan, H. R. Haldeman, WHSF-SMOF.

29. See 25 Jan. 1972 News Summary, marked "Administratively Confidential." Bruce Kehrli to Harry Dent, memo, 25 Jan. 1972, Presidential Memos—1972 Dent, Staff Secretary (box 83), WHCF-SMOF.

30. See 26–29 June 1972, 7, Annotated News Summaries, box 41, WHSF-SMOF; FBM to Bob Brown, 30 May 1972, folder 7550, FBM Papers.

31. Ibid.

32. Fred Malek to John Mitchell, memo, 26 June 1972, RG 460, Black Vote Campaign Plan, Committee to Re-elect the President (CRP), WSPF.

33. Paul DeLaney, "Report of Watergate Committee Staff Cites Plans to Use Federal Funds to Gain Black Support for Nixon," *Washington Post*, 12 June 1974.

34. See weekly activity reports of Paul Jones, from 17 January through 7 September, RG 460, Weekly Activity Reports, Planning and Coordination—Documentary Evidence (box 6), WSPF.

35. Malek to Bob Brown, Bill Murrimoto, Paul Jones, and Alex Armendariz, 3 March 1972, box 7 Ex FG 21-17, Office of Minority Business Enterprise [2 of 2, 1972–74], WHCF subject files, NPM.

36. The central feature of the Responsiveness Program was grantsmanship headed by William Gifford of OMB, likely backed by OMB director Casper Weinberger. Malek to Haldeman, memo, 16 May 1972, "Camp David Meeting," RG 460, WSPF.

37. Daniel T. Kingsley interviewed by FBI Special Agents Robert M. Satkowski and William T. Tucker, 22 May 1974, Washington, D.C., RG 460, file 46-10039, FBI Statements, WSPF. Although the GSA is technically an independent agency and therefore not part of the executive branch, its administrators are appointed by the White House.

38. Nick Akerman to the Files, memo, 20 May, 28 April 1975, RG 460, WSPF.

39. Frymer and Skrentny, "Coalition Building and the Politics of Electoral Capture," 155.

40. Malek to Haldeman, memo, 7 June 1972, RG 460, Responsiveness Program—Progress Report, 17 March 1972, Malek/Haldeman Memo RE: Responsiveness, WSPF.

41. DeLaney, "Report of Watergate Committee Staff."

42. Fred Malek to Bob Finch, memo, 2 May 1972, RG 460, White House Documents and Notes, WSPF.

43. Roy Wilkins to FBM, 5 Nov. 1973, Soul City [2 of 3], subject files, WHCF-SMOF Patterson.

44. Wayne King, "McKissick Is Succeeding Although Not 'Supposed To,'" *New York Times*, 22 Dec. 1974.

45. Edward Ashbee, "The Republican Party and the African-American Vote since 1964," in *Black Conservatism: Essays in Ideological and Political History*, ed. Peter Eisenstadt (New York: Garland Publishing, 1999), 252; Martin Kilson, "Anatomy of Black Conservatism," *Transition* 59 (1993): 15.

46. For an archetype of today's black Republican, see Dale Russakoff's *Washington Post* feature on Condoleezza Rice, "Lessons of Might and Right" (9 Sept. 2001, W23).

47. RG 460, 26 July 1972, Minutes of 25 July Meeting of Committee for the Reelection of the President, WSPF.

48. Joint Center for Political Studies, 10 Nov. 1972, folder 7687A, FBM Papers.

49. The Ripon Society, founded 1962 in Wisconsin by Republican progressives. Dick Behn to FBM, 14 July 1972, folder 7719, FBM Papers.

50. "Blacks: Soul City," *Newsweek*, 14 Aug. 1972, National Affairs sec.

51. Vernon Jarrett, "Blacks for Nixon Stress Equality," *Chicago Tribune*, 23 Aug. 1972; Vernon Jarrett, "Strange Alliance Supports Nixon," *Chicago Tribune*, 25 Oct. 1972, 26; Jeremy D. Mayer, "Nixon Rides the Backlash to Victory: Racial Politics in the 1968 Presidential Campaign," *Historian* (winter 2002): 351–66; and Jeremy D. Mayer, *Running on Race: Racial Politics in Presidential Campaigns, 1960–2000* (New York: Random House, 2002), 96–123. Members of Blacks for Nixon included presidential assistant Robert J. Brown, GOP minority affairs chief Ed Sexton, Jim Brown, Sammy Davis Jr., and Lionel Hampton.

52. W. Richard Howard to Dave Parker, memo, 8 Aug. 1972, box 7 Ex FG 21-17, Office of Minority Business Enterprise [2 of 2, 1972–74], WHCF subject files, NPM; Nate Bayer to John Campbell, memo, 26 Sept. 1972, ibid.; Commerce Secretary Peter G. Peterson to Ehrlichman, 21 Sept. 1972, ibid.

53. Matthew Lassiter, *The Silent Majority: Suburban Politics in the Sunbelt South* (Princeton, N.J.: Princeton University Press, 2005), 3–4, 252; see also Byron E. Shafer and Richard Johnston, *End of Southern Exceptionalism: Class, Race, and Partisan Change in the Postwar South* (Cambridge, Mass.: Harvard University Press, 2006).

54. Lassiter, *Silent Majority*; Shafer and Johnston, *End of Southern Exceptionalism*.

55. Shriver replaced Missouri senator Thomas Eagleton.

56. FBM, statement, 1 Sept. 1972, folder 7638, FBM Papers. Black Republicans pounced even more on McGovern's second-thought running mate, Sargent Shriver, who boasted to a white audience in Louisiana just days prior of his pride that none of his six slaveholding Confederate fighting ancestors fought for the Union. Others dredged up how Shriver, when he managed Joseph Kennedy's Chicago Merchandise Mart, failed to hire blacks above the janitorial rank, see Nixon-Blacks telegram, from Paul Jones, Director of the Black Voter Division of CREEP, folder 7551, FBM Papers.

57. See National Black Committee for the Re-election of the President campaign literature, folder 7555, FBM Papers; see also Stanley S. Scott to Presidential Surrogates, memo, 6 Sept. 1972, folders 7550, 7554, FBM Papers.

58. By Keynesianism I mean federal domestic spending, including deficit spending, while discounting more fiscally restrained notions like balanced budgets. Editorial Comment: "Four More Years," *Cleveland Call and Post*, 14 Oct. 1972.

59. "As *Black Business Digest* Sees It: The November Election," *Black Business Digest* (October 1972).

60. See National Black Committee for the Re-election of the President campaign literature.

61. Paul DeLaney, "Black Supporters of President under Fire," *New York Times*, 17 Oct. 1972; Paul DeLaney, "Blacks for Nixon Sharply Rebuked," *New York Times*, 3 Aug. 1972.

62. George Schultz was much involved in constructing of the policy of affirmative action, see Hugh Davis Graham, *The Civil Rights Era: Origins and Development of National Policy, 1960–1972* (New York: Oxford University Press, 1990), 326; Robert C. Smith, *We Have No Leaders: African Americans in the Post–Civil Rights Era* (Albany: State University of New York Press, 1996), 145–47.

63. By the time his op-ed appeared Fletcher had become a new Two-Party board member, the Republican-led black registration organization created by McKissick. Arthur Fletcher, "The Black Dilemma If Nixon Wins," *Wall Street Journal*, 25 Sept. 1972.

64. Confidential minutes of Black Executive Advisory Team/National Black Steering Committee, 15 Sept. 1972, folder 7554, FBM Papers.

65. The Black Executive Advisory Committee of CREEP included Robert Brown, Malek, Clark MacGregor, Paul Jones, Frank Herringer, McKissick, Hurst, and *Cleveland Call and Post* publisher and editor Willie Walker, see Conversation 108-1, 6 Oct. 1972, reference cassette 186, RC-1 White House Tape 108, Tape Subject Log, NPM.

66. CREEP awarded McKissick's group $7,000. FBM to Malek, 23 Oct. 1972, folder 7654, FBM Papers.

67. Ibid.

68. Lucius J. Barker and Jesse J. McCorry Jr., *Black Americans and the Political System*, 5th ed. (Boston: Little, Brown, 1980), 223.

69. Bush to FBM, 12 April 1973, folder 7703, FBM Papers. By his successful congressional bid in 1966, however, Bush had won over a sizable number of racial crossover votes, getting three times (34 percent to 10 percent) the black votes as the GOP gubernatorial candidate, see Jack Bass and Walter De Vries, *The Transformation of Southern Politics: Social Change and Political Consequence since 1945* (Athens: University of Georgia Press, 1995), 323.

70. Conference Notes for Meeting with George Bush, 30 March 1973, folder 7703, FBM Papers.

71. Ibid.

72. Larnie G. Horton to FBM, 12 April 1973, folder 7637, FBM Papers.

73. For Immediate Release, the National Committee for a Two-Party System, Inc. Soul City [2 of 3], subject files, WHCF-SMOF Patterson.

74. See Purposes and Objectives of the North Carolina Chapter of the National Committee for a Two-Party System, ibid.

75. FBM to Bush, 22 May 1973, Soul City [2 of 3], subject files, WHCF-SMOF Patterson, NPM; see Conference Notes for Meeting with George Bush, 30 March 1973, folder 7703, FBM Papers.

76. For surveys regarding conservatives versus liberals, see for instance Roper Poll, December 1974, and General Mills Poll, November 1974, respectively. For polls regarding party identification, see for instance Gallup, December 1974, and Time/Yankelovich, Skelly and White Poll, September 1974. Surveys retrieved 15 June 2008 from the iPOLL Databank, Roper Center for Public Opinion Research, University of Connecticut.

77. William Link, *Righteous Warrior: Jesse Helms and the Rise of Modern Conservatism* (New York: St. Martin's Press, 2008), 149.

78. FBM to Robert Thompson, HUD-Regional Office, 28 March 1973, Soul City [2 of 3] subject files, WHCF-SMOF Patterson.

79. Link, *Righteous Warrior*, 149.

80. Paulette Pierce, "The Roots of the Rainbow Coalition," *Black Scholar* (March/April 1988).

81. Ibid.

82. Sadauki's chief complaint was black political leaders' singular focus on electoral politics, see Harold Cruse, "The Little Rock National Black Political Convention," *Black World* (November 1974): 16; Paul DeLaney, "Hatcher Criticizes Blacks Absent from Convention," *New York Times*, 18 March 1974.

83. Besides, he told the *Chicago Daily News* reporter, "I am an integrationist." Robert Gruenberg, "Floyd B. McKissick Has Come a Long Way since the '60s," *Raleigh Register*, 20 March 1974, folder 2950, FBM Papers.

84. Indeed, Helms's reply could be described as almost Vardamanesque, referring to the colorful, late nineteenth-century white supremacist governor James K. Vardaman of Mississippi, who disdained any change in black America's political and suffrage status; not even the democratic incrementalism of white America's most beloved compromiser escaped the Mississippian's ire. Admittedly Helms, unlike Vardaman, never raised publicly black extirpation as the "final solution." FBM to Helms, Western Union telegram, 10 Nov. 1972, FBM Papers; Helms to FBM, 27 Nov. 1972, folder 794, ibid. For the Vardaman quote, see John Hope Franklin and Alfred A. Moss Jr., *From Slavery to Freedom: A History of African Americans*, 8th ed. (Boston: McGraw-Hill, 2000), 289.

85. See *Congressional Record*, 26 May 1975, 25135.

86. McKissick suspected that these motions were thinly veiled broadsides to undermine Soul City's development. "The resolution assumes wrongdoing without any substantiating evidence. It disrupts our progress and ignores the record, the accomplishments and the merits of our program." See the Senate Joint Resolution 415, General Assembly of North Carolina, sess. 1975.

87. For all practical purposes, however, Soul City had been in existence only eighteen months. The New York scandal was most likely a reference to the Senate's investigation of Nelson Rockefeller, during his vice presidential nomination hearings. The North Carolina senator and others accused Rockefeller of making illegal personal contributions to New York officials in violation of New York State law. Lee Rudd to John Freeman, Assistant Administrator for Policy Development, 9 Dec. 1974, file unit 1.10 Public Information, 1972–1978, series Program Records Relating to Soul City, Warren County, N.C., 1972–1978, subgroup NCDC, General Records of the DHUD, National Archives. For Helms's quote, see *Congressional Record* (1975).

88. "Announcement by Governor James Holshouser Establishment of North Carolina Office of Minority Business Enterprise," 21 July 1975, folder 476, FBM Papers.

89. Harry E. Payne Jr. to Waymond Burton, 19 June 1975, folder 5281, ibid.

90. Editorial, "The Needs of Second America," *Washington Post*, 6 July 1974, A14.

91. The grant was for building water lines, storm water drain line and roads, see "Soul City Receives New Funds," *Raleigh News and Observer*, 17 Dec. 1975.

92. Steve Berg, "Fountain, Helms Ask Audit for Soul City," *Raleigh News and Observer*, 6 March 1975.

93. Gary Pearce, "Review of Audit Urged by Helms," ibid., 17 Dec. 1975; *New York Times*, 21 March 1974, 1; Charles Jeffers, "Opinion Mixed on Economic Impact of Soul City Failure," *Durham Sun*, 28 June 1979.

94. James F. Dausch, Deputy General Manager, HUD to FBM, 28 June 1976, file unit 1.10 Public Information, 1972–1978, series Program Records Relating to Soul City, Warren County, N.C., 1972–1978, subgroup NCDC, General Records of the DHUD, NABII.

95. According to Shepard it was the logical outcome dictated by McKissick's blind racial impulse to see Soul City all-black. "Editors Say," *Carolinian*, 23 Dec. 1975.

96. Senator Robert Morgan to HUD Secretary Carla Hills, 12 Oct. 1976, file unit 1.13 Correspondence (Development) 1974–1977, box 2, series Program Records Relating to Soul City, Warren County, N.C., 1974–1977, NCDC, General Records of the DHUD; James F. Dausch c/o Melvin Margolies to Morgan, 21 Oct. 1976, ibid.

97. "$19 Million Fleeced—And You Pay," *National Enquirer*, n.d., author's collection.

98. FBM to Rockefeller, 17 Jan. 1976, folder 1810, FBM Papers.

99. FBM to John Marsh, 4 Oct. 1974, folder 7301, ibid.

100. FBM to Rockefeller, 17 Jan. 1976, folder 1810, ibid.; Barker and McCorry, *Black Americans and the Political System*, 215.

101. Paul Luebke, *Tar Heel Politics 2000* (Chapel Hill: University of North Carolina Press, 1998), 212; Bass and De Vries, *Transformation of Southern Politics*, 234–39.

102. Bass and De Vries, *Transformation of Southern Politics*, 235.

103. "Like every other citizen," Helms defended Nixon, when most others in the GOP urged that Nixon step down, the president "is entitled to due process and a presumption of innocence until proved guilty," Helms lectured colleagues on the senate floor. Helms, however, applied a less elastic standard of citizenship to racial liberals like McKissick and Rockefeller, whose vice presidential nomination Helms nearly ruined

with accusations of corruption. *Congressional Record*, 19 March 1974, 7174–75; see also 11 June 1974, 18664–65, ibid.; 5 Aug. 1974, 26651–55, ibid.; 15 Oct. 1974, 35677–78, ibid.; 5 Dec. 1974, 38361–63, ibid.; 9 Dec. 1974, 38537–39, ibid.

104. Goldwater's 1964 defeat of Rockefeller in California is the other. Craig Shirley, *Reagan's Revolution: The Untold Story of the Campaign That Started It All* (Nashville, Tenn.: Nelson's Current, 2005), chap. 8.

105. North Carolina Citizens for Reagan for President newsletter, n.d., James Holshouser Governor's Papers, North Carolina State Archives, Raleigh (hereafter cited as Holshouser Papers); Rowland Evans and Robert Novak, *The Reagan Revolution* (New York: E. P. Dutton, 1981), 54; Gary Wills, *Reagan's America* (New York: Penguin, 2000), 390.

106. Long Marketing North Carolina Poll, January 1976, question 4, Republican Party folder, box 501, Holshouser Papers; Wills, *Reagan's America*, 390.

107. Press Release, 19 March 1976, Republican Party folder, box: 501, Holshouser Papers.

108. See, for instance, Andrew C. Untener of Charlotte to Holshouser, telegram, 19 March 1976, Holshouser series, box 483, President Ford Political II folder, Holshouser Papers.

109. "GOP Governors Ask Reagan to Quit," Associated Press, 20 March 1976, President Ford Political I folder, box 483, Holshouser Papers.

110. The other major Political Action Committees were National Committee for Political Action, the Committee for the Survival of a Free Congress, Citizens for the Republic, and the Fund for a Conservative Majority. Val Burris, "The Political Partnership of American Business: A Study of Corporate Political Action Committees," *American Sociological Review* 52 (December 1987): 732–44; David E. Price, "Our Political Condition," *Political Science* 25 (December 1992): 681; and Luebke, *Tar Heel Politics 2000*, 162–63.

111. The Congressional Club view was a popular one. R. J. Howell of Goldsboro to Holshouser, 19 Oct. 1976, Soul City folder, box 501, Holshouser Papers.

112. See, for example, *Congressional Record*, 26 July 1975, 25133–37; 16 Dec. 1975, 40881–83, ibid.

113. *Congressional Record*, 40882.

114. "Groundbreaking for Soul City," Soul City, 9 Nov. 1973, *Addresses and Public Papers of James Eubert Holshouser, Jr., Governor of North Carolina, 1973–1977*, ed. Memory F. Mitchell (Raleigh: Department of Cultural Resources, 1978), 172–73.

115. Sharing this view, one Missouri Republican wrote, "Half of the Republicans don't want a Neville Chamberlain formulating foreign policy or one who thinks there is no alternative to appeasement or confrontation." Ruth Kressler of Kansas City, Kans., to Holshouser, 19 March 1976, President Ford Political I folder, box 483, Holshouser Papers.

116. North Carolina Citizens for Reagan for President newsletter, n.d., Holshouser Papers; "N.C. Last Stop for Wallace, Reagan?" *Daytona Beach New-Journal*, 21 March 1976, folder 3016, FBM Papers.

117. Shirley, *Reagan's Revolution*, 176; Matthew Dallek, "Reagan and His Times: Three New Looks Back at the Dawn of a New American Conservatism," *Washington Post*, book review, 17 April 2005, BW13.

118. Wills, *Reagan's America*, 390.

119. Rather than lose to Eugene McCarthy or Robert Kennedy, Johnson dropped out of the Democratic primary three days before the 2 April Wisconsin primary, see Robert Dallek, *Flawed Giant: Lyndon Johnson and His Times, 1961–1973* (New York: Oxford University Press, 1998), 528.

120. "Headline: Campaign 1976/N.C. Primary/Republicans," *ABC Evening News*, 24 March 1976, Television News Archives, Vanderbilt University, Nashville, Tenn.; "Headline: Campaign/N.C. Primary/Republicans," *CBS Evening News*, 24 March 1976, ibid.

121. See press release, Wednesday, 16 June 1976, Republican Party folder, box 501, Holshouser Papers.

122. See Hamilton Horton, 5 June 1977 interview, Southern Oral History Program, Manuscripts Department, University of North Carolina at Chapel Hill.

123. Bill Bradley and Howard Wimpey to Holshouser, 28 June 1976, Republican Party folder, box 501, Holshouser Papers; Holshouser to Bill Bradley and Howard Wimpey, 8 July 1976, ibid.; Luebke, *Tar Heel Politics 2000*, 193.

124. The seat was one of two bonus delegate seats, awarded to the state party following the respective 1972 victories of Helms and Holshouser.

125. Sen. Robert G. Shaw, 16 Feb. 1996 interview, Southern Oral History Program, Manuscripts Department, University of North Carolina at Chapel Hill. See also Joe Mosnier, "What Led to the Republican Resurgence?" *Raleigh News and Observer*, 6 July 1997.

126. "What Caused GOP's Need for Blacks?" *Chicago Defender*, 3 May 1978.

127. Holshouser to Carl L. Mayle, 15 March 1976, President Ford Political II folder, box 483, Holshouser Papers; Long Marketing North Carolina Poll, April 1976, Republican Party Folder, box 501, Holshouser Papers.

128. Wills, *Reagan's America*, 391–92.

129. "Helms Is 'Best' Senator," *North Carolina Anvil*, 2 Nov. 1974.

130. James F. Dausch, Handling of Soul City at NCDC Board Meeting, 6 Oct. 1976, file unit 1.4 NCDC Board Correspondence, series Program Records Relating to Soul City, Warren County, N.C., 1974–1979 (box 2), subgroup NCDC, General Records of the DHUD.

131. Steven F. Lawson, *Running for Freedom: Civil Rights and Black Politics in America since 1941*, 2nd ed. (New York: McGraw-Hill, 1997), 191.

132. For slightly different percentage of blacks voting for Ford, see Ashbee, "The Republican Party and the African-American Vote," 239; Barker and McCorry, *Black Americans and the Political System*, 214–19, 294; "Blacks and the GOP," *Congressional Quarterly* (April 1978): 1046–51; and Michael B. Preston, Lenneal Henderson Jr., and Paul Puryear, eds., *The New Black Politics: The Search for Political Power* (New York:

Longman, 1982), 7; Earl Black and Merle Black, *The Rise of Southern Republicans* (Cambridge, Mass.: Harvard University Press, 2002), 94–96.

133. Mayer, "Ford Gives Up on Blacks: The Absent Racial Politics of 1976," chap. 6 in *Running on Race*.

134. *Durham Morning Herald*, 27 Nov. 1976.

135. Lou Cannon, *Governor Reagan: His Rise to Power* (New York: Public Affairs, 2003), 426; see also study on Helms, Link, *Righteous Warrior*.

136. Shirley, *Reagan's Revolution*, 176.

137. James C. Roberts, book review, *Human Events*, 21 Feb. 2005.

138. Brooke to Elmer Staats, Comptroller General of the U.S., 10 May 1975, Brooke to FBM, 31 July 1975; See draft letter of "Proposed letter to be written by Senator Brooke to Secretary Hills," FBM to Brooke, 5 Dec. 1975, folder 791, FBM Papers; FBM to Brooke, 13 Jan. 1977, ibid.

139. Small, *Nixon*, 167.

140. John Dean, *The Rehnquist Choice: The Untold Story of the Nixon Appointment that Redefined the Supreme Court* (New York: Free Press, 2001), 53–54.

141. Ambrose, *Nixon*, 179, 186.

142. Brooke to FBM, 3 Oct. 1978, folder 7252, FBM Papers.

143. Avi Nelson was Brooke's opponent in the primary, see "Is Brooke in Danger?" *Chicago Defender*, 13 May 1978, ibid.; Edward W. Brooke to FBM, 28 July 1978, folder 7252, FBM Papers; Brooke to FBM, 3 Oct. 1978, ibid.

144. To see the sharp ideological departure of contemporary black Republicans from Brooke's, see Alicia Montgomery, "Elephants of a Different Color," *Salon.com*, 19 Feb. 2000; see also Edward W. Brooke, *The Challenge of Change: Crisis in Our Two-Party System* (Boston: Little, Brown, 1966), ix–xv, passim; Ashbee, "Republican Party and the African-American Vote," 239.

145. Bill Noblitt, "Hodges Sees Need for Government Aid," *Chapel Hill News*, 3 Feb. 1978, folder 7578A, FBM Papers.

146. See Luther H. Hodges Jr. to FBM, 8 Feb. 1978, folder 7578A, FBM Papers; and Hodges promotional literature, ibid.

147. For a small but accurate sampling, see Asa T. Spaulding to FBM, 5 Aug. 1974, folder 777, FBM Papers; "Minority Enterprise Small Business Investments Corporation (MESBICS)," *Winston-Salem Chronicle*, 27 Aug. 1977; National Association of Black Manufacturers, 7 April 1978, folder 5470, FBM Papers.

148. The *Carolina Financial Times*, no connection to Durham's black-operated *Carolina Times*, was a monthly business publication in Chapel Hill. Richard Bierck, "A *CFT* Interview with Floyd McKissick: Economy Cited as Reason for Delay in Soul City," *Carolina Financial Times*, 24 June 1974, folder 2946, FBM Papers.

149. Black America's financial sector was hit unusually hard. Aubrey Zephyr, "Black Businesses Feeling Brunt of Inflation," National Black News Service *Carolinian*, 15 March 1975.

150. Zephyr, "Black Businesses Feeling Brunt of Inflation."

151. By comparison, corporate company casualties generally were about one-half of one percent per year during the first half of the decade, according to Dunn and Bradstreet. For minority industries, see also ibid.

152. Timothy Bates, "The Changing Nature of Minority Business: A Comparative Analysis of Asian, Nonminority, and Black-owned Businesses," *Review of the Black Political Economy* 18, no. 2 (1989): 25–42.

153. Andrew F. Brimmer, "The Dilemma of Black Banking Lending Risks vs. Community Service," *Review of Black Political Economy* 20 (1992): 5–29.

154. McKissick cofounded NABM, "Floyd B. McKissick: Making Black Capitalism Work," 285; black mainstays like the National Business League remained active, though much of its energies was dedicated toward obtaining more equitable federal resources for black enterprises—see Berkeley G. Burrell to FBM, 12 May 1978, folder 5975, FBM Papers; MESBICS was initiated in 1972 via congressional Small Business Investment Act, not black entrepreneurs, during 1972—see Norman A. Hodges of NABM to FBM, n.d., folder 5470, FBM Papers. On Black Economic Research Center, see BERC records, 1969–82, Schomburg Center for Research in Black Culture, Manuscripts, Archives and Rare Books Division, New York Public Library.

155. For correspondence between McKissick and Rustin, see folders 5373, 7349, 7550, FBM Papers.

156. Report of the Soul City Task Force, June 1979, 16, folder 1824, FBM Papers.

157. A. O. Sulzberger Jr., "H.U.D. to Foreclose on Soul City, Troubled 'New Town' in Carolina," *New York Times*, 29 June 1979, A12.

158. Monthly Professional Staff Meeting, 7 May 1979, folder 1984, FBM Papers.

159. As of 13 June 1979: 9 letters from senators, 6 Letters from congressman, see Soul City letter tally, 13 June 1979, Soul City Task Force, box 22, series Program Records Related to Soul City, Warren County, N.C., 1974–1979, NCDC, General Records of the DHUD.

160. John P. Stewart to FBM, memo, 23 Jan. 1978, folder 528, FBM Papers.

161. Fountain and Morgan were already slowing being converted into Soul City allies, said McKissick, thanks to area mayors, the *Warren Record*, Warren County Chamber of Commerce, Democratic County Committee, and Second Congressional District black caucus.

162. FBM to Harris, 6 July 1979, folder 716, FBM Papers.

163. Seventy-six percent of whites agreed with the statement: "Minorities and women have to learn that they are entitled to no special consideration and must make it strictly on merit." *Survey by Louis Harris & Associates, January 8–January 12, 1982*, iPOLL Databank, Roper Center for Public Opinion Research, University of Connecticut, http://www.ropercenter.uconn.edu.proxy.library.vanderbilt.edu/ipoll.html, accessed 6 June 2008.

164. "Troubled Soul City Loses Support of U.S., Which Backed $10 Million of Financing," *Wall Street Journal*, 29 June 1979.

165. Helms simultaneously introduced amendment HR 3875, designed to prevent HUD from guaranteeing the remaining $14 million loan made in June 1972. FBM to North Carolina State Legislator, week of 27 Aug. 1979, folder 470, FBM Papers.

166. Settlement Reached on Soul City, press release, n.d., folder 1851, FBM Papers.

167. Quoted in "McKissick Cites Soul City's Worth," *Raleigh News and Observer*, 28 June 1980.

168. Press release, 29 June 1979, folder 1827, FBM Papers.

169. FBM to Ford, 27 Aug. 1974, folder 7269, FBM Papers.

170. Devin Fergus, "Liberalism and Black Nationalism in an American Southern State, 1965–1980" (PhD diss., Columbia University, 2002), 332.

Conclusion

1. US and BPP served as signifiers for Black Power's unraveling in the civil rights classic, *Eyes On the Prize*. Editors wrote, "Black power . . . ideological disputes undermined racial unity. . . . Agreement on the need of Black Power and pride did not prevent . . . sometimes deadly conflicts between advocates of revolutionary nationalism and advocates of cultural nationalism"; see *Eyes on the Prize Civil Rights Reader: Documents, Speeches, and Firsthand Accounts from the Black Freedom Struggle, 1954–1990* (New York: Viking, 1991), 247. In another classic work, this one on Black Power, William L. Van Deburg writes, "Nationalist Infighting Disrupted the Political Unity of the Black Power Movement," *New Day in Babylon: The Black Power Movement and American Culture, 1965–1975* (Chicago: University of Chicago Press, 1992), 175.

2. The FBI's furtive role in establishing a climate of mutual hostility is rightly ascribed, but little is written on the backdrop role of the liberal–Black Power interplay. Of course, nary a book on Black Power has been written without exploring the disruptive role played by the FBI in the late 1960s, a subject I dedicate extensive space to in chapter 3. What remains largely forgotten is the role of liberal hegemony in incorporating Black Power resistance.

3. It is easy for skeptics to dismiss so-called white money for black studies programs as cynical attempts of Black Power militants to extort liberals. Others, conversely, reduce such academic earmarks as liberal hush money to appease the campus cavils of Black Power activists. Such cynicism, particularly when coming from conservatives, seems odd—given how the amicus curiae community on the Right have insisted in federal courts over the years that money equals speech. If money is tantamount to speech, the underwriting of black studies programs seemed to indicate a mutual recognition—from administrators and Black Power activists—that a shared value regarding speech existed, and even the possibility of a common language.

4. Karenga's rapport with the young chancellor also underscores historian Scot Brown's point regarding black cultural nationalists as reactionary. Cultural nationalists like Karenga often had the ear, and at times tugged the programmatic purse strings, of some of the most progressive college presidents of the day. See Scot Brown, *Fighting for US: Maulana Karenga, the US Organization, and Black Cultural Nationalism* (New York: New York University Press, 2003).

5. For more on the BPP-UCLA shoot-out, see Black Radical Congress-News for "FBI's War on the Black Panther Party's Southern California," http://www. Hartford-hwp. com/archives/45a/077.html, accessed August 2008; see also "Young's Story," *Daily Bruin Online*, 8 June 1997; Betty Song, "Asian American Center Celebrates History,"

ibid., 20 Jan. 1995; Ward Connerly, "Confessions of an Admiring Adversary," ibid., 8 June 1997; Brooke Olson, "Chancellor, Regents Do Not Always See Eye to Eye," ibid., 8 June 1997; Scot Brown, "The US Organization, Black Power Vanguard Politics, and the United Front Ideal: Los Angeles and Beyond," *Black Scholar* 31 (fall 2001); Brown, "The US Organization, Maulana Karenga, and Conflict with the Black Panther Party," *Journal of Black Studies* 28 (November 1997); see also Gene Marine, *Black Panthers* (New York: New American Library, [1969]), 207–11.

6. The early days of Young's thirty-year tenure overshadowed subsequent events, including the publicized confrontations in the Ward Connerly–run regent years of the 1990s, which some hinted forced Young's premature retirement. "Young's Story," *Daily Bruin Online*, 8 June 1997.

7. King is referred to as a "liberal integrationist" for four reasons. First, his consistent support for individual, institutional, and state desegregation, even when the racial trade-off resulted in incremental or symbolic change. Second, his deep ambivalence about race-first black philosophies. Third, like liberalism writ large, his abiding faith in the power of dialogue, viewing black political violence, in specter or fact, not simply as morally corrosive but as a sign of failure to find the common ground. Finally, because of King himself. Despite misgivings about the "liberal doctrine of man," King never strayed far from his self-described "liberal leaning." As King wrote, "In noticing the gradual improvements of [the] race problem, I came to see some noble possibilities in human nature. Also my liberal leaning may have rooted back to the great imprint that many liberal theologians have left upon me and to my ever-present desire to be optimistic about human nature." *The Autobiography of Martin Luther King, Jr.*, ed. Clayborne Carson (New York: Warner Books, 1998), 24–25.

8. There was a salient if slim progressive strand in Memphis, as evinced in Harold Ford Sr.'s 1970 upset congressional victory over incumbent Republican Dan Kuykendall in a district where—despite massive white flight and 1970 redistricting—blacks remained a minority (40 percent) of eligible voters; see Jack Bass and Walter De Vries, *The Transformation of Southern Politics: Social Change and Political Consequence since 1945* (Athens: University of Georgia Press, 1995), 303; *Memphis Press Scimitar*, 20 Feb. 1969, microfilm, Benjamin L. Hooks Public Library, Memphis, Tenn.; see also Invaders and the Black Organizing Project vertical files, Benjamin L. Hooks Public Library. See also Nick Kotz, *Judgment Days: Lyndon Baines Johnson, Martin Luther King, Jr., and the Laws That Changed America* (Boston: Houghton Mifflin, 2005), 412, 414.

9. The most comprehensive study of New Orleans during the civil rights–Black Power years is Kent Germany, *New Orleans after the Promises: Poverty, Citizenship, and the Search for the Great Society* (Athens: University of Georgia Press, 2007), esp. chaps. 12–13; see also vertical files, particularly under subject heading "Black Politics, Main Library, New Orleans Public Library, La.; and Bass and De Vries, *Transformation of Southern Politics*, 179.

10. Other Rockefeller senate Republicans during the 1970s and 1980s included Mark Hatfield, Bob Packwood, Charles Mathias, Arlen Specter, John Heinz, Bill Cohen, Warren Rudman, John Chafee, John Danforth, Richard Lugar, Nancy Kassenbaum,

and Lowell Weicker. Their legislative agenda often overlapped on environmental, universal health care, reproductive rights, and civil rights. See Dick Meyer, "The Wreck of the U.S. Senate," *Washington Post*, 22 May 2005.

11. *Pittsburgh Press*, 17 Dec. 1980; see also Black Power vertical file, Carnegie Public Library, Pittsburgh, Pa.

12. Ads ranged from "Tony Scuro's Automatic Transmission" business to college-prep-course registration at Community College of Allegheny County, to state-run ads promoting Pennsylvania's dairy industry, see Black Power vertical file, Carnegie Public Library, Pittsburgh. For more on the *Courier* and the black press more generally, see Carl Sienna, *The Black Press and the Struggle for Civil Rights* (New York: Franklin Watts, 1993), esp. chap. 11.

13. Stax was also profitable. Black Enterprise rated Stax Records the second-most successful nonfinancial, banking, or insurance service business in black America, behind only rival Motown Records.

14. *Guardian*, 20 July 2002, Benjamin L. Hooks Public Library; *Memphis Press Scimitar*, 16 Aug. 1972, ibid.; *Memphis Commercial Appeal*, 8 Feb. 1976, ibid.; Rob Bowman, *Soulsville, USA: The Story of Stax Records* (New York: Schirmer, 1997), 266–71; Peter Guralnick, *Sweet Soul Music: Rhythm and Blues and the Southern Dream of Freedom* (New York: Little, Brown, 1997), 385–92; and remaining Stax files, Benjamin L. Hooks Public Library.

15. Werner's words ring true when one considers the global outreach agenda of Wattstax. Looking to display black unity to the world, Bell tapped Mel Stuart, trading on the filmmaker's recent commercial success with *Willy Wonka* to produce an artful documentary on Wattstax. The liberal filmmaker and Columbia Pictures took a Watts community gathering, billed as a black-controlled event that celebrated black unity against racism and oppression, and packaged the context in which black music had evolved for anticolonial transnational consumption from Lagos, Nigeria, to London. Craig Werner, movie review, "Watching 'Wattstax,'" *Point of View*, PBS, 2004.

16. Bowman, *Soulsville, USA*, 270.

17. *Guardian*, 20 July 2002.

18. See Twenty-first Century Foundation records, 1971–84, 1992, Schomburg Center for Research in Black Culture, New York Public Library; DJB [Daniel J. Bernstein] Foundation Records, 1971–75, Philanthropy Collections, Ruth Lilly Special Collections and Archives, IUPUI University Library, Indiana University–Purdue University Indianapolis; and Carol Bernstein Ferry and W. H. Ferry Papers, 1971–97, ibid. James A. Ward, *Ferrytale: The Career of W. H. "Ping" Ferry* (Palo Alto, Calif.: Stanford University Press, 2005).

19. Stephen Ward, "Scholarship in the Context of Struggle: Activist Intellectuals, the Institute of the Black World, and the Contours of Black Power Radicalism," *Black Scholar* (fall 2001): 42–53. Ward tells us that conferences brought over two thousand black scholars, from across continental America, seven African countries, and parts of the Caribbean. The black illuminati of the era resided there in the first years: C. L. R. James, Walter Rodney, St. Clair Drake, Margaret Walker Alexander, Horace Cayton,

Amiri Baraka, and Stokely Carmichael. Yet Ward never reveals who was footing the bills.

20. Peniel Joseph, "Black Liberation without Apology: Reconceptualizing the Black Power Movement," *Black Scholar* 31 (1 Oct. 2001), 2–19.

21. Although at this time the IBW was part of the newly founded King Center, no direct reference was made to it by Wesleyan trustees. See the Wesleyan University Board of Trustee Minutes for 12 April 1969, 36, University Archives, Wesleyan University. For more on Wesleyan's Afro-American Institute, see the student newspaper, its alumni magazine, and trustee minutes.

22. See, for example, *Quality Education and the Black Community*, Proceedings of a Conference Sponsored by the Institute of the Black World, January 1976, (Atlanta: IBW Publications, 1977).

23. It is left to Robert C. Smith, a political scientist belonging to an earlier generation of "stringer" scholars, to point out that IBW, like the more integrationist think-tank rival the Joint Center for Political and Economic Studies, "depended disproportionately on white corporations and foundations to survive." Robert C. Smith, *We Have No Leaders: African Americans in the Post–Civil Rights Era* (Albany: State University of New York Albany Press, 1996), 116.

24. Noliwe Rooks, *White Money, Black Power: The Surprising History of African American Studies and the Crisis of Race in Higher Education* (Boston: Beacon Press, 2006), 10–11.

25. Joseph, "Black Liberation without Apology."

26. Prasenjit Duara, "Transnationalism and the Challenge to National Histories," in *Rethinking American History in a Global Age*, ed. Thomas Bender (Berkeley and Los Angeles: University of California Press, 2002), 25–46.

27. Gary Gerstle, *American Crucible: Race and Nation in the Twentieth Century* (Princeton, N.J.: Princeton University Press, 2001), 308. As one early supporter of the nationalist organization stated in the journal *Black Dialogue* in 1966, "US means exactly that—all of US (black folks)." See also Scot Brown, *Fighting for US*, intro. Historians, public intellectuals, and pundits referring to US as "United Slaves" have adopted the designation ascribed to the group by its opponents.

28. Capturing this, one author writes, "Then the 1968 assassination of Martin Luther King, Jr., . . . opened a deep chasm between black and white America. The triumph of conservative, antiblack politics later that year convinced many black people that the majority of whites opposed their aspirations for first-class citizenship. In the face of white opposition, many African-Americans concluded they could count only on themselves"; see Nell Painter, *Creating Black Americans: African-American History and its Meanings* (New York: Oxford University Press, 2005), 299.

29. Joseph, "Black Liberation without Apology." A second oppositional narrative to the dominant interpretation might be added, that of the declensionists. The declension thesis is distilled in the scholarship of Paul Buhle, Van Gosse, Doug Rossinow, Jeremy Suri, and Jeremy Varon. More so than either Black Power or dominant narratives, declension scholars engage both the books of specialists and broader works.

Though both declensionists and the scholarly main predicate analysis on decline in the 1960s, a line should be drawn that distinguishes the respective interpretive concerns of oppositional vis-à-vis the dominant narratives. One is interested in the decline of a specific movement, typically the denouement of the New Left; the other is preoccupied with the decline of a nation. To the scholarly main, national unraveling—and how a particular struggle, often enabled by liberalism, fueled that unraveling—appears more consequential for the study of modern U.S. history.

30. Michael Flamm, review of *American Babylon*, by Robert O. Self, *Reviews in American History* 32 (December 2004): 552.

31. Thomas Bender, "No Borders: Beyond the Nation-State," *History News Network*, 17 April 2006.

32. Bill Bishop and Robert G. Cushing, *The Big Sort: Why the Clustering of Like-Minded America Is Tearing Us Apart* (New York: Houghton Mifflin, 2008); Gregory Rodriguez, "The New American Segregation," *Los Angeles Times*, 26 May 2008.

33. Warren Holmes, *National Black Independent Party: Political Insurgency or Ideological Convergence?* (New York: Garland, 1999), 29, 45.

34. See Ira Katznelson, *When Affirmative Action Was White: An Untold History of Racial Inequality in Twentieth-Century America* (New York: Norton, 2005), and Robert C. Lieberman, *Shifting the Color Line: Race and the American Welfare State* (Cambridge, Mass.: Harvard University Press, 1998).

35. Earl Black and Merle Black, *Rise of Southern Republicans* (Cambridge, Mass.: Harvard University Press, 2002), 141.

36. William Leuchtenberg, *The White House Looks South: Franklin D. Roosevelt, Harry S. Truman, Lyndon B. Johnson* (Baton Rouge: Louisiana State University Press, 2005), 224.

37. Byron Shafer and Richard Johnston, of course, present a counterthesis to the role of civil rights in spurring white southerners' mass Democratic exodus; they argue it was primarily class, not race, that undermined Democrats' hegemony in southern politics; see *The End of Southern Exceptionalism: Class, Race, and Partisan Change in the Postwar South* (Cambridge, Mass.: Harvard University Press, 2006).

38. V. O. Key, *Southern Politics in State and Nation* (New York: Knopf, 1949).

39. The Dunning artifact is a reference to the historian William Dunning and the school of thought (ca. 1901–1960s) he generated on Reconstruction, which portrayed black voters and legislators blindly following the post–Civil War Republican Party lead. For a sampling of mainstream political historians taking a monolithic view of the black electorate uncritically voting Democrat, see E. Black and M. Black, *Rise of Southern Republicans*, 250; for "herding blacks," see David Tucker, *Memphis since Crump: Bossism, Blacks, and Civic Reformers* (Knoxville: University of Tennessee Press, 1980).

40. Holmes, *National Black Independent Party*, 43–45.

41. Ibid., 28.

42. Komozi Woodard, *A Nation within a Nation: Amiri Baraka (LeRoi Jones) and Black Power Politics* (Chapel Hill: University of North Carolina Press), 252.

43. NBPA in "The Say Brother" collection, 11 June 1976, program 617, WGBH Archives, WGBH, Boston.

44. *Pittsburgh Courier*, 29 March 1975; see also Hannah Atkins, "Why I Resigned from the NBPA," *Black World* 24 (1975): 45–46. Other intellectuals have theorized how modern nationalism is consistent with and, indeed, is operational within a liberal worldview, see in particular Yael Tamir, *Liberal Nationalism* (Princeton, N.J.: Princeton University Press, 1993), 12.

45. R. Smith, *We Have No Leaders*, 306, n.114.

46. Robert C. Smith, "Black Power and the Transformation from Protest to Policies," *Political Science Quarterly* 96 (autumn 1981): 431–43; Adolph Reed, *Stirrings in the Jug: Black Politics in the Post-segregation Era* (Minneapolis: University of Minnesota Press, 1999), 79–116, 163–77; Matthew Countryman, "From Protest to Politics: Community Control and Black Independent Politics in Philadelphia, 1965–1984," *Journal of Urban History* 32 (2006): 827.

47. Yvonne King, "Barbara Easley Cox—Servant of the People—Is Honored," n.d., at www.itsabouttimebpp.com/Chapter_History/pdf/Philadelphia/BC_Servant_of_the_People.pdf, accessed August 2008.

48. Amiri Baraka, Speech to the Congress of African Peoples, 1970, in *Modern Black Nationalism: From Marcus Garvey to Louis Farrakhan*, ed. William Van Deburg (New York: New York University Press, 1997), 147.

49. Lerone Bennett, *IBW and Education for Liberation*, 2nd ed., with an IBW historical overview by Vincent Harding and an essay by Lerone Bennett Jr. (Chicago: Third World Press, 1973), 4.

50. Ibid.

51. Vincent Harding, "Letter to the Editor," December 1979, in *The Other American Revolution* (Los Angeles and Atlanta: Center for Afro-American Studies, University of California, and Institute of the Black World, 1980), vii–x; Bill Montgomery, "IBW Has Rough Sailing," *Atlanta Journal Constitution*, 28 Nov. 1971, IBW Collection, Auburn Avenue Research Library, Atlanta, Georgia. Had IBW writers completed the television script on time, the program might well have aired on WMAL. The program did not make the air for three reasons. First, scriptwriter John O. Killens was late in completing the script for the original pilot. Second, the late script was upstaged by advance promotion for *Roots*. Third, there was, in Harding's words, "the fading of black chic."

52. For Black Power and commodification of dissent, see Andreas Killen, *1973 Nervous Breakdown: Watergate, Warhol, and the Birth of Post-sixties America* (New York: Bloomsbury, 2006).

53. Benedict Anderson, "Imagined Communities," in *Nationalism*, ed. John Hutchinson and Anthony D. Smith (New York: Oxford University Press, 1994), 94–95.

54. R. Smith, *We Have No Leaders*, 116.

55. Max Horkheimer and Theodor W. Adorno, *Dialectic of Enlightenment* (New

York: Herder & Herder, 1972), trans. by John Cumming; Rob Walker, "The Alienation Market," *New York Times Magazine*, 13 June 2004.

56. See Nell Irvin Painter, *Creating Black Americans: African-American History and Its Meanings, 1619 to Present* (New York: Oxford University Press, 2006), 331.

57. See folders in Misseduc Foundation, series 3 (Grants), National Black United Fund, Karamau Foundation, Arts for Racial Identity, Black Theatre Alliance, Rockefeller Brothers Fund Archives, 1941–89, Rockefeller Archive Center, Sleepy Hollow, N.Y.

58. Herbert Klein, interview, 9 April 1970, record group (RG) 1.2, series 200R, box 385, folder 3344, Rockefeller Foundation Collection, Rockefeller Archive Center, Sleepy Hollow, N.Y. (hereafter cited as RF Collection).

59. Gwendolyn Terreri Blackstone to Herbert Klein, 15 Feb. 1978, RG A82, series 200R, box R1868, folder NBT Workshop, 1976–1980, RF Collection; Leo Kirschner, CPA, to Lynn Blackstone, 27 Dec. 1977, RF Collection.

60. Jacob S. Hacker, *The Great Risk Shift: The Assault on American Jobs, Families, Health Care, and Retirement and How You Can Fight Back* (New York: Oxford University Press, 2006).

61. Barbara Ann Teer to Howard Klein, 13 Oct. 1980, RG A82, series 200R, box R1868, folder National Black Theater Workshop, 1976–1980, RF Collection; Howard Klein to Barbara Ann Teer, 11 Nov. 1980, ibid.

62. Grant-in-Aid Application, RG 1.2, series 200R, box 385, folder 3344, ca. August 1970, RF Collection.

63. "Operational Description," RG A82, series 200R, box R1868, folder NBT Workshop (1976–1980), RF Collection.

64. Rebecca M. Painter to D. Lydia Bronte, Inter-Office Correspondence, 14 Jan. 1976, record group 1.3, series 270, box 14, folder 126, RF Collection.

65. Anne Garonzik, interview, 2 Feb. 1976, RG 1.3, series 270, box 14, folder 126, RF Collection.

66. See James Smethurst, *Black Arts Movement: Literary Nationalism in the 1960s and 1970s* (Chapel Hill: University of North Carolina Press, 2005).

67. OBAC writer workshops provided a mutually supportive atmosphere for a generation of black writers who published in black independent houses like Third World and Path presses. Of course OBAC did receive some subvention, from a benefit for writers, to private and public agencies—Community Arts Foundation, Illinois Arts Council, and National Endowment for the Arts—that aided in financing the OBAC-led mural movement in Chicago during summer 1971; see *Chicago Tribune*, 3 Nov. 1969 and 18 July 1971.

68. See Sam Greenlee's speech at OBAC Reunion, 6 Feb. 2005, Vivian Harsh Collection, Carter G. Woodson Regional Library, Chicago Public Library, Chicago (hereafter cited as Harsh Collection).

69. See OBAC Interpretive Text Panel, Chicago Black Writers Public Exhibit, May 2000, Harsh Collection; see other OBAC materials in Harsh Collection.

70. Chicago Writers and the Black Arts Movement: OBAC Reunion, 6 Feb. 2005, videocassette, Harsh Collection; Paul Breman Collection, Harsh Collection.

71. Cora Iver Rivers [mother of Conrad Kent] to Paul Breman, 24 March 1969, Paul Breman Collection, Harsh Collection; Paul Breman to Cora Rivers, 11 June 1969, ibid.

72. OBAC members and former members themselves made the argument that personal fame or fortune was detrimental to liberation struggle, citing self-interested ambition as the reason many members left the group. The contention was that, increasingly, artists conflated their own personal successes with the larger liberation aims of the movement. In other words, more commercially minded artists, in some measure, came to embody the principles of classical liberal individualism—a political philosophy that greatly alarmed the social scientist-minded members of OBAC. For scholars of the modern black political experience the best-known political parallel would be Jesse Jackson's 1988 presidential bid, when personal ambition eclipsed the larger ambition of liberation struggle, which had so inspired Jackson grassroots activists in 1984.

73. Tamir, *Liberal Nationalism*, 85.

74. Bennett Johnson and Haki Madhubuti made significant community organizing contributions for Harold Washington, notably from 1977, Washington's first run for Chicago's mayoralty, through the 1983 election. Their efforts and those of others helped to register a hundred thousand new black voters by 1983, putting Washington over the top in a three-way Democratic primary race in 1983, won by a plurality of a mere 36 percent.

75. Manning Marable, *Black Leadership* (New York: Columbia University Press, 1998), 127.

76. Dianne Pinderhughes, *Race and Ethnicity in Chicago Politics: A Reexamination of Pluralist Theory* (Urbana: University of Illinois Press, 1987), 133.

77. Elisabeth Lasch-Quinn, *Race Experts: How Racial Etiquette, Sensitivity Training, and New Age Therapy Hijacked the Civil Rights Revolution* (New York: Norton, 2001), 121, 3.

78. Baraka, Speech to the Congress of African Peoples, 1970, 151.

79. Lasch-Quinn, *Race Experts*, 120.

80. Tommie Shelby, *We Who Are Dark: The Philosophical Foundations of Black Solidarity* (Cambridge, Mass.: Harvard University Press, Belknap Press, 2005), 3, 15.

81. Ibid., 15.

82. Komozi Woodard, *A Nation within a Nation: Amiri Baraka (LeRoi Jones) and Black Power Politics* (Chapel Hill: University of North Carolina Press), 232.

83. Kwame Anthony Appiah, "The Case for Contamination," *New York Times Magazine*, 1 Jan. 2006, 30, 52. For more on Browne, see Judy Tzu-Chun Wu, "African-Vietnamese American: Robert S. Browne, the Antiwar Movement, and the Personal/Political Dimensions of Black Internationalism," *Journal of African American History* (Fall 2007): 492–515.

84. See Robert S. Browne Papers, box 1, folders 1–2, Schomburg Library, N.Y. (hereafter cited as Browne Papers).

85. "Case for Black Separatism" with responses, box 18, folder 32, ibid.; for articles by and about Browne, see box 15, folder 2, ibid.

86. Robert S. Browne and Bayard Rustin, *Separatism or Integration, Which Way for America? A Dialogue* (New York: A. Philip Randolph Educational Fund, 1968).

87. Fairleigh Dickinson University, box 4, folders 11–14, Browne Papers; Robert Browne, "Origin, Birth, and Adolescence of 'The Review of Black Political Economy' and the Black Economic Resource Center," *Review of Black Political Economy* 21 (winter 1993): 9.

88. Browne, "Origin, Birth, and Adolescence"; Dean Robinson, *Black Nationalism in American Politics and Thought* (New York: Cambridge University Press, 2001), 74–75.

89. Richard Pells, "American Historians Would Do Well to Get Out of the Country," *Chronicle of Higher Education*, 20 June 2003, B7.

90. Ibid.

91. Robert S. Browne, "The Case for Black Separatism," *Cross Currents* (fall 1968): 471–82.

92. Christopher Lasch, *The Culture of Narcissism: American Life in an Age of Diminishing Expectations* (New York: Norton, 1991), 144.

93. Ibid.; for an example in Allan Bloom, see his *The Closing of the American Mind* (New York: Simon & Schuster, 1987), intro., esp. 33.

94. Rooks, *White Money, Black Power*, 114; C. Lasch, of course, would likely have detested the bureaucratic culture that gave rise to the HEW report. Louis Menand, *American Studies* (New York: Farrar, Straus, Giroux, 2002), 198–220; Christopher Lasch, "Life in the Therapeutic State," *New York Review of Books*, 12 June 1980.

95. Gerstle, *American Crucible*, 326.

96. Benedict Anderson, *Imagined Communities: Reflections on the Origin and Spread of Nationalism*, rev. ed. (London and New York: Verso, 1991), 144.

97. Herman Graham, "Black and Navy Too," *Journal of Men's Studies* 9 (January 2001): 227; Graham, *The Brothers' Vietnam War: Black Power, Manhood, and the Military Experience* (Gainesville: University Press of Florida, 2003); Stanley Karnow, *Vietnam* (New York: Penguin, 1997).

98. Ian Tyrell, "Beyond the View from Euro-America: Environment, Settler Societies, and the Internationalization of American History," in Bender, *Rethinking American History in a Global Age*, 168–92. This is not uncommon among American Americanists. As Daniel Rodgers asked of historians living and writing about the United States in the *American Century*: "How have historians contrived to . . . cabin the Progressive and New Deal years" within an insular frame? More Beardian in method and interpretation than they imagine, isolationists' interest in group analysis, as Rodgers wrote of American Americanists, "focuses attention not on the ideational aspects of politics, with their ambiguous fluidity," but on interests and political pressures that "unconsciously magnifies difference." Rodgers, "An Age of Social Politics," in Bender, *Rethinking American History in a Global Age*, 250–73.

99. According to Anthony Smith, Basques fit more the ethnic-genealogical profile, stressing purity of blood and exclusive rights, whereas the Catalans' linguistic and

cultural nationalist orientation tended to be more open and inclusive as well as tolerant of immigrants. See Anthony D. Smith, *Nationalism and Modernism: A Critical Survey of Recent Theories of Nations and Nationalism* (London and New York: Routledge, 1998), 212.

100. Browne, "Case for Black Separatism," 47.

101. See also Robert H. Wiebe, *Who We Are: A History of Popular Nationalism* (Princeton, N.J.: Princeton University Press, 2002), 5.

102. Nor, as Anthony D. Smith tells us, have nationalisms always blindly hewed to "the road to outright independence." Instead, several nationalisms have "prefer[red] to attain maximum cultural, social, and economic autonomy for their homelands and peoples within a wider, federal sovereign state. . . . To deny them the label of 'nationalism' because their oppositional movements have not been bent on capturing state power is to overlook the centrality of national cultural and social regeneration in their movements, an ideal that is common to so many other 'nationalisms'" (A. Smith, *Nationalism and Modernism*, 90). Like Smith, this is where I also part ways somewhat with Hobsbawm, who contends that for the historian, nationalism's abiding concern and political goal is territorial, specifically the creation of a nation-state. E. J. Hobsbawm, *Nations and Nationalism since 1780: Programme, Myth, Reality*, 2nd ed. (Cambridge and New York: Cambridge University Press, 1992), intro., esp. 9–10.

INDEX

ATF (Bureau of Alcohol, Tobacco, and
Firearms), 96
Atkins, Hannah, 244
Atlanta Journal, 156
Attica Brothers, 155
Atwater, Ann, 67
Austin, Louis, 65
Avent, Harold, 99–101, 106
Axton, Estelle, 236

Bailey, James Pou, 137
Bailey, Thomas, 79
Bain, Carson, 79
Baker, James, 223
Baldwin, James, 186
Ballard-Chatman, Florence, 152
Baraka, Amiri, 55, 189, 191, 244–46, 253,
338n19
Barnes, Alexander, 62–63
Bass, Jack, 17, 145
Battle, B. J., 77
Baxter, Tom, 156
Beaufort County, N.C., 134–42, 149
Beauty of Black Week (Duke Univer-
sity), 34, 273n111
Bedau, Hugh, 141
Behn, Dick, 208
Bell, Al, 236–37, 337n15
Bell, William, 69
Bellamy, Minnie, 104–5
Bender, Thomas, 241
Bennett, Lerone, 246
Bennett College, 99
BERC (Black Economic Research Center),
228, 257–58
Bernstein, Daniel J., 237
Bernstein, Felicia and Leonard, 11, 175
Big Sort, The (Bishop & Cushing), 241
Bin Wahad, Dhoruba, 105
Bishop, Bill, 241
Black, Earl, 242
Black, James Michael, 97–98
Black, Merle, 242

Black Arts Movement, 154, 251
Black Business Digest, 211
black capitalism: and economic independence, 200; and MXLU, 82–83; and
Soul City, 227–30
—as viewed by: BPP, 171; Fuller, Howard,
58; Helms, 221; McKissick, 198–202,
230; Newton, Huey, 117; Stith,
David, 61
Black Economic Research Center
(BERC), 228, 257–58
Black Executive Advisory Committee,
212
Black Is Beautiful week, 34, 273n111
Black Manifesto (Forman), 50
black middle class, 59–62, 64–72, 79–81,
201, 204, 279n7
black nationalism. See Black Power
movement
Black Panther Intercommunal Newspaper,
98, 109, 120, 163, 175, 294n83,
294n99
Black Panther Party (BPP): and AAUO,
96–99, 106; and ACLU/NCCLU, 4–5,
93–94, 108, 113, 121–29; armed self-
defense of, 104–5, 293n72; on black
homophobia, 175; and black nationalism, 335n1; community programs
of, 94, 117–21 (see also antipoverty
programs); corporal punishment
within, 185–86; cosmopolitanism
of, 175; and Davis, Angela, 181; and
DNC, 181; feminization of, 181–82,
318n17; and Greensboro, 99–102; as
inclusionist, 116–21; international
appeal of, 174; and Joan Little case,
133, 148, 156, 167, 306n111, 306n117;
and law enforcement, 93, 95–96,
107–14, 125, 155; and legal system,
171; and liberals, 3, 114–21; Little's
commitment to, 313n4; Oakland
oversight of, 99, 101–3, 106–7;
platform of, 6, 92, 116–18, 246; and

prostitution, 183, 185; reform of, 91–94, 98–99, 113–21; sexism within, 179–83, 185–86; social democratic strategy of, 2, 114–24, 128–31, 171, 181; UCLA shoot-out, 233–37

Black Power movement: as America's nervous breakdown, 250–52; backlash against, 47–50, 231, 233–34; chauvinism of, 179, 317n59, 323n141; and commodification of dissent, 247; and cosmopolitanism, 166–79, 316n44; criminal imagery of, 92; on desegregation, 79–80; in Detroit, 47; in Durham, 20–24; and economic nationalism, 82; as federally subsidized, 196–98; and gender relations, 4; and global nationalist movements, 262; historical reinterpretation of, 238–42; and individualism, 251–52; and Invaders group, 234; and Joan Little case, 4, 166–67, 194–95; and leftist politics, 42, 176; and local realities, 56, 278n5; and mainstream blacks, 214–15; as nation-building middle class, 57–66; and new-age therapeutic model, 253–54; Newark conference of, 256; and Pan-Africanism, 41; patriarchy and misogyny among, 4, 194–95; and patriotism, 261; and Piedmont progressives, 19; and political violence, 1, 10, 34, 115, 213, 234; and sociopolitical movements, 51–57, 78, 84; surveillance of, 76, 96, 125; and UCLA, 233–37; and war on poverty, 14. *See also* cosmopolitanism; cultural nationalism; liberal–Black Power alliance

Black Scholar, 176, 190, 192, 199

Blacks for Nixon, 208–15

black student movements, 33–38

black studies, 36–40, 51, 233–42, 260, 337–38n19, 338n21, 338n23

Black Theatre Alliance, 248

black writers, 251–52, 258

Bloom, Alan, 260

Blount, Alvin, 76, 85–86

Boldt, George H., 70

Bond, Julian, 148, 155, 211, 286n141

Bowen, Bobby, 181

BPP. *See* Black Panther Party

Braden, Anne, 155

Brame, Walter, 101

Breman, Paul, 251

Brewer, James, 74

Brimmer, Andrew, 227

Brinn, Tim, 18

British Association for American Studies, 7

British Broadcasting Co., 155

Brooke, Edward, III, 212, 215–16, 222, 225–26

Brown, Charlotte Hawkins, 81

Brown, Elaine, 117, 168–73, 179, 181–82, 185–86, 193

Brown, Eric, 99–100, 106

Brown, H. Rap, 154

Brown, Robert, 201, 212

Brown, William, 206

Browne, Robert, 254–58

Broyhill, James, 219

Buchanan, Pat, 204

Buckley, William F., Jr., 95

Bureau of Alcohol, Tobacco, and Firearms (ATF), 96

Burger, Warren, 123, 159

Burke, Yvonne, 144, 149, 153

Burrell, Berkley, 208

Burt, Moses, 22

Bush, George H. W., 6, 197, 212–13, 328n69

Cabral, Amilcar, 56

Cain, Anthony, 106

Califano, Joseph, 28

Callins, Preston, 318n77

McKissick, Floyd B. (*continued*)
  Williams, 196; and Soul City, 5, 82,
  217–19, 229, 329n86
McKissick Enterprises, 199–200
media: and black nationalism/IBW,
  246–48; on Duke student protest,
  35; and Joan Little trial, 157–58; on
  Karenga, Haiba, 190; and 1967 dis-
  turbance, 298; and political aware-
  ness, 310n196. *See also individual
  news sources*
Memphis, Tenn., 336n8
MESBICS (Minority Enterprise Small
  Business Investment Corporation),
  227
Michaux, H. M., 135
Militant, 158, 160
Miller, Marvin, 156
Mills, Nancy, 147
Mills, Wilbur, 209
Minority Enterprise Small Business
  Investment Corporation (MESBICS),
  227
Misseduc Foundation, 248
Mitchell, Burley, 158
Mitchell, John, 226
Model Cities agency, 205
Monte, Robert, 23–24
Moore, Daniel K., 24, 29
Moore, Richard, 105
Morales, Carlton O., 75, 87
moral relativism/universalism, 168–72
More Representative Political Participa-
  tion (MRPP), 98, 291n33
Morgan, Robert, 218, 334n161
Mothers for Black Liberation, 104
MRPP (More Representative Political
  Participation), 98, 291n33
Mullin, Courtney, 142
multiculturalism, 33, 49, 174–76
murders: of Alligood, 157, 312n231; at
  BPP-US shoot-out, 233–37; of Chi-

cago panthers, 110–11; of Rucker,
  Carol, 182, 318n77
Murphy, Robert M., 109
Murray, Carlos, 154
music, of black liberation, 157, 236–37,
  337n15
MXLU. *See* Malcolm X Liberation
  University

NAACP (National Association for the
  Advancement of Colored People):
  and BPP, 103–4; Chavis/Stansel
  settlement by, 188, 320–21n111; legal
  activism of, 98; suit of, against
  Raleigh, 146; support of, for Joan
  Little defense, 154; view of, on
  MXLU, 65; waning influence of,
  20–21, 62–63
NABM (National Association of Black
  Manufacturers), 227–28
Nash county, 18–19, 137
Nash-Edgecombe Economic Develop-
  ment, Inc., 18–19
Nation, 161
National Alliance Against Racist and
  Political Repression, 154
National Association for the Advance-
  ment of Colored People. *See* NAACP
National Association of Black Manufac-
  turers (NABM), 227–28
National Association of Black Social
  Workers, 147–48
National Black Feminist Organization
  (NBF), 195, 323n148
National Black Political Assembly
  (NBPA), 71, 214–15, 235, 242–46
National Black Political Convention, 210
National Black Theater (NBT), 248–50
National Black United Fund, 248
National Business League, 227, 334n154
National Center for the Prevention and
  Control of Rape, 149, 306–7n122

National Committee for a Two-Party System, 212–13, 224
National Committee for Political Action, 331n110
National Committee to Combat Fascism (NCCF), 102, 104–14
National Council of Black Republicans, 213
National Council of Churches, 234
National Endowment for the Arts (NEA), 341n67
National Endowment for the Humanities (NEH), 238
National Enquirer, 218
National Jewish Community Relations Council, 256
National Negro Business and Professional Committee (NNBPC), 71–72
National Organization for Women (NOW), 152, 154, 156, 312n235
National Public Radio (NPR), 201
National Welfare Rights Organization, 210
Nation of Islam (NOI), 10, 179, 321n119
NBC Nightly News, 119
NBF (National Black Feminist Organization), 195, 323n148
NBPA. *See* National Black Political Assembly
NBT (National Black Theater), 248–50
NCADB (New Communities Development Board), 224
NCCF (National Committee to Combat Fascism), 102, 104–14
NCCLU. *See* North Carolina Civil Liberties Union
NCF (North Carolina Fund), 15–24
NEA (National Endowment for the Arts), 341n67
Negro Digest, 37
NEH (National Endowment for the Humanities), 238

Neiman, Ernest, 163
New Communities Administration (HUD), 217
New Communities Development Board (NCADB), 224
New Left, 154, 156
New Orleans, La., 235
New Review (Dutch), 155
New Right: campaign tactics of, 222–25; and elitism, 8; on liberal-Black Power alliances, 52–53; rise and development of, 2–3, 7–8, 47–50, 84, 219–25
New South politics, 153–54
Newsweek, 208
Newton, Huey: on BPP platform, 6, 92, 116–18; chauvinism of, 179–80, 182, 317n59; FBI harassment of, 110; on liberal universalism, 164, 167, 174; self-exile of, in Cuba, 164, 174; violence of, 182, 318n77; *The Women's Liberation and Gay Liberation Movement*, 180
Newton, Jerry, 105
New York Magazine, 189
New York Review of Books, 161–62
New York Times: on black capitalism, 200; Browne's writing in, 256; on Duke student protest, 36; on Joan Little case, 132, 138, 147, 157–58; on McKissick, 197–98; on Spaulding, Asa T., 66
Nguyen, Huoi, 256
Nielsen, Mark, 162, 164
Nixon, Richard: black capitalist project of, 61, 201–2; and Brooke, 226; and CBC, 325n23; civil rights actions of, 210–11; governance of, 201; as liberal, 324–25n13; and McKissick, 6; as moral relativist, 169; political strategy of, 73, 95, 203–4, 210–11; on school desegregation, 209; and

Peachey, Willis, 136
Pells, Richard, 258–59
Penney, Wade H., 68
Pentagon Papers, 155
People's Conference on Poverty, 21
Pepper, Claude, 116
Pinsky, Mark, 147
Pitt, Ernie, 128
Pitt County, 138
Pittsburgh Courier, 235
Planned Parenthood, 235
political action committees (PACs),
    220–23, 331n110
politics: and activism, 17–20, 22–24,
    66–71, 98–99, 157, 245; in Durham,
    17–19, 22–24; of judicial system,
    170; postsegregationist, 69, 145–46;
    practical versus symbolic, 150,
    307n132; public mistrust of, 173;
    resistance to, 293n73; and self-
    interest, 170
Pollock, Donald, 213
Porter, E. Nathaniel, 43
Portugal, 262
Pottinger, J. Stanley, 149
Powell, Lewis, 209
"power of the people" concept, 147–60
Power to the Ice Pick mantra, 312–13n3
pragmatism, and black cultural national-
    ism, 51–53, 171, 207, 254
Presbyterian Church, Catawba Synod, 81
Preyer, Lunsford Richardson, 18, 115–16,
    296n136
Preyer Committee Report, on BPP, 115
Programme to Combat Racism (PCR),
    287–88n168
progressivism, 201, 209, 214, 235, 239,
    336n8
protest demonstrations: at Duke, 33–38;
    led by Avent, 101; for Joan Little
    defense, 141–42, 150–53, 159–60,
    310n200; at UNC, 30
public relations: and Alligood blunder,
    151–52; in Joan Little case, 133,
    136–39, 142, 147–60; and N.C.
    attorney general appointment, 152;
    and Winston-Salem BPP, 96, 102–6,
    124
Pursell, William, 22, 27

Race Experts (Lasch-Quinn), 252–53
racial discrimination, 67–71; in criminal
    justice system, 139–42, 151, 168–73,
    177, 315n30; in historiography,
    240–41; and Joan Little trial, 69,
    137–39, 142, 302nn37–38, 304n70;
    in Raleigh, 146; in sexual assault
    sentencing, 184–85; worsened by
    liberal–black power alliances, 253
Radical Chic (Wolfe), 10–11
Radical Right. *See* New Right
Radish weekly, 68
Rainbow Coalition, 174, 252
Rainey, Thomas, 35
Raleigh, N.C., 142, 144–46, 163,
    305–6n89
Raleigh News and Observer: on Howard
    Fuller's speech, 22, 29; on Joan
    Little case, 141, 149, 154, 157–59, 163;
    on Soul City scandal, 216, 224
Randolph, A. Philip, 228
Randolph, Louis, 139
rape. *See* sexual abuse
Reader's Digest, 120, 162
Reagan, Ronald, 47–48, 219–25, 233–34
Red Cross, 119
Redding, Evangeline Grant, 184
Reed, Adolph, 245
Rehnquist, William, 123, 209
Reid, Willie Mae, 136, 155
religious fundamentalism, 49, 134–35,
    161–62
religious imperialism, 49
Religious Right. *See* New Right
Republican Party: black members of,
    201–8; and Congressional Club,

U.S. Department of Justice, Civil Rights Division, 144, 151
U.S. Freedom of Information Act, 173
U.S. House Appropriations Committee, 202
U.S. House Committee on Internal Security (HCIS), 115–16
U.S. House Committee on Un-American Activities (HCUA), 70, 282n74
U.S. House Judiciary Committee, 151
U.S. International Cooperation Administration, 256
U.S. Navy, 261
U.S. Office of Minority Business Enterprise (OMBE), 201, 203
U.S. organization, 176, 190–91, 233–37, 239, 322n131, 338n27
U.S. Small Business Administration (SBA), 203
U.S. Supreme Court, 122–27, 140–41, 143

Van Deburg, William, 6, 233
Vanderbilt Business School, 257
Volunteers in Service to America, 16
voter registration: by BPP, 118; by DCNA, 64; and disenfranchisement, 126–27, 299n189; by Johnson, Nelson, 77; in southern cities, 57, 64, 67, 134, 144–45, 278–79n6; and Spaulding, Asa T., 73
Voting Rights Act (1965), and black suffrage in North Carolina, 17

Waddell, Joseph P., 90, 112–13
Wake County. See Raleigh, N.C.
Wake Forest University, 118
Walker, Margaret, 260
Wallace, George, 47, 95, 209
Wall Street Journal, 139, 211
Ward, Stephen, 237–38, 337–38n19
Warren County, N.C., 197
Warren Regional Planning Corporation, 202

Washington, Cordell, 97
Washington, Harold, 252, 342n74
Washington, N.C. See Beaufort County, N.C.
Washington (N.C.) Daily News, 135, 143
Washington Post, 142, 146, 150, 158–59
Watergate scandal, 6, 155, 169
Watson, Douglas, 146
Wattstax concert, 236–37, 337n15
WCC (World Council of Churches), 88–89, 287–88n168
Webb, Wellington, 154
Weicker, Lowell, 336–37n10
Wellstone, Paul, 13–14
Werner, Craig, 236, 337n15
Wesleyan University Afro-American Institute, 238, 338n21
Whaley, Sara S., 191
Wheeler, John, 69
White, E. Frances, 193–94
White Rock Baptist Church, 64, 70
whites: and antiblack politics, 219–25, 239, 329n84, 338n28; and election of Lightner, 145; and ethnic consciousness, 250; excluded from IBW, 238; as founders of Stax, 236; as jury members, 163; male elites among, 172; philanthropy of, to black organizations, 237–42, 248–49, 337–38n19, 338n21, 338n23; and postblack politics, 69, 145–46; on reparative action, 229, 334n163; on self-defense by women, 137–38; as supporters of McKissick, 200, 202; as unwelcome at MXLU, 41; urban flight of, 145, 305n90
Whiting, Albert, 75
Wilkins, Roy, 71, 197, 205, 207, 215
Wilkinson, John, 151–52, 163
Will, George, 8
Williams, G. Wesley, 145
Williams, Kenneth, 288n1
Williams, Robert F., 21, 196

Politics and Culture in the Twentieth-Century South

A Common Thread: Labor, Politics, and Capital Mobility
in the Textile Industry
by Beth English

"Everybody Was Black Down There": Race and Industrial
Change in the Alabama Coalfields
by Robert H. Woodrum

Race, Reason, and Massive Resistance: The Diary of
David J. Mays, 1954–1959
edited by James R. Sweeney

The Unemployed People's Movement: Leftists, Liberals, and
Labor in Georgia, 1929–1941
by James J. Lorence

Liberalism, Black Power, and the Making of American
Politics, 1965–1980
by Devin Fergus

Guten Tag, Y'all: Globalization and the South Carolina
Piedmont, 1950–2000
by Marko Maunula